THE MAKING OF
THE POETS

THE MAKING OF
THE POETS

Byron and Shelley in Their Time

———

IAN GILMOUR

CARROLL & GRAF PUBLISHERS
NEW YORK

THE MAKING OF THE POETS
BYRON AND SHELLEY IN THEIR TIME

Carroll & Graf Publishers
An Imprint of Avalon Publishing Group Inc.
245 West 17th Street, 11th Floor
New York, NY 10011-5300

Copyright © 2002 by Ian Gilmour

First Carroll & Graf edition 2003

Library of Congress Cataloging-in-Publication Data is available.

ISBN: 0-7867-1273-2

Printed in the United States of America
Distributed by Publishers Group West

To Caroline

Contents

List of Illustrations

William Whitton, Timothy Shelley's lawyer, by James Leaky. (*Dr W. Shirley Arundell*)

Shelley's Cottage, Keswick, artist unknown. (*The Wordsworth Trust*)

Title pages of Shelley's first two published volumes of poetry, C & W Phillips. (*The British Library Board*)

15 Poland Street, London, from a drawing by D. Collins.

23 Chapel Street, London.

60 George Street, Edinburgh.

7 Lower Sackville Street, Dublin.

Thomas Jefferson Hogg. (*Mrs W. S. Scott*)

Thomas Love Peacock, by R. Jean. (*By courtesy of The National Portrait, London*)

William Godwin, by James Northcote. (*By courtesy of The National Portrait Gallery, London*)

Thomas Moore, by Sir Thomas Lawrence. (*John Murray*)

Belem Tower, Lisbon. (*Ian Gilmour.*)

Buenos Aires Hotel, Lisbon. (*Ian Gilmour.*)

Mafra Monastery, Portugal. (*Ian Gilmour.*)

Hotel where Byron stayed in Cintra. (*Ian Gilmour.*)

Mary Chaworth, by Samuel John Stump. (*Newstead Abbey Collection, Nottingham City Museums and Galleries*)

Teresa Macri, engraved by William Finden from a drawing by Frank Stone after a sketch taken from life by T. Allason. (*Keats-Shelley Memorial House, Rome*)

Ioannina, engraved by Edward Finden.

Ali Pacha Museum in Ioannina. (*Ian Gilmour.*)

Every effort has been made by the author and the publishers to trace holders of copyrights. Any inadvertent omissions of acknowledgement or permission can be rectified in future editions.

Count Maddalo [Byron] is a person of the most consummate genius ... But it is his weakness to be proud ... He is cheerful, frank and witty. His more serious conversation is a sort of intoxication; men are held by it as by a spell.

Shelley on Byron in 1818

Shelley is *truth* itself – and *honour* itself – notwithstanding his out-of-the-way notions about religion.

Byron on Shelley in 1821

> The Pilgrim of Eternity whose fame
> Over his living head like Heaven is bent
> An early but enduring monument ...
>
> *Shelley on Byron in 1821*

He is, to my knowledge, the *least* selfish and mildest of men – a man who has made more sacrifices of his fortune and feelings for others than any I ever heard of.

Byron on Shelley in 1822*

---

*Preface to *Julian and Maddalo*; E of M II, pp. 660–661; *BLJ* VIII, p. 132; *Adonais*, St.30, R & P, p. 399; *BLJ* IX, p. 119

ix

Acknowledgements

I have been lucky enough to receive a great deal of help in the writing of this book. Major M. A. T. Hibbert-Hingston of the Coldstream Guards and Michael and Melissa Bakewell provided information on the military career of Byron's father. Michael Meredith, the librarian of Eton College, showed me documents about Shelley at Eton and read the chapters on Eton and Harrow. Dr C. J. Tyerman, the historian of Harrow School, and Peter Hunter, librarian of the Vaughan library at Harrow, patiently answered many questions about Byron's school life. Sir John Smith CH showed me two books Shelley gave his friends on leaving Eton. Hubert Picarda QC gave me much material on the teaching of classics at public schools. Dr Robin Darwall-Smith, the archivist of University College, Oxford, gave me the run of his archives and showed me Shelley's rooms as well as providing advice and information. Professor Anne Barton showed the Byron Society the poet's rooms at Trinity College Cambridge and told us about his life there. Haidee Jackson at Newstead and John and Virginia Murray at John Murray (Publishers) Ltd allowed me to see the documents I requested. Ken and Dagmar Prichard Jones showed my wife and me round the Shelleys' house, Field Place in Sussex. In Spain, El Marques de Bonanza of Gonzalez Byass explained to me the intricacies of the sherry trade in 1809. In Greece Mrs Rosa Florou showed me around Missolonghi and took me to Ioannina. I am greatly indebted to all of the above for their kindness and to the late Joan Bayliss who gave me *The Military Adventures of Johnny Newcome*, first published in 1815, which provides a vivid picture of Portugal during the Peninsular War.

I am also profoundly grateful to Professor Barton, Megan Boyes, Sir Frank Kermode and Professor Timothy Webb for their assistance on particular points; to Dr Barrington Cooper for reading the medical parts of the book and giving expert advice; to Dr Emma Gilmour for doing the same on Chapter XI; and to Mark Garnett,

John Grigg, David and Andrew Gilmour, William Keegan and Jane Pleydell Bouverie for reading all or most of the book and making many valuable suggestions. To Dr Peter Cochran I owe an even larger debt. He not only read the book more than once but dispensed from his vast knowledge of the period a great deal of information, ideas, criticism and advice.

Gerald Pollinger gave me permission to consult the Lovelace Papers at the Bodleian Library. Sotheby's, the Pierpont Morgan Library in New York, the Horsham Library, Angela Campbell of the Lake History National Park Authority in Keswick, the London Library, and of course the British Library were all very helpful. The staff of the library at the House of Lords were, as always, prompt and resourceful both in acquiring books and manuscripts and in helping with research.

As well as being a source of encouragement, Penelope Hoare of Chatto and Windus was an editor who was both a judicious pruner and a planter of ideas. Diane Craig once again typed a number of sometimes impenetrable drafts with skill and genial compliance. And my wife, Caroline, endured it all with her invariable good nature.

A Note on Money

Prices and the rate of inflation varied widely between 1788 and 1812. But, as a rough guide, the sums of money mentioned in this book should for the years 1788–99 be multiplied by eighty, and for the years 1800 to 1812 by fifty, to convert them to the broad equivalent of present-day money.

Introduction: Byron and Shelley in Their Time

If politicians tend to be not very interesting people who lead interesting lives, poets tend to be interesting people who lead not very interesting lives. The early nineteenth-century diplomat and poet Lord Strangford, 'whose plaintive strain', Byron mockingly remarked, 'each lovesick Miss admires', observed that 'the memoirs of literary men' were usually 'devoid of extraordinary incident'. That was not true of Byron or Shelley. Their lives were full of extraordinary incident and controversy. They lived, too, in interesting times, and not merely in the sense of the Chinese curse – 'May you live in interesting times' – because they lived through the French Revolution and the Napoleonic Wars, but also in the sense that their era was one of intellectual and artistic as well as political turmoil. Byron's friend and biographer, the Irish poet Thomas Moore, wrote of the taste for strong excitement 'in every walk of intellect' engendered by 'the fierce and passionate spirit' of the era; and Shelley maintained that it was impossible to read 'the most celebrated writers' of the day 'without being startled with the electric life which burns within their words', adding that their 'all-penetrating spirit' was less theirs 'than the spirit of the age'.[1]

Writing to Byron, Shelley called the French Revolution 'the master-theme of the epoch'. Another master-theme was the so-called Romantic movement, which in England, though not abroad, began at much the same time. 'Romantic' was not a word that the poets of the day ever applied to themselves or to each other. The words 'Classical' and 'Romantic', Byron wrote to Goethe in 1820, 'were not subjects of classification in England'. 'Romantic' did not come into vogue until the mid-Victorian age – and it defies definition: it should be felt, not defined, said a French writer. So it will be used sparingly here, but like 'Romanticism' it cannot be banished altogether. Between about 1760 and 1830 Romanticism, which was never a single intellectual movement, produced a great reversal in human consciousness, altering ways of thinking and behaviour. The assumptions that the universe was rational and all problems had a rational answer were doubted. The balance between man's rational and intuitive faculties was tilted, and a far greater emphasis was placed on the irrational and the subjective; unseen and supernatural forces are ever present. Romanticism attempted to liberate the unconscious mind. 'Like the accompanying French Revolution', wrote F. L. Lucas, it was 'the insurrection of a submerged population'. It was also the revolt of the individual against the claims of society, government, morals and almost everything else. And finally, largely through the novels of Sir Walter Scott, Romanticism brought with it, as Lord Acton said, the discovery of a sense of history.*[2]

'The period, which intervened between the birth of Pericles and the death of Aristotle', Shelley judged to be 'the most memorable in the history of the world'; it had produced 'so unparalleled a progress . . . in literature and arts'. In the same essay he ranked Shakespeare, 'on the whole, as the greatest individual mind, of which we have specimens remaining', and the Shakespearean era as 'the golden age of our own literature'. Shelley also believed that despite much 'low-thought envy' his own times would 'be a memorable age in intellectual achievement'. Whether or not out of envy, Hazlitt, who thought it a misfortune for any man of talent to be born 'in the latter end' of the eighteenth century, contended that theirs was not 'an age of gold'; similarly, in a light-hearted essay, which shocked Shelley but would have pleased Byron if he read it, Shelley's friend, the novelist Thomas Love Peacock, called it 'an age of brass'. Yet Shelley was right. The age in which he and Byron lived was indeed golden.[4]

On the continent the last quarter of the eighteenth and the first quarter of the nineteenth centuries were the age of Goethe, Schiller and Chateaubriand in literature; Kant and Hegel in philosophy; and Mozart, Beethoven, Schubert and Rossini in music. In Britain they were the age of Turner and Constable in painting; of Gibbon, Scott, Sheridan, Jane Austen, Cobbett and Hazlitt in prose; and of Blake,

* In 1812 Coleridge summed up Romanticism in a note for a lecture: 'the infinite, & indefinite as a vehicle of the Infinite – hence more to the Passions, the obscure Hopes and Fears – the wandering through Infinite – grander moral Feelings – more august conception of man as man – the Future rather than the Present – Sublimity'.[3]

Burns, Wordsworth, Coleridge, Byron, Shelley, Keats, Landor and Crabbe in poetry. What Byron often called 'poesy' was in the ascendant. And the poets of the age were deeply concerned with such worldly matters as politics and social affairs. Peacock might claim that a writer of poetry was 'a waster of his own time and a robber of that of others', and Keats might marvel 'how people read so much of it'. But the fact is they did. Although many of them would have jibbed at Wordsworth's high-flown claim that 'poetry [was] the first and last of all knowledge', contemporary culture, Stuart Curran has said, 'was simply mad for [it]'. Or, as Byron cheerfully wrote:

> I've half a mind to tumble down to prose
> But verse is more in fashion – so here goes.[5]

Inevitably, however, it was less the golden than 'the Chinese' aspect of the age – the upheaval of the times – that chiefly affected the lives of Shelley and Byron. Eighteenth-century England had been extraordinarily successful in both peace and war. Although her wealth was very unevenly spread, she was richer than her neighbours; and she had beaten France in a succession of wars. Not unnaturally this supremacy fostered considerable complacency in the upper classes about the country's political and social system. Even the one war that Britain lost – the American War of Independence – only briefly dented that self-satisfaction. In 1780 the Gordon Riots, much the biggest civil tumult since 1685, had brought home 'to all thinking people', Gibbon believed, 'the danger of an appeal to the people'. The 1780s were hence a conservative decade; and the economic recovery that followed the American war restored national contentment with the political system.[6]

That contentment was not initially threatened by the outbreak of the French Revolution. Charles James Fox famously hailed the fall of the Bastille, even though it had contained only seven prisoners whose living conditions were far better than those in the London prisons destroyed by the Gordon rioters; he did so, not because he had suddenly adopted revolutionary and democratic ideas – he did not even become a convinced parliamentary reformer – but because he saw 1789 as the French equivalent of the 'Glorious Revolution' of 1688. Others were under a similar misapprehension: the British Ambassador in Paris thought that France should from then on be 'considered as a free country'.[7]

The Revolution's real doctrines were not widely disseminated in Britain until Tom Paine's *Rights of Man*, which had a phenomenally large sale, was published early in 1791. England's drowsy radicalism was then slowly awakened and, as Wordsworth later wrote,

> The inert
> Were rous'd, and lively natures rapt away!

Two years after *Rights of Man*, Shelley's second father-in-law, William Godwin, who regarded Robespierre as 'an eminent benefactor of mankind', as at first had Coleridge and Southey, published his *Political Justice*, the first completely worked out statement of anarchism. In his book Godwin sought nothing less than the regeneration of the species. All mischievous institutions – the monarchy, the law, the Church, the aristocracy, marriage and the domestic affections – were to vanish, and justice, equality and universal benevolence were to reign in their place. Wordsworth, Southey and many others fell briefly under Godwin's spell. In 'a republican spirit', Wordsworth wrote a Godwinian 'Letter to the Bishop of Llandaff', deploring the country's 'extremes of poverty and riches', attacking monarchy and condemning hereditary nobility for binding 'down whole ranks of men to idleness'. He was, however, too cautious to publish it.[8]

Mary Wollstonecraft, the mother of Shelley's second wife, who, as a governess, had had some experience of the aristocracy, had a similar attitude but was much braver. Maintaining in one book that an aristocrat was 'changed into an artificial monster' by his station in life, she inveighed in another, the first great feminist tract, *A Vindication of the Rights of Women*, against the 'preposterous distinctions of rank' and the ridiculous respect paid to property. Nevertheless the radicals were a small minority. Judith Milbanke, the mother of Byron's wife, was much more in the mainstream of opinion. The future Lady Milbanke referred to herself as 'my Ladyship' even when she was still Mrs Milbanke, and when canvassing for her husband in Sunderland in 1790, she found 'the honest Tars . . . perfectly sensible of the deference due to a Lady'. That was not surprising. Aristocratic influence had not diminished in the second half of the century – if anything it had increased – and the aristocracy were still generally taken at their own high

4

valuation: they were the best people in the country with a right and duty to govern it.[9]

So when in 1794 the Attorney-General, Sir John Scott, later Lord Eldon, the man whom Shelley abhorred above all others, contended in the first English treason trial of the 1790s that representative government was contrary to the British constitution, he scarcely exaggerated. The proportion of the male population entitled to vote in England was one in ten, and in Scotland less than one in a hundred. Some 6,000 people could elect an effective majority of MPs. Seventy peers were responsible for the return of one-third of the English and Welsh members. Seats were bought, sold and leased, and by 1798 two-thirds of the borough seats were filled by land-owning patrons. While all this was of course anathema to the reformers, it was still generally accepted. The British constitution was widely venerated: many agreed with George III that it was a thing of 'beauty' and 'perfection'; some may even have concurred with the previous Attorney-General's belief, expressed when prosecuting Tom Paine, that it had been growing in excellence since Julius Caesar's invasion and indeed 'from time almost eternal'.[10]

Nevertheless, there were many who feared that this almost divine excellence would not be enough to save it. The warnings of Burke in his magnificent *Reflections on the Revolution in France*, to which the books of Paine and Mary Wollstonecraft were replies, and, more important, the course of that Revolution – the September Massacres, the execution of Louis XVI and the Terror – together with social unrest at home and the revival of radicalism, produced what the young Coleridge called 'a panic of property'. Fortunately for the fearful, God was on the side of property owners. Providence, according to the Church, had placed every man in his proper sphere of life, and morality demanded obedience from the poor and their acceptance of the divinely ordained social order. 'Religion', maintained Archdeacon Paley, an author admired by Shelley's father, 'smoothes all inequalities, because it unfolds a prospect which makes all earthly distinctions nothing'.[11]

For the poor to look forward to equality and better times in heaven suited the rich; such future hopes were an antidote to revolutionary ideas. Yet those who did not want their 'inequalities' smoothed away on earth looked to morals and religion for additional protection. The French Revolution had hastened a reaction against the relative freedom of women in the 1780s, a reaction hardened by the writings of English radicals, especially Godwin, who in his *Political Justice* stigmatised marriage as an 'odious monopoly' and denigrated the 'domestic affections'; he preferred 'universal benevolence'. In France the poorer classes favoured free union between the sexes and demanded equal rights for illegitimate children and unmarried mothers. They saw sexual freedom as an important part of the revolution. Not surprisingly, therefore, republicanism, atheism and free love were lumped together in England as dangerous threats to the stability of the country. The French Revolution, the *Annual Register* believed, illustrated the connection 'between good morals and the order and peace of society'. If, as some thought, the dissolute life of the French Court in the reign of Louis XV had caused people to lose their respect for the higher classes in France, both sexual and political repression, which Blake thought were linked, were considered by many to be essential for the preservation of society.[14]

Hence, as well as more secular measures, the prosperous sought to use strict female chastity, female subordination, family feelings and religious observance as weapons to safeguard their 'earthly distinctions' from those godless and profligate French revolutionaries and their would-be English imitators: men who ignored the importance of the family and undermined the social order, while preaching the brotherhood of man. This life of virtue was more genuinely practised in the middle classes, but many of the aristocracy put on a parade of virtue, though not for long. The spectacle of the rich suddenly going regularly to church bewildered, said the *Annual Register*, 'the simple country people' who wondered what had caused it. A few years later William Cobbett, the popular journalist, whom both Shelley and Byron admired, gave them a hint. Amongst Pitt's adherents, he wrote in 1804, there was 'a strange mixture of profligacy and cant: jobbers all the morning and methodists in the afternoon.'

This growing moral conservatism, an overture to Victorianism, was allied with a strengthened political conservatism. In 1794 the Conservative or Portland Whigs joined Pitt's government, leaving behind only a factious and impotent Foxite rump, which included the Duke of Norfolk, the patron of Shelley's father and grandfather. This small Foxite remnant mounted a gallant though ineffective opposition to the suspension of habeas corpus and the government's other repressive measures, that had been, Coleridge publicly asserted, 'conceived and laid in the dunghill of despotism'. Even more hyperbolically, Fox stigmatised them as Pitt's 'reign of terror'.[13]

Yet there had been no need for property to panic nor for the Duke of Portland, a later antagonist of Byron's, to fear 'the inundation of levelling doctrines'. The aristocracy and the conservative cause triumphed. The extremism of the later stages of the French Revolution, combined with traditional Francophobia, was sufficient inoculation for most Englishmen, even those without property, against revolutionary and radical ideas. 'The inborn divinity that attends upon rank', as Godwin described it in his novel *Caleb Williams*, continued to be 'revered, as Indians worship the Devil'. Loyalist patriotic nationalism turned out to be far more popular than radical 'levelling doctrines' which were tainted by connection with France. They were also tainted with incoherence. Except for Paine, Coleridge and a few others, the radicals proposed only political reform. They had no social programme to benefit the deprived masses; they thus alienated the rich without winning the poor. In consequence the conservatives scarcely had to win the argument: the radicals themselves lost it.'[14]

Godwin, who had himself recanted on aristocracy, noted that 'even the starving labourer in the ale house [had] become [its] champion'. Earlier 'the Lake poets', Wordsworth, Coleridge and Southey, disillusioned with the French Revolution, had changed sides; they were not the only ones. As Byron said to Southey in his dedication of *Don Juan*,

> Although 'tis true that you turn'd out a Tory at
>   Last, – yours has lately been a common case. . . .
>   Apostasy's so fashionable too,
> To keep *one* creed's a task grown quite Herculean,
> Is it not so, my Tory ultra-Julian?[15]

Yet there had been no reform, and in the general conservative reaction there was little prospect of it. Many years afterwards Sydney Smith listed the things wrong with the country in 1802, the year he and others had founded the *Edinburgh Review*:

The Catholics were not emancipated – the Corporation and Test Acts were unrepealed – the Game Laws were horribly repressive – Steel Traps and Spring Guns were set all over the country – prisoners tried for their lives could have no counsel – Lord Eldon and the Court of Chancery pressed heavily upon mankind – libel was punished by the most cruel and vindictive imprisonment – the principles of Political Economy were little understood – the Law of Debt and of Conspiracy were upon the worst possible footing – the enormous wickedness of the Slave Trade was tolerated – a thousand evils were in existence . . .

– prominent among them the electoral system and political corruption.[16]

Of course England still had its litany of liberties: trial by jury, habeas corpus, which Dr Johnson considered English government's only advantage over other countries ('I like the habeas corpus – when we've got it', wrote Byron), an elected parliament, restricted ministerial powers, no absolute monarch, in all of which it was superior to its continental rivals. Despite its very real blemishes, therefore, and despite the frequent prosecutions of journalists, of which there were seventy-five in 1819, as well as the growing moral conservatism and authoritarianism of the early nineteenth century, England was still largely a free country. In 1816 calling her 'that most excellent of nations', Shelley was 'persuaded' that of all countries she was 'the most free & the most refined'. England was also France's sole undefeated enemy. She was 'the only country', wrote a great French historian, 'to oppose [France] with analogous forces: national principles and popular passions'. Yet, understandably, English critics and radicals took those blessings for granted and concentrated on the blatant abuses.[17]

And by the time Byron and Shelley were more or less adults, only one of those abuses – the slave trade – had been abolished; all the others were still there at their deaths. In 1811, when Southey met Shelley, he said that the young man was just what he himself had been in 1794, while Shelley thought Southey had been 'corrupted by the world, contaminated by custom'. Unlike Southey – and Wordsworth and Coleridge – Shelley and Byron never were in that sense 'corrupted' or 'contaminated'. They accomplished the 'Herculean' task of 'keeping[ing] one creed', remaining what Shelley's widow called 'partisans of reform'.[18]

They were less well disposed to other partisans of reform. Byron regarded most reformers as 'ragamuffins' and 'scoundrels', which accurately describes the Cato Street conspirators, who in 1820 discredited the cause of reform by their futile plan to assassinate the Cabinet; they were arrested in Cato Street near the Edgware Road, and five of them were executed. Shelley, who once wrote that Byron had 'the canker of aristocracy' which needed 'to be cut out', although he himself, as Keats and Hazlitt and others recognised, was similarly, if more slightly, infected, also viewed Cato Street as a 'mad and strange plot'. He was worried, too, by 'the strength of the popular party' and by the prospect of having 'illiterate demagogues for masters'. The Whig leader, Lord Grey, made much the same point when he told a friend in 1819 that 'the leaders of the popular party, or rather of the Mob' wanted 'not Reform, but Revolution'. Grey exaggerated, but certainly nothing resembling what is today called democracy or democratic government was even a remote possibility at that time. Indeed the words 'democrat' and 'democracy' were still terms of abuse.[19]

Both men were fully aware of the excesses of the French Revolution. 'The common feelings of humanity were openly violated', Byron said in 1816; and in the following year Shelley wrote of 'the atrocities of the demagogues'. Yet unlike Wordsworth, Coleridge and Southey, they had gone through neither the initial excitement of the Revolution nor the disenchantment produced by its subsequent course. For them the Revolution and its atrocities were history; and the present, Shelley wrote in *Laon and Cythna*, was 'the winter of the world'. In consequence 'gloom and misanthropy [were] the characteristics of the age' in which they lived, although that scarcely affected Shelley's own views. He remained a Godwinian optimist. But Byron and most of his generation were disillusioned from the start. Having missed the Revolution, he and they merely saw the conservative reaction in all its mediocrity, corruption and social repression. Hence Byron simplified his politics 'into an utter detestation of all existing governments'. He was sure, all the same, that 'God [would] not be always a Tory', that 'the king-times [were] fast finishing', and that 'the peoples [would] conquer in the end'.[20]

In his 'Ode to Liberty', Shelley similarly hoped that 'the free would stamp the impious name / Of King into the dust'. Earlier in 1817, he thought that 'the panic', which 'the excesses' of the French Revolution' had produced in England, was gradually giving way to 'sanity'. That was over-optimistic; the reaction still had some years to run. But neither poet thought France's failure to achieve freedom by her Revolution should preclude new attempts to achieve it elsewhere. Mankind, wrote Shelley, echoing Sheridan in the 1790s, should not be consigned to 'ignorance and misery' because the long-enslaved French had not suddenly been capable of acting 'with the wisdom and tranquillity of freemen'. He and Byron, who wanted 'if possible' the stones to 'rise against Earth's tyrants', both stayed much where Southey said he had been in 1794, a position which was not as naïve as Southey's remark suggested and which was largely justified by events. In any case, in the 1790s, although Britain had fought on the side of political legitimacy against Jacobinism, she was ideologically closer to her enemies than to her allies – the autocratic Austria, Prussia and Russia; and in the years of the second war, 1803–15, when the enemy was allegedly French imperial expansion, Britain achieved the greatest expansion of her own Empire since the seventeenth century. Sheridan called it 'filching sugar islands', and Shelley likened Britain's 'conquests in India' to those of 'Buonaparte' in Europe. Hence ambivalence to the war was understandable, if misguided, and opposition to the reaction was well-founded.[21]

In addition to not changing sides, Byron and Shelley differed from Wordsworth, Coleridge and Southey in their class background. The Byrons were aristocrats, though relatively impoverished; the Shelley family was *nouveau riche* and far from aristocratic. Yet they were both indubitably upper-class land-owning families, and Shelley himself was highly aristocratic in manner – 'as perfect a Gentleman', Byron said of him, 'as ever crossed a drawing room'. As such they would have been expected to stay with the rest of their class on the conservative side. Indeed John Wilson Croker, the long-serving Secretary of the Admiralty and zealous Tory, who was caricatured as 'Rigby' by Disraeli in *Coningsby*, was convinced that Byron had at heart stayed with his class. A man of his taste, talents and habits, Croker told Byron's publisher in 1820, could have 'nothing in common with such miserable creatures' as the radicals. Those at the other end of the political spectrum thought much the same. In his 'peevish invective' against Byron after his death, Hazlitt called him 'that anomaly in letters and society, a Noble poet', whose '*liberalism*' because of that anomaly was necessarily 'preposterous'. Against Shelley, too, Hazlitt had a not dissimilar prejudice.[22]

In 1817 Lord Castlereagh, who was fiercely attacked by both Shelley and Byron, claimed that 'the revolutionary spirit' had been gradually descending from the 'higher and better informed ranks' to the 'lower orders'. Arguably that happened in France. 'The patricians began the Revolution', said Chateaubriand, whose novel *René* prefigured the Byronic hero, 'and the plebeians completed it'. But it was not true, earlier or later, of England. Among the upper classes, apart from some of Byron's friends, Byron and Shelley were almost alone in their views. Both of them, as Henry James said of Byron, 'quarrelled with the temper and accent of [their] age'. That was due partly to their exceptional abilities and partly to their upbringing and family circumstances. Although superficially very different, they were more like each other than they realised; and so were their lives.[23]

Only the first part of those lives is recounted here. After Lord Rosebery, the former Liberal Prime Minister, had published his *Napoleon, The Last Phase* and *Chatham, His Early Life*, Arthur Balfour remarked that it was just like Rosebery to write about Chatham before he had become and about Napoleon after he had stopped being interesting. More encouragingly, John Hanson, Byron's indolent solicitor and business agent, thought of writing a book about him, particularly his life from eight to eighteen years old, which period, he told Byron's friend Hobhouse, 'was the most interesting of his existence'. Not many people would go as far as that; but the early years of both Byron and Shelley were certainly important; and they had few years afterwards: when Byron left Harrow, almost half his life was over; and when Shelley left Eton, only two-fifths of his life remained. By 1812 both men had lived two-thirds of their lives. Later of course they became friends.

CHAPTER I

The Byrons and Gordons

Scotland's greatest poet was 'hatched', as he called it, on 22 January 1788. The anniversary is not widely observed. No annual suppers are held in Scotland or in faraway countries; no haggis is ceremonially speared before being eaten with discomfort or relish; no emotional speeches are delivered to evoke the 'immortal memory'. There are not even any toasts to 'the lassies'. Scottish celebrations take place three days later on the birthday of Robert Burns.

Admittedly Byron was born in England and wrote in English, yet his mother was a Gordon of Gight, his father took his mother's name to ease his intended inroads on her fortune, and Byron himself (who spent his early childhood in Aberdeen) insisted as a boy on being called George Byron Gordon. He was, he told Sir Walter Scott, 'bred a canny Scot till ten years old'.[1]

In any case, whether Byron should be regarded as 'a Scottish poet', as T. S Eliot argued in one of his less persuasive essays, as one of Scotland's great poets or just as an English one, his use of English in his poetry should not disqualify him from being a Scot. The greatest figures of the Scottish Enlightenment and post-Enlightenment, David Hume, Adam Smith and (despite his liberal use of Scottish dialect) Sir Walter Scott, wrote in English; and so, on occasion, did Burns. When one of Byron's least favourite mistresses told him that he had a little of a Scotch accent, he replied: 'Good God, I hope not. I'm sure I haven't. I would rather the whole d . . . d country was sunk in the sea – I the Scotch accent!' Yet, Byron, like Mr Gladstone, did speak with a burr* and for much of his life he pronounced his name not 'Byron' but 'Birron'. He once lamented that he was 'half English as I am (to my misfortune) . . .'. Conversely, he later wrote in *Don Juan*, 'But I am half a Scot by birth, and bred/ A whole one, and my heart flies to my head/. . . . I

---

* Leigh Hunt thought, wrongly, that Byron had a 'Northumbrian burr'; Mr Gladstone's was more Lancastrian than Scottish.[3]

"*scotched,* not killed," the Scotchman in my blood'/, he went on,
'And love the land of "mountain and of flood".'[2]

'Every Scottishman', wrote Sir Walter Scott, 'has a pedigree. It is a
national prerogative, as unalienable as his pride and his poverty'.
Byron certainly had a pedigree and was proud of it:

> For I can boast a race as true
>   To Monarchs crowned and some discrowned
> As ever Britain's Annals knew.

But, unlike Don Juan who 'owed . . . much also to the blood he
showed,/Like a race-horse', Byron's pedigree was not one that, had
he been a horse or a dog, a prospective buyer would have found
reassuring. As he wrote on another occasion, he came from 'a line
of cut-throat ancestors'.[4]

The Burons or Birons came over with William the Conqueror and
appear in Domesday Book. 'Eight-and-forty manors', according to
Byron, 'Were their reward for following Billy's banners'. The
manors with which 'the conqueror William did repay' the Biron
from whom the poet's family was descended were in Nottinghamshire and Derbyshire; a century later a marriage to an heiress
brought the family an estate in Lancashire. In an early poem, 'On
Leaving Newstead Abbey', Byron claimed that his ancestors were
crusaders – 'Led their vassals from Europe to Palestine's plain' – but
the family tradition is probably wrong. He was on slightly firmer
ground in affirming that 'Paul and Hubert too sleep in the valley of
Cressy', since a Sir John de Byron did fight in that battle. Another
ancestral trait even more enduring than martial ardour emerged in
the crusading period, although it does not figure in Byron's early
poems: in 1191 Godfrey de Buron borrowed money from 'Aaron
the Jew'. The Byrons were chronically in debt, and Aaron was not
the only money-lender to have his services sought by the Byron
family.[5]

After the dissolution of the monasteries, Henry VIII granted the
Sir John Byron of the day 'all the house and site, ground and soil, of
the late Monastery or Priory of Newstede within the Forest of
Sherewode', together with some other land and buildings, 'for the
sum of eight hundred and ten pounds'. Newstead, one of many
religious houses founded by Henry II for the order of Austin
canons, had done little to refute Shelley's dismissive remarks about
monasticism: 'the monks in their cloisters were engaged in trifling

and ridiculous disputes'. Byron was more favourably disposed. 'Years roll on; to ages, ages yield', he wrote in another juvenile poem, 'Till royal sacrilege their doom decreed'. But little sacrilege was involved in closing Newstead Priory; it had long ceased to serve any useful purpose.[6]

Having no children by his wife, Sir John Byron formed an open liaison and had at least two bastards. His son, also a Sir John, carried on the family tradition of being heavily in debt, and his daughter carried on that of adultery. His great-grandson, another Sir John, also conformed; indeed, after failing to appear in court to answer a charge relating to his debts, he at one stage suffered outlawry.[7]

In the Civil War the Byrons were not backward in supporting Charles I. The fifth Sir John, a choleric man even more heavily in debt than his predecessors, served in the Royalist army together with his six brothers and an uncle, and in 1643 he was created Lord Byron of Rochdale. His career as a commander was chequered. Brave and loyal, he was successful at Roundway Down, but his rashness was damaging at Edgehill and disastrous at Marston Moor. Later, John Byron's troops massacred a number of civilians in a church. We 'put them all to the sword', he boasted, 'which I find to be the best way to proceed with these kind of people, for mercy to them is cruelty'.[8] Nevertheless, Clarendon surprisingly claimed that he had 'as unblemished a reputation as any gentleman in England'. And when Byron died in France in 1652, Clarendon called him 'an irreparable loss'. His death, though, did not end his family's services to the Royalist cause. His beautiful widow Eleanor, whom he had married in 1644 when she was seventeen, became the future 'King's seventeenth whore abroad', Evelyn told Pepys; and his brother Richard, the second Lord Byron, plotted busily but ineffectually at Newstead.

Eccentricity was probably introduced into the Byrons by the fourth Lord's third wife, Frances, daughter of the fourth Lord Berkeley of Stratton, Chancellor of the Duchy of Lancaster in Harley's 1710 administration. The first Lord Berkeley, who succeeded Byron as tutor to the future James II, was described by Pepys as 'the most hot, fiery man in discourse, without any cause, that ever I saw'. Dissolute and dishonest, he was briefly Lord-Lieutenant of Ireland and Ambassador to France, but he is chiefly notable for having given his name to Berkeley Square.[9]

The fourth Lord Byron was fifty-one when he married young Frances Berkeley, and their union produced an unusual brood. In quick succession Frances gave birth to a decidedly unconventional daughter, a cocky and disreputable heir, an admiral, a clergyman artist who became an absentee landowner in Nova Scotia and, finally, a nonentity who, not inappropriately, was the godson of George II.[10]

Their eldest child, Isabella, was married to the fourth Earl of Carlisle in 1743, when she was twenty-one and her husband forty-nine. Lady Mary Wortley Montagu found her 'very agreeable, but if I am not mistaken in her Inclinations, they are very gay'. Her appraisal turned out to be well founded. Nevertheless, Isabella lasted the final fifteen years of the Earl's life without serious mishap, giving him four daughters and a son. The year after his death, however, she married a man sixteen years her junior, whom she soon abandoned for a life of scandal and money troubles on the continent.[11] Isabella, the mother of the poet's guardian, was also something of a bluestocking, writing and sketching a little. Even so, Mme du Deffand thought it 'important que cette dame quitte ce pais – garrison, – fréquens repas, – fort agréable à tous les officers'. English ladies came to a different conclusion, thinking Isabella was right to stay abroad, 'for no mortal would go near her if she were at home'. Yet the Dowager Lady Carlisle so lacked doubts about herself, that she published a book of maxims to keep young ladies on the path of virtue.[12]

William, the eldest son, was sent to Westminster School and, when his father died, he was packed off, aged thirteen, to the navy which he left after coming of age. A gambling rake, he abducted a beautiful and intelligent actress, George Anne Bellamy, shortly before he married a Norfolk heiress who brought him £70,000. Neither his wife nor her money deterred him from continuing his persecution of the actress; only the threatened violence of her brother put a stop to that. Miss Bellamy, who had some dealings with Dr Johnson and charmed Boswell, later became a champion of women's rights (then largely non-existent) probably partly because of William Byron's treatment of her.[13]

Racing and cock fighting were William Byron's chief occupations, accompanied by vast extravagance and the building of follies. At the end of 1763 he was made Master of the Royal Staghounds, though it was not until a year later that he briefly emerged from obscurity by killing his neighbour William Chaworth in a duel, fought over the momentous question as to which of the two men had more game on his estate. Because the coroner's jury brought in a verdict of murder, William Byron as a peer had to be tried by the House of Lords. As was not unknown in 'duels of honour', honour in this affair was scarce. Purists were shocked that the duel had taken place in a small dark room without seconds, because this allowed the possibility of 'the foulest treachery'. Byron was evidently the aggressor and was the first to start drawing his sword, although Chaworth managed to make the first thrust. Byron then took advantage of Chaworth's mistaken belief that, he, Byron, was mortally wounded to stab Chaworth to death, an action which seems treacherous but was apparently within the rules of 'honour'. At all events the Lords found Byron guilty only of manslaughter, a verdict that allowed him to plead benefit of peerage under a statute of Edward VI and to be 'discharged paying his fees'.[14]

Despite the Lords' customary complaisance to one of their own, the widespread suspicion of foul play turned opinion against William Byron. He lost his mastership of the Royal Staghounds, and the case gave a fillip to his unpopularity in Nottinghamshire where he had long been known as a bad neighbour, a bad landlord and a man who did not pay his bills. He was not, however, immediately ostracised; only some years later did his wife and daughter leave him. He then consoled himself with his servant 'Lady Betty' and became a recluse at Newstead which he denuded of its pictures, furniture, timber and deer – as late as 1814 John Murray, the sixth Lord's publisher, found 'not a tree left standing'. In his last years many stories, mostly false, were told of him, and he became known as the 'wicked Lord', a legend that gave him unmerited glamour for, although he was sinister and possibly slightly mad, he was essentially dim, disagreeable, selfish and vindictive; neglectful of his heirs he despoiled his estate.[15]

Even before his disgrace, William Byron had not been close to any of his family. His next brother, the far more handsome John, followed him into the navy and stayed in it, eventually becoming a rear-admiral. When he was a young midshipman, his ship was lost after rounding Cape Horn, and he suffered extraordinary privations which he later recounted in a book that is still readable.* In the

---

* It was one of his grandson's sources for the shipwreck scene in *Don Juan* which so upset the dying John Keats on his voyage to Italy.[17]

West Indies during the American war he was struck, it was reported, with disorder and disease 'that deprived him of his reason'.[16]

At home John Byron was far from monogamous. His attractive, sociable, intelligent wife, Sophia Trevanion, was tolerant and broad-minded – she once shocked Mrs Thrale by lending her an 'obscene' poem – and does not seem to have been particularly put out by her husband's various escapades. She did draw the line, however, at finding a chambermaid in his bed, and Betsy Green was dismissed.*[18]

The Admiral was much less erratic than his elder brother William and sister Isabella, but his wife Sophia was his first cousin, which entailed a second dose of Berkeley blood in his descendants. These numbered two sons and seven daughters, three of whom died young. The Admiral had to appear in a Nottingham court to pay money to an illegitimate girl fathered by his second son, George Anson Byron. A competent and conscientious naval officer, George further disturbed his parents by returning from the West Indies with a wife, Henrietta Dallas, whom he hardly knew and whom his mother did not like even after she got to know her. The elopement of one of their daughters, Juliana, with her cousin, William Byron's only son and heir, drove the Admiral and his brother further apart. The 'wicked Lord', who had hoped his son would repair the family fortunes by hooking an heiress and who had had one lined up for him, was enraged by what he regarded as a *mésalliance*.[20]

Nevertheless, it was their eldest son Jack, born in 1756 and the father of the poet, and their eldest daughter Frances who were the chief sources of parental vexation to John and Sophia Byron. Miss Bellamy said of the 'wicked Lord' that he 'had little to boast of but a title and an agreeable face'. Jack Byron did not even have a title. Having sent Jack to Westminster and a French military academy, the Admiral bought him a commission first in the 68th Foot and then in the Coldstream Guards, and he served for a short time in the composite Guards battalion in the American war. His son claimed that he had 'the reputation of a good officer and showed himself as such in the Guards in America'. If that were true, it would have been the only time that Jack Byron did have a good reputation. But

---

* This was presumably not the same Betsy Green as the lady of whom John Wilkes said he wrote his best *North Briton* when he was in bed with her.[19]

17

the evidence for it is slight. The Coldstream Guards have no record of Jack Byron in America, and he came home well before the rest of the battalion. Characteristically, however, he got heavily into debt in Philadelphia, and left America without paying his bills. Jack Byron's sole talents were for seducing women, running up bills and borrowing money; time and time again his parents, as in Philadelphia, had to pay up for him.[21]

On his return from America, Jack Byron, known as 'Mad Jack', began an affair with Amelia, Lord Carmarthen's beautiful and accomplished wife who had both money, £4,000 a year, and a title, Lady Coningsby, of her own. This was not Amelia's first lapse or even the first one that her husband knew about. Like Jack Byron's father, she had earlier 'yielded to the impulse of her complicated passions ... with one of her own domestics'. And when the indolent and vain Lord Carmarthen, who was Lord Chamberlain to the Queen and later became an inadequate Foreign Secretary, discovered her adultery with Jack Byron, he decided he had had enough and divorced her. Amelia married Jack, whose financial position was thus improved, yet the scandal and his debts made Paris a more suitable dwelling place for the couple than London. Their first two children died in infancy, and shortly after the birth of their third child, Augusta, Amelia herself died in July 1784. The cause of her death is obscure. Gossip alleged it was due to the 'brutal and vicious conduct' of her husband; the poet claimed that it was due to her going out hunting before she had fully recovered from Augusta's birth. Whatever the reason, Jack Byron was once again penniless. So, depositing his baby daughter in Paris with we know not whom, he went in search of another heiress and selected as his prey Catherine Gordon of Gight.[22]

According to her son, Catherine Gordon was 'as haughty as Lucifer' about her ancestry. Lucifer would probably have rated it higher than Jack Byron's. The Gordons of Gight were even more turbulent than the other members of the Gordon clan, their killings, robberies and treachery easily outstripping in villainy the first Lord Byron's Civil War massacre and the 'wicked Lord's' killing of William Chaworth. The fifth Laird of Gight (d.1604) murdered at least four people, including his brother-in-law. A more famous family murderer was Colonel William Gordon who assassinated Wallenstein, the great commander of the imperial forces in the Thirty

Years War. Surprisingly only one member of the Gight family died on the scaffold, and Nathaniel Gordon was condemned not for murder but for his support of Montrose in the Civil War. The main reason why some other Gordons escaped execution was that they were in their turn murdered before such law as there was caught up with them. The Gights did not confine themselves to murder. Both the fifth and the sixth Lairds were excommunicated; the sixth Laird (d. 1640) tried to blackmail his dying mother-in-law, and the eighth Laird tried to oust his own father from the estates. Nor was the Gight violence confined to the males. A daughter of the fifth Laird assaulted one man so brutally that she 'left him for deid'.[23]

As well as possessing that roll of honour, Catherine could trace her ancestry from the Scottish royal house. Her branch of the Gordons stemmed from Sir William Gordon who was the third son of the second Earl of Huntly by his second wife, Annabella Stuart, daughter of James I of Scotland. The head of the Gordon clan, Lord Huntly, was known as 'the cock of the north'. No wonder Catherine Gordon looked down on the Byrons. Her son, too, preferred 'my mother's family – for its royalty'. Yet the two lines resembled each other more than they differed. Because of the Trevanions, the Byrons were Celts like the Gordons of Gight, and the vehemence of the Berkeleys came close to that of the Gordons. Additionally the parents of both Jack Byron and Catherine Gordon were cousins. So the two blood strains, a breeder might well have concluded, were far from complementary and should not be mingled.[24]

In the eighteenth century the Lairds of Gight were not murderous but melancholic. When her mother died in 1782, Catherine Gordon was left without parents or siblings at the age of eighteen. Her two sisters had died young, and her father had committed suicide, drowning himself in the Bath canal. Her grandfather had done the same but in the River Ythan near the Castle of Gight. Even before she was orphaned, Catherine had been partly brought up by her grandmother, but neither that lady, who was herself ignorant and illiterate, nor Catherine's parents gave her much of an education, though she was certainly no fool. One of her relations later remembered her as 'a romping, comely, good-humoured girl of sixteen, inclined to corpulency'. Like those of her Gordon ancestors, her emotions were often unbridled. Aged twenty she went to see the famous actress Mrs Siddons perform in Edinburgh. An observer noted that while 'a large proportion of the ladies were generally in hysterics at the end', the paroxysms of Miss Gordon of Gight were particularly clamorous. After she shrieked out Mrs Siddons's exclamation to another character in the play 'Oh my Biron! Oh my Biron!' she needed medical attention. As the play was Southerne's *The Fatal Marriage* and Miss Gordon had not yet met Jack Byron, who was shortly to propose such a marriage, the story would be thought too neat to be credible but for the fact that the observer was Sir Walter Scott.[25]

Miss Gordon had a dumpy figure and lacked the dress sense to help her to improve on nature; her gait was awkward, her features homely, her complexion florid. Yet, if her sex appeal was minimal, she was, as the only descendant of the twelfth Laird of Gight, an heiress with a substantial fortune; and as John Dryden, a poet later much admired by her son, had earlier pronounced, 'All heiresses are beautiful'.

Shortly before Miss Gordon came of age she went to Bath in 1785 to buy jewellery and widen her horizons. For her grand-mother and her aunt – she had no other relations – to allow their naïve young heiress to visit Bath without having taken any precautions to safeguard her inheritance was almost criminally negligent. Maybe they thought her plainness would be adequate protection against unscrupulous suitors. If so, they were as naïve as Catherine herself, for marriage in the upper classes was a market, and money was a more valuable asset than looks. 'In this island', the novelist Robert Bage wrote a few years later, 'birth is the first virtue, and money the second.' Furthermore Catherine, lacking knowledge of the market, was an ignorant seller who was bound to be worsted by an informed consumer. Miss Gordon was duly entranced by Mad Jack Byron's good looks and fine dancing, and as the Byron creditors were pressing for payment he snapped up her and her fortune.[26]

CHAPTER II

Childhood in Aberdeen

Byron: 1788–98 (birth to age 10 years)

Catherine Gordon was superstitious, yet she was so infatuated that she married Jack Byron on 13 May 1785 in the presence of only two witnesses from Bath. And as she was the only person who did not realise that Captain Byron was interested solely in her inheritance, she did not insist on any form of marriage settlement, and there was nobody else to do it for her. In consequence the Captain took not only her name, as her father's will required, but also her money. Even worse, his debts, according to the law of the time, effectively became hers – his creditors could take her property to pay them.[1]

The young couple went to Gight, where Jack Byron Gordon was his usual extravagant self. The Aberdeenshire gentry, who were impressed by neither his hospitality nor his charm, disliked him, quickly realising that, as a contemporary ballad put it, he would 'squander the lands o' Gight awa''. And his creditors were indeed as pressing as ever. Hence woods were chopped and farms sold; in a few months Captain Byron rivalled at Gight the damage his uncle, the 'wicked Lord', took years to inflict on Newstead. When Jack married the heiress, he probably thought her inheritance was much larger than it turned out to be: rumour had it that Miss Gordon was worth some £60,000. Catherine's wealth cannot be exactly computed. Jack was not interested in the proper stewardship or realisation of his wife's property. He was only concerned with getting ready money for himself, and with the rapacity of a twentieth-century asset stripper he sold off her timber, her salmon fishing rights and her bank shares. Before long the remains of the estate had to be put up for sale, and so the whole Gight inheritance became £24,450 in cash. Had Catherine's assets been carefully managed after her marriage and then sold in an orderly fashion, they would of course have realised much more; so rumour may not have been far wrong.[2]

In the spring of 1786, after going through a second marriage

21

ceremony in the Scottish form, Jack Byron had retreated with his by now miserable wife from the hostile Aberdeenshire neighbours first to Hampshire and then the Isle of Wight. Catherine's near ruin did not abate her husband's extravagance nor give her the resolve to deny him money to pay off old debts or contract new ones. Face to face she could refuse him nothing, but seeing that if she stayed inert she would soon be destitute she began an attempt to put some part of her money beyond the reach of her predatory mate. Meanwhile, Jack sought funds from other sources. His sister Frances, unhappily married to Charles Leigh, a failed general, usually contributed from her pin-money. He journeyed to Cornwall to try his mother's Trevanion relations. The previous year he had tried his father, Admiral Byron who had rebuffed him shortly before he died. In his will the Admiral administered another rebuff, leaving his eldest son only £500 on the reasonable grounds that he had already 'paid and advanced [him] considerable sums of money'.[3]

Wrongly thinking the Admiral's will must have transformed his situation, one of Jack Byron's creditors committed him to a debtors' prison. From most points of view that was the best place for him; unfortunately, in return for the assignment of the Admiral's legacy, his tailor liberated him by paying £176. Another committal to prison being likely and a repetition of his tailor's misguided intervention improbable, Byron retired to France in the summer of 1787 taking with him £700 which had been sent to his wife to pay his debts. As Catherine, who was now 'big with bairn', still had a little money left she was welcome to join him in Paris. Welcome or not, Augusta Mary, Jack's daughter by his first wife, also joined the household for the first time. The little girl, aged three and a half, soon fell seriously ill and nearly died, but Catherine's devoted nursing saved her life. 'I still recollect with a degree of horror', Catherine later told Augusta with her customary lack of restraint, 'the many sleepless nights and days of agony I have passed at your bedside drowned in tears, while you lay insensible and at the gates of death. Your recovery certainly was wonderful and, thank God, I did my duty.' Augusta, too, may have thanked God, but she never thanked her stepmother.[4]

Wearing as the sleepless nights and the tears must have been to the heavily pregnant Mrs Byron Gordon, Augusta's illness may have brought some benefit. While Jack had had to learn French at his military academy in France and moved smoothly in French society, Catherine spoke not a word of the language and lacked polish even in English circles. Dominated and neglected by a husband whom she still loved but resented, and impatiently seeing him accumulate debts, most of which she would have to meet, the ex-heiress would probably have been still more unhappy in France had she not had her stepdaughter to look after. At any rate when Augusta was better, Catherine decided to return to England. Jack stayed behind, borrowing money from a Paris bank on the security of both Catherine's money and – he was not over-scrupulous in these matters – of an assignment of the Admiral's legacy that he had already assigned to his tailor. Probably, too, he managed to cajole his brother, George Anson Byron, then living at Chantilly, into paying off some of his debts, though that claim may only have been a device to extract more money from Catherine's dwindling estate.[5]

In London Catherine rented cramped lodgings at 16 Holles Street, a road that connects Oxford Street with Cavendish Square and is now on both sides a department store. She soon sent Augusta to the little girl's grandmother, Lady Holderness, the widow of a former Secretary of State. As Catherine knew virtually nobody in London, she was badly in need of assistance. Unfortunately Lady Holderness had no reason to care for the second wife of the man whom she doubtless regarded as having ruined the life of her daughter Amelia; and although herself Dutch she shared the current English aristocratic obsession with rank, looking down on Catherine, and evidently teaching Augusta to do the same. As a result Catherine's child and Augusta did not meet until he was twelve and she was sixteen.[6]

Pregnant, friendless and short of money in a large city, the erstwhile heiress faced a dispiriting future. But however loudly Mrs Byron Gordon complained of her misfortunes either then or later, she never lacked fortitude; and at least she was not left entirely to fend for herself. In the middle of December the Edinburgh commissioners (trustees) of the Gight estate sent her £55 5s. for her 'lying-in'. Unless Jack got his hands on it, and he was on his way to England, that was enough for her immediate needs. With this money she was able to engage the services of a doctor, a male midwife and a nurse, all apparently recommended by a stranger; and with them in attendance her first and only child was delivered after a long and difficult labour. The baby boy was born with a caul (a membrane covering the head), which contrary to legend did not

turn out to be lucky, and an abnormal foot,* which caused
Byron much physical pain as a boy and mental torment both as a
child and as a man.[7]

In 1810, after bathing in the Gulf of Lepanto with Lord Sligo,
Byron pointed to his leg and foot and blamed his deformity on his
mother's 'false delicacy at my birth'. That was unjust. If he meant
that his mother was wearing corsets during her labour, he could not
have known; and even if she was, that seems to have been the
contemporary custom. If, as is more likely, Byron meant that his
mother had refused to have a male assistant at his birth, he was
wrong. Unlike Mary Wollstonecraft nine years later, she had had
two.[12]

* Curiously, for such a famous deformity, there is no unanimity on the nature of Byron's
disability or even on which foot was affected. Thirty years after Byron's death at
Missolonghi, Edward John Trelawny an adventurer and writer who knew Byron in Italy and
Greece, claimed to have seen his corpse: 'Both his feet were clubbed, and his legs withered to
the knee – the form and features of an Apollo, with the feet and legs of a Sylvan Satyr'. Had
that been so, as Swinburne pointed out, Byron would not have been able to swim; nor would
he have been able to walk without a stick; nor, as his mistress Teresa Guiccioli privately
implied, would he have been able to 'make love' except 'platonically'. And finally as
Trelawny had bathed with Byron, he would certainly have noticed such a deformity long
before the poet's death.[8]

A further twenty years later Trelawny gave a quite different account, writing that apart
from a 'contracture of the back sinews . . . his feet were perfect.' Neither was true; both were
fabrications. Trelawny, of whom Byron had observed that he 'could not, even to save his life,
tell the truth', probably did not reach Missolonghi in time to see anything at all.[9]

One of the doctors at Missolonghi, Julius Millingen, said the left foot was clubbed.
'Gentleman' John Jackson, who taught Byron boxing, and Marianne Hunt thought the same.
Others who knew Byron, such as his principal biographer, Thomas Moore, as well as John
Galt, Lady Blessington and the Contessa Albrizzi, did not know which foot was deformed;
Tom Medwin, Shelley's schoolfellow and first biographer, who saw much of Byron at Pisa,
thought it difficult to distinguish one foot from the other. Catherine Byron, however, the
most authoritative witness apart from Byron himself, had no doubts. When Byron was three,
she wrote to her sister-in-law, Mrs Leigh: 'George's foot turns inward, and it is the right foot;
he walks quite on the side of his foot'. That it was indeed the right foot was confirmed when
the Byron vault was opened in 1938.[10]

The nature of the deformity is even more problematic. The only time he mentioned his son
in his correspondence, Captain Byron said it was impossible he could walk 'as he is club-
footed'. A foot expert consulted by Byron, T. Sheldrake, also said Byron had an ordinary
club-foot, though as his sketch is of the left not the right leg his testimony is not of great
weight. Still, most people including Millingen have taken the same view. Other suggestions
have been that Byron was spastic or that he suffered from infantile paralysis (polio) or from
Little's Disease – a tightening of the Achilles tendon, which Byron named in *Don Juan* as 'the
very tendon which is most acute'. We shall never be certain. Yet Byron's valet, Fletcher, who
was in the best position to know, told Moore that there was nothing wrong with the shape of
Byron's foot except that it was smaller than the other ; and Byron's boots in the possession of
John Murray indicate that he did not have a club-foot but what one recent medical authority
has described as 'a grotesquely thin calf and a small foot'. There was 'a failure of the region
to form properly; a dysplasia and not a moulding deformity such as a club-foot'. If that is
correct, all the painful treatment Byron received as a child was useless. His disability was
incurable.[11]

Naturally anxious about her baby's abnormality, Catherine immediately consulted John Hunter, an eminent surgeon. Hunter's diagnosis has not survived but, according to Catherine three years later, his opinion was that the baby's 'foot would be very well if he could have a proper shoe'; so from birth to death Byron was dogged by bad medical advice.

The anxieties of the child's father lay elsewhere. He was not present at the birth: writing to Edinburgh four days after it to complain that his wife had not received any money, he even got its day wrong. Nor did he attend the christening on 29 February at Marylebone parish church which was entirely a Gordon affair and at which the boy was named George Gordon after Catherine's father. No member of the Byron family was present. They may not have known of the child's existence. Except for his sister Frances, who was abroad, Jack Byron was not on good terms with his family. He did not even visit his mother who was 'old and infirm' and died two years later. Clearly he had no hopes of funds from that quarter, or he would have been in assiduous attendance, probably taking with him her grandson whom she never saw.[13]

For, of course, money – getting and spending it – was always Jack Byron's overriding concern, and added to it now was the fear of being thrown into the Fleet prison by one of his creditors. Under English law debtors were immune from arrest on a Sunday; for the rest of the week Captain Byron was at risk and obliged, as he put it, 'to be at hide and seek'. That meant skulking indoors or retiring to the country. Perhaps still more worrying for him were signs that his milch-cow was drying up. Belatedly, Catherine's Edinburgh trustees were also becoming uneasy. On the day of the christening, their London representative told them that 'nothing less than £1,300 will make Mr Byron a free man', and after recalling what had happened to the £700 sent the previous summer he suggested that to discharge the present debts 'would only be paving the way to the accumulation of fresh ones'. He added that Catherine was afraid that she had 'not the resolution to refuse any request that Byron may make to her personally' and therefore hoped that the trustees would not respond to any request for money but would 'protect ... the remainder of her property'. That plea succeeded. So at last Catherine's efforts, begun two years earlier, bore some fruit: yet out of the original £24,000, after giving her grandmother an annuity of £55 11s., only £3,000 was left to be invested for herself. Everything else had gone to her husband or his creditors. And still he had not finished with Catherine's money.[14]

Between the spring of 1788 and the summer of 1789 the whereabouts of Mrs Byron Gordon and her baby son are uncertain. Probably they were most of the time near London with Captain Byron, who played 'hide and seek' with his creditors so skilfully that the family eluded not only the bailiffs but subsequent investigation. This evasive existence seems to have lasted until spring 1789 when Catherine took her son to Aberdeen. There her £150 a year would be enough to live on – though only if her husband stayed away.

That summer Jack Byron took a house on the Kent coast, entertaining his nephew, the 'wicked Lord's' grandson and heir, William John Byron. How Jack paid for the house and his 'very fine lugger', or if he ever did, is not known. According to his nephew, who was charmed by him, he only narrowly escaped being imprisoned for debt in Boulogne and then went to Scotland which was 'much the safest place for him'.[15]

Safety for the Captain spelled financial peril for his wife. Catherine, who remained passionately in love with her husband, invariably welcomed the resumption of conjugal life, however dire the consequences. A frugal regime in Scotland would have been alien to the luxurious habits of Jack Byron, even if his domestic circumstances had been peaceful; and there was no possibility of tranquillity in the cramped conditions of their life in Aberdeen. Catherine was undoubtedly a difficult person to live with. Her always fragile temper had been frayed by her misfortunes, and when the author of these misfortunes was close at hand he bore the brunt of her rages. Her scolding outbursts were followed by extravagant demonstrations of affection, and possibly Jack found their lovemaking more of a burden than their rows. At all events he soon sought refuge in separate accommodation at the opposite end of Queen Street, where he once had his little son to stay. That visit, as his nurse had predicted, lasted only one night. Shortly afterwards, having received a little money from his sister, Jack Byron retreated from Aberdeen, only to return for a second visit when he had spent it.[16]

Little Geordie, as the poet was then called, later claimed to have clear recollections of his parents' 'domestic broils' which had very early given him 'a horror of matrimony', but he always spoke well of Jack Byron, whom, he said, 'I perfectly remember'. Yet as Little Geordie was aged two when he last saw his father, not six as he claimed, his alleged feat of recall must have been largely the fruit of his later experiences – of his own marriage, presumably – and his imagination. Like Augusta, Byron always, as he said, 'loved the memory of our father', but that memory was based on little, if any, reality. He later lamented that

> Stern Death forbade my orphan youth to share,
> The tender guidance of a father's care –

yet it was debts and indifference as much as death which prevented Jack Byron from providing tender guidance to his son, whose memory even misrepresented the finances of his parents. 'If he dissipated his fortune', Byron told a correspondent shortly before he left for Greece, 'that concerns us alone; for we are his heirs'. Unquestionably Jack Byron would have dissipated his fortune, had he had one. As it was, he dissipated his wife's, and his son inherited only his debts.[17]

Byron's admiration for his father stemmed partly from pride of ancestry and partly from his memory of his mother's ungovernable temper while having seen only his own, not his father's, aggravations of it. Captain Byron's principal provocation was of course his demands for money. By the time he left Catherine for the last time he had driven her deeply into debt; she had to write begging letters to borrow £300, and he was reduced to writing notes asking her for a guinea. The knowledge that there were no more guineas to be had rather than his wife's complaints of his extravagance sent Mad Jack back to France in September 1790 to join Fanny Leigh, his sister, who was almost equally dissolute.[18]

Jack Byron showed to even worse advantage in Valenciennes than in Aberdeen. On the death of their mother, Fanny returned to England in quest of legacies. Her brother's letters suggest that he preferred the physical attractions of his sister* to those of his

---

* Thirty years afterwards his son thought it ridiculous to deny that we 'inherit our passions, as well as the gout or any other disorder'. In that case, if he and Augusta in their turn later committed incest, it may have been hereditary. Yet, as neither Augusta nor Byron knew of the sexual union between their father and their aunt (who was also Augusta's mother-in-law), they were not consciously indulging in ancestor worship or copying the Ptolemies.[20]

wife. 'I can find no Woman so handsome as you', he confided. 'I have tried several, but when I do anything *extraordinary* I always think of you'.[19]

The absence of his sister's charms did not cause Jack Byron to relapse into celibacy. 'I have more on my hands than I can do,' he told Fanny, 'as La Henry [a brothel madame], who does the business well, is always after me, and I love to oblige her Dames now and then.' In another letter he claimed to 'have had one third of Valenciennes', an arrogantly inaccurate boast, even though Valenciennes was a fairly small town. Jack Byron was politically arrogant as well. When the theatre audience shouted 'Vive La Nation!' it was not a foreigner's place to shout 'Vive Le Roi!' even if he was drunk. He was worse than arrogant to his servants. Josephine 'gets no money and plenty of abuse, it is the only way to treat her'. On another occasion he felt 'obliged' to kick her downstairs so that she fell headfirst 'in a state of intoxication'.[21]

Maybe he was himself intoxicated when he expressed the hope to Fanny that 'you will be able to get me what little remains of my mother'. Then came the sad intelligence that he would not be receiving his mother's legacy of £500 because he had already assigned it to somebody else when he was at Deal. When Fanny told him she had had a letter from his wife, he had the gall to reply: 'what can the correspondence of Mrs Byron be? I hope not for money, as she has had quite enough, and never would give me a farthing.' Catherine had indeed been desperately seeking a loan – 'me nor my child have not at present a farthing' – but Fanny had evidently kept that from her brother who then deftly headed off the possibility of Catherine's letter leading to some of Fanny's funds being diverted to his wife and son instead of to their proper recipient.[22]

Apart from one remark about Byron's foot, Jack Byron never gave a recorded thought to his son. He did, however, more than once enquire after his daughter; Augusta, after all, was living with a rich family. Despite Fanny sending Jack Byron the occasional remittance, both his health and his finances were in decline. His clothes were seized, yet his extravagance continued. He kept on his sister's box at the theatre, even though he was too ill to use it. But he was well enough to continue his ill-treatment of his servant. 'I forgot Miss Josephine ['s] sex, & knocked her down & beat her so that she has kept her bed for these two days', he told Fanny in May

1791. He died two months afterwards. His son later thought he had committed suicide, and he may well have been right.[23]

In her letter informing Catherine of her husband's death, Fanny understandably assumed that Catherine's sorrow would not be overwhelming. She was mistaken. Mrs Byron was not one to forgo the chance of a good paroxysm. She was no less 'loud in [her] wail' than 'the widows of Ashur' whose grief was memorably depicted by her son; her shrieks could be heard in the street. Having been deceived often enough by her husband in life, she deceived herself on his death. She assured Fanny that the loss of her husband had made her 'very miserable'; and that she and Mr Byron had parted out of 'necessity, not inclination'. She now believed further that her husband's ill-treatment of her had amounted to no more than 'foibles'. Fanny probably stayed sceptical – only recently had her brother, while conceding that Mrs Byron was 'very amiable at a distance', defied his sister 'and all the Apostles to live with her two months'. In any case it was now their son who had to live with her – for much more than two months, and although he was well and her 'only comfort', she told Frances, George before long showed himself to be far from an Apostle.[24]

Catherine was not affluent; her income had been further reduced by Captain Byron's depredations to £135 a year. But in a Scotland where few lived above the poverty line, she was still well within the Scottish middle class – the widow of a Scottish clergyman gained a pension of £25 a year. Catherine adjusted to her diminished circumstances and avoided running into further debt. She could afford a reasonable flat in the main street of Aberdeen and a nurse and another servant.

Catherine undoubtedly loved her son; indeed he was 'a complete spoiled child', as Byron conceded after her death. And she had a number of good qualities – she was brave, intelligent and warm-hearted – but her Gordon temperament was far too wayward to make up for her son's double disadvantage of being an only child with a single parent. Byron was subjected to the same excesses of anger and affection that she had lavished on his father. The difference was that Mad Jack, who had brought his troubles on himself, could escape and was not emotionally scarred by the rows. Byron could not escape, and his mother's unpredictable swings from lavish spoiling love to shrewish fury inevitably fostered insecurity.[25]

Of course, like every other child, her son occasionally deserved parental wrath. One Sunday in church Byron aged seven or eight was seen to be every now and then sticking a pin in his mother's podgy arms, of which she was unaccountably vain. Either they were so fat that she did not feel the pricks or she exerted unusual self-restraint, for she did not react to such an apparently annoying disturbance of her devotions. On other occasions Byron was less fortunate and received an outburst of rage and a buffeting. Yet Catherine's temper seems to have been less volcanic than it became after her son inherited the title, when her pretensions swelled and her life became more complicated.[26]

Inexcusably, however, she sometimes taunted George with his lame foot, which rankled.* And when a nurse of another child remarked to Byron's nurse on his prettiness, adding 'what a pity he has such a leg!', the boy struck at her with a little whip, saying 'Dinna speak of it'. Yet he had a friend who was similarly afflicted, and would say laughingly: 'Come and see the twa laddies with the twa club feet going up the Broad Street'. If he was rather less morbidly sensitive about his lameness in Scotland than later on, it was partly because he had not yet been subjected to the tortures that a quack in Nottingham later prescribed for his incurable deformity.[28]

There was nothing poetic in the life of Jack Byron, but his death may have paved the way for his son's poetic development. Evidently an absent father can inspire poetry. Many twentieth-century American poets lost their father at an early age. In eighteenth-century England Chatterton's father died before he was born. Coleridge and Keats were eight and Wordsworth thirteen when their fathers died; notoriously, however, Shelley's father outlived his son by more than twenty years.[29]

Whatever influence his father's death had on Byron's writing of poetry, it affected his intellectual development in politics and religion. Maybe Catherine had been radicalised by her financial decline, or maybe she had long held her political opinions. At all events in the 1790s her view of the French Revolution was the

---

* Written many years later, Byron's drama *The Deformed Transformed* opens with the parent's command 'Out, hunchback!' to which the son responds, 'I was born so, mother'.[27]

opposite of that of her late husband. 'I fancy you and I are on different sides', she told Fanny at the end of November 1792, 'for I am quite a Democrat and I do not think the King, after his treachery and perjury, deserves to be restored'. 'To be sure,' she admitted, 'there has been horrid things done by the People, but if the other party had been successful there would have been as great cruelty committed by them'.[30]

Aberdeen was still peaceful, Mrs Byron went on; elsewhere in Scotland there were riots and tumult. Although these were economic in origin, the government was already worried by popular societies pressing for peaceful reform. Many minds were changed by the war with France and the Terror – the poet Cowper said the French had made him 'sick of the very name of liberty'; but there is no sign of Catherine having changed hers. Even if she did waver, she was probably shocked by the treatment meted out to the Scottish reformers accused of sedition. The charges were inventive: the young and brilliant Thomas Muir was effectively tried for recommending Paine's *Rights of Man* to his barber; the juries were packed; the judges, especially Braxfield, who maintained that 'in this country ... the landed interest alone has a right to be represented', were biased and brutal, and the sentences savage. The government strongly defended the Scottish judges; in contrast Robert Burns, on hearing that Muir had been sentenced to fourteen years' transportation, composed his defiantly nationalist 'Scots wha hae': 'Lay the proud usurpers low!/ Tyrants fall in every foe!/ Liberty's in every blow!/ Let us do, or die!'[31]

Mrs Byron evidently remained set in her political attitudes. A few years later in the Nottingham election of 1803 she made herself unpopular with the local gentry by supporting the Whig candidate. There was in fact little to choose between him and his Tory opponent. Like other Whigs he had no social programme, but he claimed that the election was a contest between rich and poor. Catherine's opinions influenced those of her son; had her husband been alive, they would have been strongly challenged.[32]

Jack Byron would have found the religion, which was natural to Catherine and was instilled into his son in Aberdeen, even less congenial, and here his influence would have been beneficent. Many years later Byron said he had read the Bible 'through and through before I was eight years old – that is to say the Old Testament – for the New struck me as a task – but the other as a pleasure'.

In the fourteenth century Boccaccio, who was highly praised in *Childe Harold's Pilgrimage* and on whose stories both Shelley and Keats based poems, wrote in *The Decameron* that 'by perversely construing ... the Holy Scriptures' many people had 'led themselves to perdition'. In 1796, shortly after George Byron Gordon had begun to read the Bible, Matthew Lewis, whom Byron later liked but thought 'a damned bore', expressed more contemporary if lighter fears in *The Monk*, a novel which influenced Shelley at school: 'the annals of a brothel', Lewis claimed, 'would scarcely furnish a greater choice of indecent expressions' than the Bible, which 'frequently inculcates the first rudiments of vice, and gives the first alarm to the still sleeping passions'.* At his trial for treason in 1794 Horne Tooke made a similar point; and writing from a very different point of view four years later, William Blake feared that 'to defend the Bible in this year – 1798 – would cost a man his life'. In any event in the 450 years between Boccaccio and Blake nothing much happened to dispel the impression that for the unsophisticated the Bible could be a heady and dangerous brew.[33]

Shelley later thought that the Old Testament was 'a record of such grovelling absurdities and enormities so atrocious' that it gave 'a picture of the Deity ... characteristic of a demon'. Yet indiscriminate reading of even the most bloodthirsty parts of the OT with what Shelley called its *'loathsome and minute obscenities'* would probably not have done the little George Byron Gordon great harm, had it not been accompanied by heavy doses of Calvinism; these were administered by his superstitious mother and various schoolmasters, as well as by his nurse Agnes Gray, who told him stories and taught him a number of psalms, and her sister May, who succeeded her as his nurse. The teaching of Calvin which was most damaging was his claim that God had predestined some of his creatures to salvation and others to damnation. Of course the great majority of believers in this doctrine, which Cardinal Newman considered 'detestable', scarcely doubted that they were among the elect who were predestined for salvation. But Byron perversely conceived the idea that he was destined for evil and damnation. He thought himself one of those

---

*A furious outcry led by the Bishop of London, followed by a prosecution, forced Lewis to remove this paragraph from later editions of the novel.[34]

> Deeming themselves predestin'd to a doom
> Which is not of the pangs that pass away.

This idea was reinforced by his reading of 'Gothic' novels, especially John Moore's *Zeluco*, with whose repulsive and murderous hero he later often compared himself. The mark of Cain is on most of his own heroes in his tales and dramas; and however much he later excoriated orthodoxy and the ministers of the Church, the idea continued to lurk in his mind until he died. Many years after his death his widow, not always a reliable witness, ascribed what she called 'the misery of his life' to his belief 'in the gloomiest Calvinist tenets'.[35]

At Byron's first school in a grimy room like a workhouse, the schoolmaster, by fear of the tawse (a leather strap), kept both sexes in some sort of order for the fee of one guinea a year (which was double what schools cost in the rural areas). George learned little, he later recorded, 'except to repeat by rote the first lesson of monosyllables – God made man, let us love him'. That was not surprising, for he was not yet five when he entered the school, and his mother's primary objective seems to have been discipline, not learning. Nevertheless, she boxed his ears when she discovered how little knowledge he had picked up in a year. Only after Byron had left and his 'intellect had been consigned to a new preceptor', he later wrote, did he make 'astonishing progress'. As soon as he could read, his grand passion was history. He began Latin under his next tutor, a rigid Presbyterian, and continued with him until he went to Aberdeen Grammar School.[36]

Before that, Little Geordie had become the heir to the Byron barony, the 'wicked Lord's' grandson having been killed in battle in Corsica: at the siege of Calvi, where Nelson lost his eye. Although there were at least two members of the family in a position to do so – old Lord Byron himself and Fanny Leigh, with whom Catherine had corresponded – they were both too self-absorbed and cold-hearted to bother to inform Catherine of an event which was bound to transform the lives of her son and herself. When she did learn of it, Catherine understandably thought it might bring some immediate improvement to their current privations, and tentatively sounded out Fanny on the possibility of aid from Newstead. She was unsuccessful. Himself under financial pressure, Lord Byron preferred to disregard the plight of his new heir.[37]

Accordingly, shortly before his seventh birthday, Byron entered Aberdeen Grammar School under the name of 'George Bayron Gordon', the misspelling being the result, presumably, of his or Catherine's broad Scottish pronunciation of 'Byron'. The school consisted of some 150 boys of the middle class and the gentry who were taught by four masters, a far better pupil–teacher ratio than that at Eton or Harrow. The sole subject taught for five hours a day was Latin, with an hour's instruction in handwriting as an optional extra. Unsurprisingly, Byron was bored and his academic performance undistinguished.[38]

Fortunately the relentless grind of Latin did not stunt Byron's appetite for reading, which was encouraged by his mother. Catherine Gordon's spelling and grammar were often shaky, yet she had a shrewd intelligence and was interested in books as well as politics and public affairs. As she could not afford to buy books, she must have had a library subscription, as a result of which her son was able to get his hands on a remarkable number of volumes. Before he was ten he had read 'all travels, histories or books upon the East I could meet with', as well as 'Don Quixote, Smollett's novels, and Gestner's Death of Abel and I was passionate for the Roman history'. And all that was in addition to his readings of the Old Testament.[39]

Away from his books, George Byron Gordon seems to have been outwardly a fairly normal schoolboy: brave, loyal, disorderly and mischievous, though much more intelligent, volatile, shy, sensitive and violent than his comrades. One observer thought indeed that he 'had a damnable disposition', and Byron himself later said that in his 'sullen moods' he 'was always a devil'. After having been beaten for some misdemeanour at the suggestion of an Aberdeenshire neighbour, Lady Abercromby, whom his mother was visiting, he struck her in the face, saying 'That's for meddling. But for you I should not have been beaten.'* Sometimes his violence took a self-destructive form. When, aged about ten, he was in one of what he later called his 'silent rages', a knife which he had 'applied' to his breast had to be wrenched away from him. On an earlier occasion after a reprimand for having soiled a new frock, he seized it and rent it from top to bottom, a biblical action which probably, however, owed less to Ahab, Elisha and other Old Testament

* When Coleridge's mother was similarly advised to beat her son, Coleridge took no similar reprisal but twenty years later had not been able to conquer his antipathy to the woman who had recommended a beating.[40]

renders of clothes than to his mother who, when angry, frequently mutilated her caps, gowns and other garments.[41]

Probably at the age of seven (though he once later said he was nine) Byron felt his first violent attachment to a girl. His distant cousin, Mary Duff grew up to be a woman described by Ruskin as 'still extremely beautiful in middle age'. When she was a pretty little girl, Byron used to pester his mother's maid to write to her on his behalf. Byron was later surprised by the strength of his feelings, asking 'how the deuce did all this occur so early?' Earlier he had written:

> Yet it could not be love, for I knew not the name,
> What passion can dwell in the heart of a child?

Whether it was or was not love, it was certainly powerful; Mary Duff remained in his mind for years.[42]

According to Byron, he 'certainly had no sexual ideas for years afterwards'; yet he had sexual experiences. These were provided by his nurse May Gray. As the boy subsequently told his solicitor (who after the poet's death told Byron's closest friend, J. C. Hobhouse), his sternly Calvinist nurse 'used to come to bed to him and play tricks with his person'. How often this happened in Aberdeen is not known. The geography of the flat and the presence of Mrs Byron may have been inhibiting; some of the incidents may have occurred later, at Newstead. Nor it is known what Byron's feelings were. According to Hobhouse, May Gray's tricks were 'much *less* romantic and *more* satisfactory than his amour with Mary Duff'; Byron very likely did enjoy them, but Hobhouse may have been guessing. Byron himself wrote that his 'passions were developed very early' – so early that he thought that few would believe him if he were to state the period and the circumstances – adding that 'perhaps this was one of the reasons which caused the anticipated melancholy of my thoughts – having anticipated life.'[43]

Child abuse, as it is called today, may indeed have helped to induce what Byron called his 'constitutional depression of spirits'. Almost certainly it had other effects as well. To ensure George's secrecy at the time, May Gray's attentions must have been accompanied by threats of violence in this world and hellfire in the next, if he breathed a word to his mother or anybody else of what was going on. His sense of being damned was therefore reinforced. More healthily, having been thus 'versed in hypocrisy, while yet a child' by his nurse's behaviour, Byron acquired a deep suspicion of ostentatious religious piety and a hatred of cant and hypocritical mumbo-jumbo. Much less healthily, May Gray's activities probably did more than anything else to give him his lifelong disdain for women. They helped to embed the belief that women were inferior beings, an opinion that the current climate and the state of the law did nothing to weaken, giving him the conviction that, as Rudyard Kipling later put it,

> They're as like as a row of pins –
> For the Colonel's Lady an' Judy O'Grady
> Are sisters under their skins![44]

Unlike the death of his second cousin which had made George the heir to the barony, the death in May 1798 of the fifth Lord Byron did not come as a shock; Catherine had even taken legal steps to preserve her son's inheritance at Newstead. Both mother and son had grown accustomed to the idea of George becoming a peer of the realm. When a neighbour said he hoped that Byron would make good speeches in the House of Commons, Byron interjected, 'the House of Lords, I hope'. And Catherine doubtless devoted much thought and no little talk to her son's lordly prospects. Yet the first time he was called Dominus de Byron on the school roll, George burst into tears. Byron told Hobhouse that only after his school-master gave him tea and cake did he realise how important he was. When he asked his mother if he looked any different now that he was a Lord, because he did not think he did, he was probably trying to curb her ecstasy. Yet he may have been serious. The extent to which Britain was then a hierarchical society, the vast prestige of the peerage and the extraordinary deference paid to it, are today difficult to comprehend. Even forty years later the young W. E. Gladstone, on taking up his first ministerial appointment, could write: 'People call Lord Lincoln my friend and he acts as such. But it is well for me to remind myself of the difference of rank between us'.[45]

Aberdeen was too bleak to leave any trace in Byron's poetry; not so the Highlands where he spent his last three summer holidays in Scotland. 'Years have roll'd on, Loch na Garr, since I left you', he wrote in 1807. 'Years must elapse, e'er I tread you again'. Byron never did tread Scotland again, but the scenery of Deeside had left lasting memories:

> England! thy beauties are tame and domestic,
> To one who has roved on the mountains afar,

he wrote in the same poem, and at the end of his life Scotland still held its magic:

> He who first met the Highlands' swelling blue,
> Will love each peak that shows a kindred hue. . . .
> The infant rapture still survived the boy
> And Loch-na-Gar with Ida looked o'er Troy.

Byron remembered not only the Scottish mountains, but also the 'little events' of his early days. He retained a 'warm feeling' for the friends of his youth, and despite occasional denunciations of the Scots he loved Scotland. While Scottish education was not as good as is often supposed, he was probably better taught there than he would have been in England: he always admired the Scottish educational system, but he said he was 'early disgusted with a Calvinist Scotch school where I was cudgelled to church for the first ten years of my life'. Though the Byron household was fairly comfortably off amid the pervading penury of Aberdeen, the relative poverty of his Scottish youth was also a valuable experience; it helped to set him apart from his later associates in fashionable London.[46]

On the whole, the years of Byron's Scottish childhood were quite happy – perhaps the happiest of his life – yet the accumulated disasters of those years guaranteed much unhappiness later. His Harrow friend, William Harness, exaggerated when he said that Byron had 'virtually never known a father's love or a mother's tenderness'. Catherine could be very tender, but her wild swings of mood ruled out a balanced home life. With his Gordon and Byron blood and his lame leg, Byron would anyway have been a difficult child; Catherine ensured that by upbringing as well as by blood he had no tranquillity. And her taunts about his being a lame brat were unforgivable and unforgiven.[47]

Yet it was May Gray who did the worst damage. The Jesuits allegedly used to say: 'Give us a child until he is seven, and you can do what you like with him afterwards'. Much the same was true of Protestant teaching in the late eighteenth century. May Gray's imprint on her charge was as lasting as the Jesuits' on theirs. She was probably the most influential person in Byron's life, more so even than his mother. Her Calvinism and sexual 'tricks' were a

37

much more fatal combination than Catherine's amalgam of frenzied anger and over-indulgence. Inevitably, Byron was riddled with complexes. Desperately shy, femininely sensitive and craving affection, he was sometimes known as 'Mrs Byron's crocit deevil' or, more charitably, as 'a very takin' laddie, but not easily managed'. The women in his household fostered his later misanthropy and exacerbated his violent temper. Yet, in spite of everything, he was an attractive and engaging little boy.[48]

CHAPTER III

The Shelleys and Field Place

Shelley: 1792–1802 (birth to age 10 years)

Byron was born in what he called 'the Gallic era "eighty-eight"' when 'the devils had ta'en a longer, stronger pull'; he may have extended 'the Gallic era' to include his birth year, though others, including William Godwin and, later, Shelley himself, took a rather similar view of 1788. But, whenever the Gallic era began, the man who became possibly England's greatest lyric poet and certainly her greatest radical poet was unquestionably born within it. Percy Bysshe Shelley, the son of Timothy and Elizabeth Shelley, was born at 10 p.m. at Field Place, Warnham near Horsham in Sussex on 4 August 1792 and had his first baptism an hour later. On that day the French National Assembly decreed that all religious houses should be sold for the benefit of the nation; on the previous day forty-seven of the forty-eight Paris sections had demanded the deposition of Louis XVI; and within a week the French monarchy had been overthrown.[1]

The coinciding events in Paris were the only features of Shelley's birth that were in any way unusual, and his parents had no reason to doubt that the life of their heir would be as prosaic as their own. Although he is said to have been proud of his connection with the Sidneys, Shelley had little interest in pedigrees, and despite attempts for a time by his family and admirers to make it seem otherwise, his own was undistinguished, although it would certainly have been more reassuring to breeders than that of Byron. The main branch of the Shelley family, the Shelleys of Michelgrove, who may have come over with the Conqueror, had been substantial Sussex landowners for generations, but the Worminghurst or Field Place Shelleys were very tenuously related to them – Timothy Shelley was about the eighth cousin once removed of the current holder of the Michelgrove Shelley baronetcy. He was descended from Edward Shelley, who was probably one of the masters of Henry VIII's household, but whose descendants had sunk in the world. None of them did anything much of note or of particular use, and they were only just gentlemen.[2]

Timothy Shelley's great-grandfather, John, through marrying Helen Bysshe became the owner of Fen Place, which was worth £200 a year. They had eight sons, the third of whom, Timothy, was an apothecary or, in the words of the poet's friend, second cousin and first biographer Thomas Medwin, 'a Quack doctor' who emigrated to America. There he had two sons, John and Bysshe, before returning to England about 1740. As his eldest brother had died and his second one was 'an esquire and a lunatic', Timothy soon took over Fen Place as head of a still obscure family, and a few years later he inherited Field Place from an uncle. It was, however, Timothy's son Bysshe who founded the family fortunes. He did so by eloping twice with heiresses.*[3]

Bysshe's first heiress was Mary Michell, the sixteen-year-old orphaned daughter of the late vicar of Horsham. In 1752 they underwent a Fleet marriage – so-called because in the early eighteenth century many clandestine marriages had been performed by parsons incarcerated for debt in the Fleet prison – at Keith's Dissenting chapel in Mayfair.† Bysshe's first wife bore him one son, Timothy, and two daughters before dying after nine years of marriage.[4]

Having had his wife's substantial property settled on him, the widower could afford to wait and make a careful choice of his next heiress. Bysshe was tall and good looking with an impressive manner, attributes which nine years later at the age of thirty-eight enabled him to carry off one whose social position was far superior to his own. Elizabeth Jane Sidney Perry, who was on her mother's side a Sidney and who inherited from her father large estates in three counties, bore Bysshe seven children.

Bysshe's two official families were not, however, his only offspring; he founded another family, providing for his four bastards in his will as well as making belated and meagre provision

* Since his grandson, the poet, also eloped twice, though not with heiresses, one might think that, like gout, elopement is hereditary but misses a generation, were it not that two of Bysshe's daughters also eloped – which saved their thrifty father the expense of giving them proper dowries.
† A year later Hardwicke's Marriage Act afforded some protection to heiresses by making a marriage service invalid unless performed by an Anglican clergyman after the banns had been called for three successive Sundays in the parish church; from then on elopers had to travel to Scotland – usually Gretna Green – to be wed.[5]

for his two legitimate daughters who had eloped to get away from him.[6]

Becoming a widower again in 1781, Bysshe presumably felt too old or too satiated to attempt the ensnaring of a third heiress. In any case he had never relied solely on rich wives for augmenting his property. He made money on his own account, though exactly how is not known, and he cultivated the friendship of his most powerful neighbour, the Duke of Norfolk. On the death of his childless elder brother in 1790 he inherited the Fen Place and Field Place estates, previously the family's main property but now dwarfed by the properties he had himself accumulated. One of the richest men in West Sussex, he had achieved his ambition of founding a substantial landed family, which according to Dr Johnson was the main motive for making money. In 1806 when at the behest of the Duke of Norfolk Bysshe was given a baronetcy, he was worth, the Duke estimated, £10,000 a year, the same income as that of Mr Darcy in *Pride and Prejudice*.[7]

More, however, was expected of landed families – even the most *nouveau* ones – than just wide acres and large investments. The ownership of land was thought to demand a house and park of suitable magnificence, and a style of life and hospitality appropriate to the rank and wealth of the landowner; but Bysshe was not prepared to adopt that style. Although Field Place is a beautiful house, which has recently been sensitively restored by its present owners, and although it has fine grounds, Bysshe did not wish to live in it; for this reason his son Timothy had taken up residence there in his uncle's day and continued to live there when Bysshe inherited it in 1790; nor did Bysshe live on any of his other estates. Admittedly he built an imposing house overlooking the sea, Castle Goring, which was designed by J. B. Rebecca and was said to have cost £80,000, but he never occupied it. Instead, for the last twenty-five years or so of his life, he lived with only one servant in a smallish house in Horsham. His overriding concern was to make yet more money and to spend as little of it as possible. According to Medwin, Sir Bysshe was 'still remarkably handsome' in old age 'with a noble and aristocratic bearing'. Yet an acquaintance, who probably knew him later than Medwin, wrote that 'he was as indifferent to his personal appearance as he was to his style of living. He wore a round frock, and passed a portion of his time in the tap-room of the Swan Inn at Horsham, not drinking, indeed, with its frequenters, but arguing with them in politics'. In short Sir Bysshe was a miser, and avarice taken to the extremes that he practised it – when he died, almost £13,000 in banknotes was found scattered about his house – was deemed by Sir Thomas Browne in the seventeenth century 'a deplorable piece of madness'. Indeed, one of Sir Bysshe's later acquaintances thought he had 'a dash of insanity'.[8]

In a country where birth was still so important, Sir Bysshe's demotic way of life was a constant reminder to his son, Timothy, on whom devolved the duty of behaving like a country gentleman, that the Field Place Shelleys were parvenus. This inevitably dented Timothy's social confidence, leading him to cling to respectability and conformity. Nor can his confidence have been strengthened by his relations with his father, whose feelings for him oscillated between contempt and hatred; according to his grandson, who 'always regarded him as a curse on society', Sir Bysshe seldom met Timothy without discharging a volley of oaths at him. Like his father, Timothy was good looking, but there the resemblance ended. Whatever Sir Bysshe's many defects, he was out of the ordinary. In contrast Timothy was as commonplace as it is possible to be. Ill-educated – some of his letters are barely literate – he nevertheless went to University College, Oxford, to which on leaving he donated a silver candlestick. He also went on the Grand Tour without being discernibly affected by his experiences. That would not have surprised Lord Chesterfield, on whom Timothy tried unavailingly to model himself. Chesterfield thought most young men returned from the Grand Tour as ignorant as they had been when they left, while Adam Smith considered that the typical Grand Tourist returned 'more conceited, more unprincipled [and] more dissipated' than before. Pope, Lady Mary Wortley Montagu, Johnson, Smollett and Cowper thought much the same.[9]

In 1790 Timothy Shelley became MP for Horsham. The eleventh and Protestant Duke of Norfolk, who until his father's death in 1786 had been MP for Carlisle, was intent on extending his political power and, as a first step to broadening his sway in West Sussex, the Duke had decided to contest Horsham, a borough which had long been under the control of the Ingram family. Timothy Shelley was an obvious choice for one of the Norfolk candidates, not because of his political talents – he had none – but because of his father's wealth; moreover, the wife of Thomas

Charles Medwin, the Duke's new steward, who ran his electoral affairs in Horsham, was a cousin of the Shelleys. As candidate Timothy Shelley was not overworked. There were only twenty-four voters, and no meetings, speeches or addresses were required. Others fought the election for him with fraud and skulduggery, and Medwin as chief poll clerk secured the election of the Duke's candidates. Yet neither his election nor his property brought Timothy influence. The influence was all the Duke's; Timothy voted as Norfolk wished, and not even that for long, for, by disqualifying too many of the Ingram supporters, Medwin had overdone the skulduggery. On petition the Duke's candidates were unseated in March 1792, and the Ingram nominees put in their place.[10]

Timothy Shelley had a wife and, shortly afterwards, an heir to console him for the temporary end to his parliamentary career, a heavy blow to so self-important a man. At the age of thirty-eight he had married the beautiful twenty-nine-year-old Elizabeth Pilfold. She is said to have been 'in a certain sense a clever woman, and though of all persons most unpoetical was possessed of strong natural sense'. Apparently she wrote 'admirable letters' – none has survived – but 'took a narrow and cramped view of men and things, and was as little capable of understanding Shelley, as a peasant would be of understanding Berkeley'. Within nine years of the birth of their heir, Percy Bysshe Shelley in 1792, the Shelleys had four surviving daughters, followed by a second son in 1806. Timothy also had an illegitimate son.[11]

Very little is known about young Bysshe's early years. 'Perhaps the most remarkable single fact of Shelley's childhood', as Richard Holmes, the poet's leading post-war biographer, has written, 'is that while both parents comfortably outlived him, neither left a single word of reminiscence about his early boyhood.' Shelley himself was similarly reticent about his childhood – probably the only attribute he shared with the Duke of Wellington, who, like Shelley, was unhappy at school. Nor is much known about either Timothy or Elizabeth Shelley, but there was evidently something odd in their upbringing of their children. If they are judged by results, they were bad parents. They were failures with their eldest son, and they ill-treated his widow. With their daughters they were not much more successful. All their daughters were beautiful and far from penni-less, yet three of them remained unmarried; and the fourth, Mary, after marrying and having three children, left her husband and in the Shelleyan style eloped, the marriage ending in divorce proceedings in the House of Lords.[12]

Apart then from their second son, a buffoonish nonentity who seems to have heeded his father's advice – 'never read a book, Johnnie, and you will be a rich man' – not one of the lives of the Shelleys' children turned out even remotely as their parents would have liked. In view of what happened later, the obvious suspect as author of the trouble is Timothy Shelley. Yet early on he seems to have been on reasonable terms with his eldest son who, according to one story, waited anxiously outside the door when his father was seriously ill, although that may not mean much, even if true. Timothy himself thought he had been a forbearing father. 'I never before oppos'd or closely pursued him', he wrote later, while his son's reference in a letter to going to a ball with 'Il Padre' suggests neither hostility nor reverence.[13]

Outside the family circle Timothy Shelley was recorded as being 'sincerely respected', a 'kind benefactor' to agricultural labourers and a 'constant rewarder of honest industry', who 'possessed in a high degree the best qualities of a country gentleman'. This glowing tribute cannot, though, be taken at face value; it appeared in Sir Timothy's obituary in the *Gentleman's Magazine* whose pages were adorned with similar encomia on departed squires and baronets.*[14]

Timothy Shelley was nearly always out of his depth. He himself suspected his defects; hence his habit of boasting. Yet his piercing blue eyes, handsome face and erect bearing helped to conceal his deficiencies, something which was done even more effectively by his wealth. In *Mansfield Park* Edmund Bertram, when he met Mr Rushworth, used to say to himself: 'If this man had not twelve thousand a year, he would be a very stupid fellow'. Timothy had almost as large an income, or at least he would have when he at last succeeded Sir Bysshe; hence he could not be a stupid fellow. He more than passed muster with the neighbouring gentry and his tenants; and if, though he thought himself a seasoned legislator, he was one of those MPs, dubbed by Byron as 'Mute, though he votes,

---

* The obituary on the same page as that of Timothy Shelley claimed that the death of Sir John Lowther, Bt would 'by none be more sincerely lamented than by his tenantry and the poor in the vicinity of his extensive property', while on Lord Sidmouth's death in the same year the *Gentleman's Magazine* eulogised the former Addington, who when Home Secretary had ordered P. B. Shelley to be watched in 1812, as though he had been Cincinnatus.[15]

unless when call'd to cheer,' there were many other silent ciphers in Parliament. At home his faults were less easily concealed, but we do not know how soon or how clearly his family, and in particular the poet, became aware of his inadequacy.[16]

Timothy was certainly a conscientious landowner, and work on his estate and his attendance at Westminster ensured that the joy or burden of bringing up their children fell mainly on his wife. Elizabeth Shelley is a shadowy figure. To her children, though, she was doubtless substantial enough, and she may, at least as much as her husband, have been the root of the trouble. After his expulsion from Oxford Shelley told Thomas Jefferson Hogg, his very close friend and second major biographer, that his mother was 'mild and tolerant, yet a Xtian' which Hogg translated as 'narrow-minded'. Edward Dowden, the poet's authorised biographer who had the full cooperation of the Shelley family, wrote that Elizabeth's 'temper was violent and domineering', adding that 'she had a special grievance against the boy' because he preferred reading books to killing animals. Brought up in a sporting household, she was determined to instil proper habits into her elder son. Accordingly Shelley was forced to fish from a boat under her supervision from the bank. She also drove him out to shoot with the gamekeeper, but then Shelley was out of her sight and able to foil her, getting on with his reading while the keeper amassed corpses sufficient in number – if attributed to the boy – to satisfy his mother.[17]

If Elizabeth Shelley was in any sense 'a clever woman', as she is said to have been, she must soon have conceived a very limited regard for her husband's attainments. How much that was evident to the children, and whether it caused quarrels in front of them, is not known. But in 1813 Shelley contended that the current system of matrimony turned people into 'hypocrites or open enemies' and that the early education of the children of ill-assorted couples took 'its colour from the squabbling of the parents; they are nursed in a systematic school of ill-humour, violence, and falsehood'. Shelley was arguing a case, he had literary sources, he may not have been writing primarily from experience and, if he was, he almost certainly exaggerated, yet his words surely had some foundation in his parents' household. Maybe Elizabeth adopted an obedient yet condescending attitude to her husband which communicated itself to her children. In any case Shelley later on showed a marked lack of filial piety and obligation to his father. We do not know when his attitude progressed through disdain to hatred and contempt, but one incident makes the transition understandable. One day Shelley accompanied his father to Horsham where they met the prison chaplain who had just been ministering to a convict at his execution. 'Well,' exclaimed the jocular Timothy, 'old soul-saver! How did you turn the rascal off?' That exhibition of tasteless waggishness must surely have hastened Shelley's evolution from obedience to rebellion. And unfortunately the absence of a close bond with his father was not balanced by a great affection for his mother. Even when Shelley was young, his relationship with his mother seems not to have been close; consequently she had little influence on his later life.[18]

Almost the only source of information about Shelley's childhood is a series of letters written by his sister Hellen half a century later, which not surprisingly read more like legend and propaganda than history; in addition Hellen was seven years younger than her brother, so she knew nothing at first hand of his earliest years.

At the age of six Shelley was sent daily to the vicar of Warnham to be grounded in Latin and Greek. The sermons of Mr Edwards, who was Welsh, are said to have been unintelligible, but Shelley plainly understood what Edwards taught him and, having an outstandingly retentive memory, absorbed it. Otherwise, when not reading and not exiled with rod or gun, he spent his time playing with his sisters, who enjoyed his fondness for 'eccentric amusements', for which the park and gardens of Field Place were ideal. Shelley might be an alchemist with a grey beard casting spells in a garret, or his sisters had to wear strange clothes 'to persuade spirits or fiends', or they had to hold hands round a table 'to be electrified'. Later on Shelley described his family home as 'this temple of solitude'; apart from the company of his sisters he grew up in virtual isolation. Strangely, his parents made no effort to introduce boys of his own age into Field Place to play with him, a neglect which had important consequences when he grew up. He yearned then to be surrounded, as in his childhood, by adoring women, sister substitutes, whom he could lead and teach.[19]

Byron's ancestry and early years carried the likelihood of some sort of revolt; they virtually precluded a conventional career as a minor peer. With the important exception of eccentricity or madness stemming from his grandfather and namesake, Shelley's lineage and upbringing provided no such obvious seeds of rebellion. Yet he revolted against his family and background far more drastically than Byron. His revolt, it has been authoritatively claimed, cannot have been against a stuffy, conservative home, since his father was a Whig and was not a devout, still less a bigoted, churchman. That claim is worth examining in some detail.[20]

Timothy Shelley was certainly a Whig, but then almost everybody in the political world regarded himself as a Whig of some sort; William Pitt never called himself a Tory. And although British parliamentary politics were not quite one-party, they were one-class. The claim that the landed interest alone had 'a right to be represented' in Parliament was not legally or constitutionally correct, but it accorded with the current position. Except possibly for Poland, the British aristocracy was more firmly in control of the state than any other in Europe. And it was well rewarded for its pains. Many peers profited from 'Old Corruption' – the government's wholesale distribution of sinecures, pensions and other payments to those it wanted to benefit. Further, before Pitt's wartime taxes, the taxation system in Britain was even more biased in favour of the rich than that in pre-Revolutionary France. Hence, not surprisingly, the great English magnates were both absolutely and relatively richer in 1800 than they had been a hundred years earlier.[21]

While the rich were getting richer, the poor were getting poorer. Although the fast expansion of the economy in the second half of the century had brought a consumer boom and a wider holding of property, growing prosperity had barely trickled down to three-quarters of the country. The growth of the population and the slow growth of agricultural productivity kept the wages of many families well behind prices. Indeed the slave trade was sometimes defended on the grounds that the conditions of the lower classes in England were worse than those of Negro slaves in the West Indies. Acute poverty was certainly widespread, peaking in the crisis years, 1792, 1795–96 (when Timothy Shelley was said to have been generous to the poor) and worst of all 1799–1801, when real wages reached their lowest point for 250 years. The people were nearly 'starving for want of food', the first Lord Liverpool told the Cabinet in 1800, and in the coming winter were 'likely to starve also for want of raiment'. Coleridge put it more vividly: the poor were 'dying with grass in their bellies'.[22]

Together with Napoleon and many others, Edmund Burke was convinced that only if religion was able to keep the poor, if not contented, at least quiescent, could great inequalities of wealth survive. Thus to the Church – long an important part of the state – fell the task of providing 'divine cement' to hold society together by urging the poor to seek their consolation in the next world, not this one.* At the height of the war in 1809 the second Lord Liverpool, the Secretary for War, considered the 'class of men, who, of all others, were the most serviceable to their country' to be not, as one might expect during a war, soldiers or sailors, but clergymen. Unquestionably the bishops strongly upheld 'the gradations of civil society' though, to be fair, by 1790 most of them regarded slavery as an excessive gradation. William Wilberforce, who took a much stronger line on slavery, of course, also urged the poor to be grateful for having to withstand fewer temptations than the rich; consequently they should be content to have 'food and raiment' (even though many of them did not have enough) since 'their situation' was better 'than they deserved at the hand of God'.[24]

If the Church's defence of the social order and its identification with the state, displayed not merely by the bishops in the House of Lords but by the plethora of clerical magistrates and the involvement of many clergymen in elections, had led a youthful idealist to suspect that the contemporary Church had more in common with the Pharisees than with Jesus Christ, Timothy Shelley's own attitude would have done little to dispel such a suspicion. Timothy had all his children baptised twice, once very soon after their birth and then publicly about a month later, which indicates some degree of bigotry or superstition, yet according to Medwin his religious opinions were 'very lax'. He even signed his order for two copies of a book of Unitarian sermons 'A friend of religious liberty'; and, possessing not 'true devotion' himself, made no attempt to inculcate it in 'his son and heir'. Nevertheless he 'made his servants regularly attend divine service'. While his son might have admired this paternal emulation of Voltaire, who also thought that his servants, his lawyer, his tailor, 'the common people' and even his wife but not himself should be 'yoked' by 'belief in future rewards and

* It was quite 'possible', Mary Wollstonecraft told Burke, 'to render the poor happier in this world without depriving them of the consolation which you gratuitously grant them in the next'.[23]

punishments', Shelley was more likely to despise both of them for dissimulation and hypocrisy.[25]

The comfortable view that God had ordained the inordinately unequal social hierarchy was common to nearly all parliamentarians, including the Foxite Whigs. Timothy Shelley was a Foxite because his patron the Duke of Norfolk was, and he followed the Foxite line during his first brief sojourn in Parliament. Yet Foxism like Whiggery in general did not preclude Field Place from being a conservative home; it was at best a very minor deterrent to adolescent revolt. Charles James Fox did go though two phases of being 'the man of the people', but for most of his career his politics were aristocratic – in 1791 he urged the introduction of aristocracy into Canada. Hence to be a follower of Fox was fully compatible with a conservative attitude.[26]

The young Wordsworth had the government in mind when he railed against 'the insolence and presumption of the aristocracy', but his words applied equally well to the Foxites, who were, indeed, almost as unrepresentative as the Pittites and even more oligarchic. Foxism, of course, spanned divergent attitudes. The Whiggism of Field Place was far distant from that of the Byron household. Neither Timothy nor Elizabeth Shelley would have dreamed of calling themselves 'a Democrat' and both would have been shocked by Catherine Byron's hostility to field sports. Like the father of Sir Robert Peel, who always considered 'a fox-hunter an enemy to God and man', Mrs Byron thought society would be considerably improved if not only foxes but 'the breed of fox-hunters' could be exterminated.[27]

Mr and Mrs Milbanke, Byron's future parents-in-law (they became Sir Ralph and Lady Milbanke in 1798), would also have disagreed with Catherine on fox-hunting, but their political views were rather nearer to hers than to Timothy Shelley's. Ralph Milbanke, the good-humoured, tolerant son of a northern landowner and coalowner, was the brother of Lady Melbourne and the nephew of Lord Rockingham's sister. A natural Whig, therefore, he entered the House of Commons at the same time as Timothy Shelley as MP for Durham, where there being some 3,500 electors he, unlike Timothy, had had to do some energetic canvassing.*

* His domineering wife, Judith, the sister of Lord Wentworth, had been relieved to find that, so far from heavy drinking being obligatory when electioneering, the strictest sobriety was required. Her husband had to have 'his senses always about him' and could 'seldom

Milbanke did not, however, rely solely on his eloquence to win the seat; he spent £15,000 on the election, expenditure which was met by mortgages. These eventually crippled his estates, with important consequences for his daughter and future son-in-law. Milbanke's maiden speech supporting the abolition of the slave trade was said to be 'short and good'. Six weeks later, on 17 May 1792, after fifteen years of marriage and at the age of forty, Judith Milbanke gave birth to their first and only child, Anne Isabella, the future Lady Byron. The Whiggism of the Milbanke household was sufficiently liberal for their daughter to react against it: in 1803 Anne Isabella self-importantly told her mother that she was 'an impartial Tory'. The Whiggism of the Shelley household was sufficiently illiberal for their son later to react against it in the opposite direction.[28]

Percy Bysshe Shelley, though, was not yet ready to rebel in 1803. Unlike his almost exact contemporary, Miss Milbanke, he was neither precocious nor spoilt; nor at the age of eleven was he interested in politics. When a few years later he did rebel, his leanings towards defiance and heresy might have been quelled by the kind of indulgent parental response always accorded to Miss Milbanke. Instead, they were fuelled by resentment against the uncongenial atmosphere at Field Place.

And, in the first decade of the nineteenth century, a clever, discontented young idealist had no shortage of causes to espouse. Although conditions in Britain were less dire than elsewhere in Europe, 'the increasing disproportion' between low wages and the high cost of necessities, Wordsworth told Fox in 1801, weakened or destroyed 'the bonds of domestic feeling among the poor'; poverty, hardship and misery abounded side by side with luxury, extravagance and what such a staunch defender of the *status quo* as Burke called 'the fortunes of those who hold large portions of wealth without any apparent merit of their own'. Britain's one-class politicians largely neglected the social problems which only afflicted other people; few Pittites or Foxites were well equipped to deal with such difficulties or even know what they were. Hence a youth's inclination to rebel against 'the lamentable and gross deficiencies', in Hazlitt's words, 'of existing institutions' would not be stilled or

spare more than an hour and a half or two hours for dinner'.[29]

diverted by the attitudes prevailing in a Whig household. Indeed, as Leigh Hunt suggested a few years after Shelley's death, the 'licensed contradictions' and hypocrisies of the Whigs were likely to stimulate a young man to revolt – and all the more so if Whiggery was seen to be embodied in Timothy Shelley and expressed at Field Place with cant and without charm or distinction.[30]

Because so little is known about Shelley's childhood, almost anything said about it contains an element of guesswork. Yet the absence of evidence is in itself a sort of evidence. That there was so little parental regard for Shelley, that eleven years after his death his sisters were still not allowed to mention his name at Field Place and even his sister Hellen had at that time no admiration or sentiment for him, support the impression of an unhealthy family atmosphere. When he was twenty, Shelley told Godwin that he had never loved his father; and writing of 1811 when he was Shelley's closest friend, Hogg said that Shelley 'was passionately fond of his sisters'. Even if young Shelley was not fully aware of it at the time, Timothy and Elizabeth seem to have been cold and unresponsive, even neglectful, parents. His mother's relative indifference evidently led him to transfer his main affections to his sisters. Even they, in the end, proved unfaithful. Yet, in later life, 'sisters' of one sort or another were far more important to Shelley than either his mother or his father.[31]

CHAPTER IV

Isleworth and Dulwich

Shelley: 1802–4 (aged 10–11 years)
Byron: 1798–1801 (aged 10–13 years)

In 1802 at the age of ten Shelley was sent to Syon House Academy, Isleworth, an establishment containing some sixty boys, aged between eight and eighteen, who were mainly the sons of London shopkeepers. As the Field Place Shelleys were by then one of the leading landowning families in Sussex and were Whigs, not radicals or democrats, this was surprising company for their son and heir, all the more so since Syon House had no claim to academic or any other kind of distinction. It was vastly inferior, for instance, to Clarke's School at Enfield to which John Keats was sent a year later, and 'must have been', as Shelley's close friend, the satirical novelist and poet Thomas Love Peacock, later judged, 'a bad beginning of scholastic education for a sensitive and imaginative boy'.[1]

Timothy and Elizabeth Shelley's choice of school has been defended on the grounds that they had not been infected by the spirit of aristocratic exclusiveness and still saw themselves as middle class. That is implausible. Earlier in the year, under the aegis of the Duke of Norfolk, Timothy had once again become a Sussex Member of Parliament, this time for New Shoreham, and he certainly would not have gone out of his way to call his social position into further question; besides, only two years later Shelley was sent to Eton, the most aristocratic of all the great public schools. Shelley seems to have been dispatched to Isleworth for two reasons: Old Bysshe's meanness – the Shelley daughters were later sent to a similar school in Clapham – and Timothy and Elizabeth's lazy indifference. Rather than search for the best school available within the financial constraints imposed by old Bysshe, it was less trouble to plump for Syon House to which the Duke's steward, Thomas Medwin, and his wife, who was a cousin of Elizabeth Shelley, had already sent their son Tom.[2]

Before describing Shelley's arrival at the Academy, Tom Medwin who had 'preceded him' by some four years wrote that Shelley had been 'brought up in retirement at Field Place'. In the early twentieth century, George Santayana put it rather differently. 'Shelley seems hardly to have been brought up', he wrote; 'he grew up in the nursery among his young sisters, at school among the rude boys, without any affectionate guidance, without imbibing any religious or social tradition'. It was in the passage from nursery to school, from sisters to boys, that the lack of affectionate guidance was most conspicuous.

Shelley's parents could not have been unaware that boys' boarding-schools were rough and tough arenas in which their son with his girlish looks and ways would be particularly vulnerable to the bullying of his contemporaries and elders. Yet they did nothing to prepare him for his ordeal. On top of failing to provide any boys to be his companions at Field Place, they did not have him taught the ordinary schoolboy games and pastimes. Above all they did not ensure that he had at least some knowledge of how to defend himself when 'the rude boys' taunted or assaulted him or even that he knew to clench his fists on such occasions. One of his schoolfellows later recorded that Shelley was 'like a girl in boy's clothes, fighting with open hands'.[3]

In Shelley's time Syon House (not, of course, *the* Syon House) was largely an early eighteenth-century building with extensive playgrounds behind a wall which ran along the London Road.* Walking past it with Shelley a few years later, Jefferson Hogg, who was then Shelley's closest friend, thought it a 'gloomy brick house'. Shelley told him that the headmaster, Dr Greenlaw, 'was a hard-headed Scotsman, and a man of rather liberal opinions'. Greenlaw, a Scottish clergyman, had a choleric temper, and his liberalism did not extend to his methods of maintaining discipline. He used to deliver heavy blows to the heads of his pupils and, like most headmasters of his time, was an assiduous wielder of the birch; by contrast, at the enlightened school Keats attended at Enfield, there was no flogging. Greenlaw was a tolerably good classical scholar, who sometimes entertained the boys by introducing lavatorial humour into his Latin translations; such interludes pleased Shelley no more than did the manners and language of the boys, which shocked 'his pure and virgin mind'.[4]

---

* Having survived both world wars, the house and the gazebo on the wall were still there when I moved to Isleworth in 1953. Sadly, it was pulled down later that year.

In his biography of Shelley, Medwin describes him as being at that time 'tall for his age, slightly and delicately built, and rather narrow chested, with a complexion fair and ruddy, a face rather long than oval. His features, not regularly handsome, were set off by a profusion of silky brown hair, that curled naturally.' He had large and prominent blue eyes, and a sweet and innocent expression. Sir John Rennie, afterwards a distinguished engineer, who was also at the school, gave in later years a similar description, adding that Shelley's 'countenance [was] rather effeminate, but exceedingly animated'.[5]

Both unprepared and unfitted for communal life with boys, Shelley would have had a wretched initiation at almost any boarding-school. But at Syon House he was despised by the other pupils (who were, says Medwin, the sons of men 'of rude habits and coarse manners') not only because of his girlishness and his ignorance of schoolboy pastimes, but because he was not 'one of them' and was therefore subjected to some class warfare. As he was not equipped or inclined to enter into their sports or to fight, he was mercilessly bullied; he also had to suffer the ordinary persecution from older boys who used their juniors as quasi-servants. Consequently Syon House was 'a perfect hell to him'.[6]

Among his loving sisters Shelley's equanimity had seldom been found wanting. In the very different surroundings of Syon House and among his tormenting fellows he turned out to have a violent temper. 'The least circumstance that thwarted him', wrote Rennie, produced 'paroxysms of rage', which led him to throw anything that came to hand at those who were teasing him. All that is doubtless true, but Rennie stretches our credulity when he claims that Shelley 'not infrequently astonished his schoolfellows by blowing up the boundary palings on the playground with gunpowder, also the lid of his desk in the middle of schooltime, to the great surprise of Dr Greenlaw and the whole school'. Just possibly, after one such incident with both the palings and the lid, Dr Greenlaw might have limited his reaction to astonishment, but any succeeding ones would surely have earned a heavy flogging; so however badly Shelley wanted to attract attention, frequent explosions are barely conceivable.[7]

Even one or two explosions must have given Shelley great pleasure, whatever the retribution that followed. His interest in science had been generated by a talented itinerant inventor and lecturer, Adam Walker, who also performed at Eton. Through Walker, Shelley gained a fascination not just with gunpowder but with chemistry in general, and with electricity and astronomy. The adult Shelley was reviled as a dangerous revolutionary and heretic, who sought to undermine the principal institutions of Church and state. Hence his schoolboy addiction to explosives, the emblematic weapon of later anarchists, was gratifyingly appropriate. Yet his pyromania, more clearly indicated by his practice at Field Place, until prohibited, of carrying a flaming fire stove about the house, is associated by some psychologists with boys who are in doubt about their masculinity.[8]

Partly, perhaps, because of his explosions he was at times, Rennie wrote, 'considered to be almost upon the borders of insanity', but when treated kindly he was 'very amiable, noble, high spirited and generous.' Yet he was regarded 'as a strange and unsocial being'; he did not join in the sports and games of his schoolfellows, preferring to remain engrossed in his own thoughts. The only boy with whom he was at all intimate was Tom Medwin to whom he confided his sorrows, and apart from occasionally walking up and down with his much older second cousin, his only pleasures came from reading and his own imagination. His first extant letter, written in July 1803, shows that already he wrote well and could add a touch of humour. Although the letter was to Medwin's aunt, Catherine Pilfold, he began it 'Dear Kate' and ended 'I am not your obedient servant, P. B. Shelley'.[9]

The novels of Fielding and Smollett, which were prominent in the circulating library, should have appealed to him. But 'they exhibited life pretty much as it is'; so they were, according to Medwin, 'little to his taste', since 'poets of all ages have despised the real'. In general, of course, that is not true – Byron liked both Smollett and Fielding – and in so far as it was true of Shelley, it was to the detriment of his poetry. Not only, however, did Shelley later prefer the Gothic unreality of the second-rate Charles Brockden Brown to far superior realistic novelists, he also disliked Sheridan, only reluctantly sitting through *The School for Scandal* and hating, according to Peacock, 'the withering and perverting spirit of comedy'.[10]

At Syon House unreal 'Blue books' were the staple literature of Shelley and the school. The initial stock was brought back after the holidays; when exhausted, it was replenished by the bigger boys

THE MAKING OF THE POETS

dispatching their juniors out of bounds to fetch a new supply from a circulating library in Brentford. Blue books 'embodied stories of haunted castles, bandits, murderers and other grim personages' and were avidly read by the boys. However, these 'Penny dreadfuls', as a later age dubbed them, did not have a monopoly of such themes. The Gothic novel, which became increasingly popular in the second half of the eighteenth century, an appetite satirised by Jane Austen in *Northanger Abbey*, catered for similar tastes on a far higher plane, later reaching its peak with *Frankenstein*, the first novel of the poet's second wife. Shelley read and was influenced by the poems and novels of 'Monk' Lewis and Ann Radcliffe, some of which can still be read with much enjoyment. He was also influenced by Paltock's *Peter Wilkins*, a book admired by Coleridge, Southey, Lamb and Scott, which tells of a shipwrecked sailor who arrives in a land where the inhabitants can fly and eventually marries a beautiful one who had crashed outside his hut. 'How much', says Medwin, 'Shelley wished for a winged wife and little winged cherubs of children'. Perhaps he always did.[11]

Presumably because of his unhappiness at school and because of his constant reading of tales of terror and horror which fired his vivid imagination, Shelley had 'frightful' nightmares at Syon House and, in Medwin's words, was 'haunted by apparitions that bore all the semblance of reality'. At least once, too, he walked in his sleep, arriving at Medwin's dormitory, for which involuntary activity, so boundless was the contemporary ignorance of such matters, he was severely punished. He continued, however, to have what Medwin called 'waking dreams, a sort of lethargy and abstraction that became habitual to him, and after the *accès* was over, his eyes flashed, his lip quivered, and his voice was tremulous with emotion, a sort of ecstasy came over him, and he talked more like a spirit or an angel than a human being.'[12]

Medwin sounds as though he were describing the Shelley of later years, mistakenly attributing similar behaviour to the ten- or eleven-year-old boy, but, if he is accurate, Shelley's so-called 'visitation' may have taken place at Syon House. Opinions have strongly differed as to whether it occurred there or at Eton, or at all. The 'visitation' is the name given to the spiritual experience described in the dedicatory verses 'To Mary', at the beginning of *Laon and Cythna*, and in one of Shelley's best poems, the 'Hymn to Intellectual Beauty'. Here are the relevant lines of the former:

Thoughts of great deeds were mine, dear Friend, when first
The clouds which wrap this world from youth did pass.
. . . a fresh May dawn it was,
When I walked forth upon the glittering grass,
And wept, I knew not why . . .

And then I clasped my hands, and looked around –
But none was near to mock my streaming eyes . . .
So, without shame, I spake: – 'I will be wise,
And just, and free, and mild, if in me lies
Such power, for I grow weary to behold
The selfish and the strong still tyrannise
Without reproach or check.' I then controlled
My tears, my heart grew calm, and I was meek and bold.[13]

Had the poem been written in the last 150 years, the 'streaming eyes' would point to Syon House, crying having by then become the infirmity of little boys, not bigger ones; not long after the deaths of Byron and Shelley, as W. H. Auden put it in his *Letter to Lord Byron*, 'crying went out and the cold bath came in'. But as it was written in the early nineteenth century the tears are neutral. It was a weeping age, at least in literature,* and Shelley's poems brim with tears. During his rages at Syon House, Shelley very likely did feel at war with the world and breathe the spirit of revolt against 'the selfish and the strong', yet the whole incident seems less improbable at, say, sixteen than at eleven. The opening lines, quoted above, plausibly fit a boy who had been through puberty; 'the clouds' between youth and the world could hardly be said to clear away at the age of eleven.[14]

Much the same applies to the relevant lines in 'Hymn to Intellectual Beauty', when again the hands are clasped, although the eyes streamed later:

While yet a boy I sought for ghosts, and sped
      Through many a listening chamber, cave and ruin,
      And starlight wood with fearful steps pursuing
Hopes of high talk with the departed dead. . . .
      When musing deeply on the lot . . .
      Sudden, thy shadow fell on me;

---

* In the last 100 or so pages of *A Simple Story*, a very readable novel written in 1791 by Elizabeth Inchbald, who was once described by Godwin as 'a piquant mixture of a milkmaid and a fine lady', tears are shed on approximately every fourth page. And in Ann Radcliffe's *The Mysteries of Udolpho* there are tears or weeping on 41 of the first 100 pages.

I shrieked, and clasped my hands in ecstasy!

I vowed that I would dedicate my powers
>To thee and thine – have I not kept the vow?
>With beating heart and streaming eyes . . .

At Field Place Shelley did seek ghosts and spirits in the holidays from Syon House as well as Eton, but he seems very young to be 'musing deeply on the lot of life' at Isleworth. And although he was evidently a touch priggish at Isleworth, it is far-fetched to think that an eleven-year-old boy, even a boy like Shelley, could have made a vow to dedicate his powers to intellectual beauty. If the experience (or experiences) actually occurred, Eton seems the far more likely venue. Equally, if Shelley really had sensed the intimations that he wrote of in those two poems, he would surely have told Hogg about them at some point during the period of their intense intimacy at Oxford and afterwards. Further, if Shelley had wanted to write a piece of accurate autobiography, he would have written it in prose.[15]

Even in conversation and prose Shelley was often more inventive than accurate and, naturally, he was all the more inventive in his poetry. 'The poet & the man are two different natures', he told two friends in 1821. And, in any case, the voice of the speaker in a poem should not be identified with the poet. In another letter, Shelley told Leigh Hunt that he 'had undertaken in early life' the task of fighting evil. Following bouts of anger and folly many boys make resolutions not to repeat such conduct, and Shelley doubtless did so with far more than normal intensity after raging in his 'violent paroxysms' against the cruelty of authority and his schoolfellows. Yet the dedicatory verses 'To Mary' and the 'Hymn' were based not merely on his memories of schoolboy unhappiness but also on his feelings in 1816 when, as he told Hunt in the same letter, he was 'opposing myself, in these evil times and among these evil tongues, to what I esteem misery and vice'; with his powerful imagination he fused a number of distressing episodes of violence and repentance at school into one quasi-mystical moment. In so doing, he may well have been influenced by the mystical experience undergone by St-Preux in *La Nouvelle Héloïse*. Shelley conceived his 'Hymn' while voyaging with Byron round the Lake of Geneva and reading Rousseau's novel for the first time. He was 'charmed by [its] passionate eloquence', his widow wrote, and felt an affinity with St-Preux. In any event Shelley was aiming for and achieving poetic, not literal or historical, truth. Hence, almost certainly, his so-called 'visitation' at Eton (or Isleworth) was no less mythical than the Duke of Wellington's alleged remark that the Battle of Waterloo was won on the playing fields of Eton.[16]

Though he was not interested in what he was being taught (except by Adam Walker), Shelley's ability and retentive memory enabled him to more than hold his own in the classroom without effort or even much attention. He acquired the dead languages, Medwin wrote, 'as it were intuitively, and seemingly without study', while Rennie remembered his writing English and Latin verse 'with considerable facility'. Shelley's scholastic proficiency did not save him from the usual pedagogic punishment. Another schoolfellow described him as 'rolling on the floor when flogged, not from the pain, but from a sense of indignity' – although the pain probably had something to do with it.[17]

Both Medwin and Shelley so hated Syon House that they never discussed it together in after life. Similarly, except for his remark about Dr Greenlaw when walking past the school, Shelley never gave Hogg any account of that period of his life; nor did he mention it to Peacock. Unquestionably, therefore, he must have continually longed to get home to see his sisters. At the Easter holidays in 1804 that pleasure was postponed. Shelley went to stay with his Grove cousins in Wiltshire. He suggested they should play carpenters, so they got carpenter's axes and cut down some of his uncle's young fir trees. Shelley later acquired a proper respect for trees, even once peremptorily dismissing a gardener for having despoiled one. Shortly after his own tree-felling, which was tolerantly regarded by his uncle, he left Syon House for good, going to Eton in the summer of 1804.[18]

Newstead and Dulwich

If Shelley suffered from his parents' lack of interest, Byron suffered first from his mother's negligence and then from her excessive interference. Despite her anxiety to protect her son's inheritance 'from embezzlement' – she had engaged a former Scottish MP, George Farquhar, to safeguard his interests – they could not leave for Nottinghamshire as soon as they heard of the death on 21 May 1798 of the fifth Lord Byron. Catherine was short of money for the journey, and the Newstead estate seemed almost equally bereft; the fifth Lord's executor and creditor was reluctant to pay for the funeral of the dead man, who consequently remained unburied for almost a month. Eventually having raised from the sale of her furniture in Aberdeen nearly £75, a sum sufficient to meet the £35 the journey cost and to pay May Gray her year's wages of £9, Catherine, with her son and Gray, set out for Newstead in August.[19]

An earlier visitor to Newstead, John Evelyn, remarked in 1654 that it was 'situated much like fontaine Belauw in France . . . with brave woods and streams; it has yet remaining the front of a glorious Abby Church'.* In 1798 it still had, and anybody who has seen Newstead since can easily appreciate the profound impression the sight of it and the realisation that it belonged to him are likely to have made on a clever, imaginative little boy, accustomed to living frugally in a small flat in Aberdeen. Byron's abrupt change of circumstances – his inheritance of Newstead and his peerage at so young an age – was thought not only by the poet Tom Moore, who was his friend and principal biographer, but also by many others to have damaged his character. He was certainly proud of his ancestry and always very conscious of being a lord, but then so were many peers who, reared in luxury, had inherited their titles as adults.[21]

On their arrival at Newstead, the Byrons were met by Mr and Mrs John Hanson. Farquhar had gone to Hanson, a Chancery solicitor, for legal advice, and Hanson, who possessed an engaging manner and knew a good thing when he saw it, became the Byrons' man of affairs. Before long he had proved a disastrous choice. In a profession notorious for procrastination, Hanson was praeternaturally idle and inefficient. Initially, however, his influence was benign: though short of scruples, he was kind and intelligent and took an immediate liking to Byron. 'The young Lord is a fine sharp boy', he told Farquhar, 'not a little spoilt by indulgence but that is scarcely to be wondered at'.[22]

Newstead, however beautiful and romantic, was scarcely habitable. The fifth Lord had let it fall into decay, and in places it lacked a roof. Most of the furniture had either been sold by him or seized after his death by his creditors. Though not encumbered with debt,

---

* In fact, all the time Newstead was a religious house, it remained a mere priory; so despite Byron's limping line, 'Abbots to abbots in a line succeed', Newstead never had an abbot. Only after it had been secularised and the church destroyed, was it given the title of abbey.[20]

the Newstead estate was in disarray; despite the war having brought agricultural prosperity through high food prices, which greatly increased rents elsewhere, the rent roll was a meagre £850 a year. In addition to Newstead the Byron family still owned their potentially valuable estate in Rochdale. Unfortunately, the 'wicked Lord' had illegally sold some valuable parts of it. Byron was made a ward in Chancery, and ineffectual proceedings, hampered by a shortage of funds and the lassitude of his lawyers, were begun to recover the property.[23]

In his redundant will, Byron's father had requested his cousin Lord Carlisle to be guardian of both his children. Now Hanson persuaded Carlisle to take on Byron in addition to Augusta. Like Hanson himself, Carlisle proved an unfortunate choice. The right guardian for Byron would have been a man of strong character, actively interested in his welfare, who could influence him and control his mother. Carlisle failed on all counts. He was in poor health, had never met Byron, no longer had any connection with the family, and although a despot with his own large family he found Catherine Byron too appalling to tangle with. Nevertheless, neither he nor Hanson should be blamed. Carlisle did not want the job, only accepting it on the understanding that he would not be expected to do more than advise; as for Hanson, he was more or less bound by Jack Byron's will, and there was no other suitable candidate.[24]

Hanson fared better with his attempt to procure a pension for the indigent Catherine who now had only £122 a year of her own. In July 1799, in words devised by Hanson, Catherine wrote a letter to the Home Secretary, the Duke of Portland, asking for a pension from the King. Her petition, supported by Carlisle, was successful, the Home Secretary telling her a month later that 'the King had been graciously pleased' in the light of her circumstances to allow her £300 a year out of the Civil List. Portland expressed the hope that Catherine would consider the pension 'a testimony of the respect I have professed for the great house to which you belong'.[25]

In fact Mrs Byron's pension was a testimony to the privileges of the peerage and to the strength of 'old corruption'; Catherine was relatively poor, but millions of people were very much poorer. Pensions were one of the ways the Crown and the government bought or secured the allegiance or quiescence of people who might be useful or troublesome. Moreover Portland, who was himself very far from poor, had a personal motive for pleasing Catherine. As a result of a mortgage taken out a few years earlier the Duke owed £3,000 plus interest to the Byron estate, and the grant of a pension might inhibit Mrs Byron from pressing for its repayment. In the event the pension proved a bad investment for both the government and Portland. Politically Byron was always hostile to George III, while Mrs Byron and, later, her son tried to get Portland to pay up.[26]

Byron told Hanson's wife that he had no regrets at leaving Aberdeen save for 'the scenery and one associate, a little girl named Mary Duff'. His mother probably had none at all. She had lived in Aberdeen only because her husband had sent her down in the world by dissipating her fortune. Now she had risen anew and saw the prospect of making her son much more than she herself should have been. Her elevation did not, however, improve her temper or her figure, enhancing her pretensions but not her self-control. Her rages became still more violent and her body even more corpulent. Yet she evidently treated her servants well – they stayed with her – and she set about making Newstead a seat worthy of a Lord Byron who was a Gordon and a descendant of the Scottish royal house. In so doing she had to contend not only with the havoc wreaked by the fifth Lord but with the incorrigible dilatoriness of her man of affairs. Hanson customarily took weeks to summon the energy to deal with a request or even answer a letter. As late as 1803 Catherine was complaining to him that the house would 'soon be in ruins' because he had not carried out instructions to spend the necessary money. All the same, by the previous year she had at least got the house into a condition in which it could be let.[27]

Earlier in November 1798, partly because of Newstead's dilapidated state and partly because she thought her son's foot was getting worse, the Byrons had gone to live in Nottingham. Mrs Byron herself soon returned to the Abbey, leaving Byron and May Gray in another house in the town, where the nurse's shocking treatment of the little boy became a general topic of conversation. Equally misguidedly Catherine entrusted his foot to the care of one Lavander who had some local repute as a healer of damaged limbs and called himself a 'surgeon'. In reality he was a 'trussmaker to the general hospital', and that was evidently his only expertise. Had he made a truss for Byron, he would have done little damage and inflicted no pain. Instead, apparently, after rubbing the foot with oil the quack twisted it into the position he wanted and then screwed it up in a wooden machine, which was more torture than treatment.[28]

Either from economy or neglect Mrs Byron had provided no education for her child since they had left Scotland. Writing to her from Nottingham in March 1799 Byron showed that he could already write a good letter, though one less polished than Shelley's at a similar age. Having suggested that he should be tutored every night by an American called Rogers, Byron expressed astonishment that his mother did 'not acquiesce in this scheme ... because if some plan of this kind is not adopted I shall be called or rather branded with the name of a dunce which you know I could never bear'. Such a reminder of the importance of education usually comes from the parent, not the child. But whether or not Mrs Byron was stung, she did acquiesce. Rogers was engaged to teach Byron Latin and found him well advanced for his age. On one occasion Rogers conveyed his discomfort at seeing his pupil agonised by Lavander's machine. 'Never mind, Mr Rogers,' Byron replied, 'you shall not see any signs of it in *me*'.[29]

Rogers gained Byron's respect and affection. Lavander, of course, did not. One day Byron decided on a reversal of roles, making Lavander his victim. Having jumbled up some letters of the alphabet randomly but in the form of words, he asked Lavander what language they were in. When the quack confidently answered 'Italian', Byron had satisfyingly exposed him as a fraud. Mrs Byron, however, stuck to her foolish delusion. In July she told Lord Carlisle that Lavander had much improved the foot. Still, she had absorbed her son's letter, telling Carlisle that Byron's education was as important as treatment to his foot. Probably for that reason she agreed to let Hanson take him to London to meet his guardian, to find a school for him and to have his foot properly examined.[30]

The expedition was least successful in the first objective. At Byron's interview with Lord Carlisle in Grosvenor Place, his guardian spoke kindly to him but scarcely had the chance to study him because after a short time Byron turned to Hanson and said, 'Let us go.' Although his rudeness may be partially explained, if not excused, by a surgeon also being there and Byron not wanting his foot discussed in front of his guardian, the episode demonstrates how badly he had been brought up.[31]

Together with May Gray, Byron stayed at the Hansons' grand house in Earls Court, where on his arrival the Hanson children studied him carefully before one of them pronounced: 'Well, he is a pretty boy, however.' The introduction to Carlisle might have gone still worse. Though probably caused, not by his enhanced status, but by the pain inflicted on him by Lavander, Byron's temper, like his mother's, grew more violent in England. When the young Lord Portsmouth pulled his ears at Hanson's house, Byron picked up a heavy conch shell and hurled it at him, luckily missing and only breaking a window. Mrs Hanson's attempt at peacemaking by claiming that Byron had not meant to hit Portsmouth was foiled by Byron's insistence that he did 'mean it. I will teach a fool of an earl to pinch another noble's ear'. Another incident was nearly far more serious. After quarrelling with the cook, Byron pointed a loaded gun at her and pulled the trigger. The woman's cap was riddled with the shot, but she was unhurt. This time the Hansons did not try to make peace. Byron was horse-whipped. His violent temper was all the more dangerous in that, probably influenced by the stories of the 'wicked Lord', he liked to have arms near him, and it was his practice, according to Byron's friend, Thomas Moore, 'when quite a boy to carry at all times small loaded pistols in his waistcoat pockets'.[32]

Two days after the meeting with Carlisle, Byron's foot was properly examined. Dr Baillie, who with Dr Laurie treated it for the next three years, was of the opinion that 'if the proper means had been taken at the first in infancy, the malformation might have been brought round'. Almost certainly that was wrong, but Baillie's conclusion that 'little could be done after a lapse of ten or eleven years' was probably correct and effectively spelled the end of painful treatment. Special appliances – chiefly a leg iron – were made from time to time, but they seem to have done little harm or good, especially as Byron was careless in his use of them, also disregarding his doctor's advice not to take more than moderate exercise. Eventually a special boot was constructed, which was probably the best solution.[33]

After summer holidays spent with the Hansons, Byron was sent at the suggestion of George Farquhar to Dr Glennie's Academy, a small school in Dulwich Grove, Dulwich being then largely rural though no longer a spa. An assiduously self-anglicised Scotsman, Glennie was a cultivated man and a friend of Campbell the poet; he was also even more of a worshipper of rank than most of his adopted countrymen. As a result, Hanson was able to write to Mrs Byron – characteristically some ten days later – that he had 'succeeded in getting Lord Byron a separate room, and I am persuaded the greatest attention will be paid to him'. And so it should be, Catherine probably thought, especially as Glennie charged £86 a year, a stiff increase on the minuscule sums she had had to pay in Aberdeen.[34]

The rest of Hanson's letter contained less welcome news. While expressing reluctance to interfere in Mrs Byron's 'domestic arrangements', Hanson thought it 'absolutely necessary to apprize' her that the conduct of Mrs Gray 'towards your son was shocking'. He had found it was the general topic of conversation in Nottingham. 'My honourable little companion', Hanson continued, 'told me that she was perpetually beating him, and that his bones sometimes ached from it; that she brought all sorts of company of the very lowest description into his apartments . . . that she would take the chaise-boys into the chaise with her. . . . But, Madam, this is not all; she has even – traduced yourself.' Hanson continued by recording his 'very great affection for Lord Byron'. He had 'ability and a quickness of conception, and a correct discrimination that is seldom seen in a youth, and he is a fit associate of men, and choice indeed must be the company that is selected for him'.[35]

By concluding with that tribute, Hanson was perhaps trying to ensure that as the messenger of very bad news he did not suffer along with May Gray, and maybe for the same reason he kept from Mrs Byron what her son had told him of his nurse's sexual practices. Even without that intelligence Catherine should surely have dismissed her straight away. Yet Byron wrote to Hanson probably in November, 'since you are going to Newstead I beg if you meet Gray send her packing as fast as possible'. The relations between Byron and his nurse had deteriorated sharply during the year. Possibly Gray had ceased her sexual tricks with him because of her dalliances with 'the chaise boys' and her other 'lowest' company, and taken to beating him instead. Shortly afterwards she was indeed sent packing to Aberdeen, together with a miniature of Byron given to her by his mother. She left behind a malign legacy. Being solely in the care of females as a child would have been bad enough for Byron; but to have been brought up only by very unbalanced women was much more damaging.[36]

Unlike May Gray, Dr Glennie did not beat Byron or his other

pupils; discipline was not ferocious at his school. Byron's 'separate room' was Glennie's own study where there were plenty of books, while his mother was liberal with clothes and pocket money. Admittedly he had to wear his leg iron, which according to Hobhouse he one day threw into a pond, but his foot was causing him annoyance and discomfort rather than pain. Bullying was evidently slight or non-existent so that Byron's violent temper, in contrast to Shelley's, was more manifest in the holidays, when he would sometimes scream 'Don't come near me! I have a devil', than at school. Either because of his privileged position in Glennie's study or because of his boasts that his ancestry was superior to those of Pitt's new peerages, he was nicknamed 'the Old English Baron'. Yet he was popular and had at least one close friend, a clever boy named Lewis. Both friends predicted that the other would distinguish himself in the world. Lewis died very young, however.[37]

All in all, therefore, Dulwich should have been a fairly pleasant experience for Byron, but it was not. In later life he scarcely ever referred to Glennie or Dulwich Grove. Much of the trouble may have arisen from his dislike of his first experience of boarding-school, which his extreme shyness was bound to make difficult. Added to that, the work was uncongenial. Because Latin grammar was taught differently in Scotland, he had to retrace his steps and hence was behind the other pupils; maybe even the word he dreaded, 'dunce', was applied to him. But there seems to have been something else as well.*[38]

According to Glennie, Byron 'entered upon his tasks with alacrity and success. He was playful, good humoured and beloved by his companions.' Glennie's remarks are more eulogy than evidence. There is much more in the same strain about Byron's 'intimate acquaintance with the historical parts of Holy scriptures', his wide reading, and his belief in 'the divine truths' unfolded 'in the Sacred Volume'. 'I have never been able to divest myself of the persuasion,' the pedagogue continued, 'that, in the strange aberrations which so

---

* It probably concerned Byron's deformed leg and foot. According to T. Sheldrake, who was an expert, Glennie was ordered to send for him to remedy Byron's affliction. Instead, Glennie summoned another man calling himself Sheldrake, who was 'stupid, ignorant and neglectful'. Nevertheless, Glennie continued to employ him. When Byron was nineteen and at last saw the right Sheldrake, he 'expressed great indignation at the baseness of Glennie, who had deliberately left him in the hands of a worthless, mercenary empiric, to whose misconduct he owed much of his suffering . . .' If, as is probable, that is right, Byron had ample reason for disliking Glennie and Dulwich.[39]

unfortunately marked his subsequent career, he must have found it difficult to violate the better principles early instilled into him'. If the eleven-year-old Byron spotted the smugness and pompous snobbery of Dr Glennie as unerringly as he detected the quackery of Mr Lavander, the absence of happy memories of the school is easy to understand.[40]

Byron spent the Christmas holidays with the Hanson children: John Hanson and his wife went to Newstead and then paid an ineffective visit to Rochdale to investigate the position of the Byron estates. On their return Mrs Byron accompanied them to Earls Court. One of the Hanson children, Newton, thought she 'showed a great fondness for her son, but it was occasionally interspersed by a contrary disposition'. Byron's habit of biting his nails sometimes brought from his mother 'violent ejaculations of disgust accompanied by a box on the ear or hands'. Although she was certainly fickle in her treatment of him, 'on the whole they were very fond of each other'.[41]

Meanwhile, Catherine quarrelled with Glennie. According to the headmaster, the blame was all hers; he himself was guiltless. Mrs Byron, he told Moore, 'was a total stranger to English society and English manners; with an exterior far from prepossessing, an understanding where nature had not been more bountiful, a mind almost wholly without cultivation, and the peculiarities of northern opinion, northern habit and northern accent'. That was pretty rich coming from a Scot, and all the richer for being told to an Irishman, but Glennie may have thought that Moore felt as Anglicised as he did.[42]

Glennie's main complaint was that, instead of leaving her son at the school and paying him the occasional visit, Mrs Byron was constantly coming down and taking him to her lodgings in Sloane Terrace from Saturday to Monday, sometimes for even longer periods. Taking Byron for a weekend at home may seem to us a sensible habit, but keeping him away for longer periods was clearly mistaken. What is more, Catherine used to make scenes on her visits. These were probably caused by Glennie's opposition to what he regarded as the abduction of his pupil. But sometimes, apparently, she would roundly abuse Glennie for Byron's lack of progress, and on one such occasion, according to Glennie, another boy remarked to Byron, 'your mother is a fool', to which he replied, 'I know it'.[43]

At this time the neurotic Catherine Byron was even less balanced than usual. She had fallen in love, we are told, with a French dancing master – not that that in itself points to lack of balance although in those hierarchical times ladies were thought guilty of a grave indiscretion if they were attracted by their social inferiors – and intended to elope with him to France, taking Byron with them. All this seems to have come from Glennie who told Hanson, who told Carlisle and, later, Hobhouse. As Britain was then at war with France, it seems unlikely that the lovers would have used Napoleonic France as the equivalent of Gretna Green. Yet however exaggerated the story, there was evidently something in it. Because of the danger or merely because of the frequency of Byron's absences from school, Hanson, at the insistence of Glennie, persuaded Carlisle to give the headmaster a formal order denying Mrs Byron access to Byron at weekends. That naturally provoked Catherine into furious rows with both Glennie and Carlisle. According to Glennie, her altercation with Carlisle led that feeble peer to tell the headmaster, 'I can have nothing more to do with Mrs Byron – you must manage her as best you can.'[44]

The difficulty in assessing Catherine's conduct is that we have only a witness for the prosecution. That Mrs Byron sometimes kept Byron at home instead of sending him back to Dulwich Grove is not in dispute. The question is why she did so. Possibly she just wanted to be with him; possibly she listened to his pleas to be allowed to stay away from school; possibly she intensely disliked Glennie, finding his pretensions to southern manners as objectionable as he found her unaltered, unaffected northernness. All that may be so. Yet we know that she had told Hanson the previous November that Byron's education had been too much interrupted since he had been in England. And we also know that, earlier, Byron himself had been worried at being deprived of teaching and being thought a dunce. They seem an unlikely pair, therefore, to have thrown away, without severe provocation, the chance of him gaining proper instruction. The likelihood is that Glennie's teaching was poor and the atmosphere at the school unpleasant. In any case, whereas Byron was thought by Rogers to be remarkably good at Latin for his age, when he reached Harrow he was found to have been so badly taught that he needed special instruction. This turn-around is less likely to have been the fault of Catherine and her son than of the headmaster and his school.

In the summer of 1800 Byron made what he later called his 'first dash into poetry', though May Gray told Moore that Byron had composed the following lines in 1798:

> In Nottingham county there lives at Swine Green,
> As curst an old lady as ever was seen;
> And when she does die, which I hope will be soon,
> She firmly believes she will go to the moon.

If these were genuinely original, they were pretty good for a boy aged ten.[45]

Byron's 'dash' was generated by his passion for his first cousin, Margaret Parker – a much closer cousin than the object of his earlier attachment, Mary Duff, who to Byron's dismay had recently married. More than twenty years afterwards he could 'not recollect scarcely anything equal to the *transparent* beauty' of Margaret Parker. In view of May Gray's practices and his very early reaching of puberty, this was evidently more than an ordinary schoolboy crush. Byron could not sleep, eat or rest. 'It was the torture of my life' to wait the usual twelve hours before they could meet again. 'But I was a fool then, and I am not much wiser now'. Byron thought his passion was returned, but their schooling kept them apart, and two years later Margaret Parker was dead. Byron wrote 'a very dull' elegy on her. Another poem on the same subject which has been attributed to him is much livelier, beginning with the startling lines: 'Cease, cease thou hoary lying priest;/ Deceive me not with hopes of Heaven'. This is a remarkable production for a fourteen-year-old but, if Byron composed his 'Swine Green' epigram at ten, he may well have been able to write this poem four years later.[46]

By Christmas 1800 either Catherine or Hanson or both had come to the conclusion that Byron should be removed to another school. Accordingly, after Hanson had been to see the headmaster of Harrow, Dr Drury, and Carlisle's agreement had been secured, it was settled that Byron should go to Harrow in the summer, a decision that was welcomed by the schoolboy and resented by his headmaster in Dulwich.[47]

Probably because of Dr Glennie, Byron did not like Dulwich, but apart from his deformity the school, unlike Shelley's, was nowhere near being 'a perfect hell to him'. Of the four other great 'Romantic' poets, Blake's father though it prudent to 'withhold' him from school; Wordsworth was well treated at a dame school in Penrith, as was Keats at Enfield; only the nine-and-a-half-year-old Coleridge was miserable at Christ's Hospital – his widowed mother could only afford a charity school. The Shelley family had no such excuse. Their son had been brought up in much greater isolation than any of the other budding poets and had a 'pure and virgin mind'. So his parents surely should have taken all the more pains to see that he went to the most suitable school. Instead they took no pains at all, merely accepting the Medwins' choice. If their son ever felt betrayed and rejected, he had good cause.[48]

CHAPTER V

Harrow and Eton

Byron: 1801–5 (aged 13–17 years)
Shelley: 1804–10 (aged 11–17 years)

Byron went to Harrow aged thirteen and three-quarters; later in the nineteenth century, when Shelley's character was still in low repute, a headmaster of Eton 'rather wish[ed]' that Shelley, too, 'had been at Harrow'. For he had in fact been at Eton, going there shortly before he was twelve. Although some boys went to public school as young as six, twelve was then the average age for new entrants to Eton. Byron was older than most new boys at Harrow, where his surname was pronounced Birron.[1]

'By a public school', the Reverend Sydney Smith wrote in 1810, 'we mean an endowed place of education of old standing to which the sons of gentlemen resort in considerable numbers where they continue to reside from eight or nine to eighteen years of age'. Although some 'gentlemen' had been sending their sons to these schools for many years, only since the middle of the eighteenth century had the practice become almost universal. In 1795 William Cowper, who himself had been happy at Westminster, could still find it a matter for surprise. Writing of the half dozen great 'public-schools' – Eton, Winchester, Westminster, Harrow, Rugby and Shrewsbury – he wondered,

> What causes move us, knowing, as we must,
> That these menageries all fail their trust,
> To send our sons to scout and scamper there,
> While colts and puppies cost us so much care?

As Cowper suggested, the English gentry would not have dreamed of subjecting their horses or dogs to the treatment they considered suitable for their sons. Some, though, did stand out against the fashion. So scarred was he by his sufferings at Eton that Lord Chatham had William Pitt and his other sons educated at home.[2]

'The most important peculiarity' of a public school, Sydney Smith thought, was 'its numbers, which are so great, that a close inspection of the master into the studies and conduct of each individual is quite impossible . . .'. Boys were therefore 'left to their own crude conceptions and ill-formed propensities'; this neglect was called 'a spirited and manly education'. At a public school, Smith continued, every boy was 'alternately tyrant and slave', a system which he considered an evil because it inflicted 'upon boys, for two or three years of their lives, many painful hardships and much unpleasant servitude'.* The unreformed public schools did indeed combine the worst features of the reformed post-Arnold schools – fagging, flogging, enforced as well as voluntary homosexuality and a narrow classical education – with much savage bullying of the weak and a remarkable lack of supervision by the masters.[4]

Fags started the day, often still numb with cold, by cleaning their masters' boots and shoes, then waited on them at breakfast, and ran errands for them during the rest of the day. Fagging was accurately described by the Etonian 'Monk' Lewis as 'the only regular institution of slave labour enforced by force which exists in these islands'. Disobedience and faults, real or imagined, were punished with beatings and other cruelties. In the early nineteenth century fagging amounted to a system of institutional violence.[5]

Far worse, however, was the uninstitutional violence. Bullying went largely unchecked. Even boys who caused grievous bodily harm were not expelled from Eton. Indeed, when Shelley was there, two boys who had nearly killed another were only a few days afterwards entertained at dinner by the headmaster. At Harrow, a little later, Augustus Hare found the bullying 'terrible'; Charles Lamb found it 'heart-sickening' to recall 'the oppressions of the young brutes' at Christ's Hospital; and Robert Southey had a friend who was 'almost literally killed' at Charterhouse 'by the devilish cruelty of the boys'.[6]

The excessive fagging and cruel bullying largely stemmed from the public schools' 'most important peculiarity': a horde of boys and a scarcity of masters. When Keate became headmaster of Eton in 1809 (the year before Shelley left), the school had 515 boys and seven assistant masters. Byron's Harrow was slightly better-off, having five assistant masters for some 300 pupils. In contrast Aberdeen Grammar School had four masters for only 150 boys, and Clarke's School at Enfield, where Keats was educated, had five masters for some 80 pupils.[7]

---

* Smith knew what he was talking about. He had been at Winchester where the system was one of 'abuse, neglect and vice'.[3]

Clearly such a spectacularly large pupil–teacher ratio also had far-reaching effects on the quality of education and on other matters. It was only one cause of the compulsive flogging habits of so many headmasters. William Godwin was mercilessly flogged although he was his master's sole pupil. And some fairly gentle headmasters, such as Drury at Harrow when Byron was there or Goodall at Eton when Shelley went there, managed with little or no flogging, at least of the older boys. A flogger like Keate did not maintain better school discipline than his predecessor or his successor who were far more lenient.[8]

Pope, and before him Steele, had derided this 'custom of educating by the lash'. Yet the custom had become engrained if not sanctified; when Southey at Westminster School described flogging as 'beastly', 'idolatrous', and 'an abomination', his headmaster treated his attack as sacrilege and expelled him. Over flogging as in other things the public schools were so conservative as to be ossified. The second reason for the endless flogging was its strong sexual element; many schoolmasters enjoyed beating boys. As *Don Leon* the indecent pseudo-Byron poem put it, 'Flog, lechers, flog, the measured Strokes adjust:/'Tis well your cassocks hide your rising lust'. Some of the birch's recipients were also sexually affected. William Lamb, later Lord Melbourne, became an addict of flagellation, telling Queen Victoria truthfully, if misleadingly, that 'flogging had an amazing effect on him'.[9] Being flogged at Eton may also have had an amazing though different effect on another Victorian Prime Minister, W. E. Gladstone, who in later life frequently flagellated himself.[10]

Flogging was of course not the only, or even the main, cause of sexual stimulation in the public schools. That chiefly came from herding together a large number of boys of varying ages with very little adult supervision. How much homosexual activity these conditions generated cannot be known. In the 1850s homosexuality was rampant at Harrow, as the writings of a future biographer of Shelley, A. J. Symonds, put beyond doubt. And the agonised appeal from the Provost of King's College, Cambridge, to the Provost of Eton in 1850 not 'to deluge our College with vicious and immoral boys' shows that Eton's state was then the same. That there was less homosexuality at Harrow and Eton in the early 1800s than half a century later, by which time the Victorian obsession with masturbation and 'unnatural' vice had hit the public schools, is scarcely conceivable. Hence, although adult homosexual relations were strongly deprecated and savagely punished, a *laissez-faire* attitude to such practices prevailed in the public schools. Naked boys often shared beds, and schoolboy homosexuality seems to have been taken for granted and largely ignored – as was inevitable, given the dearth of masters.[11]

The relaxed attitude and the lack of supervision also provided scope for heterosexual activity. While at Eton Lord Hinchinbrooke fathered a bastard in Windsor, which was not considered a particularly serious offence; he was merely subjected to ten strokes of the cane.[12]

However diversified was the sexual education obtainable at public schools, the scholastic education they provided was stunningly tedious and unvaried. More than a hundred years earlier, John Locke had complained that forcing boys 'to learn by heart great parcels' of ancient authors served no purpose but to 'give them a disgust and aversion to their books'. Schoolmasters nevertheless had not changed their ways. The school curriculum was still almost exclusively classical, and it was still taught by requiring endless repetition and learning by heart, thereby giving a boy, in Cowper's words,

> No nourishment to feed his growing mind
> But conjugated verbs and nouns declin'd.[13]

Perhaps the only advantage the unreformed schools had over their successors was that their inmates were spared often excessive doses of organised games. Muscular – and indeed any other sort of – Christianity was largely absent; both Shelley and Byron had plenty of free time.

Harrow

'I am going to leave this damned place at Easter', Byron wrote from Dulwich to a cousin in February 1801. Predictably, however, Harrow, to which Hanson took him at the end of April, also proved to be a damned place. 'I always hated Harrow till the last year and a half', Byron later wrote, but at least Harrow had a headmaster whom he could like and respect.[14]

Though not much of a scholar, Dr Joseph Drury was a remarkable headmaster under whom Harrow enjoyed a golden age.

When he was appointed in 1785, Harrow had only 150 boys and was not one of the great public schools. After remaining fairly static for a time, the numbers jumped from 141 in 1797 to 345 in 1803. Under Drury Harrow educated four future prime ministers: Goderich, Peel, Palmerston and Aberdeen. Palmerston, who left Harrow shortly before Byron went there, was always fulsome about the school. He thought it taught 'self-control [to be] better than indulgence', believed 'buffeting' to be 'wholesome' – he had had at least two black eyes – and even defended the education. His father did not altogether agree. Because senior boys were confined to 'the common routine of classical instruction', he removed him from Harrow at the age of fifteen and a half and sent him to Edinburgh.[15]

Drury had a liking for staying in great houses, and under him Harrow's clientele became at least as aristocratic as Eton's. That Byron was a peer, even if an impoverished one, did him no harm with Drury. On an earlier visit Hanson had warned Drury that Byron's education had been neglected, but 'he thought there was a cleverness about him'. Drury himself soon found, he later wrote to Byron's biographer, that 'a wild mountain colt had been submitted to my management'. Learning that the boy feared the humiliation of being graded below many younger boys who were ahead of him in their studies, Drury reassured him that he would not be placed until he had caught up with his contemporaries. Byron remained shy, but 'his manner and temper soon convinced me', Drury continued to Moore, 'that he might be led by a silken string to a point, rather than by a cable; – and on that principle I acted'.*[16]

Like Glennie's at Dulwich, Drury's words were full of hindsight. At the time he made frequent complaints of Byron's 'negligence', idleness, and 'childish practices', and when the 'mountain colt' was sixteen Drury wanted to return him to the mountains, asking Hanson to take him away from the school. All the same, Drury was far superior to the average headmaster of his time – Byron later described him as 'my great patron' and as 'the best, the kindest (and yet strict, too) friend I ever had'. Drury took a close interest in his boys, or in many of them, and, even more remarkably, he exempted the older boys from flogging, leaving corporal punishment to be

---

* Shelley's widow was evidently so impressed by these words that she echoed them in the new edition of *Frankenstein* which appeared a year after Moore's biography of Byron. Frankenstein says of his parents, 'I was so guided by a silken cord that all seemed but one train of enjoyment to me.'[17]

administered by ten monitors or prefects, which presumably increased his popularity. He did not often even give lines as a punishment, preferring to rely on sharp verbal rebukes, or 'Jobations', as Byron called them; Palmerston later maintained that Drury's rebukes were such a positive pleasure that they almost tempted boys into transgression.[18]

Drury ran Harrow as a profitable family business and amassed a large fortune. He had paved his way to the top job by marrying his predecessor's sister, and by the time Byron arrived he was employing his son Henry, his brother Mark and his brother-in-law Bromley as masters. He selected Henry to be Byron's tutor, and the boy went to live in Henry's house. Byron's shyness on which Drury commented was fully understandable. Arrival at a large public school was enough to overawe all but the most self-confident newcomers, and an unusually sensitive boy, accustomed to a school containing very few fellow pupils and worried at being thought a dunce, was inevitably apprehensive. At least this last anxiety was soon removed. Henry Drury's tutoring was successful enough to enable his father to place Byron in the Upper Fourth, alongside Edward Long, who had already become a friend, and Robert Peel. Such a placing did more than salve Byron's self-esteem: since the Upper Fourth was in the Upper School, he did not have to fag.[19]

But no amount of Drurys would have saved the new boy from being bullied at Harrow. It was all the more inevitable because Byron was, as he later said, 'a most unpopular boy'. Neither by blood nor by upbringing was he of such tractable material to appeal to schoolmasters or to other boys. He was still a spoilt child, and abnormally sensitive, quick to take and give offence. Socially insecure, he had what Moore called 'high notions of his rank', once asking a monitor not to beat Lord Delawarr on the grounds that he was 'a brother peer'. Especially in a school which was riddled with peers or sons of peers of more distinguished lineage than his own, such pretensions were bound to attract dislike as well as derision and violence.[20]

In facing the violence Byron had two advantages and one large handicap. At nearly thirteen and a half – more than twice the age of the youngest boy – he was older and stronger than other newcomers, and Aberdeen Grammar School had taught him to fight and look after himself. He also had courage. On the other hand, boys being what they are, his lameness was an irresistible target for the taunts of his schoolfellows. When in later life a newspaper said he was deformed, he commented that such information was not very new to a man who had spent five years at public school. And still later Leigh Hunt wrote that 'the usual thoughtlessness of schoolboys made him feel [his lameness] bitterly at Harrow. He would wake, and find his leg in a tub of water.'*[21]

Byron's later physical adventures are better documented, but by then he was usually the protector of younger boys. The only stories we have of his early Harrow days show him not as mere victim but as victim-hero. Thus William Harness arrived at the school a year after Byron, aged twelve and pale and thin. He also had a limp, which helped to arouse Byron's sympathy. Seeing Harness being bullied by a much older boy, Byron intervened, and the next day told him, 'if any fellow bullies you, tell me; and I'll thrash him if I can'. That story is undoubtedly true; another one which tells of Byron offering to take half of a punishment being administered to Peel is legend.[23]

Byron's unhappiness at Harrow was not unusual. Anthony Trollope, who went there not long after him, was much more miserable, and Byron's exact contemporary, Robert Peel, was so out of sympathy with his surroundings that his removal from the school was considered. Although an even more accomplished scholar than Palmerston, Peel took a much less roseate view of the school. 'I was at Harrow myself', he later wrote, 'but I would not send my boys there unless I believed what I have reason to believe, that it is better conducted now than it was when I misspent my time there.'†[24]

'As a scholar', Byron correctly wrote, Peel 'was greatly my superior', adding that 'as a declaimer & actor' he was reckoned at least as Peel's equal. Whereas Byron 'was always *in* scrapes', Peel never was and unlike Byron always knew his lessons. 'In general information, history, etc. etc.' Byron thought he was Peel's 'superior as well as of most boys of his standing'. As Byron himself suggests, he was idle over his schoolwork, because it did not interest him. The syllabus, based on the Eton system, was wholly devoted to the classics, which were probably taught at Harrow better than elsewhere. Greek was given unusual prominence, and Dr Drury,

---

*Byron was relatively lucky. The Keppel family believed that in 1804 their eldest son died because of ill treatment at Harrow.[22]
† Peel did in the end send his three eldest sons to Harrow, but the two youngest went to Eton.[25]

who liked modern English poetry, encouraged his pupils to translate Latin and Greek poets into English verse. Yet Byron, it has been calculated, spent nearly 2,500 hours in school imbibing Latin and Greek – and learning them by rote. Hence his verdict in *Childe Harold* – 'I abhorred/. . . . The drill'd dull lesson forced down word by word' – was not unfair. There were, anyway, far too many boys in a class for much good teaching to be feasible. For schoolwork, the entire school was crammed into one building and four rooms.[26]

Any boy who relied for his education solely on what he learned from schoolmasters was likely to leave school almost entirely ignorant. Not surprisingly and not to his discredit Byron, like the earlier Harrovian writer and later friend, R. B. Sheridan, did not waste more time on his school studies than was necessary. And that was not much. The hours spent in the schoolroom were few. At Harrow on Mondays, Wednesday and Fridays they were five; on Thursdays and Saturdays which were half-holidays they were only three; and Tuesdays were a whole holiday. Thus, leaving aside the time spent in preparation (not long in Byron's case), the boys worked a twenty-one-hour week. In contrast, at Hawkshead Grammar School, Wordsworth worked seven hours a day in winter and an additional two hours a day in summer. All the same, Byron's inattention and idleness have often been exaggerated. Peel and he, as he later wrote, 'were both at the top of our remove' (i.e. form), and the School Bill Books show him at the top of the Fifth Form in 1803 and as a monitor and the third boy in the school in 1805. Admittedly promotion up the school was largely automatic: in the 1820s Trollope achieved seventh position in the school 'by gravitation upwards'. Yet Byron's name would not have appeared at, or near, the top of the list in those years, had he not acquitted himself with some credit in the schoolroom. His later writings, especially *Childe Harold's Pilgrimage*, show that at Harrow he gained a sound knowledge of Greek and Latin and an admiration for Greece and Rome.*[27]

For those so inclined, the short working week left plenty of time for reading, as well as for drinking, fighting, gambling and other pleasures. Byron's reading was certainly prodigious. Towards the end of 1807 he made a hasty compilation of the books he had read,

* Both remained with him. When they visited the beautiful Palladian Theatre in Vicenza in 1816, Hobhouse recorded that Byron was able to declaim from the stage a speech from the *Aeneid* and a chorus from Euripides.[28]

most of which he had 'perused before the age of fifteen', adding that since he left Harrow he had 'become idle and conceited, from scribbling rhyme and making love to women'. The list is impressive: the major histories of England, Rome, Greece and most Western European countries and many biographies including Johnson's *Lives of the English Poets*; many philosophers including Hobbes whom he 'detest(ed)'; under Poetry, 'all British classics ... with most of the living poets; and under Divinity: 'Blair, Porteus, Tillotson, Hooker, – all very tiresome. I abhor books of religion, though I reverence and love my God, without the blasphemous notions of sectaries, or belief in their absurd and damnable heresies, mysteries and thirty-nine articles' – a good summary of his fairly consistent attitude to religion. In a postscript Byron added that he had 'also read (to my regret at present) above four thousand novels', and said that Burton's *Anatomy of Melancholy* was 'the most amusing and instructive medley of quotations & Classical anecdotes I ever perused'.[29]

Byron's reading list has been much doubted, initially even by Hobhouse when he first read it in Moore's biography, though he soon retracted his doubts. Certainly Byron's assertion that he had read 4,000 novels even with 'regret' is hard to accept literally but it was probably not so intended, and doubtless he had not read every word of every book on his list – he would have been a fool if he had – as his choice of word 'peruse' indeed suggests. But, as he wrote on another occasion of his Harrow days, 'the truth' was that although he was 'never *seen* reading, but always idle and in mischief or at play ... I read eating, read in bed, read when no one else read, and had read all sorts of reading since I was five years old'. Byron's fund of information impressed his school contemporaries, and both his poetry and his letters show him to have been widely and deeply read. Indeed Ruskin considered Byron's early power to have been founded on reading, which he thought 'utterly unparalleled in any other young life'. Finally, an obscure youth of nineteen would hardly have bothered to write a private fictional memorandum on the off-chance of deceiving some unknown reader many years later. So Byron's list was surely a true record of his early reading.[30]

His relations with the Harrow masters were strained not by his schoolwork but by his behaviour both in the schoolroom and elsewhere. The masters objected to his 'scrapes' and to his attitude to the school. The absence of a father during his childhood may have aided his poetical development – which burgeoned at Harrow – but it made him unamenable to authority. The angry outbursts and the occasional cuffs of his mother amid a normal diet of affection and spoiling were no substitutes for some male parental governance which would have prepared the boy for the Harrow regime. Never having had to submit to a father's authority, the spoilt schoolboy was not ready to accept that of a schoolmaster. School rules and the wishes of schoolmasters were of little account to the adolescent Lord Byron. In a poem written shortly before he left Harrow he warned the Duke of Dorset, who was his fag, not to believe

> That books were only meant for drudging fools,
> That gallant spirits scorn the common rules.

Two years earlier the second of those lines should have been addressed to himself.[31]

Byron's unruliness was aggravated by his lack of respect – except for Dr Drury, whom he admired – for the Harrow schoolmasters. While disclaiming 'any personal allusions', he wrote in the same poem of 'passive tutors' who 'View ducal errors with indulgent eyes/ And wink at faults they tremble to chastise'.

Byron's strictures on sycophantic pedagogues hoping for future preferment from their aristocratic pupils had some force, but certainly in 1802–3 the Reverend Henry Drury, in whose house he still was, could not have been accused of viewing *lordly* 'errors with indulgent eyes'. Rather his refusal to 'wink at faults' had caused Byron to decline to go back to Harrow in January 1803 unless he was moved from Henry Drury's house. His dislike of Harrow and the attractions of Bath, where he was spending the Christmas holidays, may have had something to do with Byron's defiance, but the reason for his failure, his mother told Hanson, was that Henry Drury 'has used him *ill* for some time past'. Anticipating the obvious reaction, she added, 'you may perhaps be surprised that I don't force him to return but he is rather too old and has too much sense for that', words which to Hanson may have seemed doubtful in logic as well as fact.[32]

Apprised of the schoolboy's haughty complaint, the headmaster explained how his son had 'used' Byron 'ill'. He had had the temerity to make several complaints of Byron's 'inattention to business and his propensity to make others laugh and disregard their employment as much as himself'. Henry Drury, it turned out, had repeatedly requested his father 'to withdraw Byron from his tuition'. The headmaster had relied, however, on his own remonstrances to rectify Byron's errors and had been 'unwilling to accede to my son's wishes'. But now that 'Lord Byron' had 'made the request himself', Dr Drury was glad to effect the separation, transferring Byron, who returned in the middle of February, to Mr Evans's house, in the hope that it would lead to a considerable improvement in his conduct. While the relationship between head and housemaster may have been a complicating factor, Byron was on the face of it wholly in the wrong. Yet, later in his career, Henry Drury provoked the animosity of Trollope's elder brother and other boys, which led one historian of Harrow to doubt if he was the right kind of tutor 'for an extremely sensitive, erratic and impressionable boy of genius'.[33]

Henry Drury and Byron subsequently became such close friends that after the poet's death Drury adopted two of his dogs, but at the time the boy's removal to another house did not end their feud. On 1 May 1803 Byron wrote to his mother that Henry Drury had 'behaved himself to me in a manner I neither *can* nor will bear'. Drury had seen Byron talking in church – Harrow did not have a chapel and so used the parish church – but said nothing about it afterwards to Byron. Instead he took the other boy to his pupil-room where he abused Byron 'in a most violent manner, called me blackguard [and] said he *would* and *could* have me expelled. . . .' Byron, whose inscription in a Harrow schoolbook, 'His Holiness Byron 1804', does not indicate deep piety, conceded that he had been idle and should not talk in church but claimed he had 'never done a mean action at this school to him or anyone'. Reminding his mother that he had warned her that Henry Drury would seek revenge, and telling her that if he were treated in this manner he would not stay at the school, he asked her to write to Dr Drury, who, he said, 'has behaved to me, as also Mr Evans, very kindly'. While Byron's reaction seems inordinate, he was on this occasion evidently in the right. Drury conceded as much, expressing sorrow to Hanson that 'a hasty word' had ever been uttered, while maintaining that 'it was never intended to make so deep a wound as his letter intimates'. The headmaster went on to display tact; he was 'deeply interested in Lord Byron's welfare', admired his 'mind that feels and can discriminate reasonably', and looked forward to his exercising his talents to 'supply the deficiencies of fortune by the exertion of his abilities and by application'. Admirable as Dr Drury's diplomatic skills and the trouble he took with Byron undoubtedly were, they can have done nothing to diminish the schoolboy arrogance or the excessively high notions of rank from which Byron was currently suffering.[34]

That storm ended well for Byron. In June he reported to his mother he had been placed in a higher form, and, he continued, 'Dr Drury and I go on very well'. The calm at Harrow did not last, however, and even before it had ended, Mrs Byron, too, had suffered from her son's rebelliousness. Ever since her husband had consumed her fortune, Catherine had been in financial straits, but they had lately been made more acute partly by the expense caused by her son's foot. Byron's touchiness about his deformity did not lead to a consistent effort to mend it. 'I much fear', wrote his doctor, who advised resting the leg, and keeping the brace in place, 'this extreme inattention will counteract every exertion on my part to make him better'. But Byron's inattention continued – he wanted to act as much like other boys as possible – and the largely wasted treatment had to be paid for. The doctor's fee came to £150 a year which, understandably, Catherine thought 'a great deal of money'.[35]

When her son went to Harrow, Mrs Byron stayed on in London, only moving from Sloane Terrace to 16 Piccadilly. But when possible she took him away from London for the holidays. In the summer of 1801 they went to Cheltenham and the Malvern Hills, which, though 'miniature', made Byron nostalgic for the Scottish Highlands. They returned to Cheltenham the following year and went to Bath that Christmas. The Easter holidays of 1802 were spent in London. At that time, Mrs Byron could have used her son's phrase of Dr Drury and said that she and her son were 'going on very well'. Pryse Gordon, a Scottish friend of Catherine, remembered him then as a 'spoiled child' who was allowed too much of his own way, but also as 'a fine, lively, restless lad' who never, Catherine told Gordon, 'did anything to disoblige or vex' her.[36]

A year later Gordon would not have been told the same. Byron's pride of rank was showing itself at home as well as at Harrow. By then Newstead had been leased to the young Lord Grey de Ruthyn for five years at the hardly extortionate rent of £50 a year, although

Grey did also have to pay taxes and a gamekeeper. And in May 1803 Mrs Byron, who had been living in lodgings in Nottingham, had taken Burgage Manor, which the Newstead gardener and steward, Owen Mealey, thought 'a handsome new house', on the green of the pleasant small town of Southwell, some twelve miles from Newstead, at a rent of £23 a year. When her son appeared there for the summer holidays, however, he took an instant dislike to the place, later complaining to Augusta that it had 'no society but old parsons and old maids'.[37]

Admittedly Southwell was clerically over-populated, having sixteen prebendaries, but, as well as old maids, it was also blessed with plenty of young maids eager to meet the noble newcomer. At fifteen, though, Byron was far from being the object of beauty he later became. Small and fat with his hair plastered down on his forehead, he was both shy and disdainful of his neighbours, a combination which made him reluctant to mix with them. Hence, to his mother's natural chagrin, which she did not hesitate to communicate to her Southwell acquaintances, he took himself off to Newstead, where he stayed with Owen Mealey. The last person the shifty steward would have chosen to have in his home, keeping an eye on him and causing him additional work and trouble, was his employer: 'My Lord has been a great hindrance to me', he complained to Hanson. But he did not have to put up with him for long. Luckily for Mealey and unluckily for Catherine Byron, Lord Grey suggested to Byron that he visit Annesley, the home of the descendant of William Chaworth who had been killed by the 'wicked Lord' in 1764.[38]

Byron was made welcome at Annesley by Ann and William Clarke, the mother and stepfather of the eighteen-year-old heiress Mary Chaworth, and soon spent almost all his time there. Ann Clarke was genuinely fond of Byron, who would, she thought, make an excellent match for Mary. His peerage more than made up for his relative indigence, while the nearly adjacent Annesley and Newstead estates could be conveniently run as a unit and the latter soon brought up to the high standard of the efficiently run Annesley. Such a union would deliver an additional benefit: the happy young couple would live at Newstead, enabling the Clarkes to continue enjoying the comforts of Annesley. When Hanson had taken Byron over to Annesley in 1798 to introduce him to the Clarkes and to Mary, he had laughingly said to him, 'Here is a pretty young lady, you had better marry her', and had elicited the rejoinder, 'What, Mr Hanson, the Capulets and Montagues intermarry?' Now six years later a Byron-Montague quickly fell in love with a Chaworth-Capulet but, unfortunately for the Clarkes and probably, as Byron later thought, for both Mary and himself, there was never any serious chance of a Montague–Capulet marriage. Mary was two years older than Byron, he was not attractive, and her heart was already engaged elsewhere.[39]

The object of her affections, Jack Musters, the son of an extravagant and hard-up Nottinghamshire landowner, was a handsome, womanising, musical fox-hunter who, according to Nimrod,* 'was as regularly educated for hunting as a Church-man for Church', and who, according to himself, had never read a book in his life. His mother, Sophia, was a noted beauty, and his real father may have been the Prince of Wales, whom he closely resembled. Mary fell in love with Jack Musters as soon as she met him, and Musters was attracted to the vivacious, pretty and above all rich Annesley heiress. Understandably, the Clarkes opposed the match and, having failed to persuade Mary to call it off, successfully petitioned for her to be made a ward of court; the Lord Chancellor, Eldon, forbade Musters to see or correspond with Mary, and prohibited marriage without the consent of the Clarkes or the court. These edicts did not, however, end the romance which was invigorated by secret notes and clandestine meetings.[40]

With Mary already infatuated with Musters, Byron's calf-love was doomed to disappointment. Yet he spent his days reading with Mary and her plain, malicious cousin, Ann Radford, moping and showing off by firing his pistol at a door on the terrace. By inventing a story that he had seen a ghost on his way home the previous evening, he managed from then on to stay at Annesley at night. Mary looked on him as the schoolboy he was, but she found him amusing and endearing. Byron was so severely smitten that he refused to return to Harrow for the Michaelmas term.[41]

Naturally his mother was distraught. In September in reply to her letter summoning him back to Southwell, he promised to return the next day and, having said he knew it was time to go to Harrow, signed his letter 'your unhappy son, Byron'. Yet he insisted on remaining unhappy at Annesley rather than at Harrow. In answer

* The sporting writer of the early nineteenth century, whose real name was Charles James Apperley. He had a passion for hunting.

to an enquiry from Dr Drury about Byron's absence, his mother wrote that although she had 'done all in my power for six weeks past', she could not get him to return. 'He has no indisposition that I know of, but love, desperate love, the *worst* of all *maladies* in my opinion'. Mrs Byron had of course experienced that malady. Some weeks later her son was partly cured by the cause of it. After Byron's constant attendance had begun to pall on Mary, he either overheard her saying to her maid or had her words repeated to him by Anne Radford: 'Do you think I could care anything for that lame boy?' Enraged and mortified, Byron fled back to Newstead.[42]

Yet he never forgot Mary Chaworth. While she may have had a more profound effect on his memory and imagination than the facts of his brief unsuccessful love for her warranted, she left an indelible impression on his mind. His vow in a very early poem (1804) 'For ever I'll think upon you' turned out to be almost true. In his autobiographical poem 'The Dream', written in the dark time of 1816, he described his love for Mary and how on his wedding day

> he spoke
> The fitting vows, but heard not his own words
> And all things reel'd around him

because Mary and the past 'came back/ And thrust themselves between him and the light'. He said much the same in his memoirs.* Perhaps his antipathy to his wife overcame autobiographical truth and he was, in Wordsworth's words, confounding his 'present feelings with the past'. Characteristically, Hobhouse was later sceptical about the strength and duration of Byron's passion for Mary Chaworth, yet the poet had in a sense anticipated his friend, writing in 1821 in his Detached Thoughts that his 'hopeless attachment' had been 'sedulously concealed'.[43]

Still Byron did not join his mother at Southwell. Instead he stayed at Newstead to the dismay of Mealey who, having enjoyed a respite while Byron was at Annesley, lamented to Hanson that most of his time was again spent waiting on his employer. According to the steward, Byron and Lord Grey, who was eight years older, 'goe out those moonlight nights and shuitt pheasants as they sit at Roost' – behaviour which Byron would not have contemplated in later years. Then Grey came to Mealey's rescue. He did something which caused Byron to leave Newstead, vowing never to see Grey again.

* Burned after his death.

The cause of their quarrel was clearly some sexual advance to the younger boy, and the incident is made perplexing only by the comment Hobhouse wrote in his copy of Moore's biography: 'A circumstance occurred during this intimacy which clearly had much effect on his future morals.' But since Byron plainly rejected Grey's advance, it can scarcely have affected his future morality. Hobhouse may have been suggesting that Grey and Byron were having a sexual relationship, but if they were why did Byron end it so abruptly and decisively? Probably Hobhouse's comment was muddled and appears to suggest something he did not intend.[44]

With both Annesley and Newstead no longer casting a spell, Harrow had increased attraction for Byron. On his return in January he was moved from Evans's house to that of the headmaster, presumably because after his long absence Dr Drury wanted to keep a close eye on him. Even though he had necessarily lost ground in his schoolwork, Byron's truancy had not lost him his place in the school, and his attitude to Harrow soon began to change. This was partly due to the transition he described in a note on one of his Harrow poems: 'the junior boys are completely subservient to the upper forms . . . but after a certain period, they command, in turn, those who succeed'. Byron was now in the upper forms and, in the language used by Sydney Smith, no longer 'a slave' but 'a tyrant'.[45]

He does not seem to have abused his position as 'a tyrant', although one schoolfellow, Sir Thomas Bernard, who said he had shared a bedroom with Byron, later called him 'a terrible bully'. That is quite possible (although there is confusion about when Bernard went to the school); but, if so, it almost certainly relates to the earlier period when Byron admitted he was 'most unpopular'. From 1804 onwards, when he was a senior boy, he was a protector not a persecutor of the weaker boys. Thomas Dundas, who had been bullied by Lord Herbert, well remembered Byron saying 'I like licking a Lord's son' and proceeding to do so. Byron later wrote that he had had seven battles at Harrow and lost only one, when his opponent cheated. Probably nearly all those took place in his earlier Harrow years and anyway do not come into the category of bullying. Nor did his fight with Lord Calthorpe for writing 'D . . . .d Atheist' under his name. Byron seems to have treated his fags kindly, and he left a reputation for benevolence with the local tradesmen.[46]

By the summer of 1804 the long hours spent in all weathers brooding and sometimes crying, 'As reclining, at eve on your tombstone I lay', in Harrow churchyard with its magnificent views of the surrounding countryside were a thing of the past. Byron's sunnier attitude to Harrow may have been aided by the resumption of relations with his half-sister Augusta. On the death of Augusta's grandmother, Lady Holderness, in October 1801, Catherine wrote a characteristically tactless letter of condolence to the young girl, ending with the words, 'your brother is at Harrow School, and, if you wish to see him, I have now no desire to keep you asunder'. Evidently they did meet at least once some time afterwards, and Augusta began a one-sided correspondence until March 1804 when Byron apologised for his lack of response, attributing it not to a want of affection but to the shyness 'naturally inherent to my disposition'. Having conquered his shyness, he fired a volley of letters at Augusta, sending her four long ones in less than three weeks. In the last one, after expressing reservations about his approaching '*Debut* as *an orator*' he told her: 'By the bye, I do not dislike Harrow. I find *ways* and *means* to amuse *myself very pleasantly* there.'[47]

What were those ways and means? As well as reading, occasion-ally drinking, making people laugh and annoying the masters, Byron's chief way and means of pleasure lay in his friendships. Because of his social insecurity, these were largely with young aristocrats, although peers and sons of peers were so thick on the ground at Harrow at that time that it would have been difficult to avoid them. 'My school-friendships were with *me passions* (For I was always violent)', Byron wrote in his Detached Thoughts; 'that with Lord Clare began one of the earliest and lasted longest'. Clare, who eventually became a Privy Councillor and Governor of Bombay, was more than four years younger than Byron – a vast disparity at that time of life. In another reminiscence Byron wrote of six boys who 'were my juniors and favourites, whom I spoilt by indulgence'. It was his friendship with these mainly much younger boys that were passions. Thus he told Augusta that, if she deserted him, 'I have nobody I can love but Delawarr', who also became a Privy Councillor but only a Lord of the Bedchamber to George IV and the Lord Chamberlain of Queen Victoria.[48]

Byron had earlier ended a poem to the 'remarkably handsome' Delawarr, who though nearly four years younger than him, was his 'principal ... and particular friend', with the lines: 'On *thy dear* breast I'll lay my head/ Without *thee*! *where* would be my *Heaven*?' And in lines about the same boy in a later poem he said that his name was 'yet embalm'd, within my heart' which did 'palpitate' when it heard 'the sound' of it. Of course Byron was not alone in using very sentimental language for his school friendships. Leigh Hunt wrote of 'a disembodied transport' and of having 'loved [his] friend for his gentleness, his candour, his truth', etc.; and Wordsworth wrote of a schoolfriend that he was 'Then passionately lov'd'. Yet Byron did not just use sentimental language. His friendships were punctuated with absurd tiffs and jealousies. What he called 'some childish misunderstanding' caused estrangements with Lord Delawarr, William Harness and others; and he was affronted when Lord Clare addressed him as 'My Dear Byron' instead of as 'My dearest Byron'. Clare was barely thirteen when this tiff took place shortly before Byron left Harrow.[49]

Hence the question arises whether Byron's sentimental friendships with younger boys were just that or whether in at least some of them the sentimentality took physical expression. Homosexuality, as was seen earlier, was common in the public schools of the time with no fuss being made about it; later in Greece when parting from a boy Byron used the phrase 'as many kisses as would have sufficed for a boarding school'. Moreover during some stages of his later life Byron was strongly attracted to boys or young men. There is also more particular evidence. Faced with his friendships with younger boys at Harrow, his chief biographer, Thomas Moore, wrote an orotund paragraph explaining that they were merely the natural result of the English public school system. Against that paragraph in his copy of Moore's book Hobhouse wrote: 'M. knows nothing, or will tell nothing of the principal cause and motive for all these boyish friendships.' And the fact that Moore does seem to have had some knowledge and worries about them confirms what Hobhouse was implying about Byron.[50]

Three other pieces of evidence do the same. At Cambridge Byron fell in love with a choirboy, John Edleston. In always stressing that this love was 'pure', he was evidently contrasting it with other loves or relationships; he never claimed that his relationships at Harrow were 'pure'. Secondly, early in 1807, he wrote a short autobiographical poem 'Damaetas' (whose suppressed title was 'My Character') which began, 'In law an infant, and in years a boy,/ In mind a slave to every vicious joy'. Admittedly Byron could conceivably have been referring solely to the period since leaving Harrow eighteen months before, but that is improbable. Admittedly, too, as his young Harrow friend William Harness later wrote, echoing Bolingbroke on Swift, Byron had a 'tendency to malign himself – this hypocrisy reversed'. Despite, however, Byron's undoubted habit of calumniating himself, his poem is unlikely to have been based on nothing at all, especially as in another of his comments on Moore Hobhouse wrote: 'Certainly B had nothing to learn in the way of depravity either of mind or body when he came [to Cambridge] from Harrow.' Finally, according to Lady Byron, Lady Caroline Lamb told her in 1816 that Byron had confessed to her that 'from his boyhood he had been in the practice of unnatural crime . . . he mentioned three schoolfellows whom he had thus perverted'. Caroline Lamb, who once defined truth to be what one thinks at the moment, was an untrustworthy witness, especially where Byron was concerned; yet even she can hardly have invented the whole conversation, though she no doubt exaggerated it and recounted it as luridly as she could.[51]

The overwhelming probability then is that some at least of Byron's 'school friendships' were, as he said, 'passions', and were the most important of his 'ways and means' of amusing himself 'very pleasantly' at Harrow. The transition from Byron's heterosexual, though unconsummated, passion to a series of homosexual ones was not unusual. Many adolescent boys, especially if they live in an exclusively male society, go through a homosexual phase which does not preclude their being attracted to women. Writing to Tom Moore many years later, Byron attributed 'all the mischief I have ever done or sung' to the book of poems, which Moore published under the name of 'the Late Thomas Little' in 1801 and Byron read in 1803, an allegation which has been endorsed by later authorities, though Byron was surely only teasing the Irish poet. By the standards of the time 'Thomas Little's' slight but enjoyable poems were, in the contemporary term, fairly 'warm' – 'Be an angel, my love, in the morning,/ But, Oh! *be a woman to-night*!' – but the idea that they stimulated Byron's erotic impulses, either hetero- or homosexual, is surely fantasy. 'Thomas Little' influenced Byron's poetry, not his morals. The erotic impulses of fifteen- or sixteen-year-old boys seldom need stimulation, and Byron's certainly did not. His 'passions' had been 'developed very early' by May Gray.[52]

Byron's various sexual or romantic attachments helped to alter his view of the school without changing his behaviour. He was still in one 'scrape' after another. So while he was now enjoying Harrow, the authorities were still not enjoying him. In May Dr Drury complained that Byron was making his house a scene of riot and confusion and indicated that he should leave at the end of the term. At the same time Mark, Dr Drury's brother and the Lower Master, apparently said that Byron was a *'blackguard'* – evidently the Drurys' favourite term of abuse – and, inexcusably, reproached him for the meagreness of his fortune. In one respect, however, Byron did win the approval of the Drurys. At Byron's 'first declamation' the headmaster was impressed by the boy's ability to 'diverge from the original composition' without losing his flow, and at the subsequent speech day he also did well. Yet in December Drury once again hoped for Byron's departure from the school. Although Byron represented it to Hanson as his own wish to do so and gave a leaving present to the school library, Drury told the lawyer that the boy's conduct had given him 'much trouble and uneasiness' and the wish for his departure had originated with him. In the end, nevertheless, Drury was persuaded to allow Byron to stay until the following summer, and though subjected to lengthy and no doubt justified 'Jobations' from the headmaster, Byron continued to like and respect him.[53]

If the Harrow authorities were unable to control or discipline Byron at school, his mother had little chance of being able to do so at home. Indeed, while his relations with his schoolmasters had not improved despite his more favourable view of Harrow, his relations with his mother had been deteriorating. He had long had rows with her, and the customary rebelliousness of adolescence made them worse. Catherine loved her son, but he found her easy to exasperate. On important issues such as his refusal to return to Harrow, she was strikingly forbearing. On small ones her tolerance was replaced by violent rages. She could never deliver an impressive 'Jobation' in the style of Dr Drury; instead she flew into a passion and might even throw things at him.

As her son grew older, he naturally found her vulgarity more embarrassing, while mother-and-son disputes were 'heightened' by the near presence of Lord Grey. Catherine had complicated matters by falling in love with Grey – 'Whatever he says is right with her', Mealey told Hanson – and demanded a reconciliation between her son and their tenant. Byron refused, telling Augusta that 'I *never will*' be reconciled with Grey and that he could not explain even to his 'dear sister' his reasons for 'ceasing that friendship'. He found his mother's 'penchant' for Grey, for whom he still had a 'cordial, deliberate detestation', demeaning and ridiculous. Even if there had been a reconciliation, Mrs Byron's love affair would not have prospered; Grey preferred her son.[54]

Byron's various emotional entanglements also contributed to their growing estrangement, as did his new relations with his half-sister Augusta to whom he poured out complaints against his mother. He was honest enough to concede that the trouble was his own fault and that she was generous, but he had difficulty in restraining his 'dislike' of her. After cataloguing Catherine's ill-treatment of him in a succession of letters, Byron confided to his sister that she was 'certainly mad', her 'conduct being a happy compound of derangement and folly'. Meanwhile in May 1804 Catherine gave Hanson a good sketch of her wayward son: 'What is to be done with him when he leaves Harrow God only knows. He is a turbulent unruly boy who wants to be emancipated from all restraint, his sentiments are however noble.'[55]

Despite his professed dislike of Southwell – 'this horrid place' where he was, he told Augusta, 'oppressed with ennui' – Byron liked the Pigot family who lived some thirty yards away across the green from Burgage Manor. Elizabeth, the eldest Pigot daughter, was only a few months older than Augusta but far more sensible. Indeed she was one of the nicest and most level-headed women Byron ever met; sadly he never saw her after 1807. She soon dispelled his shyness, and from April 1804 they were firm friends. Charming and attractive with a sense of humour, Elizabeth was nearly two years older than Mary Chaworth which should have comforted Catherine; even so, scarred by that earlier experience, Mrs Byron still had her worries. Mrs Pigot assured her that Elizabeth regarded him very much as a friend, saw all his faults clearly and that there was not a spark of anything like love. She probably exaggerated. Byron wrote poems to Elizabeth which suggest there was a spark or two: 'For he who views that witching grace,/ That perfect form, that lovely face,/ With eyes admiring, oh! Believe me/ He never wishes to deceive thee.' And Elizabeth's treasuring of the locks of his hair and her directions that a packet of his letters be buried with her 'speak', as a member of the family later wrote, 'of something a little closer than friendship'. Yet Elizabeth was sufficiently judicious to prevent any possibility of a fire.[56]

Byron's reprieve at Christmas 1804 resulted in his staying longer at Harrow than the man who had granted it; because of his wife's ill health Dr Drury left the school at Easter. In the struggle for the succession Byron, despite their quarrel in the previous year, was a fierce supporter of Mark Drury. After the votes of the six governors split evenly between Drury and his chief opponent, Dr George Butler, a Cambridge don, the Archbishop of Canterbury's casting vote went to Butler. The Archbishop's uninformed choice caused resentment among the boys and is usually said to have produced a rebellion led by Byron in which a trail of gunpowder to blow up the school was laid and not lit only because of a last minute recognition that the explosion would destroy the signatures of generations of Harrovians carved on the walls. In the late eighteenth and early nineteenth centuries rebellion was endemic at public schools – the violent regimes bred schoolboy violence; one at Rugby in 1793 needed the militia to suppress it. Nevertheless, the Harrow rebellion in 1805 is legend. A few squibs were no doubt let off; that is about all. Byron fell out with Butler because of some offensively witty verses he wrote about the new headmaster, not because of rebellious violence or other misdemeanours.[57]

Augusta later told Byron that between 1804 and 1805 his 'temper and disposition' had changed so much as to make him almost unrecognisable. (Catherine Byron had noted an improvement in August 1804.) To have really led a rebellion would have been more consonant with the Byron of 1804 than the one of 1805. In fact for almost the whole of his last (and Dr Butler's first) term Byron got on well with the headmaster who insisted on Byron speaking on the second as well as on the first speech day. A good speaker himself, Dr Butler took a keen interest in the boys' speeches, and Byron evidently performed well on both occasions, as he had also done the year before when with Robert Peel he acted a scene from the *Aeneid*. The fame of his oratory, his mother told Hanson, had reached Southwell. Byron had unavailingly hoped that Augusta would come down for the second speech day to hear him declaim a passage from *King Lear*. Augusta's absence was just as well, for, though Byron wrote in a poem, 'Till, fir'd by loud plaudits, and self adulation,/ I regarded myself, as a Garrick reviv'd', he was ill and so overcome by his exertions that he had to leave the room after he had finished his speech.[58]

Only in July did war break out between him and Dr Butler when Byron produced his lampoon, 'On a Change of Masters at a Great Public School':

> – Of narrow brain, yet of a narrower soul,
> Pomposus holds you, in his harsh controul; . . .
> Mistaking pedantry, for learning's laws,
> He governs, sanction'd but by self applause.

Understandably Butler was not amused, his anger at being called pompous even leading him to insist, quite wrongly, that Byron had been expelled. Yet two years later Byron was reconciled to the headmaster and suppressed the poem.[59]

The end of the term did not end the young satirist's connection with the school. In August the first Eton v. Harrow cricket match (Harrow 'were most confoundedly beat') was played at the old Lord's Ground which is now Dorset Square. The 1805 contest was not the formal occasion it later became; it was organised by the boys themselves, probably including Byron, largely to provide an excuse for debauchery in the evening. Although Byron's foot was so improved that he could wear an ordinary boot, it was still an athletic handicap. The Captain of Harrow said afterwards that if he had chosen the team Byron would not have been in it and that he had played badly. But he batted better than the Captain who scored 0 in each innings. In the usual account, Byron made 7 runs in the first innings, going in immediately after A. Shakespeare who scored 8, and in the second, only 2. However, in a letter addressed to 'My Dearest Gordon', Byron claimed '11 notches in the first innings and 7 in the second'. No doubt because of his lameness, Byron always made the most of his athletic achievements. But he is unlikely to have lied to Gordon, whose brother Byron saw at the game and would have known what had happened, and since the usual version is not free from doubt, Byron's claim may have been accurate. In the evening, as planned, both teams got drunk and made so much noise in the theatre that none of their neighbours could 'hear a word of the drama'; the next morning Byron could not remember how he had found his way to bed, or, perhaps, how many runs he had made.[60]

CHAPTER VI

Eton and Harrow

Shelley: 1804–10 (aged 11–17 years)
Byron: 1801–5 (aged 13–17 years)

Taking into account his absences from the school, Byron was at Harrow for less than four years and was lucky to last for even that abnormally short span. Shelley was at Eton for six years – much the longest period in his short life that he spent in the same surroundings. As with Byron, many of the stories of Shelley at public school are legend, but unlike those about Byron some originated from Shelley himself. He was not to blame, though, for the misdating of his entry into Eton. Shelley, it has been almost invariably stated,* signed the headmaster's 'Entrance Book' on 29 July 1804 and joined the school in September. In fact he both signed the book and joined the school on 29 June, the general mistake being caused by a misreading of the 'Entrance Book' and an erroneous belief that then, as later, boys entered the school only at the beginning of the half (the Eton word for term). In the early nineteenth century they came at all times of the year; indeed Shelley was not the last entrant in the summer half of 1804.

Just why Timothy and Elizabeth Shelley chose to send their son to Eton at the end of June is not known. Maybe he had got into trouble at Isleworth and had been more or less expelled; or maybe it was just more convenient for Timothy to take him to the school in June than in September. Whatever the reason the decision was fully consistent with their habitually inconsiderate handling of their son's education and upbringing. At whatever time of year Shelley had gone to Eton he would have been bullied – partly because that happened to almost all new boys and partly because he was so different from his fellows – but his arrival by himself towards the end of the half was almost an incitement to ill-treatment. And once

---

* Except by Michael Meredith, a master and the College Librarian at Eton, in an unpublished lecture which was summarised in his article in the *Daily Telegraph* on 6 August 1992. For this information and much else I am greatly indebted to Mr Meredith, who showed me the relevant documents.

again, evidently, nothing had been done to prepare him for his ordeal.

The herd instinct is strong among schoolboys, and while we need not go all the way with Mary Shelley in believing that, among his 'fellow creatures' at Eton, Shelley was 'like a spirit from another sphere', he was certainly never one of the herd. And he did little to endear himself to the herd, shunning or despising, said a near contemporary, 'the usual games and exertions of youth'.[1]

As no good portrait of Shelley was ever painted, nobody can now 'see Shelley plain', even as a man, let alone as a boy. There is no unanimity even on the colour of his eyes, though they were probably deep blue. His features were delicate rather than regular. He had 'a small turn-up nose', he himself said, a receding but pointed chin – his side face was not strong – a very small head and, according to his sister Hellen, 'an eccentric quantity' of dark brown wavy hair. When he went to Eton he was tall for his age and slightly and delicately built, but the personal fascination, that for many he undoubtedly possessed as an adult, was evidently not present in the schoolboy. His clothes were untidy, if not dishevelled, and he did not wear 'strings in his shoes'.[2]

Furthermore, he was clever and good at schoolwork. Whatever the defects of Dr Greenlaw and Syon House, Shelley was well grounded in the classics. In consequence he was placed in the Upper Fourth, which meant that he was in the Upper School. This placed him safely beyond the flogging attentions of Keate, who then had charge only of the lower boys, while making him still more conspicuous and a focus of jealousy. Yet, unlike at Harrow, being in the upper school did not give a boy exemption from fagging for older boys. One of the Shelley legends, invented by himself and given wide currency by his widow, was that he was persecuted at Eton because of his 'systematic and determined resistance to . . . denominated fagging'; he has even been said to have headed a conspiracy against the system. No such conspiracy took place; hence Shelley did not lead one, though he may have initially refused to fag for Henry Matthews – later an author and a colonial judge. Even that limited defiance is probably a myth. If it did happen, it probably stemmed less from insubordination or innate love of liberty than from a misunderstanding. At Harrow something of the sort happened to Robert Peel, who refused some fagging duty because he thought his place in the school gave him immunity from fagging commands. If Shelley also refused for the same reason, his rebellion, like Peel's, was short-lived; in the autumn he was obediently fagging for Matthews.[3]

Mary Shelley was on stronger ground in thinking that her husband was mercilessly bullied at Eton. According to Peacock, who wrote *Memoirs* of Shelley, the poet often told him of his 'persecutions' by the elder boys with 'feelings of abhorrence' which Peacock had only heard equalled when Shelley spoke of Lord Eldon. But the evidence of ill-treatment does not come only from the Shelleys. More than forty years later the then headmaster of the school, Edward Hawtrey, who had been there with Shelley, spoke in a sermon of Shelley's life having been made 'miserable' by the 'injustice' with which he had been treated. Hawtrey believed that such 'ill-usage' might lead to 'misanthropy' or the 'more fatal errors of doubting the justice of Providence' and the truth of Christianity. Hawtrey knew what he was talking about: he himself had been nearly killed at Eton. There is of course a world of difference between a small boy being bullied by one or more larger ones, as was then commonplace, and a single boy being set upon, derided and tormented by several hundred others. Mass bullying causes humiliation as well as pain and distress, and that was the fate of Shelley. One of Coleridge's nephews later claimed to be the only boy he knew who did not join in the teasing of Shelley.[4]

Almost every day about noon there used to be a 'Shelley-bait'. The cry would go up 'The Shelley! Shelley! Shelley!' Shelley would be hunted up the street. His books would be knocked from under his arm and his clothes pulled and torn. Inevitably Shelley lost his temper, which delighted his tormentors and drove them to further excesses. A near contemporary, W. H. Merle, recalled him being 'surrounded, hooted, baited like a maddened bull' and thought he remembered 'the cry which Shelley was wont to utter in his paroxysm of revengeful anger'. If forty years later a bystander could remember the actions of the mob and the cry of the hunted, we can well imagine the effect on the victim. He was known as 'Mad Shelley', but his alleged 'madness' seems likely in this instance to have been more the consequence than the cause of what Mary Shelley called the 'revolting cruelty . . . and oppression which . . . it was his ill-fortune to encounter'.[5]

For the herd Shelley was almost ideal bullying fodder, but Shelley-baits must have eventually palled and other prey have been pursued. Shelley was never the sole target of the hunters and was probably their principal victim for less than a year, though that was quite long enough to scar him. His persecution may have been ended as much by his own efforts as by the satiety of the mob. Shelley had suffered at Syon House from being no good with his fists and from his unwillingness to fight. At Eton fights were common and bloody: in 1824 Francis Ashley, the youngest son of Lord Shaftesbury, was killed in one. Shelley had to engage in at least one fight if he was to gain the respect of his fellows, and in the spring or summer of 1805 he challenged (or he may have accepted a challenge from) one of his persecutors, George Lyne. The son of a tailor in the Strand, Lyne was smaller and younger than Shelley and 'was soundly beaten'.[6]

Shelley's first housemaster was Hexter, a major in the militia, a stern disciplinarian and a JP, who might have been more usefully employed in the army. Not a full member of the teaching staff, he was not allowed to wear a gown and was merely the writing master. By diligent application, the dull but ambitious Hexter was eventually able to teach a modicum of maths, but as he himself had mastered only simple arithmetic he cannot have imparted much knowledge. Hexter's fifty-year career at Eton is a further demonstration of the defective infrastructure that 'the great public schools' thought adequate for their allegedly privileged inmates. Hawkshead Grammar School had mathematics masters who could teach Wordsworth Euclid; Eton made do with a teacher who may never have heard of Euclid. Hexter had in his house only two other boys of Shelley's age. One of them, Andrew Amos, an intelligent boy who later became a barrister, ate with Shelley and was his first Eton friend. They amused themselves writing and performing plays together, though the authors outnumbered the audience, which consisted of the only other lower boy in Hexter's house.[7] Most of the stories about Shelley at Eton are from Shelley himself, and as a source of historical fact he was seldom reliable. He was capable of recounting in painstaking detail an incident that had allegedly occurred shortly before, but which was then found to be pure invention; and his stories of his remoter past were even more subject to his mythopoeic inclinations. He was, wrote Hogg, his close friend at Oxford and later, 'the unsuspecting and unresisting victim of his irresistible imagination'.[8]

In 1850, Walter Halliday, who was by then a clergyman, wrote that he used to go for long walks with Shelley through 'the beautiful neighbourhood of dear old Eton'. They walked in Windsor Park and to Stoke Poges Church where Gray is buried and was said to have composed his *Elegy*, a poem echoed in one of Shelley's earliest efforts. Halliday, who 'loved Shelley for his kindliness and affectionate ways', delighted in his friend's telling of marvellous stories of fairyland, spirits and haunted ground, a development no doubt of the stories and 'eccentric amusements' with which Shelley had entertained and frightened his small sisters.[9]

According to his widow, Shelley was 'passionately attached' to the study of the 'occult sciences'. And (as already quoted) he himself wrote in 1816 that

> While yet a boy I sought for ghosts, and sped,
> Through many a listening chamber, cave and ruin,
> And starlight wood

Mary Shelley recorded two such occasions. The first was at Field Place, when 'he got admission to the charnel house [at Warnham Church] and sat harrowed by fear yet trembling with expectation to see one of the spiritual possessors of the bones piled around him'. The second was at Eton when he 'stole' out of his house at night, and as he walked along a path through long grass 'he heard it rustle behind him' and was 'convinced that the devil followed him'.* Then standing astride a small clear stream he made an 'incantation', to which the devil made no response. Shelley later told Godwin that he used to pore over 'the reveries of Albertus Magnus & Paracelsus', but that his fondness for ghosts and magic had abated as he grew older. It does not, however, seem to have diminished much during his time at Eton.[10]

Shelley also kept up his interest in science which had been awakened by Adam Walker at Syon House. Science of course, like Euclid, was not taught at Eton. Indeed, the authorities' aversion to introducing any part of the contemporary world into the education syllabus may have been strengthened by a boy being burnt to death

---

* In *The Prelude*, which of course neither Shelley nor his widow could have read, Wordsworth recorded how on one of his 'night-wanderings'

> [He] heard, among the solitary hills
> Low breathings coming after me, and sounds
> Of undistinguishable motion, steps
> Almost as silent as the turf they trod.[10a]

after Lord Cranborne had maliciously lit the fireworks in his pocket.[11]

At all events chemistry, Timothy Shelley recorded, was 'a forbidden thing at Eton'. As was his custom, Timothy may firmly have grasped the wrong end of the stick, for the same Adam Walker who had lectured at Syon House also lectured at Eton, and Shelley and many other boys bought electrical machines from 'Old Walker's' assistant. So, however suspect, chemistry was not totally prohibited at Eton. Possibly only books on chemistry were forbidden. Or Timothy may just have meant that chemistry was 'forbidden' to his son, which would not have been an unreasonable injunction, since Shelley's experiments probably were a danger to others as well as himself.[12]

He does seem to have managed to blow up part of a dead tree by laying a trail of gunpowder which he ignited with the aid of a glass and the sun. He probably also gave his housemaster a small electric shock. That master was no longer Hexter. Halfway though his Eton career Shelley moved to another house. (Amos also moved, though to a different one.) Unfortunately Hexter's successor was little improvement, for 'Botch' Bethel was at least as dull and, though more of a scholar, a poor one. Accordingly he was a suitable victim for a practical joke. Shelley is said to have electrified his door handle and failed to warn his housemaster when Bethell came in to put a stop to the disturbance caused by the electrical experiments. In another more credible version of the story Bethel touched the machine itself and was thrown back against the wall in pain. Both versions are probably exaggerated or false. The door handle story is also told of W. M. Praed, the poet, while electrical appliances were sufficiently common at Eton for even Bethel to be wary of risking a severe shock. What is most likely to have happened was that he got a mild one, which was then inflated into a major event by his gleeful pupil.[13]

Neither at Eton nor at Field Place, where chemistry might have been more easily studied, did Shelley make any serious attempt to gain much scientific knowledge. That came later. He had perused, he told Godwin in 1812, 'ancient books of Chemistry and Magic ... with an enthusiasm of wonder almost amounting to belief', but even if he had pored over Albertus Magnus and Paracelsus – and, according to Hogg, he had not read the former – it would have been no substitute for studying modern science, such as it was. Shelley was then a dreamer rather than a scientist. He was never a mathematician; his electrical experiments were more a quest for excitement than for knowledge, and combined, as they were, with a lack of serious intellectual interest in the subject they suggest an element of exhibitionism. The blowing up of trees and the administering of electric shocks were a means of drawing attention to himself and of demonstrating that he was in his own way distinguished.[14]

Both Amos and Halliday later thought that Shelley had suffered from his intellectual interests and studies not being properly supervised. At Wordsworth's Hawkshead Grammar School, where four or five masters taught only just over a hundred boys, close direction preserved no such difficulty. But in Upper School at Eton where 300 boys were taught in one room by three or four masters, supervision was virtually impossible. Discipline was at the same time violent and inadequate. Of course Shelley could have been provided with a personal tutor, as were some other boys. His grandfather could easily have afforded to pay for one. But almost certainly Timothy and Elizabeth were too ignorant and uninterested even to be aware of such a possibility; so old Bysshe was not given the chance either to display or to overcome his miserliness. In any case, even if Shelley's studies had been lovingly overseen, he probably would not have gained more than he lost.[15]

As at Harrow, little of value took place in the schoolroom. Education was almost wholly confined to the study of dead languages: Shelley, it has been calculated, got through some 75,000 lines of Greek and Latin poetry and prose during his time at Eton, many of them being endlessly repeated. Eton gave priority to three authors: Homer, Virgil and Horace (who was Bowdlerised, of course). Yet Pote and Williams, Eton publishers, produced other books of classical authors which were used at Eton, Harrow and other schools. The 1806 edition of *Poetae Graeci*, which Shelley would have read, included extracts from *inter alia* Homer, Hesiod, Theocrates, Euripides and even Sappho. Other books published at this time included Aeschylus, Aesop's fables and selections from Ovid and Tibullus.[16]

Although this was not a restrictive classical curriculum, the dreary teaching methods and the exclusive concentration on the classics easily persuaded an intelligent boy to pay only enough attention to schoolwork to escape corporal or other punishment.

And since Shelley had been well taught before he came to Eton, absorbed knowledge at astonishing speed and had a 'marvellous' power of versifying in Latin, he did not have to spend much time on preparing his schoolwork, even if he did help others with theirs. Hence, like Byron at Harrow, Shelley sensibly neglected his official studies, later writing that, 'Nothing that my tyrants knew or taught, I cared to learn'. Far more truly than Sir Osbert Sitwell who a hundred years later was 'educated during the holidays from Eton', Shelley and Byron and many other public schoolboys in the early nineteenth century were educated in their free time away from the classroom.[17]

Shelley had plenty of free time to educate himself as well as do other things. For the lower boys, school hours at Eton were similar to those at Harrow. For the upper school they were even shorter: some 16 hours a week as opposed to 21. And in many weeks they were even fewer than that because of additional whole holidays. Shelley did not use the resulting abundance of free time solely for self-education. He was also educated by at least one congenial adult, James Lind, who was not on the Eton staff and so could not be regarded as a 'tyrant'. Lind – not to be confused with his namesake, a fellow Scot and near contemporary, who discovered the cure for scurvy – was physician to the royal household at Windsor, though other people, according to Fanny Burney, 'thought him a better conjuror than a physician'. Tall and extremely thin with a 'fat, handsome wife who [was] as tall as himself and six times as big', Lind was an intelligent and learned man, a Fellow of the Royal Society since 1777, who on his travels had amassed antiquities and curiosities which filled his house and delighted Shelley. The two probably met when Lind, who was then in his seventies, gave a lecture at Eton, and they soon became intimate. Lind 'loved me', Shelley afterwards wrote, 'and I shall never forget our long talks, where he breathed the spirit of the kindest tolerance and the purest wisdom'. Shelley also revealingly maintained that he owed Lind far, far more than he owed to his father. Lind was indeed a substitute father for him. Despite his gratitude to Lind, however, there is in most of Shelley's later poems, as Walter Bagehot long ago pointed out, 'an extreme suspicion of aged persons'. Presumably he regarded his real father, who was nearly forty years older than him, as aged, and no doubt he found most old men cynical and stripped of all idealism.[18]

Shelley was largely reconciled to Eton, and Eton to him, by the time he began his association with the royal physician. Almost certainly he exaggerated Dr Lind's virtues as much as he exaggerated 'the tyrants' vices. Lind was a far from ideal tutor for a boy like Shelley. He was a mischievous even slightly sinister old man whose reading and knowledge were wide rather than deep. All the same the doctor afforded a wondrous contrast to the dullness of Bethel and Co. – though one of the assistant masters, Francis Hodgson, later became a friend of Byron and another, John Sumner, went on to become Archbishop of Canterbury. No doubt Shelley would have read extensively anyway, but Lind widened his range of reading. Shelley apparently translated half of Pliny's *Natural History* into English, and he greatly admired Lucretius as the best of the Latin poets. Both writers strongly influenced his sceptical opinions on religion. Almost certainly Lind also steered him towards reading Plato, Benjamin Franklin, Condorcet, Erasmus Darwin and Godwin's *Political Justice*. Only an old man far removed from events and the ideas of the time would have introduced a sixteen-year-old boy to *Political Justice*, which by 1809 was virtually dead. And, in doing so, Lind did his pupil a notable disservice, for, as will later be seen, *Political Justice* inflicted as much harm to Shelley's head as its author later did to the poet's pocket. More usefully the doctor encouraged Shelley to teach himself French* and a smattering of German.[19]

Although Lind was alive for two years after Shelley left Eton, the poet never visited him. Nevertheless he put Lind into both *Laon and Cythna*, where 'The shape of an old man did then appear/ Stately and beautiful', and *Athanase* where 'an old, old man' fills his pupil with 'philosophic wisdom, clear and mild'.

Earlier, according to Shelley's account, Lind had displayed his philanthropic wisdom in saving his pupil from the madhouse. After Shelley had been very ill in the holidays from a fever which had attacked his brain, a servant overheard his father talking about sending him to a private madhouse. Warned by the servant of what was in store for him, Shelley managed to send an express letter to Lind who, having rushed to Field Place, persuaded Timothy by 'his menaces' to abandon his plan.[21]

This story, which Shelley told many times, is similar to the

* At his non-public school at Enfield Keats did not have to rely on his own efforts to learn French: the school employed a popular French abbé to teach the language.[20]

paradox of the liar (a Cretan says: 'Cretans always lie'). For, if we may eliminate the theoretical possibility that Timothy wanted to incarcerate his son even though he knew he was not mad, we are left with only two possibilities: either the story is true and Shelley's doctor and father genuinely thought he was mad at the time and were justified in discussing whether he should be sent away, or the story was quite untrue and Shelley showed a touch of madness in inventing it. 'It appeared to myself, and others also,' Hogg commented, that Shelley's 'recollections were those of a person not quite recovered from a fever which had attacked his brain, and still disturbed by the horrors of the disease'. Peacock was not sure of the truth of the matter, but was certain that throughout his life Shelley was haunted by the paranoid idea that his father was continually on the watch for a pretext to lock him up. The belief that Timothy was about to carry out his intention was, Peacock added, the reason Shelley gave for 'changing his residence and going abroad'.[22]

Shelley's fondness for such authors as Pliny and Lucretius may have been partly the cause of his being styled 'Shelley the Atheist'. At Eton, according to Hogg, that title merely meant a boy who conspicuously opposed 'the gods of Eton', the school authorities. And certainly 'Atheist', like 'Leveller' and 'Regicide', was part of what Sydney Smith called 'the Billingsgate' of the age. Yet the word 'atheist' was clearly more than mere Billingsgate at Harrow, or Byron would not have fought Lord Calthorpe for calling him one. And it surely meant more at Eton than Hogg claimed, especially as Shelley was not then a notable adversary of the established powers of Eton. Influenced, though, by Godwin's *Political Justice*, he was already a radical adversary of the established powers of England; he was a republican and an enemy of both religion and war – apart from one short interval England had been at war since 1793. Written at Eton, the most mature of his early poems contains the striking lines:

> Bearing Britannia's hired assassins on
> To victory's shame or an unhonoured grave

and again

> Religion! hated cause of all the woe
> That makes the world this wilderness. Thou spring
> Whence terror, pride, revenge and perfidy flow . . .

Admittedly Shelley did not, strictly, become an atheist until shortly before he was expelled from Oxford, but such schoolboy titles and nicknames do not aspire to scholarly accuracy. Very probably he gained the appellation from his chemical and electrical experiments as well as from his religious opinions. At this time the pietistic, ultra-religious Mrs Trimmer, an avid censor of children's books, whom in *Don Juan* Byron bracketed with his wife and the moral reformer Hannah More, was cautioning parents against 'books of Chemistry and Electricity', which she feared would lead their readers to subversion and atheism.[23]

Whatever caused Shelley's sceptical anti-Christian stance, it was not a surfeit of Christianity or religiosity at Eton. As at all the public schools, attendance at chapel was compulsory, but the boys' behaviour was often as irreverent and heathen there as it was during the rest of the day. Barracking of prayers and the sermon, sticking pins into neighbours, striking bets, trying to trip up processions, eating, and displaying pets – rabbits, mice and occasionally snakes – helped the boys to alleviate their boredom during the services. Apart from a usually inaudible sermon, Shelley and Byron, in common even with those intended for a career in the Church, were not subjected to any form of religious instruction. Indeed Sumner, the future Archbishop, found that the Eton system 'practically debarred him from saying a word about God to his pupils'.[24]

Shelley's boredom with his official studies of the pagan writers of Greece and Rome or his 'artificial education', as he called it, did not hinder his progress up the school any more than his abilities accelerated it. As at Harrow, promotion was largely automatic or 'by gravitation upwards'. In two years he rose from the Upper Fourth through the Remove to the Lower Fifth. He then remained in the Fifth Form – Lower, then Upper – for three years. So many boys were ahead of him in the queue that he did not reach the Sixth Form until September 1809 for his last three halves. As he went up the school, his life changed from miserable to tolerable and then to reasonably enjoyable. Even though he was not, in Sydney Smith's language, 'alternately tyrant and slave', since he never became a tyrant, he did pass, in Byron's words, from 'subservience' to 'command'. The allegedly sworn enemy of fagging became himself a fagmaster, though a conspicuously humane one.[25]

Unlike Byron, Shelley never in later life mentioned his school friends. Yet Mary Shelley claimed that he formed 'several sincere friendships' at Eton and was 'adored' by his contemporaries. Thinking that an unusual number of leaving books had been given to Shelley, Hogg believed that they and the many calls that old Etonians made on him at Oxford confirmed his popularity at the school. The giving of such books, however, could be more a politeness than a genuine token of friendship, and Shelley was not the sort of boy who was ever likely to be widely popular.* Peacock was probably nearer the truth in saying that he had 'several attached friends' at Eton. Certainly the only specific mention of Shelley's Eton days in his poetry – in his late poem 'The Boat on the Serchio' – suggests that he had had some friends and that not all his memories of the school were unhappy ones.[26]

Near the end of his life Shelley wrote a prose fragment of autobiography concerning his friendship with another boy. Since he thought he was eleven or twelve at the time, it could have been composed at Syon House after Tom Medwin had left or, more probably, at Eton. Shelley had 'a profound and sentimental attachment . . . exempt from the smallest alloy of sensuality . . . [to a] generous, brave and gentle' contemporary with a delicate and simple manner which he found 'inexpressibly attractive'. Every word pierced his heart, so that 'the tears often have involuntarily gushed from my eyes'. He recollected thinking his 'friendship exquisitely beautiful. Every night, when we parted to go to bed, I remember we kissed each other.'[28]

Shelley also remembered that in his 'simplicity' he wrote a long account to his mother of his friend's great qualities and of his 'own devoted attachment'. Owing to the fear and loathing with which homosexuality, though common enough both at school and later, was then viewed, most mothers would have been disquieted by such a letter from their son. Their fears would in most cases have been unwarranted. Such attachments are fairly frequent, and even those contracted during or after puberty, which are not exempt from the 'alloy of sensuality', are usually a passing phase and not an indicator of a boy's mature sexual orientation. Here, though, the indicator was not wholly inaccurate, for the mature Shelley evidently had a significant bisexual component. Indeed it is one of

---

* Shelley chose at least some expensive volumes, published much earlier, for the leaving presents he gave other boys. Possibly he lifted them from his father's library in the confident belief that they would not be missed.[27]

the oddities of our story that its four main characters – Shelley, Byron, Mary Shelley and Lady Byron – all had a strong strain of bisexuality, although only Byron was fully aware of it.[29]

If Elizabeth Shelley was disquieted by her son's letter, she did not bother to answer it. Shelley later supposed that she 'thought me out of my wits'; at the time he would not have made such a supposition and must have been surprised and hurt by his mother's silence. Presumably Elizabeth was just being her usual unresponsive self; her failure to answer is a revealing example of her attitude and performance as a mother.[30]

Shelley's first 'devoted attachment' to one of his own sex made a deep impression on him – an indication of his bisexuality; otherwise he would have forgotten the episode instead of treasuring its memory. His fragment on 'Friendship' was not his only reference to it. Describing the statue of Bacchus and Ampelus in Florence in 1819 he likened 'Ampelus embrac[ing] the waist of Bacchus' to 'a younger and an elder boy at school walking . . . with that tender friendship towards each other which has so much of love'. Dilating on 'the motions of their delicate and flowing forms', Bacchus' 'sublimely sweet and lovely' countenance, 'the flowing fullness and roundness of the breast and belly', and 'the arch looks of Ampelus', he concluded that the Bacchus was 'immortal beauty'. Shelley particularly delighted in such androgynous Greek statues. In Rome he thought it 'difficult to conceive anything more beautiful than the Ganymede'. Yet his 'favourite', according to his widow, was an Apollo which possessed 'a woman's vivacity of winning yet passive happiness and yet a boyish inexperience exceedingly delightful'. Shelley much preferred the 'sweet and gentle figures of adolescent youth' to the many female figures in Rome and, as they were only statues, his appreciation of the male body no longer had to be quite 'exempt from the smallest alloy of sensuality'.[*31]

Whether Shelley's other Eton friendships were all similarly 'exempt from the smallest alloy of sensuality' is not known. In later life he never showed any of Byron's liking for young boys, but even if he had no erotic feelings for any Etonian contemporary, he may

* He was similarly impressed by a statue of a hermaphrodite. One of the fragments for his 1822 poem *Epipsychidion* contains the lines: 'Like that sweet marble of both sexes/Which looks so sweet and gentle that it vexes/The very soul. . . .' And in *The Witch of Atlas* he wrote of 'A sexless thing it was, and in its growth/It seemed to have developed no defect/Of either sex, yet all the grace of both'. Théophile Gautier shared Shelley's admiration for the statue.[32]

well have suffered from the attentions of others. Both Wilberforce and John Bowdler agreed on shunning the public schools for their sons for fear of endangering their 'eternal state'. And Mary Wollstonecraft, who had in the 1780s spent some time in an Eton house, thought boarding-schools 'hot-beds of vice and folly', while a few years later an authority deemed it 'almost impossible' for a boy to pass through Eton 'without acquiring an acquaintance with evil'. Shelley's fastidiousness may have achieved the near impossible, but if he was forced into such 'an acquaintance' that would account for his later homophobia.[33]

Even in the twentieth century when supervision was vastly more pervasive, a well-known headmaster once observed that the only way to avoid homosexuality in a public school would be to establish a brothel. And in 1798 the *Gentleman's Magazine* accused Eton of 'the systematic arrangement of a *Fifth-Form Seraglio*', with 'pestilential consequences' resulting from it. For public schoolboys to contract venereal disease was certainly common enough: Westminster kept a surgeon whose chief duty was to treat boys thus infected. But probably at Eton the Fifth Form's heterosexual procedures were less institutionalised than the *Gentleman's Magazine* claimed, though prostitutes were numerous and no doubt many Etonians found their 'first love', in Cowper's words, in 'some street-pacing harlot'. Shelley probably had at least one encounter with a prostitute at Eton or, possibly, Oxford which resulted in 'pestilential consequences', real or imagined.[34]

The evidence for such an encounter is cumulatively persuasive, though far from conclusive. The initial evidence comes from Thornton Hunt, the son of Shelley's friend, the poet and journalist Leigh Hunt. As a boy he had met Shelley, who had been nice to him, and as a man he admired him. The crucial words appear in a laudatory and affectionate assessment of him, published in 1863. 'Accident has made me aware', wrote Hunt, 'of facts which give me to understand, that, in passing through the usual curriculum of a college life in all its paths, Shelley did not go scatheless, – but that, in the tampering with venal pleasures, his health was seriously, and not transiently, injured. The effect was far greater on his mind than on his body . . . he felt bound to denounce the mischief from which he saw others suffer more severely than himself'.[35]

Thornton Hunt, who after a stint on the *Spectator* was editor of the *Daily Telegraph* for eighteen years, cited as evidence for

Shelley's 'college experiences' the well-known passage in *Epipsychidion*:

> There, – one whose voice was venomed melody
> Sate by a well, under blue night-shade bowers;
> The breath of her false mouth was like faint flowers,
> Her touch was as electric poison, – flame
> Out of her looks into my vitals came,
> And from her living cheeks and bosom flew
> A killing air, which pierced like honey-dew
> Into the core of my green heart, and lay
> Upon its leaves; until, as hair grown grey
> O'er a young brow, they hid its unblown prime
> With ruins of unseasonable time.

Although Hunt did not mention it, Shelley had evidently referred to the same incident two years earlier in his prose fragment 'Una Favola'. In the early nineteenth century it was generally believed that venereal disease turned the hair of those infected prematurely grey, and Shelley's hair was growing grey well before he died aged twenty-nine.[36]

Thornton Hunt undoubtedly was right about Shelley's attitude to 'the mischief' of prostitutes. It was a subject, wrote Leigh Hunt, 'that at a moment's notice would overshadow the liveliest of his moods'. Only a person blinded by superstition, Shelley himself wrote in 1818, could think Greek homosexuality 'more horrible than the usual intercourse endured by almost every youth of England with a diseased and insensible prostitute'. And earlier he claimed that prostitutes 'formed one tenth of the population of London'. Unquestionably prostitution in the capital (and elsewhere) was a pressing social problem, and many other writers – Wollstonecraft, Blake, Wordsworth and Byron – and visitors to London from Dostoevsky onwards throughout the nineteenth century noted the army of women on the streets, but none of them came up with such an implausible estimate as Shelley's.[37]

Shelley's claim that 'almost every youth' had had intercourse with a diseased prostitute was less extreme. One of Keats's lecturers at Guy's Hospital asked, 'how many [youths] arrive at the adult age without having to use mercury?' – the commonest treatment for venereal disease. The answer, if poets were representative of English youth, is not many. Keats used it, having caught gonorrhoea from a prostitute in Oxford – though not at the university. Byron contracted gonorrhoea more than once. Coleridge, like Keats, frequently bought sex when he was young. He later dreamed that 'a frightful pale woman' wanted to kiss him and give him 'a shameful disease'. Later still, he feared that he actually had the disease, having contracted it when he was twenty-one. At Eton Shelley did not take mercury, but he did take arsenic – by mistake, he claimed – and arsenic was then one of the remedies for venereal disease.[38]

Whether or not Shelley lost his virginity with an Eton prostitute and was venereally infected by her, or merely thought he was, *Zastrozzi*, a Gothic novel that he wrote at the school, was said by a writer in the *Critical Review* to be 'fit only for the inmates of a brothel', and his book, which is mainly about lust, does not make it improbable that Shelley visited one.

Shelley was not the only Etonian novelist of his time. Charles Summer, the younger brother of the future Archbishop, and himself a future Bishop of Winchester, had published *The White Nun* in 1808, shortly after his eighteenth birthday. Shelley managed to write most or all of *Zastrozzi* when he was sixteen and to publish it well before he was eighteen. His liking for Gothic novels, which began at Syon House, had intensified at Eton; he was particularly taken with *Zofloya* or *The Moor* by Charlotte Dacre when it appeared in 1806.* Though also indebted to Mrs Radcliffe and 'Monk' Lewis, Shelley borrowed most from Charlotte Dacre, including his title.[39]

Zastrozzi received two reviews. The *Gentleman's Magazine* called it 'a short, but well-told tale of horror, and, if we do not mistake, not from an ordinary pen'. Shelley had asked a friend to see that the reviewers were 'pouched', and that reviewer had evidently been bribed, but even he said that the author had 'availed himself of characters and vices which . . . thank God are not to be found in this country'.† The writer of the other notice had clearly

---

* The young Byron was also influenced by Dacre, but by her poetry not her novels.
† In 1818 Shelley used similar language about Byron in Venice, alleging to Peacock that he associated 'with wretches who seem almost to have lost the gait and physiognomy of man, and who do not scruple to avow practices which are not only not named but I believe seldom even conceived in England.' The letter is not altogether reliable: since seeing Byron, Shelley had written three earlier letters to Peacock without mentioning any of this; in the same letter he complained that the Italian women were the most 'contemptible', being 'ignorant', 'bigotted', 'filthy' and 'disgusting'; and he himself was going through a crisis at the time. Finally and ironically Shelley's letter seems to be partly based on language used about the Venetians by Byron, himself in his 'Venice: An Ode', which had recently been fair copied by Mary Shelley:

not been 'pouched', for he complained of a 'discordant, disgusting, and despicable performance', of the book's 'open and barefaced immorality and grossness', and of 'vicious unrestrained passion' being dignified by 'the appellation of love'. Certainly there is a great deal about females having a 'symmetrical figure', but that had become a cliché, arising presumably from the change of fashion round about 1790 which had made women's clothing more revealing; and at other times the female form is 'fair', 'fragile', 'elegantly proportioned', 'celestial' and 'ethereal', with an 'interesting softness'. Certainly, too, the main female character is, as the review claimed, 'a lascivious fiend' – 'wild with passion she clasped Verezzi to her beating breast and overcome by an ecstasy of delirious passion, her senses were whirled around in confused and inexpressible delight'. As for Verezzi, 'the fire of voluptuous, of maddening, love scorched his veins . . .'. No doubt much of the extravagant sex in the book stemmed from Shelley's sexual feelings and, very possibly, from his sexual initiation, but some of it is evidently a parody of the Gothic genre. More significantly, perhaps, the heroine-villainess is a commanding figure, while the hero is wholly ineffectual, spending much of his time in convulsions or fainting. *Zastrozzi* is frequently absurd and is not in the same class as its model, *Zofloya*, but it is a striking achievement for a sixteen-year-old.[41]

'Does the author', asked the *Critical Review*, 'think his gross and wanton pages fit to meet the eye of a modest young woman?' Shelley certainly thought they were fit for the eyes of at least one young and modest woman, for he sent her an early copy of *Zastrozzi*. He had fallen in love with his pretty cousin, Harriet Grove, whom he had first met in his last holidays from Syon House when he had played 'carpenters' and cut down some of his uncle's new trees at Fern. A year older than him, Harriet was the sixth of nine surviving children of Thomas Grove, a large landowner in Wales as well as in Wiltshire, and Charlotte Pilfold – the sister of Elizabeth Shelley. She was outstandingly beautiful; Tom Medwin, who never met anyone to compete with her, thought her, quoting Shelley in *Julian and Maddalo*, 'like one of Shakespeare's women' – adding, 'like some Madonna of Raphael'. The two comparisons seem inconsistent today, but would not have done so then.[42]

and thus they creep
Crouching and crab-like, through their sapping streets[40]

None of Shelley's letters to this beauty has survived, but by January 1809, when Harriet's diary begins, the cousins were writing frequently to each other. Harriet's reference in her diary to Shelley's house as 'that delightful place' shows that she had recently been there at least once. As she was the first pretty girl of his age to have entered 'this temple of Solitude', as he called Field Place, her visit unsurprisingly sparked a romance and correspondence. But partly because of some obscure family quarrel that simmered among the Groves, the Pilfolds and the Shelleys, and partly because of Shelley's Eton schooling, the lovers seldom met; so the affair was largely epistolary.[43]

They did, however, have four days together with their families at the Groves' house in Lincoln's Inn Fields in April 1809. Harriet recorded that she was 'very glad to see' 'dear Bysshe', who had arrived in London with his father, but thought 'Mr Shelley appear-[ed] cross [deletion] for what *reason I know not*'. The young lovers enjoyed themselves sightseeing, theatre-going and visiting Shelley's sisters at Clapham; Harriet thought them 'the nicest girls I ever saw'.[44]

After their successful sojourn in London, Harriet continued to make affectionate entries in her diary about Shelley and his letters and to record her own frequent replies until September, when there was a rift and mentions of her correspondence with him, though not with other members of the Shelley family, became much less frequent. That Harriet first met her future husband, William Helyar, in September was a coincidence and not the cause of this break. Her diary shows that she had no interest in him at least until December when she danced with him twice. At about this time Shelley had started writing letters to Felicia Browne (later Hemans), a promising young poetess in her early teens, who eventually had larger sales than any other nineteenth-century English poet. Shelley had never met her, but he had learned from Dr Lind that there was nothing wrong in writing to people he did not know under his own or an assumed name. Eventually her mother, alarmed by the religious scepticism of Shelley's letters, had to ask that he be made to desist. The Groves may well have had the same feeling, unless they just thought he was too unstable for their young daughter.[45]

In any case, the breach was soon healed – to Harriet's satisfaction if not to that of her parents – but not soon enough to prevent Shelley expressing his feeling of betrayal in poetry:

> On her grave I will lie,
>   When life is parted,
> On her grave I will die
>   For the false hearted.

But at the beginning of March Shelley sent her a poem, probably an early version of *The Wandering Jew*, and at the end of the month *Zastrozzi*. According to Medwin she had written some of its chapters. Admittedly she resented her brother's 'abuse [of] Shelley's romance', but nothing in her diary indicates her joint authorship. And while she may have commented on some of it, both the tone and the contents of the book put Medwin's claim out of court.[46]

Harriet had been worried that this year, as last, they would not be going to Field Place when 'Dear Shelley' was there. Even after the Shelleys had invited them, Harriet feared that 'owing to some fancy my mother has in her head we shall not go'. However, the day before *Zastrozzi* arrived, Mrs Grove agreed to go for the minimum period of one day. In the end they went for two nights, getting 'to dear F.P. [deletion]' on 16 April; Harriet found the atmosphere 'very strange'. And after a walk to Saint Irvyne, a long conversation with Shelley and another moonlight walk this time to Stroud she was 'more perplexed than ever'. The mystery has not been solved. Possibly Harriet's bewilderment arose from the two sets of parents having given their children differing accounts of the cause of the autumn break and how they saw the future. Certainly it was not caused by any disappointment with Shelley, who soon became 'Percy' in her diary. And despite her perplexity Harriet regarded her two nights at Field Place 'as the pleasantest party in the world' before going on to 'the most unpleasant' one with her Pilfold cousins.[47]

On one account Shelley, too, seems to have been fully satisfied with the visit. Fifty years later Charles Grove thought that 'at the time' Shelley was more attached to 'my sister Harriet than I can express' and that 'an engagement' had been 'permitted both by his father and mine'. Yet, immediately Harriet had left, Shelley sent a poem to Edward Fergus Graham, a close friend in Sussex and London, which would have been better attuned to the period of the estrangement:

> O'er this torn soul, o'er this frail form
>   Let feast the fiends of tortured love,
> Let lower dire fate's terrific storm

I would, the pangs of death to prove.

Then after a hit at 'prating priests', the last stanza ran:

Within me burns a raging Hell.
Fate, I defy thy farther power,
Fate, I defy thy fiercer spell,
And long for stern death's welcome hour.

That does not sound much like a lover who, according to Charles Grove, was 'very well pleased with his successful devotion to my sister'. But perhaps Shelley, remembering the schism in the autumn, could not believe his current luck; or perhaps he just thought that was the way that young poetic lovers should write, and sought to dramatise himself as the unfortunate victim of fate, resigned to death.[48]

The ten days in London which followed closely on the Field Place visit were a success, to judge from Harriet's diary, even though she hurt her foot. But that was not all loss since the others went to the play and she stayed at home with 'Mama and Percy'. At one point Percy became 'Dearest P'. They went to the opera together but she 'hated it more than ever, [so does P—]'. When the Shelleys left on 5 June, Harriet was 'very sorry'. Percy returned to Eton, and although the correspondence continued she never saw him again.[49]

If Shelley did catch gonorrhoea or syphilis at Eton, the most likely times are the summers of 1809 and 1810. Shelley's chronology was seldom exact, but for what it is worth either year would roughly accord with his statement to Godwin in March 1812 that two years before he had been 'plunged [into a] state of intellectual sickness and lethargy' of which his novels were 'the distempered visions'.* Some two years after this letter, Shelley told Godwin's daughter that his enforced absences from her because of his fear of arrest for debt made him vulnerable to 'impurity and vice'; hence his more distant and far less satisfactory love for Harriet Grove does not rule out such an encounter. If he was venereally infected, his 'madhouse' story may have contained a shred of fact: his father and the doctor might well have wanted to send him away not because he was mad but because of an erroneous belief that he

---

* While of course neither gonorrhoea nor syphilis is an 'intellectual' illness, they are not aids to creativity and may induce lethargy. In addition, Shelley elsewhere uses the verb 'plunged' in connection with sexual degradation.[50]

might infect his sisters. According to Shelley's friend, Trelawny, Shelley was not only taught but treated by Dr Lind, and Lind would have been the obvious man to send for since, as a former ship's surgeon, he would have had much experience of venereal disease. Nevertheless, if Shelley was thus infected, the likelihood is that he was treated for it at Eton by Lind and himself and that his family never got to hear of it.[51]

The summer half of 1809 was Shelley's last in the Fifth Form, and the Michaelmas one was Goodall's last as headmaster. He became Provost in December and was succeeded by Keate whose aim of tightening school discipline threw him into conflict with the boys, who objected to his assault on their privileges. Yet Shelley kept clear of the trouble; for the time being he was not a rebel.[52]

He had become both a good shot – once killing three snipe with 'successive shots' – and something of a dandy. According to the recollection of his sister Hellen he ordered smart clothes at Eton and wore 'beautifully fitting silk pantaloons'. No doubt he believed that the suitor of a beautiful girl could not do otherwise, much as the seventeen-year-old Coleridge asked for new breeches as his present pair were not 'altogether well adapted for a female eye'. Otherwise Shelley spent most of his time writing. Some of the money he earned from *Zastrozzi* – a good deal less than the £40 he was said to have been paid – he spent on a leaving dinner for his friends, and on 30 July 1810, his last day at the school, he performed at 'speeches'. This was Keate's first speech day as headmaster and, although his views about who should be allowed to attend differed from Goodall's, he had not made them fully known. This resulted in a degree of chaos and an overcrowded room. But all the boys spoke well, Keate's sister-in-law thought, singling out for particular praise two of them, though not Shelley, who declaimed Cicero's condemnation of Cataline. Shelley then said goodbye to Keate and left Eton for good.[53]

Despite that harmonious finale to his school career, Shelley, without giving the reason, told Godwin two years later that he 'was twice expelled' from Eton 'but recalled by the interference of my father'. Two expulsions and two recalls are inherently implausible, and nothing else suggests that he was expelled even once – or even that he ever did anything which would have remotely merited expulsion. A few years later still, Shelley did give a reason for his

Byron aged seven. He was later described in Aberdeen as 'Mrs Byron's crockit deevil' and 'a verra takkin' laddie, but ill to guide'.

Byron in 1807. Between the autumn of 1806 and May 1807 he lost two-and-a-half stone in weight.

The only authenticated portrait of Shelley as a boy. Aged seven or eight, he already excelled at Latin and Greek.

The only surviving portrait of the adult Shelley. Unfortunately, even the artist, Amelia Curran, the daughter of Shelley's Dublin acquaintance, John Philpot Curran, thought it a poor likeness.

Shelley's father, Timothy.
An MP from 1790 to 1792
and 1802 to 1818, he made
his first and last speech in
Parliament in 1817.
Earlier he had told his son
that he would provide for
any number of illegitimate
children but would never
forgive his making a
mésalliance.

Shelley's mother, Elizabeth.
Although Shelley once called
her 'mild and tolerant, yet a
Xtian', she is said to have had
a domineering temper and to
have resented her son's lack of
enthusiasm for field sports.

Byron's mother, Catherine. Her husband, Jack Byron, defied 'all the apostles to live with her for two months'. Her violent temper did indeed make her difficult to live with, but she was an intelligent woman with a deep affection for her son.

Byron's father, Captain Byron – 'Mad Jack' (*right*) – and his first wife, Amelia (*left*), who had been divorced by her first husband, Lord Carmarthen, because of their adultery. Amelia died when their daughter, Augusta, was one year old.

Byron's half-sister, Augusta. She was brought up by her maternal grandmother, Lady Holdernesse, and did not meet Byron until 1803, when he was fifteen and she was twenty.

Two of Shelley's adored sisters, Margaret and Hellen, neither of whom married. Shelley thought that 'in no other relation could the intimacy be equally perfect' as that between brother and sister.

Field Place, the Shelleys' house near Horsham in Sussex. Shelley called it 'a temple of solitude' because he rarely saw any children other than his sisters. His room was at the right-hand corner of the first floor.

Newstead Abbey, Nottinghamshire. 'Thro' thy battlements, Newstead, the hollow winds whistle,' wrote Byron in 1803, 'Thou, the hall of my fathers, art gone to decay.' Newstead indeed was scarcely habitable when he inherited it in 1798.

Syon House Academy, Isleworth, where Shelley was at school from 1802 to 1804. He was so much bullied that the place was 'a perfect hell to him'.

Upper School at Eton, where some 300 schoolboys were taught in one room by three or four masters. Few boys learned much in school, but the time spent there was only sixteen hours a week.

Byron in nobleman's robes at Trinity College, Cambridge. He reported that in them his 'appearance in the Hall was *superb*' but the effect was spoiled by his '*Diffidence*'.

Byron's travelling companion John Cam Hobhouse. He was Byron's staunchest friend.

having been made to leave Eton, but at the cost of producing a third expulsion, this time without a reprieve. 'He told me', wrote Peacock, 'that he had been provoked into striking a pen knife through the hand of one of his young tyrants, and pinning it to the desk, and that this was the cause of his leaving Eton prematurely: but his imagination often presented past events to him as they might have been, not as they were'. A violent act of that sort by Shelley is fully conceivable – Peacock used to talk privately of Shelley's violent bouts of anger – but since there was no such premature departure from Eton, doubt is inevitably cast on its alleged cause. After his death Mary Shelley told Leigh Hunt that Shelley had often told the story of his having stabbed 'an upper boy with a fork'. Yet, as Peacock pointed out, the incident would surely have been remembered by others, had it actually occurred. And even if it had occurred, it would not, in view of Eton's easygoing attitude to physical violence, have caused Shelley's expulsion.[54]

Byron eventually persuaded Dr Drury to withdraw his request that he leave Harrow, because he was worried that his friends would think that that amounted to an expulsion, and he was angry when Dr Butler later put it about that he had been expelled, although he had not. In contrast, although Shelley had not been expelled, he wanted his friends to think he had.*[55]

So in the end both Shelley and Byron served their allotted span at public school, which in Shelley's case, ignoring holidays, amounted to one-fifth of his life. Eton gave Shelley an ease of manner which he had not formerly possessed, though he might well have acquired it anyway. Even on first acquaintance people in later life usually took to him; Keats, Haydon, Hazlitt and others of the Hampstead set were exceptions. Harrow did not do the same for Byron, who had charm of manner but remained shy with strangers. Their public schools also had deeper effects on them both. Byron had effectively not had a father; Shelley had one who was inadequate. Since both boys despised their schoolmasters – with the important exception in Byron's case of Dr Drury, who was a father figure to him – their schools did not supply a substitute or reconcile them to authority.

* Shelley had a need to feel persecuted and to claim that he had been ill-treated when he hadn't. Hence the mytho-poet, who had come to believe – and wished others to believe – that he had been a rebel and had been victimised, would have been pleased to learn that his most hostile biographer, J. C. Jeaffreson, was to claim that Shelley had left Eton in disgrace in 1809 when in fact he left it with full respectability in 1810.[56]

And their dislike of their school rulers and their knowledge of how badly the schools were run helped to insulate them from any comfortable conviction that all was well with the world and England was a happy, well-governed country. Their years at Eton and Harrow thus strengthened rather than curtailed their natural rebelliousness, which probably helped their poetry but hampered their happiness.[57]

Shelley's experiences at Eton anticipated or caused many of his later views. His republicanism mirrored his attitude to his masters and his father; his hatred of organised Christianity and the Church mirrored his dislike of the absurdities and hypocrisy of Eton College Chapel; and his dislike of direct action and his fear of the mob probably stemmed from the 'Shelley-baits' and other bullying. Thus, ironically, the original 'polluting multitude' which Shelley hated was the aristocratic mob of Etonians who had persecuted him. In his maiden speech in the House of Lords, Byron defended 'the mob' – 'It is the Mob that labour in your fields . . . that man your navy, and recruit your army' – but he was no more a member of the crowd than Shelley was. 'Yet why should I mingle in fashion's full herd?' he asked a year after he left Harrow, 'why crouch to her leaders, or cringe to her rules?' Seeing the behaviour of boys in the mass or individually did nothing to raise his opinion of human nature which had been brought low by May Gray.[58]

Harrow gave Byron abundant opportunity to indulge his taste for young boys. In another environment it might have remained latent, as did Shelley's bisexuality, but that probably would not have much lessened his melancholy, for which there were other good reasons; it might even have increased it. On balance it was probably better for Byron to have been fully aware of his dual nature than for it to have remained concealed from him like Shelley's.

Shelley was the more damaged of the two by the bizarre education, or the lack of it, provided by their schools. Byron had no Lind-figure to stimulate him, but his reading was wider and better balanced. While the translating of Pliny and the learning of French and some German was meritorious and useful, Shelley largely concentrated on the classics and philosophy, though he did spend time on the English poets, even knowing by heart most of Southey's *Thalaba*, which was surely a waste of effort. Yet he read and knew almost no modern history. So the lines Byron wrote a year after leaving Harrow

> Though marv'lling at the name of Magna Charta,
> Yet, well he recollects the laws of Sparta

were applicable to Shelley. That vacuum in his education made him all the more likely to fall victim to ideas or doctrines, such as Godwin's, which he found intellectually appealing but which a modicum of historical knowledge might have led him quickly to discard. Ironically, a few years later Godwin himself advised him to lose his historical innocence, but even then Shelley continued to regard modern history as the mere 'history of titles', unlike the history of Ancient Greece which was 'the history of men'.[59]

The Duke of Wellington thought boys 'learnt nothing at public school and less at College', and certainly for the budding poets the chief benefit of Eton and Harrow was the opportunity they provided to write and read. Shelley was astonishingly prolific at Eton. In his early years he wrote a play with his sister Elizabeth and used to recite other plays to audiences of derisive Etonians. In his last year he wrote a second novel, *St Irvyne*, a third one with Medwin which was never finished, and an ambitious poem of more than 1,400 lines, *The Wandering Jew*, as well as a good deal of other poetry. Before the first publication in 1964 of the poems in the Esdaile Notebook,* his early poetry was generally considered to be almost as bad as his novels. Yet a few of the 1809 poems in the Esdaile Notebook are far better than nearly all the poetry he published in 1810, clearly presaging the mature Shelley. Written in late 1809, *Henry and Louisa*, his first long poem, is a strong statement of two of his lifelong themes: the damage done by war and by religion. Elsewhere Shelley was sometimes influenced by Tom Moore, but his verse was warmer than Moore's, and if Byron had been able to read it as early as he read Moore, he would have been led even further astray than he jokingly claimed to have been by Moore. As it was, when he did read 'the works [Shelley] wrote at seventeen', he thought them 'much more extraordinary than Chatterton's at the same age'.[60]

Byron did not publish a novel when he was sixteen or at any other age. Nor, though he circulated his lampoon on the new headmaster, did he publish anything else while at Harrow. Yet he wrote a lot of poetry there. Much of it is mawkish mush about his

---

* Which Shelley gave to his first wife, and which contained many promising unpublished poems.

'passions' for younger boys or long poems on such classical quasi-homosexual couples as 'Nisus and Euryalus'. Despite his knowledge of history, Byron was much less politically aware than Shelley. He did not write about Napoleon, though he kept a bust of him in his room – in strong contrast to Shelley to whom Napoleon was already, and remained, 'the Tyrant of the World'. Yet some of the poetry that Byron wrote at Harrow or just afterwards showed that he had already acquired his satirical touch, and his style was more mature than Shelley's.[61]

After leaving Harrow, Byron wrote nostalgic verses about the school – 'Yet scenes of my childhood, whose lov'd recollection/ Embitters the present, compar'd with the past;' – and his nostalgia endured. His happy last year with its romantic friendships remained uppermost in his mind. Harrow, he wrote, was to him 'A home, a world, a paradise' – much more so, indeed, than his real home was. Shelley was at the other extreme. He only once mentioned Eton in his poems, and did not make a single cheerful reference to his schooldays until 1821. Not surprisingly, he remembered not his last untroubled year but the period of his persecution. Keats's mother wanted to send her son to Harrow, an ambition which was foiled by the deaths of his father and grandfather. That was fortunate for Keats, who was surely far better off at Clarke's School at Enfield. Almost certainly Shelley and Byron, too, would have been happier either there or at Wordsworth's Hawkshead Grammar School. And in both places they would certainly have been far better taught. The major writers who escaped public school, Wordsworth, Keats and even Blake, who 'Thank[ed] God I never was sent to school/ To be Flogd into following the style of a fool', had far happier schooldays than those who were caged in Cowper's 'menageries': Byron, Shelley, Southey, Coleridge and Lamb. But of that five Shelley was probably the only one to be permanently maimed by the other animals.[62]

CHAPTER VII

Oxford and Cambridge

Shelley: 1810–11 (aged 18 years)
Byron 1805–7 (aged 17–19 years)

None of the great writers of the day distinguished themselves at Oxford or Cambridge. That was not the fault of Walter Scott, who went to Edinburgh University, or of Blake, Burns, Keats, Hazlitt, Lamb and Peacock, who for financial or other reasons were given no chance of a university career. England's two ancient universities were expensive and confined to members of the established Church. Nobody could enter them without declaring himself a member of the Church of England; and attendance at chapel was compulsory.

Of those writers, however, for whom these requirements were no barrier to entry, Wordsworth boasted on his way to Cambridge that he would be 'either Senior Wrangler or nothing'. Yet he spent his opening months there, he later wrote, 'in vague and loose indifference'. In subsequent years he became 'detached . . ./ From every hope of prowess and reward', ending up in 1791 with a simple BA without honours. That was near enough to 'nothing'. Shortly afterwards, at Cambridge, Coleridge initially worked hard, winning a medal for a Greek ode. But then, he claimed, he became 'a proverb . . . for idleness', before penury and debts led him to abscond and join the army. Allowed back to his college, he left without taking a degree. Southey, who regarded his years at Oxford in the 1790s as 'the least beneficial' of his life, similarly left degreeless, as did De Quincey a few years later. Landor, an Oxford contemporary of Southey's was rusticated for firing a gun at the closed shutters of a college fellow's rooms, and never returned. Hence, in spending a short and largely barren time at their universities, Shelley and Byron were not out of line with their peers.[1]

Poets were not the only people to leave university early. In 1787 the head of the senior branch of the Shelley family, Sir John Shelley, remained at Cambridge for only one term. At that time, his pretty heiress wife helpfully explained, 'gaming, drinking and every kind

of licentiousness were the fashion'. Although Lamb felt 'defrauded
... of the sweet food of academic institution', in reality the food
was seldom sweet, and like Shakespeare he missed little by not
having had a university education. Yet a distinguished academic
career was just possible, and the universities did produce some good
scholars. Hence some blame for their failures must also fall on the
poets, even if the chief fault lay with Oxford and Cambridge.[2]

If the ancient universities were not as bad as they had been in the
early eighteenth century, they were still narrow, somnolent and self-
indulgent, the dons paying more attention to their drinking and
their own comfort than to the undergraduates' education. Jeremy
Bentham, who went to Oxford aged twelve, later wrote that he 'was
a child, without a guide, idling, trembling and hiding myself'. Adam
Smith saw little of his tutor or the lecturers when he was at Balliol
College, Oxford; all he had to do was to attend prayers twice a day
and lectures twice a week. Lord Chesterfield saw Cambridge dons
as pedants 'of [an] illiberal seminary', 'rusting' in their cells, and he
summed up the prevailing torpor and idleness by recommending a
Greek professorship to his son, as 'a very pretty sinecure and
requiring very little knowledge'.[*3]

That was not far-fetched. When the poet Thomas Gray was
appointed Regius Professor of History at Cambridge in 1767 – his
predecessor had died after falling off his horse while drunk – he
assumed that his professorship was a sinecure. Unfortunately, the
history professorship at Oxford fell vacant a month later, and to
Gray's dismay the Oxford Heads of Houses suggested to the King
that Regius Professors should remain in residence throughout the
term and deliver fifty lectures a year. That was far too much for the
new Cambridge Professor of History. Gray did, nevertheless, feel
bound to submit some proposals for his tenure of office. In these he
went so far as to undertake to live in Cambridge for half the term
and deliver one public and a few private lectures. Making promises,
however, was all he did. Gray never delivered a single lecture, not
even an inaugural one.[5]

Not long afterwards things began to improve, but only slightly
and slowly. Stagnation, corruption and incompetence were not

* In his poem *Jubilate Agno*, written when he was in a madhouse, Christopher Smart, who
as a former Fellow of Pembroke College knew his university, prayed 'God for the Professors
of the University of Cambridge to attend and to amend'.[4]

easily dethroned. And evidently by 1782 there had been little change. In that year a German Lutheran pastor, having arrived in Oxford near midnight and been taken to an alehouse by an English clergyman, was astonished to find already there a great number of other clergymen in full clerical garb, 'each with his pot of beer before him'. Drunken arguments about the Bible ensued, followed by confused discussions of less weighty matters. 'At last, when morning drew near,' Morritz records, 'one of them suddenly exclaimed, "Damn me, I must read prayers this morning at All Souls"; and 'off he went'.[6]

Nevertheless there were stirrings. St John's College, Cambridge, began examinations in 1775; Trinity, Cambridge, did the same in 1790, also improving the quality of its Fellows, though other colleges lagged behind. At the beginning of the nineteenth century Oxford introduced serious examinations for those who aimed at distinction in addition to the ordinary examinations which had long been a farce. All the same the dons' drinking scarcely diminished – Cobbett thought it was their 'chief vice' – and reform was not far advanced until well after Shelley and Byron had left university. As late as 1831 Oxford was attacked for 'a hideous laziness, an enormous and insatiable greediness, and a crapulous self-indulgence'.[7]

Oxford

Shelley's university destination had never been in doubt. In that, if in little else, he had good reason to follow his father's example, and in April 1810 he enrolled or matriculated at University College, Oxford, before returning to Eton for his final half. Either on that occasion or at the beginning of the Michaelmas term in early October, Timothy accompanied his son to his old college. Proud of Shelley's literary activities, Timothy took him to Oxford's leading bookseller and authorised him to buy 'whatever he required in books and stationery'; he then confided to Slatter, the bookseller, that his son was already an author, and requested him to indulge Shelley 'in his printing freaks'. His language was more accurate than he knew.[8]

In his early days at Eton, Shelley had been known as 'Mad Shelley', although his furious rages against his persecutors had had sufficient reason without imputing madness. At Oxford he had no such rages, yet in the months between leaving Eton and leaving Oxford his lack of judgement and common sense was striking.

Before he went up to the university, Shelley devoted much of his time to making arrangements for the sale of his latest book, which was heavily influenced by Thomas Moore's *Irish Melodies*, and to furthering – by letter – his romance with Harriet Grove. In neither of these pursuits was he successful, and in both his failures were his own fault. In the middle of September *Original Poetry by Victor & Cazire* appeared. The young poet had asked a printer at Worthing to run off 1,500 copies – an absurdly large number – of a very slim volume of poems by himself and his sister Elizabeth. Finding that he could not pay the printer's bill and introducing himself as the eldest son of Mr Timothy Shelley MP, he persuaded the firm of Stockdale to take over the debt and the poems. John Joseph Stockdale later had a colourful career as a publisher and a pornographer, if not as a blackmailer, printing the Memoirs of the celebrated courtesan Harriet Wilson; later still, he was the winner in the leading case of *Stockdale* v. *Hansard*, a success which produced a statute protecting with privilege everything said in Parliament. His dealings with the Shelley family were not as exciting as his association with Harriet Wilson or his struggle with Parliament. They did, however, enable him to be one of the first to publish some of Shelley's letters and to say some pleasant things about him after his death, despite his failure to persuade Shelley or his father to pay him what they owed.[9]

Mediocre though it was, *Original Poetry by Victor of Cazire* revealed Shelley's lack of judgement less in the calibre of the poetry than in the inclusion of two particular poems. The first – one of up to six poems probably written by his fifteen-year-old sister Elizabeth – referred to Charlotte (older sister of Harriet) Grove's pursuit of a Sussex land-owning soldier. This had been acceptable as a private joke but was tasteless in a published book, even though names were omitted. 'Received the poetry of Victor & Cazire', Harriet Grove, the subject of several of the poems, noted in her diary. 'Charlotte offended and with good reason as I think they have done wrong in publishing what they have of her'.[10]

The inclusion of another poem was similarly ill-judged. Leafing though the 64 pages of the book a few days after its publication, Stockdale noticed for the first time that one of its two long poems, *St Edmund's Eve*, was by 'Monk' Lewis. When he drew his author's attention to this plagiarism, Shelley's response was to claim that he had been deceived by his collaborator and to entreat Stockdale 'to destroy all copies' of the book. Shelley's self-exoneration was of course untrue. He was very fond of Lewis's poems and could not possibly have thought that his sister was the author of one of them. Presumably, therefore, he had included *St Edmund's Eve* partly to thicken an otherwise over-thin volume and partly as a joking attempt to fool the reviewers.* That would make some sense of the otherwise curious title *Original Poetry* – 'there is no "original *poetry*" in this volume', wrote one reviewer; only 'downright scribble'. Lewis was not the only author plagiarised: Chatterton also suffered. Shelley's joke might have been permissible, had the print order had been a very small one and had he been in a position to pay the bill. As it was, the expense of the joke fell on Stockdale.[12]

Shortly after that 'printing freak', Shelley left Field Place for Oxford, which was probably the occasion when his father gave him some friendly advice. Timothy told his son 'that he would provide for as many natural children as he chose to get, but that he would never forgive his making a mésalliance'. According to Medwin, who was present, Shelley was not favourably impressed by this paternal pronouncement. That may have been due to resentment of Timothy's (older) illegitimate son – especially if, as was rumoured, Timothy preferred his natural son to his son and heir. Yet, granted the general callousness to lower-class 'fallen women' and the shakiness of his social position, Timothy's attitude was not illiberal, and was at least in accordance with his own and his father's practice. Thus fortified, Shelley went up to University College which, after a distinguished period in the latter half of the eighteenth century, was then in decline. He was a Leicester scholar, a distinction which had nothing to do with academic ability – his father had also been a Leicester scholar – and everything to do with patronage. The Shelleys were relations of the Leicester family.[13]

Like Tom Medwin at Syon House, T. J. Hogg, a fellow student and friend at Oxford, became one of Shelley's biographers, though their approaches differed. Medwin frequently makes mistakes through ignorance or carelessness, but he tries to tell the truth. Hogg's inaccuracies are often intentional. He minimises both his

---

* They were duly fooled. None of the book's three reviews, all of which were unfavourable, noticed the presence of a poem by Lewis.[11]

own and Shelley's religious scepticism and political radicalism, purposely distorting his narrative to convey the impression that, if at Oxford he was not quite the encrusted Tory that he later became, he was, nevertheless, the amused and sympathetic observer of his friend's extraordinary religious and sexual ideas. In fact he was as radical as Shelley, led his friend towards, or into, 'atheism', and was the prime mover in, not a spectator of, one of Shelley's bizarre sexual plans.

Again, although Medwin sometimes claims to have been Shelley's co-author when he was usually nothing of the sort, Hogg conceals his co-authorship of a pamphlet which was fraught with consequences for the life of his friend. Shelley's widow once complained in a book review of an author having 'made reality and fiction, who are brother and sister, and who may not therefore too closely unite, marry and produce an offspring which is neither true nor false' but often 'confusing'. Hogg's book is guilty of similar incest or what is now dubbed 'faction'. But while it is often misleading and unfair to Shelley; dishonestly mangles if not forges Shelley's letters in the author's interest; does not balk at resorting to fiction to conceal Hogg's own transgressions; sometimes strays into self-glorifying autobiography, telling us much more about Hogg's own life than we want or need to know; and is frequently more of a caricature, as Peacock thought, than a portrait, it still manages to convey, despite its veiled hostility, a wonderfully vivid impression of Shelley at Oxford and afterwards.[14]

Thomas Jefferson Hogg was named not after the American statesman but after his grandmother, a minor heiress, who had also provided the Hogg family with its home and land near Stockton-on-Tees. A well-educated, hard-working and intelligent young man, Hogg had joined the college the previous February. He sat next to Shelley one day at dinner in hall, and they immediately took to each other; after seven or eight hours' conversation that evening their friendship was forged.[15]

Hogg describes Shelley's figure as slight and fragile; he was tall but with such a pronounced stoop that he did not seem so. His complexion was delicate, almost feminine. His features were not symmetrical, and they and his face and his head were all unusually small; yet the effect of the whole was extremely powerful: breathing animation, enthusiasm and preternatural intelligence. His hair was long and bushy, which at a time when hair was almost invariably cropped like that of soldiers, was a striking eccentricity. His clothes were rumpled and unbrushed. Only his voice was discordant. Initially Hogg thought he could never endure that 'excruciating' voice. Soon, however, it was forgotten. Hogg does not mention the poet's eyes, which according to his widow were 'brilliant'.[16]

Hogg's is the best description of Shelley we have despite his exaggeration of the horrors of the poet's voice. Although Tom Medwin found the voice 'a cracked soprano' and Lamb 'the most obnoxious squeak I was ever tormented with', Thornton Hunt thought it 'a high natural counter-tenor'. Charles Grove had 'no unpleasant recollections of his [cousin's] harsh voice'. And to Peacock it sounded 'discordant' chiefly when Shelley was excited; it was scarcely dissonant when he spoke calmly and not at all so when he read. Trelawny and Mary Shelley both seemed to praise Shelley's voice, but both were equivocal. Trelawny wrote that Shelley's first sentence 'riveted your attention', and then praised him as an orator, but did not say anything about his voice. And in her novel *The Last Man*, written after Shelley's death, his widow described the Shelleyan character's voice 'as thrilling like sweetest melody', yet she also wrote of the Byronic character: 'His voice, usually gentle often startled you by a discordant note, which shewed that the usual low tone was rather the work of study than nature.' As Byron was generally agreed to have had a fine, musical voice – the novelist Amelia Opie thought it so exquisite that the Devil might have corrupted Eve with it, and children of a house Byron frequently stayed in called him 'the gentleman who speaks like music' – Mary evidently transposed them.[17]

Shelley and Hogg immediately became 'intimate and altogether inseparable companions'. Shelley had excellent rooms in Front Quad, while Hogg's were conveniently close in the adjoining Radcliffe Quad. There was little to keep them apart. Hogg appears not to have made friends in the college before Shelley arrived; some of Shelley's Eton friends occasionally called on him, but according to Hogg 'he generally avoided their society'. Shelley did however have a friend, George Marshall, the son of the rector of Horsham, who was a Fellow of Wadham. Meeting Shelley with Marshall, the future editor of *The Times*, Thomas Barnes, found him a 'fine looking youth' and received an enduring 'impression of the frankness and uprightness of Shelley's character'.[18]

Nor was there much in the university curriculum to interrupt the two friends. Hogg had already decided that Oxford education was a towering disappointment. Shelley went to one lecture which he found dull and languid; he left before the end and resolved never to go to another, though he probably attended a few on logic. 'They are very dull people here', he said to Hogg shortly after his arrival. He was talking of the dons, who, like all Oxford and Cambridge Fellows, were obliged to take Holy Orders and to be unmarried, if not celibate. One of them had sent for him and repeatedly told him that he 'must read'. As Shelley frequently read for some sixteen hours a day – De Quincey claimed to have read at one point for eighteen hours a day – the admonition was hardly necessary. The 'little man' particularly urged him to read Euclid and, above all, Aristotle – counsel which, probably because Aristotle, unlike Plato, deals with the real world, did not particularly appeal to his pupil.[19]

In deriding Oxford education, Shelley and Hogg were not exhibiting arrogance or bad judgement. One of Congreve's characters thought that, while a university was well enough for the breeding of a servant, 'the education [was] a little too pedantic for a gentleman'. A century later the trouble was still a surfeit of pedantry but also a scarcity of education. A lecturer said to Southey at Oxford: 'you won't learn anything from my lectures, sir, so if you have any studies of your own, you had better pursue them'. And a contemporary of Shelley's, at Balliol, complaining of being 'plagued' by the college lectures, doubted whether without 'the ideas furnished by Aristotle to these numbskulls' (the lecturers), they would have a single notion in their heads. Out of 23 professors in Shelley's day, 14 enjoyed sinecures. Gray would have felt at home.[20]

Yet the uselessness of the official education did not stop Hogg and Shelley enjoying themselves or doing a colossal amount of reading at Oxford. Most of Shelley's reading was beneficial, but not all of it. In November he asked Stockdale to send him *Political Justice*, which Lind had lent to him at Eton. Shelley later said that Godwin's book had 'opened to my mind fresh & more extensive views' and that he 'rose from its perusal a wiser and a better man'. Certainly *Political Justice* was the most important and influential book in his life; it effectively became his religion. But it did not make him a wiser man. 'The fresh & more extensive views' it opened to his mind had no factual basis and were devoid of common sense; they were the products of pure reason, which Godwin thought was infallible, and virtually all of them were mistaken. Instead of taking him out of an 'ideal world', as Shelley maintained, *Political Justice*, which outlined an anarchist utopia, drove him further into one. Godwin's philosophy thus did him lasting damage, accentuating his tendency to ignore reality and lumbering him with a cluster of untenable views. All the same, Shelley's studies, damaging or beneficial, made him regret that he and Hogg could only stay at Oxford for four years; considering the vast amount there was to learn, he would have preferred six or seven.[21]

Still, however much the friends revelled in their freedom at Oxford and however much they enjoyed each other's company, they were far from popular. After morning chapel they rushed back to their rooms, and as often as possible avoided dinner with the rest of the college in the hall. According to a friend of Hogg's father, they 'dressed differently from all others and did everything in their power to show singularity, as much as to say, "we are superior to everybody."' Another witness thought Shelley was 'slovenly in his dress' without 'a proper regard for decency'. In a large college all this might not have been noticed, but theirs was not large. Estimates of the number of undergraduates at Univ. have been as high as 200; in fact there were only thirty in residence. Unquestionably, Shelley was an outstandingly generous and benevolent boy, and to Hogg he was 'a whole university in himself', whose charm was patent. Yet to those who did not know him well, he seemed hardly part of the college or university. He and Hogg appeared tiresome, stand-offish and supercilious exhibitionists. To the authorities they were worse than that. Writing thirty-four years later Elizabeth Grant, the Master's niece, thought 'the ringleader in every species of mischief . . . was Mr Shelley, afterwards so celebrated, though I should think that to the end half-crazy. . . . He was very insubordinate, always infringing some rules, the breaking of which he knew could not be overlooked.'[22]

Hogg portrays Shelley as a young man with very frugal tastes, who liked the common fruit of stalls, oranges and apples. He did have a sweet tooth, but 'his beverage consisted of copious and frequent draughts of cold water' and cup after cup of tea. Wine was drunk in 'singular moderation' and usually diluted with water. The College Buttery Book suggests, however, that Shelley was rather less ascetic than Hogg makes out. In his first term he was the second-highest spender of any undergraduate, and in the first quarter of

1811, just before he was expelled, he was the highest spender, with expenditure of £25. Similarly, despite complaints of his 'slovenly' appearance, Shelley seems to have been less 'indifferent' about his clothes than Hogg suggests. When a dog badly damaged his coat, he was so angry that at first he intended to shoot the dog and sue its owner. And a bill which was not paid until 1814 discloses that in his short time at Oxford he spent more than £25 at his tailor's.[23]

A month before he sent Harriet Grove his unwelcome *Original Poetry by Victor & Cazire*, Shelley had asked Edward Graham to send her Scott's *Lady of the Lake*, Locke's *Essay on Human Understanding* and a novel. Whether she ever received them is not known, but, whereas he had in previous weeks not been mentioned in her diary, at the end of August it records her writing to 'Percy'. In any case *Victor & Cazire* more than undid whatever good Shelley's other gift may have done. Harriet and her parents as well as Charlotte were affronted, and Harriet ceased writing to him. Probably Shelley continued to write to her; certainly he expressed in verse his dismay at the change in her attitude.[24]

Unabashed by the fiasco of *Original Poetry by Victor & Cazire*, Shelley began a new volume at Oxford. Evidently, though, he was sufficiently embarrassed by the fate of his earlier book not ever to tell Hogg about it; nor, until the project was almost complete, did he tell him about its successor. Hogg pretended in his biography that the new collection was 'burlesque poetry' – an apparently tenable claim since at that time the book was presumed lost. In fact the poems were an improvement on the earlier collection and almost their only burlesque element was the title (which may have been suggested by Hogg): *Posthumous Fragments of Margaret Nicholson; Being Poems Found amongst the Papers of that Noted Female who Attempted the Life of the King in 1786. Edited by John Fitzvictor.* The printer, Henry Slatter, noted 'the ease with which [Shelley] composed the stanzas', and that was true of course. Yet not many stanzas were composed. Though much more lavishly produced (but not 'waggishly' or grotesquely printed, as Hogg claimed) than *Original Poetry by Victor & Cazire*, *Margaret Nicholson* was even shorter than its predecessor, running to only 22

---

* Yet 'Nicholson', may have appealed to Shelley because the mother of four of his grandfather's illegitimate children was called Eleanor Nichols. One of their sons was called John, as was Timothy's illegitimate son – which may have given added point to Shelley's choice of 'John Fitzvictor' as the editor of the volume.[25]

quarto pages and less than 400 lines, whereas *Victor & Cazire* had managed nearly 700, including the 120 lines pilfered from 'Monk' Lewis.[26]

Of the six poems in the volume, all written between 10 October and the middle of November, three are concerned in one way or another with Shelley's rupture from Harriet Grove, and another is a compendium or miscellany of Gothicisms. The first of the two more substantial poems, 'Ambition, power, and avarice', is an attack on war, less accomplished than Shelley's earlier poem on similar themes and influenced by Godwin's *Political Justice*. In Shelley's view, kings are the 'oppressors of mankind', and theirs 'are crimes for which [their] subjects bleed'; they are 'Swelled with command and mad with dizzying sway'. In short a monarch's work 'is the work of hell'. Margaret Nicholson, who despite the title of Shelley's volume was in no sense 'Posthumous' but living in Bethlehem Hospital, had nothing against kings as such. She had tried to kill George III merely because she thought that she, not he, was the rightful monarch. Such pedantry was not for Shelley. He wanted to attack George III, and even under the pseudonym of Margaret Nicholson that could only be done with reasonable safety by attacking monarchy in general.[27]

The second of the two longer poems is an epithalamium of two people who, unlike Margaret Nicholson, had succeeded in their assassination attempts, Francis Ravaillac, who murdered Henry IV, and Charlotte Corday, who disposed of Marat. The core of the poem is not murder, however, but sex. Shelley told Hogg and another friend that its 'indelicacy' would make the book 'sell like wildfire', while presenting no danger to himself because his identity was a 'profound secret'. Clearly, therefore, this poem was at least in part 'burlesque poetry'. Shelley prudently ensured that the copies sent to his mother and a few others did not contain the scandalous passage, which appears to depict fellatio. Although attempts have been made to deny the seemingly obvious meaning on the grounds that the idea would have been both repugnant to Shelley and unthinkable to his audience, neither contention is convincing.

> Soft, my dearest angel, stay,
> Oh! You suck my soul away:
> Suck on, suck on, I glow, I glow!
> Tides of maddening passion roll,
> And streams of rapture drown my soul.

Now give me one more billing kiss,
Let your lips now repeat the bliss,
Endless kisses steal my breath,
No life can equal such a death.

Admittedly, that passage is not wholly original. Both Marlowe and a Latin poet had said something on the same lines, and the verse has affinities with an obscene poem printed with John Wilkes's *An Essay on Woman*. Yet Shelley added the suggestive line: 'Suck on, suck on, I glow, I glow!' And he has the couple 'mingling', which was code for sexual intercourse, as also, at that time, was the word 'kiss'. If Shelley was not describing oral sex, it is hard to imagine what he had in mind.[28]

Shelley and Hogg both claimed that the book had sold well and created a stir, but they were evidently as mistaken in that as in their belief that Shelley's anonymity had been preserved. Their publisher's verdict that *Margaret Nicholson* was 'almost stillborn' is more reliable; luckily only 250 copies of the book were printed. And a letter written in Oxford three months later shows that the identity of its author was known at Christ Church. Charles Kirkpatrick Sharpe, a Scottish bachelor, antiquarian, minor artist, mini-Horace Walpole (as a letter writer) and a man who invariably saw the worst in everybody – including Byron – and loathed Shelley, found the poems 'extremely dull' and the 'Epithalamium' 'foul-mouthed', and also 'impudent', a word which, like 'mingling', then carried sexual connotations. More interestingly, Sharpe wrote that its author, 'a Mr Shelley . . . lives upon arsenic, acqua fortis [and] half an hour's sleep a night'.[29]

Arsenic and aqua fortis (nitric acid) were then used together to treat venereal disease, and such treatment was often painful – hence Sharpe's remark about Shelley's lack of sleep. That sentence and other references in his correspondence show that Sharpe believed Shelley to be venereally infected, which raises questions about his health at Oxford and his sexual activities there; were the latter solely literary? On 1 November Shelley wrote that he had been 'confined these two weeks with a fever'. Early in their friendship, Hogg reports him saying that he was very unwell, though Hogg thought he had only 'a slight aguish cold'. Medwin, visiting Oxford in the same month, says nothing about Shelley's health but, in appropriating Hogg's description of Shelley and his room, makes one significant alteration; while Hogg has Shelley's hands, clothes and books 'stained . . . by mineral acids', Medwin has them stained with 'medical acids'. That could be due merely to Medwin's customary carelessness or to the printers being unable to read his writing; more probably, Medwin was telling the truth either on purpose or through 'a Freudian slip'. In addition, Shelley's interest in chemical experiments had evidently waned in his last year at Eton and is unlikely to have waxed strongly at Oxford, where he was more interested in metaphysics and morals than in physics. Certainly Hogg had doubts about his science. All in all, therefore, what Hogg calls Shelley's 'chemical operations', which seemed to him 'to promise nothing but disasters', were probably in part the scientific equivalent of *Margaret Nicholson*: chemistry was, as it were, a pseudonym to conceal his dosing himself for a sexually transmitted disease, real or imagined.*[30]

Of course, Shelley might well have been treating himself for a disease caught at Eton; he had after all, on purpose or by mistake, swallowed arsenic there, which, he said, had 'scarcely injured his health', and Thornton Hunt wrote that his health had been 'not transiently damaged'. But if Shelley did go whoring at university, he was in good company. He joined not merely rich young rakes like his older kinsman, Sir John Shelley, but also impoverished young intellectuals. Few young men of university age were 'From dangerous passions free', as Wordsworth later claimed to have been, though at the time he probably was not. Coleridge was certainly not free from them. He had encounters at Cambridge; a few years later he remembered his 'vices' and his 'unchastities' with many 'loose women', though not their names or their faces. Shelley could hardly have matched Coleridge's record, if only for lack of time at university. True, Hogg extols his purity – as Victorian morality and

* Shelley's later life showed that he was something of a hypochondriac. According to Hogg, Shelley in 1813 was convinced that he had contracted elephantiasis and feared that other people might also be infected; so when many young ladies stood up for 'a country dance', Shelley placed 'his eyes close to their necks and bosoms' and felt 'their breasts and their bare arms', until 'the lady of the house' told him to desist. Since the story seems improbable as it stands and Hogg is unlikely to have resorted to pure invention, and since he tells the story in a style of a pornographic novel, the twentieth century scholars, Crook and Guiton, think it possible that he transposed what happened in a brothel in 1811 – with Shelley examining the inmates for traces of syphilis, not elephantiasis – to a respectable gathering in 1813, in which year, unlike 1811, he could have attended a country dance and would not have visited a brothel. Hogg was fully capable of such juggling, and the second version is no more improbable than the first. Both of them suggest a degree of hypochrondria.[30]

his concern for Shelley's reputation so demanded – but somewhat equivocally, and at one point he exclaims 'How sadly should we disparage the triumphs of Love were we to maintain that he is able to lead astray the senses of the vulgar alone!' And C. K. Sharpe and others were far from thinking that Shelley led a life of virtue at Oxford, though on any view he was far less dissipated at university than, say, Byron or most undergraduates from a similar background. Indeed a little more dissipation or some experience of women might have enhanced Shelley's knowledge of the real world. In any case, whether his whoring was at Oxford, Eton or both, worries about a sexually transmitted disease,* real or merely psychosomatic, would certainly help to explain his erratic behaviour in the months following his departure from Eton.[33]

Back at Field Place in December for the Christmas vacation, Shelley wrote to congratulate Stockdale on his advertisement for the second novel he had written at Eton and to ask him to send copies to Medwin and Hogg. Yet the publication of *St Irvyne; or The Rosicrucian* by 'A Gentleman of the University of Oxford' did not enhance either the moral or the literary reputation of its author. Elizabeth Barrett Browning 'could never believe Shelley capable of such a book', which contains, incidentally, two plagiarisms of Byron's 'Lachin-y-Gair' and, like *Zastrozzi*, many borrowings from the more accomplished Gothic novelists. In *St Irvyne* 'symmetrical forms' and 'alabaster bosoms' reappear from *Zastrozzi*, as do such passages as 'the anticipation of gratified voluptuousness swelled her bosom even to bursting', and 'the wild transports of maddening desire raved terrific within her breast'. In addition, following Godwin, Shelley stigmatises the belief that marriage is necessary for a union between man and woman as 'stale and vulgar prejudice', marriage being 'but a chain' which binds the body, not the soul. *St Irvyne* received two and a half reviews, the 'half' consisting entirely of extracts. The critic of the *Anti-Jacobin Review* accused the author of libelling the female sex of which he evidently had 'no knowledge, but such as may be collected in the streets or in a brothel'. Once again, despite the attempted anonymity, Shelley's authorship was known in Oxford.[34]

---

* Because of a brave but faulty experiment by a leading eighteenth-century surgeon, syphilis and gonorrhoea were still generally believed to be not two diseases but a single affliction. Shelley refers merely to 'the venereal disease'.[32]

Though rather better written, *St Irvyne* is a worse novel than *Zastrozzi*, being two stories imperfectly joined together. When Stockdale understandably complained of the plot's inconsistencies – one of the characters appears to die twice – the author airily brushed aside his objections: 'I do not myself see any other explanation that is required'. With Godwin having displaced the Gothic in Shelley's mind, he could not be bothered to straighten out the plot. Unfortunately, his changing outlook did not immediately produce improved literary perception; nor did loss of interest impair his confidence. *St Irvyne* is shorter than *Zastrozzi*, but he thought it would make two volumes and told Stockdale that it was 'a thing which almost *mechanically* sells to circulation libraries etc.' In fact it hardly sold at all, Stockdale incurring a substantial loss which was never made good.[35]

The publisher avoided a similar loss with Shelley's poem *The Wandering Jew; or, The Victim of the Eternal Avenger*. Despite his later claim to the contrary, Stockdale evidently did receive the manuscript of Shelley's first long poem, written at Eton, but decided not to risk its publication, presumably because of its irreligious title and opinions, the view of two other publishers. The legend of a man condemned to everlasting life for insulting Christ on his way to crucifixion – called by Byron shortly afterwards 'the fabled Hebrew Wanderer' – had an enduring fascination for Shelley. This version of the poem, of which Medwin erroneously claimed to have been part author, gave some faint signal, unlike *Original Poetry*, of Shelley's future greatness. Yet it was to the benefit of his reputation, as well as to his publisher's pocket, that it was not published until well after his death. It was dedicated to Sir Francis Burdett, the MP for Westminster and a patrician Radical, whose committal to the Tower in April 1810 on a trumped-up charge of breach of parliamentary privilege had led to four days of fierce rioting in London, the Guards charging in Piccadilly, and artillery parked in Berkeley Square. Both the Duke of Norfolk and Timothy Shelley had been in the large minority of MPs – 152 against 190 – who had opposed the government on Burdett; Byron thought him 'the general football . . . kicked at by all and owned by none'; they later became friends.[36]

Shelley's enthusiastic championship of radical politics was more successfully demonstrated in 1811 by his subscription to a fund to help the radical journalist, Peter Finnerty, who had been imprisoned for allegedly libelling the government over Castlereagh's disastrous mishandling of an expedition to the Low Countries, and by his writing a poem to help support Finnerty. Shelley also wrote to congratulate Leigh Hunt, the editor of the *Examiner*, on having been acquitted on a similar charge, and to advocate the formation of a society to join together all radicals and independents to resist 'the enemies of liberty'. He was thus as far away from his father in politics as he was in religion, yet still he expected, he told Hunt, to succeed him as an MP when he was twenty-one.[37]

Two days after his letter to Stockdale about the advertisement for *St Irvyne*, Shelley discovered that the publisher had betrayed him to his father. Already wary of Shelley's sceptical opinions, Stockdale was further unnerved by reading the manuscript of Hogg's never-published novel *Leonora*. Having decided, after investigation, that Hogg was 'the master-spirit' leading Shelley into heresy, he alerted Mr Shelley, whom he thought 'not particularly bright', to Hogg being a deist, which was in fact an overestimate of Hogg's orthodoxy. Whether Stockdale was chiefly concerned with Shelley's spiritual welfare or his own financial future, he probably thought he was doing both the Shelley family and himself a good turn. His mischief-making did not, however, help him. Mr Shelley thanked him for 'his open and friendly communication' which he would ever 'esteem and hold in remembrance', but where money was involved Timothy seldom felt or remembered an obligation, and after his son's death he repeatedly refused to settle the family debt.[38]

Stockdale's information cannot have surprised the Shelleys, who must have already received similar intelligence from Harriet Grove's parents, whose annoyance at *Victor & Cazire*'s humiliation of Charlotte in September 1810 expanded Harriet's worries over Shelley's sceptical, heretical letters into wider doubts about him. Having consulted her mother and father, Harriet reluctantly decided that Shelley was not for her. Although she immediately stopped writing to him, her decision was not conveyed to the Shelley family until well into December. Consequently Shelley's poems about Harriet in *Margaret Nicholson* are only a little gloomier than some he had written when their relationship seemed to be prospering. Hogg gives no hint of Shelley being in despair about Harriet while they were still at Oxford, and Shelley evidently sent a copy of *St Irvyne* to the Grove family. Until, therefore, a day or two after he had returned to Field Place, he did not know that the answer to the question he had asked in his most recent poem about Harriet really was yes.

> Art thou indeed for ever gone,
> For ever, ever lost to me?[39]

Peacock thought far too much had been made both of Shelley's failed love affair with Harriet Grove and of Byron's infatuation with Mary Chaworth. Peacock never knew Byron, but he knew Shelley well, though not in 1809–10, and he never met Harriet Grove. Undoubtedly Shelley's outraged reaction to the ending of his romance contained much self-dramatisation; and Peacock's view was widely accepted until Shelley's poems in the Esdaile Notebook showed conclusively that he was deeply affected by Harriet's breaking of their understanding. The wound he felt did not stop him soon falling in love with another Harriet, any more than Byron's dismay at being spurned by Mary Chaworth prevented him immediately afterwards having relationships with younger boys at Harrow. Yet the fickleness of an adolescent heart does not stop it being wounded by rejections. So Shelley's friend, Peacock, was as much mistaken and kept in the dark about Shelley's feeling for Harriet Grove as was Byron's friend Hobhouse about Byron's feeling for Mary Chaworth.[40]

The friendship of Shelley and Hogg had earlier ripened, in the words of Richard Holmes, Shelley's biographer, 'into a passionate attachment, so that far more truly than Harriet Grove one can say that Thomas Jefferson Hogg was Shelley's first love affair'. Winifred Scott, Hogg's biographer, had taken a similar view: 'Jefferson's feeling for Shelley at this time partook of the emotions of adolescent love without the embarrassing implications of sex'. Certainly the relationship was non-carnal, like the young John Milton's platonic homosexual relationship with Charles Diodati, but it had sexual ramifications or implications that did become embarrassing. At Oxford Shelley gave such a glowing account of his sister Elizabeth that his friend fell in love with her. In accordance with the tenets of Godwin and St Irvyne they would not marry but would be 'irrecoverably united [with] no priest but love'. For Hogg to fall in love and desire to live with somebody whom he had never met or even seen* was surely an extension or transfer of his feelings for

---

* The young Goethe also plotted a love affair with the sister of two friends even though he had never seen her.[41]

Shelley, while Shelley's encouragement of Hogg's love of Elizabeth was similarly an extension or transfer of his feelings for Hogg and, probably, of his incestuous platonic feelings for his sister whom he strikingly resembled.*[42]

Indeed feelings and behaviour of that sort became something of a habit with both Hogg and Shelley. Shelley had an urge to share his women – sisters or spouses – with Hogg, which was very Godwinian, but, although Shelley said that *Political Justice* had 'materially influenced [his] character', deeper forces and feelings than Godwin surely underlay his disposition to share. Hogg, having failed to win Elizabeth Shelley, went on to seek sexual relations with both of Shelley's wives and eventually lived to the end of his days with Shelley's last attachment, Jane Williams.[44]

By the Christmas vacation, if not before, Shelley and Hogg were not just sharing 'the emotions of adolescent love'; they were engaged in what is known as a *folie à deux*. In that state a couple feed on each other's fantasies and eccentricities, become impermeable to outside advice and influence, and progressively lose touch with reality; they both become far madder than either of them would have been by themselves. And Hogg and Shelley's condition was made still more acute by their both having suffered heavy blows, in Shelley's case two of them: the loss of Harriet Grove and his parents' knowledge of his anti-religious views. The blow to Hogg was Elizabeth Shelley's rejection of his epistolary advances.

Separated by the vacation, the two youths engaged in constant letter writing. Between 20 December and 20 January Shelley wrote

---

* Shelley was of course not the only poet of the day to have such feelings. Byron loved his half-sister Augusta; and Wordsworth and Dorothy Wordsworth had passionate, though unconsummated, feelings for each other. Neither the Byron siblings nor the Wordsworths grew up together. Byron was brought up by his mother, Augusta by her grandmother; and after the deaths of the Wordsworth parents, William and Dorothy, who were then aged nine and seven, were separated for the next eight years. Shelley, who quite wrongly regarded Wordsworth as 'a solemn and unsexual man' and 'a kind of moral eunuch', alluded in his preface to *Laon and Cythna* to 'one circumstance' in the 'personal conduct' of his hero and heroine, which was that the lovers were siblings, before carefully adding that the sentiments connected with that 'circumstance' had 'no personal reference to the writer'. Although the painter Robert Haydon later alleged that Shelley 'would lie with his sister and sophisticate himself into a conviction of its innocence', Shelley's claim was true. But he did in his works usually treat incest as a positive good and he did have a fixation about sisters, once telling Hogg that 'in no other relation could the intimacy be equally perfect'. Coleridge was a partial exception to the contemporary poetic fascination with sisters. Although he and Southey married sisters from ideology as much as from love, his later horror at the thought of sexual congress with Mrs Coleridge, he told a friend, was 'as though my wife were my very own sister'.[43]

thirteen letters to Hogg, none of which was a brief note. Hogg's letters have not survived, but he evidently sent at least ten in reply. The flavour of the correspondence can only be savoured from extracts:

> There is now need for all my art, I must resort to deception. . . . I am now surrounded, environed by dangers to which compared the Devils who besieged St Anthony's all were inefficient – they attack me for my detestable principles I am reckoned an outcast, yet defy them and laugh at their inefficient efforts. . . . Oh! I burn with impatience for the moment of Xtianity's dissolution, it has injured me; I swear on the altar of perjured love to revenge myself on the hated cause of the effect which *even now* I can scarcely help deploring – *Indeed* I think it is to the benefit of society to destroy the opinions which *can* annihilate the dearest of its ties. Inconveniences would now result from my *owning* the novel which I have in preparation for the press. I give out therefore that I will publish no more; everyone here, but the select few who enter into its schemes believe my assertion – I will stab the wretch in secret. . . . My father wished to withdraw me from College I *would* not consent to it. . . . So much for egotism. . . . On *one* subject I am cool, (religion) yet that coolness alone possesses me that I may with more certainty guide the spear to the breast of my adversary, with more certainty ensanguine it with the hearts blood of Xt's hated name. Adieu. – Ecrasez l'infame. . . . [*unsigned*]
>
> . . . .Thanks, *truly* thanks for opening your heart to me, for telling me your feelings towards me. Dare I do the same to you? I dare not to myself how can I to another, perfect as he may be? I dare not even to God, whose mercy is great. My unhappiness is excessive; . . .
>
> I have wandered in the snow for I am cold wet and mad – Pardon me, pardon my delirious egotism . . . but mortality is not Godhead amiable as it may sometimes be – I am at treason however. I will check my volubility. . . .
>
> . . . .Is Suicide wrong? I slept with a loaded pistol and some poison last night but did not die. I could not come on Monday my sister would not part with me. . . .
>
> [Harriet Grove] is gone, she is lost to me forever – she is married, married to a clod of earth, she will become as insensible herself, all those fine capabilities will moulder . . . My mother fancies me in the High Road to Pandemonium, she fancies I want to make a deistical coterie of all my little sisters.
>
> I here take God (if a God exists) to witness . . . Am I not mad? Alas I am, but I pour my ravings in the ear of a friend who will pardon them. . . .[45]

This obsessive correspondence, totalling 23 letters in 31 days, also contained much solemn and tedious discussion of religion. But even leaving aside that and the prevailing tone of hysteria and mental instability, which makes parts of the letters read like some of the more absurd passages in Shelley's novels, the letters have a number of notable features. Shelley deceived both himself and others. His despair about Harriet Grove was partly paranoid: she was not even engaged to another man, let alone married to a clod of earth. And he clearly had no inhibitions about deceiving his parents. He also, it seems, deceived Hogg about his movements and his reasons for not being able to meet his friend.[46]

The letters further show that, unusually, both Shelley's parents displayed some good sense during the vacation. If Timothy Shelley had had his way and Shelley had left Oxford at Christmas, everybody would have been happier. Shelley's mother's fear that he wanted to make his sisters deists was the simple truth. He wanted his sister Elizabeth to live in an eternal union with Hogg without the 'chain' of marriage; and three months later he wrote of his youngest sister, Hellen, 'this dear little girl, she would be a divine little scion of [religious] infidelity, if I could get hold of her. I think my lessons here must have taken effect.' Hellen was then ten years old.[47]

Shelley's father soon regained his obtuseness. Having been strongly prejudiced against Hogg because of Stockdale's revelations, Timothy conceived a prepossession in his favour after discovering that he came from a respectable family in the North-East, and told Shelley to invite him for Easter.*[48]

The Shelleys were no strangers to atheism. According to the young Shelley, his grandfather was 'a complete atheist'. But Timothy and Elizabeth could not do anything about Shelley's grandfather. They could, however, at least in theory, do something about their son. Shelley's espousal of unbelief was deeply alarming and likely to ruin their hopes of his becoming a Member of Parliament and a leader of the country. Religion was considered essential not only on social grounds – it helped to keep the poor in order – but on personal grounds as well: religious infidelity, Coleridge believed, almost invariably led to 'sensuality' and other

---

* Evidently it never occurred to Timothy that anybody in similar circumstances who allowed himself to be reassured about P. B. Shelley because his father was a respectable Sussex MP would have been seriously misled.

serious vices; and although empirical evidence for such a belief was scarce, and impeccable religious orthodoxy often comfortably coexisted with 'sensuality', that was the general view.[49]

But in practice Shelley's parents could do little about their son's atheism which was probably connected with his rejection of his father. In any case Mr and Mrs Shelley were reaping where they had sown, or rather not sown; they were paying the penalty for their cold and negligent upbringing of their eldest child, which had lost them their influence over him.

Shelley had long been hostile to those whom Wilberforce and others called 'nominal Christians'. A few months later, particularly disillusioned by meeting Southey in Cumberland, he wrote in 'A Sabbath Walk':

> The village bells are sweet but they denote
> That spirits love by the clock, and are devout
> All at a stated hour. The sound
> Is sweet to sense but to the heart
> It tells of worship insincere,
> Creeds half believed, the ear that bends
> To custom, prejudice and fear,
> The tongue that's bought to speak,
> The heart that's hired to feel.

Under that show of outward piety such people led selfish lives the rest of the week. Shelley had also for some time been aggressively anti-clerical, seeing parsons and bishops as enthusiastic apologists for the war and energetic supporters of an unjust society, a stance which can only have been strengthened by Oxford's dull, dogmatic clerics. But, while for Shelley's anti-clericalism there was a good rational case, there was nothing rational about the vituperation he unleashed on Christ and Christianity when he learned that his 'understanding' with Harriet Grove had been ended because of his sceptical letters to her. His letters to Hogg make fully credible the later remark of Gibbons Merle, an acquaintance at the time, that Shelley was a mild and modest man but behaved like a maniac when discussing religion. It was that zealotry – Shelley's own missionary instinct and compulsion to proselytise – not Christianity, which had destroyed his relationship with Harriet Grove. His atheism was at this time almost a form of religious exultation or enthusiasm which even extended, as we have seen, to an indecent wish to convert his ten-year-old sister.[50]

The arguments (not quoted here) about religion in Shelley's letters show that Stockdale was right: Hogg was the leader in atheism. For some time Shelley defended a deistic position, only succumbing to his friend's arguments for atheism shortly before his return to Oxford. These religious passages, like the rest of Shelley's letters, are desperately serious and contain no hint of humour. Shelley once complained that Hogg 'laughed at everything. I am convinced', he went on, 'that there can be no entire regeneration of mankind until laughter is put down.' No doubt Shelley was partly parodying himself, but according to Hogg he 'habitually and vehemently expressed' a 'strong aversion for laughter and ridicule'. Shelley's dislike of comedy is confirmed by the more reliable Peacock. At a performance of Sheridan's *The School for Scandal* Shelley said to him: 'I see the purpose of this comedy. It is to associate virtue with bottles and glasses, and villainy with books.'[51]

If only somebody at University College had been able, as Shelley's friend at Wadham seems to have attempted, to tell either Hogg or Shelley or both of them not to take themselves quite so seriously and to bear in mind that two eighteen-year-olds would be lucky to solve in a couple of months problems which had puzzled, in Bishop Berkeley's words, 'very great and extraordinary men' for centuries, a lot of trouble might have been avoided. Unfortunately Hogg, on a walking tour or at his college where there were only two other undergraduates in residence, was as isolated as Shelley at Field Place. They only had their letters for company, and their *folie à deux* intensified. Shelley seems at times to have realised that he was in the grip of a *folie à un*. He used the word 'mad' about himself with disconcerting frequency. Certainly his letters are not conspicuously sane, and some people at Oxford thought him insane or at least half-mad.[52]

Like Byron, Shelley was fond of pistol practice and, like him, he had a pair of duelling pistols and was a good shot. However theatrical his intimations to Hogg that he was contemplating suicide – nobody genuinely intent on suicide would sleep with both poison and a loaded pistol at his side – his sister's fears that he might take his life were evidently real enough to make her reluctant to let him out of her sight.[53]

But wherever exactly Shelley was hovering over the unfixed frontiers of madness and sanity, his letters show the various parts of him to have been at markedly different stages of development.

Physically, sexually and mentally, he was a man, and a wonderfully clever one. Emotionally and morally, he was still a boy, and one who was not even old for his age. His ranting against Christianity because he thought it had thwarted him was at best adolescent, while even a fairly obtuse schoolboy would have known that to inculcate his small sisters with dangerously outlandish ideas was inexcusable. A large part of his 'madness' probably stemmed from the tension between his laggard emotional growth and his advanced intellectual maturity.

Shelley had caught from Dr Lind the habit of writing under a pseudonym to people who were allegedly experts in their field, and then engaging them in argument – an enjoyable way of annoying the pompous and wasting their time. As his current interest was metaphysics and the question of whether or not a creating deity existed, Shelley had persuaded a friendly girl called Philadelphia Phillips, who liked him, to print at Worthing a pamphlet containing his and Hogg's arguments. He thereby subjected her to the risk of prosecution for blasphemy, but the printing saved Hogg and Shelley having to write out their argument in full to each new victim of their letter-writing zeal.[54]

In his biography of Shelley Hogg suggested that the pamphlet (or syllabus) called by Shelley *The Necessity of Atheism* was entirely Shelley's work and maintained that it was 'never offered for sale'. Neither claim was true. While Shelley wrote the final version at Field Place and provided the title, what he had earlier called Hogg's 'systematic cudgel of Christianity' was evidently the first draft of much of the pamphlet. And, so far from it never having been offered for sale, it was advertised in an Oxford paper.[55]

The Necessity of Atheism was a curious title to choose. Admittedly Hume had shown that the difference between deism and atheism was largely verbal. But as Shelley had early in January been a deist, he can hardly have thought it absolutely essential to be an atheist a few days later.* Admittedly, too, putting the word 'Necessity' into the title was not unprecedented in pamphlets of this type, but as Godwin was then much in Shelley's mind and as 'necessity' plays a key part in the Godwinian system, that may have

---

* Even then his atheism was limited. He became, he told Godwin, 'in the popular sense of the word "God" an Atheist'. While denying 'a creative Deity', he accepted 'the hypothesis of a pervading Spirit co-eternal with the universe.'[56]

been the reason for its use. In any event, the title was disastrous. Although the syllabus was one of the first overtly to argue in favour of atheism, it is fairly innocuous in content and, a mere thousand words long, much more mature than Shelley's recent poetry or his novels. Only its title made it inflammatory.[57]

Its argument was derived from Locke and Hume. If, as has been suggested, Locke started with his conclusions and then worked back, Hogg and Shelley should not be harshly censured for embedding their conclusion in their premises. Their chief premise that 'the senses are the sources of all knowledge to the mind' – 'We bring into the world with us no innate principles', Godwin maintained in *Political Justice* – was a postulate as dogmatic and unprovable as the Christian propositions they loved to scorn. Blake maintained the opposite: 'Innate ideas are in Every Man Born with him'. And according to Coleridge, when 'Mr Locke's followers had repeated "there is nothing in the mind which was not before in the senses", Leibnitz added, "except the mind itself".' With their conclusion foreordained, Shelley and Hogg had little difficulty in showing 'that there is no proof of the existence of a Deity, Q.E.D.'[58]

The authors sent their tract, Shelley told his printers, to every bishop in the Church, which as he could not at Oxford use his father's privilege of free postage – MPs and peers could frank letters – would, if true, have been expensive. To beard a few bishops was rash but not suicidal; to circulate the pamphlet in Oxford was far more dangerous. Apparently Shelley sent it to many of the heads of houses. Not content with that, he plastered Slatter and Munday's shop with it, telling the shopman to sell it for sixpence. The display lasted for less than an hour. A Fellow of New College, seeing it in the window, entered the shop, and having glanced at its contents 'advised the principals' to destroy all copies – which they did.[59]

The shop incident was early in March. The authorship of the 'anonymous' syllabus was widely known by the 15th. Yet the college authorities did nothing, inactivity which shows that they were not thirsting for Shelley's punishment but hoping that with the pamphlet withdrawn from circulation the incident would soon be forgotten. Very probably it would have been, had Shelley not sent a copy to Edward Copleston, the Professor of Poetry, later a bishop, and a pugnacious man, who had in the previous year unsuccessfully tried to answer the damaging criticisms levelled against Oxford by the *Edinburgh Review*. Shelley's inclusion of Copleston in his pamphlet's recipients looks suspiciously like deliberate provocation. His erroneous claim that he had twice been expelled from Eton suggests that at Oxford he may have been courting expulsion; as over Harriet Grove's non-marriage 'to a clod of earth' he had a need to feel persecuted. In any case Copleston, not a man to let sleeping dons lie on a matter of this kind, apparently demanded action from Shelley's college.[60]

Shelley was accordingly summoned before the Master and two or three of the very few Fellows in residence. None of the conflicting versions of what happened next is fully convincing. The one usually accepted is Hogg's splendidly graphic account. This has the Master asking Shelley if he was the author of *The Necessity of Atheism*, a copy of which was waved in front of him, and Shelley refusing to answer on the untenable grounds that such questioning was unlawful and unjust and the college was behaving like a court of inquisitors. He was therefore expelled, whereupon Hogg, honourably if misguidedly, volunteered for the same treatment, similarly refused to answer and was similarly expelled. In two respects this version is plausible: it fits in with the possibility that Shelley was inviting expulsion, and it goes far to explain the imposition of that harsh penalty. But contrary to Hogg's claim, Shelley evidently had warning of his summons to see the authorities; and he can hardly have seriously thought that the Master had no right to ask him questions about the pamphlet. Walter Scott shortly afterwards refused to confirm or deny that he was the author of the Waverley novels. But for a famous writer to shelter behind anonymity is clearly very different from an undergraduate refusing to answer questions about the authorship of a thin pamphlet attacking the major tenet of the educational establishment in which he is a pupil. Nevertheless, Hogg apparently thought that his account cast a favourable light on the conduct of Shelley and himself before the college tribunal.[61]

Since the college had been slow and reluctant to move against Shelley, the Master and Fellows, when pressed into activity, probably hoped that he would deny authorship. A denial would have been slightly implausible because of the obvious similarity between Shelley's handwriting and that of Jeremiah Stukely, the pseudonym he used when circulating the pamphlet. Yet a disavowal would have closed the matter. Over Christmas Shelley had thought nothing of deceiving his family about his future writing; in February he had assured his father that in examinations at Oxford he would 'perfectly coincide with the opinions of the learned doctors', and early in March he had told Leigh Hunt that, on account of the responsibility to which his 'residence at this university' subjected him, he dared 'not publicly to avow all' that he thought. A disavowal of authorship would therefore have been consistent with the rest of his behaviour.[62]

Over the years Shelley himself gave four different versions of the expulsion, at least one of which is more convincing than Hogg's. A year afterwards he told Godwin that, after he had been sent for, he was informed 'that in case I denied the publication, no more would be said. I refused and was expelled.' Earlier he had said much the same to Merle. Like Hogg's, this version would accord with the college's official verdict of expulsion: 'for contumaciously refusing to answer questions and also repeatedly declining to disavow' the publication. And it is not only more plausible than Hogg's, it fits better with what Shelley wrote to his father four days after his expulsion. In that letter, after telling Timothy that 'refusing to disavow the publication I was expelled', he complained that the college authorities had treated Hogg and himself 'not as our fair, open, candid conduct might demand, no public argument was publicly brought forward to disapprove our reasoning . . .'. Not even Shelley, at his most over-wrought, could have believed that an undergraduate's refusal to answer legitimate questions about an anonymous pamphlet could possibly be described as 'fair, open, candid conduct', whereas a straightforward refusal to deny author-ship might, conceivably, just come within such a description.[63]

Nobody came well out of the expulsion. The college authorities began with sensible restraint, but ended with excessive severity. After Coleridge had absconded and joined the army, Jesus College allowed him to return to Cambridge. University College, Oxford, could have emulated that intelligent leniency by merely rusticating Shelley and Hogg for a term or two. That would have been treating them as if they were boys, which, however intellectually gifted, is just what they were.*[64]

If the college acted harshly, Timothy Shelley did not act at all.

* When nearly fifty years later Swinburne, who thought his 'connection with Oxford' was something like Shelley's, 'was rusticated and all but expelled', Benjamin Jowett, who was no admirer of the earlier poet, feared that Balliol might make 'itself as ridiculous as University had made itself about Shelley'.[65]

The previous month, Shelley had sent Timothy an insolent reply. His father's exposition of religion had much pleased him, he told Timothy, because it had proved to his 'complete satisfaction' that those who did 'not think at all' should be 'restrained by the bands of *prejudicative* religion' because they did not have 'sufficient principle to discharge their duties without leaning on some support'. Despite that insult, which even Timothy must have understood, he should surely have hastened back to his old college as soon as he heard the news of the expulsion and tried to negotiate a lighter sentence. That, after all, is what Coleridge attempted when his son was deprived of his Oriel fellowship a few years latter. Coleridge failed, but Mr Shelley might well have succeeded.[66]

Yet Shelley and Hogg were the chief culprits. 'The publication of this syllabus', as Medwin, who regarded the pamphlet as a 'silly work' with 'a most ridiculous title', justly wrote, was 'a reckless – a mad act'. To challenge Oxford on the subject of the deity when no one could enter or belong to the university without subscribing to acceptance of the Anglican Church was an absurd venture, about as sensible, say, as preaching to a cannibal the virtues of vegetarianism. Then Shelley's refusal either to deny the offence, which was his obvious course if he wanted to stay at Oxford, or to apologise for it invited the retribution it received.[67]

According to a college contemporary, later a junior Fellow, C. J. Ridley, most people were afraid of Shelley's 'strange and fantastic pranks' and of his 'still stranger opinions', but everybody acknowledged him to have been 'very good humoured and of kind disposition'. Hogg, he added, had great intellectual powers, but 'was not popular'. Although one Fellow, J. M. Rolleston, whose lectures on logic were probably heard by Shelley, was sorry for Hogg, but 'not for Shelley', Ridley thought that no one 'regretted their departure'. They did nevertheless conduct themselves well in their last few hours at the university. However inwardly depressed, they put on a public show of bravado, walking up and down the quad. Even that normally hostile witness, C. K. Sharpe, thought Shelley had 'behaved like a hero'. The next morning after Shelley had borrowed £20, which he never repaid, for his journey from Slatter's brother, he and Hogg took the stagecoach for London.[68]

CHAPTER VIII

Cambridge and Oxford

Byron: 1805–7 (aged 17–19 years)
Shelley 1810–11 (aged 18 years)

Byron had gone up to Cambridge in October 1805 and finally went down at Christmas 1807, but, as he was absent more often than he was present, he was resident for only three terms. He had wanted to go to Christ Church, Oxford, where many of his Harrow friends were bound, but was told that there was no room for him. That was probably the true reason for his rejection, although Christ Church may not have wanted him, as earlier it had not wanted Southey. In consequence Byron, at Dr Drury's suggestion, had journeyed from Harrow on 1 July to enter himself at Trinity College, Cambridge, which was by any standards not a bad second choice.[1]

Many years later, nevertheless, he wrote to John Murray that when he went up to Trinity a few months before his eighteenth birthday he had been 'miserable and untoward to a degree', owing to being 'wretched' at leaving Harrow, at going to Cambridge instead of Oxford, and at various 'domestic circumstances'. That was not what he was writing at the time. Two days after his arrival at Trinity, having asked Hanson to order four dozen bottles of wine, Byron told him that he was beginning 'to *admire* a College Life'. And five days later he told Augusta that he liked 'a College life extremely', especially as he had escaped from his 'domestic tyrant' his mother, and that he was 'most pleasantly situated in *Super-excellent* rooms'. He was 'comfortable' at Trinity, 'having one of the best allowances in College'. His allowance had been increased to £500 a year, largely at Mrs Byron's expense, a fact which her son ignored. So his complaints to Augusta were of his mother, not of Trinity or Cambridge.[2]

Byron's deepest Harrow friendships had been with much younger boys, who were of course still at Harrow. At Cambridge he became 'very great friends' with Edward Noel Long, whom he had known at Harrow and to whom in 1807 he addressed a poem extolling their 'joyous days' at university; he was also 'intimate' with another

Harrow friend William Bankes. But because he would have had more friends at Oxford, he might well have found Christ Church even more congenial than Cambridge, just as Shelley would have been better off at that less theological university whose Anglican orthodoxy, seasoned with Newton, Euclid and a pinch of scepticism, was slightly less rigid than Oxford's. Certainly Byron used his regrets for Oxford and his alleged 'dislike' of Cambridge to justify his non-residence to his tutor; he could not consider 'Granta' his 'Alma Mater'. Yet his excuses are contradicted not only by his contemporary letters, in which he called Cambridge 'so excellent an Alma Mater', but by the sentiments that he expressed a mere two months after his letter to Murray. In his Ravenna Journal in early 1821, he wrote that his Cambridge years had been 'the happiest, perhaps, of my life'.[3]

In the 1805 version of *The Prelude* Wordsworth discovered 'something . . . of a republic' at Cambridge. Something of one, no doubt, but not very much, and his succeeding lines that 'all stood thus far upon equal ground' and were 'brothers' in 'one community' were more aspiration than reality. While class distinctions were less pronounced at Cambridge than elsewhere, they were still prominent. As 'a nobleman' Byron paid higher fees, had a number of privileges and wore special clothes. His appearance in the hall in his 'State Robes', he reported, was '*superb*' though the effect was spoiled by his '*diffidence*'. Wordsworth was truer to life in writing of the Fellows as 'grave elders', men unwashed, 'grotesque in character, tricked out like aged trees'. Byron saw them at close quarters – noblemen dined with them at the Fellows' table where a slightly later Trinity man noted their 'goutiness and Falstaffry' – and quickly came to a similar conclusion: 'The Master eats, drinks and sleeps, the Fellows drink, dispute and pun . . .'. In his first published volume of poems he described them as:

> In manners rude, in foolish forms precise,
> All modern arts, affecting to despise;
> Yet pricing BENTLEY'S, BRUNCK'S, or PORSON'S note,
> More than the verse, on which the critic wrote;
> Vain as their honours, heavy as their Ale,
> Sad as their wit, and tedious as their tale . . .

Richard Porson, Fellow of Trinity and Regius Professor of Greek, was a famous classical scholar, who would, it was said, drink ink rather than not drink at all. Byron found the notoriously ill-mannered Porson 'always – that is – daily, intoxicated to brutality', and remembered that at a party the 'bestial' Porson 'once [took] up a poker' to one of the undergraduates who, according to Hobhouse, was Byron himself.[4]

Noblemen were exempt from university examinations, and at Trinity, where they were more prevalent than at any other college, they had what one of them described as 'an acknowledged licence . . . to abstain from all lectures'. Indeed, as a later Master put it, they were invited to be idle. Byron's tutor, the Reverend Thomas Jones, had in his earlier days been one of the pioneers of university reform, proposing that noblemen should lose their exemption from examinations. But in such an ambience of drink, decadence and aristocratic privilege, he would even in his prime have had difficulty in getting much academic work out of Byron. The poet had done as little as possible at Harrow, where boys were not invited to be idle, and naturally did less at Cambridge where they were; he quickly concluded that 'study' was the last pursuit of the university. Nobody, he wrote, seemed 'to look into an author ancient or modern' if he could avoid it. In fact some did, and Byron satirised their pursuit of 'unprofitable knowledge':

> Renouncing every pleasing page,
> From authors of historic use;
> Preferring to the lettered sage,
> The square of the hypothenuse.

Such industry, though, was largely confined to the poorer under-graduates. Even Palmerston, who was at the more diligent St John's, only worked some two hours a day there, later claiming that the two years he had spent at Cambridge were 'passed very much in forgetting what he had learned at Edinburgh'. Byron did less, telling his tutor that as he was not going to join the army he had no predilection for mathematics and that he did not intend 'to bewilder [himself] in the Mazes of Metaphysics'.*[5]

Shelley did not bewilder himself with 'Metaphysics' at Oxford, but he was certainly caught in its 'mazes'. Though more philistine,

---

* Such a view had high authority. Bishop Berkeley, the philosopher, whom Byron included in his list of authors he had read and who later was a strong influence on Shelley, wrote of 'the fine and subtle net of abstract ideas, which has so miserably perplexed and entangled the minds of men'. And Byron's later admirer, Goethe, told Eckermann that man was 'born not to solve the problems of the universe, but to find out where the problem begins, and then to restrain himself within the limits of the comprehensible.'[6]

Byron was probably wiser.* Unlike Shelley he never, it seems, attended a single lecture on metaphysics or anything else. Yet eschewing metaphysics did not make him much better disposed to the Church than Shelley. He did not believe in heaven or hell and thought that 'men without religion [were] priests,' and that there were 'fools in all sects and impostors in most.'[8]

Escaping the mazes of metaphysics, Byron instead 'ran through' what, in an autobiographical poem written a few months later, he called 'all the maze of sin'. When his tutor told another undergraduate that Byron was 'a young man of tumultuous passions', he did not have sexual passion chiefly in mind. But, with Byron having little else to do and a good allowance, a spell of debauchery was virtually inevitable. He sat down to write, he told Hanson after a month at Trinity, with 'a head confused with dissipation', which he hated but could not avoid, adding that he was 'the most steady man in the College', a claim no more plausible than his earlier one to Augusta that he went on 'gaily, but not extravagantly'. Byron was himself one of those he called

> the imprudent
> Whose daring revels shock the sight,
> When vice and infamy combine;
> When drunkenness and dice unite,
> As every sense is steep'd in wine.[9]

Unlike his 'imprudent' companions, however, he did not long enjoy these 'daring revels'. He took 'his gradations in the vices' promptly, he wrote in 1821, but they were not to his taste. His early passions were 'violent' but 'concentrated', and he 'hated division or spreading abroad'. That does not quite tally with a light-hearted poem he wrote in 1806:

> You say 'when I rove
> I know nothing of love',
> 'Tis true I am given to range,
> If I rightly remember,

---

* 'Our days', he wrote in *Don Juan*,

> are too brief for affording
> Space to despise what *no one* ever could
> Decide, and *every body* one day will
> Know very clearly – or at least lie still –

Toward the end of his life Shelley held a rather similar view. 'Let it not be supposed', he wrote, 'that I mean to dogmatise upon a subject concerning which all men are equally ignorant.'[7]

I've lov'd a good number,
Yet there's pleasure, at least, in a change.

At Cambridge, though, the 'commonplace libertinism of the place
and time' disgusted him. No doubt he sampled the women against
whom a year later undergraduates were warned in *Hints to
Freshmen at the University of Cambridge*: 'Suspect danger from
women; those women, I mean, who haunt the lanes, and ends and
corners of the town. . . . But for them the once healthful Horatio
would not now be secluded from his friends'.[10]

Unlike Horatio, Byron did not contract a venereal disease – for
the time being at least. Nevertheless his revels cost money;
according to the accounts Hobhouse kept of his own expenditure,
prostitutes cost one pound a time. Byron was not one to be outdone
even by his much richer contemporaries and, in addition to his
dissipations and other extravagances, he kept three horses and two
men servants at Cambridge; hence he was living in a style which his
income could not sustain. Instead of being grateful to his mother for
having slashed her own income to increase his, he complained of
her meanness. With her long experience of poverty and her anxiety
to get out and stay out of debt, Mrs Byron was terrified of her son
squandering his inheritance as his father had squandered hers.
Unfortunately the frequent violence of her expressions and behaviour neutered her sensible and justified remonstrances. After
indulging in some wearisome pomposities and ignoring the good
reasons for his mother's exasperation, Byron summed up to
Hanson, who had sought to defend Catherine, her treatment of him
as 'a *peevish*, *harassing* system of Torment . . . now & then
interrupted by Ridiculous Indulgence. . . .' Ending his letter in a
more engaging vein, he confided to Hanson that he was 'still the
schoolboy and as great a rattle as ever, and between ourselves
College is not the place to improve either Morals or Income'.[11]

As to his morals and income that was certainly true. Byron was
'still the schoolboy' not only in his adolescent ingratitude and ill-
treatment of his mother, but in having conceived what he later
called 'a violent, though pure, love and passion' for John Edleston,
a Trinity choirboy, although not only schoolboys do that. He had
been attracted first, he told Elizabeth Pigot, by Edleston's voice,
then by his countenance and then by his manners. In the same letter
he said the chorister, who was two years younger than him, had
been his 'almost constant associate since October 1805'. If that had

been true, they would have had to be astonishingly discreet. While there was much less of it than at Harrow, there was inevitably some homosexual activity at Cambridge. William Bankes, whom Byron called his 'collegiate pastor, and master, and patron' in his first year, was homosexual though he later proposed to the future Lady Byron. So, too, was Charles Skinner Matthews, a later Cambridge friend of Byron's. And Edleston was far from the only choirboy to catch the eye of an undergraduate. Yet, if Byron had been frequently seen in the company of a young chorister, there would soon have been a pile of gossip. In one of his poems Byron he wrote:

> Ours too the glance none saw beside;
> The smile none else might understand;
> The whisper'd thought of hearts allied,
> The pressure of the thrilling hand.

Presumably all that took place in private; even so, the absence of gossip is remarkable, particularly as Edleston was equally fond of Byron and gave him a 'Cornelian' heart.[12]

With his customary generosity Byron doubtless gave the choirboy some money, but Edleston is unlikely to have been the cause of his being deeply in debt. He wrote to Augusta from London immediately after Christmas, swearing her to secrecy and asking her to go joint security with him for a loan from money-lenders. This was a common expedient for young men due to come into some money when they came of age, but a dangerous one. Because repayment was uncertain, money-lenders exacted a ruinous rate of interest – according to Byron 100 per cent. Frightened by his proposal, Augusta offered him some of her own money, which he refused. Unable to come to London to put her name on the 'bloodsuckers'' bond, she explained Byron's predicament and his suggested remedy to his guardian. Carlisle's advice that she should see Hanson caused a two-year estrangement between Augusta and her half-brother, who thought she had betrayed his confidence. It did not prise Byron from the money-lenders; his landlady at 16 Piccadilly, Mrs Massingbird, took Augusta's place on the bond. Byron's transaction – in the family tradition stretching back to Godfrey de Burun's recourse to Aaron the Jew in 1191 – was only the first of several with what he called 'the Tribe of Levi'.[13]

Flushed with what he regarded as a success, Byron arrogantly told his mother that though he happened to have 'a few hundred in ready cash lying by me' he found it 'inconvenient to remain at

College', as it did not suit his constitution. 'Improvement at an English university to a Man of Rank', he added, was 'impossible and the very idea ridiculous'. (Though irritatingly worded, that was only a slight exaggeration.) Accordingly he wished to go abroad for a couple of years where his time would be better and more cheaply employed than 'at our English Seminaries'. He ended by saying that after remaining 'a month in Town' he would perhaps bring his horses and himself down to her residence in that 'execrable kennel'. He hoped she had engaged 'a Man Servant – else it will be impossible for me to visit you, since my servant must attend chiefly to his horses, at the same time you must cut an indifferent figure with only maids in your habitation'. That was an even more obnoxious missive than Shelley's patronising letter to his father about religion; however attractive Byron and Shelley were to their close friends, assuredly they were, when at University singularly tiresome youths to their parents and many others. Even a calm and controlled mother would have been appalled by Byron's letter, and Catherine, who was neither, had already been shaken by his bills, which were coming in at double the amount she had expected. She correctly supposed to Hanson that Byron had got himself 'inveigled' into some emotional attachment and was in the hands of money-lenders. 'That boy will be the death of me,' she wrote; he will 'drive me mad'.[14]

'That boy' did not go back to Cambridge for the Easter term on 5 February. The reasons he gave his mother for wanting to leave university were quite sound – understandably, he was uninterested in 'College studies' and there was little point in his being there – but they were not the only ones. Earlier, in 'sinking spirits', he told Augusta of his 'melancholy', something to which from now on he was always prone, assuring her that it was not caused by ill health, money worries or 'Love', by which he presumably meant love for a girl. Of course, melancholy, now called depression, does not necessarily have a clear-cut cause; it may be the result of mental illness, or what Byron called his 'perhaps natural temperament', or the outcome of upbringing, religion or guilt. Besides, a sufferer from depression may be, as Dr Johnson (who was himself one) accused Boswell of being, 'proud' of his melancholy, as Byron sometimes came near to being. But in so far as there was a distinct cause, other than medical or financial, of his low spirits at this time, it was probably his love for John Edleston.[15]

Byron did condescend to return to Cambridge for the summer term of 1806. 'The Detail of a Cambridge life', he told Hanson in June, 'can be neither amusing or interesting', which is just as well since few details of his life there are known. Finding fencing and boxing useful diversions during his negotiations with the money-lenders, earlier in the year in London he had been a frequent visitor to 13 Bond Street, where Henry Angelo, who had taught him fencing at Harrow, shared rooms with the great boxer, 'Gentleman' John Jackson. Byron now hoped that Angelo would set up rooms in Cambridge, but to his intense annoyance the Mayor of the town refused permission, a decision which in view of the many other much less desirable activities of undergraduates was unfathomable. The Master of Trinity, Lort Mansel, who felt strongly about such matters as undergraduates wearing trousers instead of proper breeches at dinner, declined to intervene.[16]

Though deprived of fencing and boxing, Byron had his friendship with Long and his passion for Edleston, which was, he later wrote, the 'then romance of the most romantic period' of his life. Yet that period was not sufficiently romantic to persuade him to repeat it in any of the next three Cambridge terms. Much of the next year he spent at his mother's house, Burgage Manor on the green at Southwell. Byron was always scathing about Southwell, railing about 'your cursed, detestable and abhorred abode of Scandal, antiquated virginity and universal infamy' to Elizabeth Pigot, who did not take his imprecations too seriously. His precarious finances, wrecked by his extravagance – he was 'detained in Cambridge by the painting of [his] carriage', he told Mrs Massingbird in July – was the main reason why he spent so much time there; he could not afford Cambridge, he said. Yet Southwell, which was his base for a year, had its compensations. He was fond of the Pigot family, especially Elizabeth and her brother John; and though he was irked by Southwell's small town atmosphere and gossip, he enjoyed its amateur theatricals. And not all its virgins were 'antiquated'. As with Shelley's much more complex passion for Hogg, Byron's for Edleston did not inhibit attraction to the other sex. There were plenty of pretty girls with whom he could and did flirt; they also provided material for his poetry. Byron unfairly mocked his mother as an 'Upas Tree, that Antidote to the Arts'. In fact she was a sensible critic when given the chance, and his poetry flourished at

Southwell, much helped by the influence of Elizabeth Pigot, one of the most sympathetic people he ever knew.[17]

In August after a particularly violent quarrel with his mother, Byron 'decamped from Notts' in the middle of the night. While staying with Long near Worthing, he received the news that he was £30,000 richer as a result of apparently winning back control of his Rochdale estate at Lancaster Assizes. That, though, soon proved an illusion. The law's delays were far from exhausted, and it was seventeen years before his friend Douglas Kinnaird finally settled the case. Meanwhile the hope of becoming very considerably richer because of Rochdale – the following February he thought he had gained £60,000 – unsurprisingly did nothing to abate Byron's extravagance.[18]

When he fled to London, Byron already had poems at a printer which, after a great many changes, emerged in November as *Fugitive Pieces*. As with Shelley's first book of poems, they showed the influence of Thomas Moore, though from an earlier volume, *The Poetical Works of the Late Thomas Little Esq*, which Coleridge thought 'wanton', and which Byron said he had known by heart in 1803; Byron's poetry was also influenced by the sentimental poems of Charlotte Dacre. Two early copies of his privately printed book went to John Pigot and his uncle, the Reverend J. T. Becher, a cleric whom Byron liked and respected. One of them was read by a Mrs Sherbrooke, called by Byron a 'portly female', who together with other 'Ladies in Years' pronounced the poet 'a most profligate sinner' and a 'young Moore'. As Becher's father-in-law owed his living to Sherbrooke's husband, Becher was forced to protest, expostulating in verse to Byron at his varnishing scenes 'With guilty lustre, and with amorous lay', and urging him to 'Forbear to taint the Virgin's spotless mind,/ In Power though mighty, be in Mercy kind,/ Bid the chaste Muse diffuse her hallowed light'. Becher and the gossips at Southwell took particular offence at the poem 'To Mary' which, though more sexually conventional, was as erotically explicit as Shelley's 'Epithalamium'. Like the 'Epithalamium', too, Byron's poem contained some unintentionally funny lines:

> No more that bosom heaves for me,
> On it another seeks repose,
> Another riots on its snows. . . .
>
> No more the genial couch we bless
> Dissolving in the fond caress;

Yet some of its lines were a prelude to Byron's later humorous style:

> And smile to think how oft we've done.
> What prudes declare a sin to act is,
> And never but in darkness practice,
> Fearing to trust the tell-tale sun.

Another offending poem was 'To Caroline'. 'Mary' was probably a Londoner of, according to Moore, 'humble even equivocal station', but 'Caroline' was probably Julia Leacroft, a Southwell girl whose station was not humble, but still capable of improvement. This her parents were intent on achieving, Byron thought, by ensnaring him into marriage. They seemed to have their chance when Byron was caught emerging from 'a shrubbery' at night with their daughter and another girl. The next morning her brother called, but finding that Byron, whom he knew to be a good shot, 'preferred fighting to matrimony', he retired, and that was the end of the affair. Byron was less combative over his book. Though nettled by the 'the censorious throng's attacks' on his poetry, he cannot have been greatly surprised, as he had earlier told John Pigot that one of the poems was 'improper for the perusal of Ladies'. He withdrew the book, burning all the copies he could. Only four survived, including the one belonging to the original complainant. The Reverend J. T. Becher doubtless believed that Byron's 'amorous lay' could not 'taint' *his* 'spotless mind'.[19]

So Byron's first volume of poetry, like Shelley's, ended in destruction. Like Shelley, too, he was not deterred from another attempt, though unlike Shelley's his next book, *Poems on Various Occasions*, was, he regretfully said, '*vastly* correct and miraculously *chaste*'. Unavoidably, such a miracle could be achieved only at the heavy cost of omitting most of his poems that were erotic or irreverent. Byron also deleted some lines expressing a view of marriage which Shelley would have applauded:

> No jargon of priests o'er our union was mutter'd,
> To rivet the fetters of husband and wife.

But, while also mutilating another poem, he did leave in a stanza containing the prophetic line: 'Though women are angels, yet wedlock's the Devil'. Yet the volume as a whole, unlike *Fugitive Pieces*, was more sentimental than satirical.[20]

Poems on Various Occasions was ready for private distribution in early January 1807, its appearance coinciding with a temporary change in its author's finances and in his appearance. Byron negotiated another loan from the money-lenders on the usual extortionate terms – in return for £3,000 now he had to pay back £5,000 when he became twenty-one – and began an intensive effort to slim. Though never as corpulent as his elephantine mother, he had been overweight all the time he was at Harrow, and at Cambridge, where an Aberdonian schoolfellow failed to recognise him, he had become fatter still, going up to fourteen and a half stone in the autumn despite his boxing and fencing. His height was 5 feet 8½ inches, and, although in *Mansfield Park* Mr Rushworth thought a man who was less than 5 feet 9 was 'under-sized', 5 feet 8 was then slightly above the average; the Duke of Wellington, usually regarded as a tall man, was only 5 feet 9. Even so, for his height, Byron's weight was almost as excessive as the interest charged by his money-lenders.[21]

So, whether because of his health, the additional strain that his weight placed on his deformed leg and foot, or the presumed wishes of the Southwell ladies, Byron had at last decided to do something about his figure. In February he wrote to Clare, one of his much younger friends at Harrow, whom he still addressed 'My dearest Clare', that he was 'making *love* and taking physic'. Other slimming aids were 'violent exercise' while wearing 'seven waistcoats and a great coat', eating 'animal food' only once a day, drinking no spirits and only a little wine, and '*hot* bathing'. Apart from 'making love', of course, these were roughly the recommendations of a Southwell doctor, Benjamin Hutchinson, whom Byron had consulted in November. Hutchinson's regime resulted in a loss of 35 pounds in four months without any loss of humour. '*Wine* and *Women* have *dished* your *humble Servant*', he told Hanson, 'not a *Sou* to be *had* ... condemned to exist, (I cannot say live) at this *Crater* of Dullness, till my *Lease* of *Infancy* expires'.[22]

Byron's recourse to Dr Hutchinson may not, however, have been prompted by vanity or the fear that excess weight was endangering his health and making his deformity more painful. An undated letter from Long expresses the hope that he had entirely recovered from his 'Gonorrhoea (Virulanta)'. Hutchinson's prescription included 'powders to be taken two or three times a day', and as Byron, who was usually unable to keep a secret, never told anybody that he was acting on doctor's orders, possibly the chief reason for his slimming regime was that he had been 'clapped'. If so, the combination of gonorrhoea and the slimming regime presumably produced 'The Adieu, Written under the impression that the author would soon die'. In this poem which was probably composed at this time, Byron lamented,

> My name obscure, unmark'd my birth,
>> My life a short and vulgar dream:
> Lost in the dull, ignoble crowd,
> My hopes recline within a shroud ...
>> My fate in Lethe's stream

and asked the Almighty to 'Instruct me how to die'.[23]

'The Adieu' and the disease would accord with his remark in his February letter to Clare that though his health was not 'perfectly re-established' he was 'out of all danger'. On the other hand rest, not exercise, was the usual cure for gonorrhoea, and Byron would probably have preferred not to consult his mother's doctor over such an ailment. At all events Byron certainly caught the disease in the years 1807–9, and not for the last time, though he never emulated Casanova's eleven venereal attacks or Boswell's nineteen. Unlike Shelley's, none of Byron's doses of clap had lasting physical or psychological effects.[24]

Yet his slimming regime did have a result which lasted a long time. It gave him his famous face. In Genoa many years later Byron irritably said to Hobhouse: 'Now I know you're looking at my foot'. 'My dear Byron,' his friend replied, 'nobody ever thinks or looks at anything but your head'. Like Shelley, Byron had an unusually small head, but all his features, one of his female biographers maintained, were 'exquisite'; he was 'preposterously beautiful'.[25]

Byron's second volume, part of his 'juvenilia' as he aptly called his early poems (though his juvenilia are rather better than those of the other 'Romantics') was generally well received, despite his friend William Bankes, to whom he had not given a copy, sending him a letter in which the proportion of criticism to flattery was too high for an author's comfort. Byron was ambitious for fame which, as he told Hanson, could not be gained through his oratory until he came of age. Hence the only way of achieving it now was through his poetry, but he had doubts and hesitation about seeking a wider audience. In the end his 'own vanity', he said, induced him to make the 'hazardous experiment'. The resulting *Hours of Idleness*, his first published volume, excluded six of the good poems in its privately printed predecessor, while only two or three of the new ones were worth their place. With nearly all his satirical pieces and his 'amatory effusions' thus cut out, although one poem, 'Nisus and Euryalus', had a strongly homosexual tinge, the chastity of the new volume was even more 'miraculous' than before, and the collection was pretty dull, humourless and conventional. Both his book's title and its preface were partly derived from Charlotte Dacre's *Hours of Solitude* published in 1805, but that did not stop Byron later savaging its author for writing

> Prose is masquerade,
> Whose strains the faithful echoes of her mind,
> Leave wondering comprehension far behind.[26]

Indeed the deterioration between *Poems on Various Occasions* and *Hours of Idleness* was even greater than that between the former and *Fugitive Pieces*, confirming Byron's remark to Long that no man was 'a proper judge of his own productions'. The chief new feature was a preface which, having begun by stressing the author's youth, explained that poetry was not his 'primary vocation', but something indulged in 'to divert the dull moments of indisposition, or the monotony of a vacant hour'. Having thus made himself seem condescending, Byron strengthened that impression by an allusion to his 'title' and his 'noble relation', the Earl of Carlisle. In a poem written in November 1806 are the lines:

> In Southwell there happened to be at this Time,
> A singular Creature, a Dealer in Rhyme:
> No very great praise of this Youth we afford,
> His merit consisted in being a Lord.

And in a poem written a month later he wrote:

> When Peers are Poets, Squires may well be Wits.

So Byron then, as in later life, was well able to laugh at himself and his title, but as neither poem was included in *Hours of Idleness*, and the Preface was all too conspicuous, readers could be forgiven for thinking that the author took himself too seriously.[27]

In his reply to Bankes, Byron had said that he would return to Cambridge in the spring 'to dismantle' his rooms. In fact he did not do so until the end of June just after *Hours of Idleness* had been published, and then only because his mother who, though believing that he did nothing there except 'drink, gamble and spend money', was anxious to prevent him becoming still further enmeshed in money-lenders; accordingly she had raised a loan of £1,000 on her own security from Byron's aunt, another Mrs Byron, who lived in Nottingham. He was now so much thinner than when he was last at Cambridge – his hair had also changed colour from dark 'to a light chestnut' which was mysterious to Byron but is now known to be a result of eating insufficient protein – that at first even John Edleston did not recognise him. Byron found the choirboy 'much grown and rather improved', he told Long, who had earlier been let into the secret of the 'Cornelian'.[28]

The strength or 'violence' of Byron's passion for Edleston seems to be attested by both his poetry and his prose. Nor is there much doubt about the 'purity'. Byron seldom used that word about his relationships, but of Edleston he wrote:

> The kiss so guiltless and refin'd,
> That Love each warmer wish forbore;
> Those eyes proclaim'd so pure a mind,
> Ev'n passion blush'd to plead for more.

That Byron's passion for Edleston was exceptional is clear, but much else about the relationship is obscure. If he was so fond of Edleston, why had his love not drawn him back to Cambridge for the Easter term in 1806? And after he had at last returned to Cambridge for the following term, why did he then stay away from the university for a whole year? Now that he was back again, he told Elizabeth Pigot, he certainly *loved* Edleston 'more than any human being' and 'neither *time* or Distance [had] had the least effect'. Indeed he seemed almost to go out of his way to put distance between himself and Edleston and to stay away from him for as long as possible.[29]

On 30 June he told Elizabeth Pigot that he was quitting Cambridge 'for ever' because his set had 'vanished' and because Edleston, who was sitting opposite him as he wrote, was going to work in an eminent 'mercantile house' in London. Yet, just five days later, immediately after he had parted from Edleston, he told her that he had decided to stay another year at Cambridge, which was an odd decision to make just when his 'Cornelian' was leaving for London. Even odder, Byron said he probably would not see him again until 1809. Why ever not, one wonders? Meeting in London would presumably have been easier than meeting in his rooms in Cambridge, even if Byron had adhered to his decision to stay at

Cambridge for three more terms. In the end he stayed for only one more term, but neither in Cambridge nor London did he ever see Edleston again. In other words the relationship seems to have depended on, or been nourished by, prolonged periods of separation. Maybe his passion was not so violent until he returned to Cambridge, and maybe he then thought that separation was the only sure way of preserving his idealised notion of Edleston and maintaining the purity of their love. It could then live unsullied in his memory like his love for Mary Chaworth.[30]

And why was the passion 'pure'? Evidently it did not have anything to do with the difference in their social position – 'Yet envy not this gaudy state/ *Thine* is the pride of modest worth', Byron wrote in a poem almost certainly addressed to Edleston – nor, probably, with the danger attending homosexual activity. Even in its purity the relationship had to be secret; and later Byron engaged in some casual homosexual acts with his social inferiors without, apparently, fearing the criminal law. He did, however, have a yearning for innocence, no doubt stemming from his early loss of it through the attentions of May Gray. In a contemporary poem about Edleston are the lines:

> And Youth is sure the only time,
>> When Pleasure blends no base alloy;
> When Life is blest without a crime,
>> And Innocence resides with Joy.

Yet 'innocence' in Byron's relationships was usually involuntary: his potential partner – Mary Duff, Margaret Parker, Mary Chaworth – was unavailable or unconsenting. That was not so with Edleston, who was strongly attached to him.[31]

One cause, perhaps, of this unusual purity was Byron's revulsion from his fairly squalid activities with loose women in Cambridge and his desire to have an island of innocence in his life. Probably a more important reason for it, as well as for his earlier separations from Edleston, was an attempt to conquer his bisexuality – a word not coined by Coleridge until the year of Byron's death. Byron would not have been disturbed by his homosexuality at Harrow, where it was nothing out of the ordinary, but may well have thought that at Cambridge he was, or should be, growing out of it. That, according to the late Dr Kinsey, is what happens to many homosexually inclined youths. 'And Manhood claims his stern dominion', Byron wrote in his poem to Long. The fact that in his case 'manhood' seemed to be losing and homosexuality asserting its dominion would also help to account for the melancholy that Byron could not explain to Augusta. Maybe by 1807 Byron was more reconciled to his condition, for his letter to Elizabeth Pigot in July of that year contains no trace of guilt or embarrassment about the subject. To Elizabeth he is frank about Edleston, and proud of him. She, level-headed and intelligent as ever, expressed no disapproval and was delighted that he talked of his 'Cornelian in such affectionate terms'.[32]

Because of his changed appearance, his greater maturity and his recognition as a poet, and also, perhaps, because of his freedom from Edleston, Byron was now much more attractive to his Cambridge contemporaries than he had been during his previous two residences, making in a few days many new acquaintances. He was taken up by people such as John Cam Hobhouse, Douglas Kinnaird and Charles Skinner Matthews, who the year before had barely noticed him, disapproved of him – throughout his life the insecure Hobhouse did a lot of disapproving – or disliked him, and whose friendship compensated for the departure of Long who had joined the Guards. His new popularity and Edleston's removal to London evidently persuaded Byron that he should return to Cambridge in the autumn. Meanwhile, buoyed up by the good reception of himself and his poems, he left for London and a 'perpetual vortex of dissipation'. He also swam in the Thames for three miles and was still getting thinner, falling below eleven stone.[33]

Dissipation, including gambling, continued in the Michaelmas term at Cambridge in the congenial company of his new friends, human and otherwise. Byron had noticed that while the Trinity statutes forbade the keeping of a dog, they said nothing about other animals. Accordingly he bought a 'tame bear', and when he was asked what he meant to do with him, he replied that 'it should sit for a fellowship'. Since this was a sharp dig at the boorish manners of many of the Fellows, his answer, he told Elizabeth Pigot, not surprisingly 'delighted them not', adding later that it was 'the jealousy of [the bear's] Trinity contemporaries' that had prevented his 'success'. Apparently Byron used to parade the streets with the bear which followed him like a dog. But after the immense animal had too enthusiastically hugged a 'small college-man', his owner was persuaded to send him to Newstead.*³⁴

Matthews had gone to London, but Byron quickly gained new acquaintances; they 'formed a coterie', Scrope Berdmore Davies and Francis Hodgson becoming two of his closest friends. They were almost polar opposites: Davies was a witty, gambling dandy and rake,† while Hodgson, a former Eton Master, was an earnest, pious and orthodox scholar-parson.

Byron joined the Whig Club, founded by Hobhouse, which must have pleased his Whiggish mother. At the same time, though less than at Harrow, he read and wrote poetry, producing several hundred lines of a satire which eventually became part of *English Bards and Scotch Reviewers*, as well as much other verse and 200 pages of a novel. Encouraged by the reaction to *Hours of Idleness*, he prepared a second edition, wisely but belatedly deleting his patronising, self-advertising Preface, and unwisely deleting some of the few surviving good poems; he dedicated the book to his guardian, Lord Carlisle, who had written a flattering letter about the first edition. Byron claimed with only slight exaggeration that he had been reviewed in '20 different publications'. In fact, of the fifteen reviews which appeared in 1808, two-thirds were favourable and only two were hostile, although despite the omission of the 'amatory' poems the *Eclectic Review* pronounced the volume 'unsuitable for any refined reader and well regulated family'. At least it did not say that the book was fit only for a brothel.³⁷

Byron left Cambridge voluntarily after three terms; Shelley left Oxford involuntarily after less than two. Both of them could have echoed De Quincey's remark that he owed his university 'nothing', and neither of them could even have endorsed the almost equally harsh judgement of Southey that all he had learned was 'a little swimming and a little boating', since Byron was already a strong swimmer, and Shelley never learned.³⁸

* Had Byron been at Oxford, his behaviour would have been considered less eccentric. The Professor of Biology kept bears, monkeys and jackals in his house in Christ Church.³⁵
† In later life Scrope Davies bore some resemblance to Hogg with Shelley in that he had a liking for Byron's former loves: Ladies Caroline Lamb, Oxford, and Frances Webster. Unlike Hogg, however, Scrope waited until his friend had discarded them – and succeeded with none of them. Byron's other great friend at this time, Hobhouse, was rather differently affected. At least while Byron was alive, he seems to have been unable to form a substantial relationship with a woman outside his family.³⁶

Except for providing a mass of time for intensive reading which could have been found in other places, Oxford did Shelley no good. His university did not even provide him with later valuable friendships – he did form a close relationship with Hogg, but that did him as much harm as good – and being expelled did him lasting damage. When Hogg told Shelley's mother that the university had blasted 'every prospect of public advancement or domestic happiness', he exaggerated, but his claim that the expulsion had sown 'the seeds of domestic dissension' and created 'discord amongst relations' was correct. Of course, if Timothy Shelley had acted with some degree of sense and tolerance, or if Shelley had made a serious effort to conciliate his father, peace could have been made and the effect of his dismissal greatly diminished. But, as it was, his expulsion caused a breach with his family which was never healed.[39]

Cambridge did not cause a breach between Byron and his family; in some moods, indeed, he thought he did not have a family, and while there was a breach between him and Augusta for most of his Cambridge years it was not caused by the university. But if Cambridge did Byron no harm, virtually the only good it did him was that, with the important exception of Shelley, he met there those who became his closest friends until death or exile divided them. Otherwise he, too, might just as well have been somewhere else.

CHAPTER IX

Post-University Blues I

Byron: 1808–9 (aged 19–21 years)

Yet when they did go 'somewhere else' (to London), Byron in 1808 and Shelley in 1811, life became worse for each of them. They both had objective reasons for gloom and, probably, medical ones as well. Both of them were separated from their families – Byron because he did not wish to live with his mother and was still estranged from his sister, and Shelley because of his expulsion from Oxford. Byron was entirely alone. Six years later he wrote in *Lara*:

> Left by his sire, too young such loss to know,
> Lord of himself; – that heritage of woe, . . .
> With none to check and few to point in time
> The thousand paths that slope the way to crime;
> Then, when he most required commandment, then
> Had Lara's daring boyhood govern'd men . . .
> Short was the course his restlessness had run
> But long enough to leave him half undone.[1]

That was a very heightened picture of Byron's life in London, but unfortunately none of his Cambridge friends was in town when he was staying at Dorant's Hotel at the beginning of 1808. He was in touch with Henry Drury, but Harrow had temporarily lost most of its charms; and he made no attempt to see John Edleston. This isolation made him vulnerable to the importunities of R. C. Dallas, an author, Tom Moore wrote twenty years later, 'of some novels popular, I believe, in their day'. On the strength of his sister having been married to Byron's uncle, Dallas gushed to Byron at inordinate length that 'the name of Byron [was] extraordinarily dear' to him, while showering extravagant praise on the young man's poetry. Had Byron been as cynical as he claimed to be, his loneliness would not have stopped him from seeing his distant relation for what he was: no fool, but an elderly – he was thirty-four years older than Byron – boring, grasping, and well-polished toady, as self-satisfied as he was self-serving, a man to be kept at a distance. Instead, Byron demonstrated his naïvety by accepting Dallas's praise and friend-ship. Consequently the latter's letter proved an excellent investment for its writer and an expensive one for its recipient. Despite being allegedly too poor to return to Cambridge, Byron gave Dallas £200 then, and much more later.[2]

Although he did not cavil at Dallas's adulatory comments on his poetry, Byron was quick to repudiate his imputation of 'virtue'. Seldom missing an opportunity to make himself seem worse than he was – much later William Harness and Henry Drury agreed that they knew nothing bad about Byron but what he had told them himself – he informed Dallas that he had been held up as 'the Disciple of Infidelity' and that his religious friends had likened him to the Prince of Darkness. The Calvinist dogmas of predestination, sin and divine retribution that had been forced into him in Aberdeen left a permanent mark on Byron, but, intellectually, he had long since abandoned them and much else.

> Let bigots rear a gloomy fane,
>   Let superstition hail the pile,
> Let priests, to spread their sable reign,
>   With tales of mystic rights beguile,

he wrote in 'The Prayer of Nature' at the end of 1806 before asking,

> Shall man confine his Maker's sway
>   To Gothic domes of mouldering stone?

Like Shelley, he had become more irreligious at university. Why should he 'believe mysteries no one understands?' he asked Long. Like Shelley, before Hogg persuaded him into an atheism of a sort, Byron was a deist who disbelieved in heaven and hell. Hence his remarks to Dallas.[3]

That fervent moralist disclaimed the intention of answering Byron's reply with 'a sermon', though characteristically he came near to doing so. Probably provoked by Dallas's ostentatious piety and religiosity, Byron's second response was to give his relation what he called 'a brief compendium of the Sentiments of the *wicked* George, Lord B'. In morality he preferred 'Confucius to the Ten Commandments and Socrates to St Paul', in religion, he 'refused to take the sacrament', and believed 'Truth the prime attribute of the Deity and Death an eternal Sleep, at least of the body', observations which Dallas initially considered 'flippant'. He soon discovered that they represented Byron's real opinions.[4]

Dallas's prosy lay-preaching – in his writings he aimed to be 'the auxiliary of the Divine' – might well have turned any young man's thoughts to profligacy. Not that Byron's inclinations needed any such stimulation. As well as losing weight – he was down to ten and a half stone – writing poetry, and watching for reviews of *Hours of Idleness*, he was leading a dissipated life in London. 'I am buried in an abyss of sensuality', he told Hobhouse. 'I have renounced hazard however, but I am given to Harlots and live in a state of Concubinage'. Quite apart from Byron's later admission that he had 'no coolness or judgement' at the gaming table, that was a sensible decision – even though the renunciation was not quite total. In an age when many young men, Scrope Davies for one (and old men, too), ruined themselves by gambling, harlots were a safer pastime than hazard.[5]

As young upper-class girls were closely chaperoned, married women were the only 'respectable' females who might have joined Byron in his 'abyss of sensuality'. But in London he knew no women of his own class, married or unmarried; so harlots and servant girls were the only alternatives to celibacy or homosexuality – and indeed fears of his bisexual instincts were probably a contributory cause of his dissolute life.[6]

Another cause may well have been the onslaught on *Hours of Idleness*, which the Whig *Edinburgh Review* published in late February. Byron erroneously believed the author of the anonymous piece to be Francis Jeffrey, the *Edinburgh*'s editor; it had in fact been written by Henry Brougham, a brilliant, shifty, ambitious barrister and politician, who had been in charge of the Whig press campaign at the general election in the previous year. As has been seen, Byron had laid himself open to attack by his pretentious Preface and his self-Bowdlerisation of his poems – 1807 was the year the Bowdler family first published their *Family Shakespeare* which took the sex out of Shakespeare, even expunging *Romeo and Juliet* altogether.* He therefore certainly deserved a wounding shot or two, but not a salvo with heavy artillery.[8]

Shelley in 1816 thought the *Edinburgh Review* was as well qualified to judge poetry as Homer would have been to write a

* In 1820 the *Edinburgh Review* endorsed the *Family Shakespeare*, saying that 'it is better every way that what cannot be spoken and ought not to have been written should now cease to be printed'; and a few years afterwards Murray engaged Byron's old friend the Reverend William Harness to produce 'a family edition' of the plays of Shakespeare's contemporaries.[7]

commentary on Newton; and in a satirical attack on the paper in 1807 Shelley's scourge at Oxford, Edward Copleston, had advised a young reviewer to concentrate on prefaces and above all to find fault. Brougham acted on both bits of advice. Yet, if the poetry was as bad as he alleged it to be, it did not merit the attention he gave it; in addition, his review reeked of inverted snobbery. These reviewers attack 'a lord and a minor', Wordsworth told a friend, 'as if no one may write poetry unless he lives in a garret'. Scott was so astonished by the 'undue severity' of the 'offensive article' that he made a protest to Jeffrey. Moreover, Brougham's salvo was dishonest as well as inappropriate. He quoted three particularly dull stanzas of a poem which he claimed had been written in 1806 when Byron was 'a youth of 18', even though the book showed that they had been written in 1802 when Byron was a boy of fourteen.* Brougham then 'positively' asserted that there was nothing better in the volume than those three stanzas, which was palpably false. Understandably, he kept his authorship of the *Edinburgh*'s laborious denunciation secret for as long as he could; and he did not forgive Byron for the wrong he had done the nineteen-year-old peer.[10]

Not surprisingly, Mrs Byron was incensed by Brougham's review; her son was 'cut to atoms' by it, he confessed to Hobhouse, who thought he had come close to suicide. He felt better after drinking three bottles of claret, but two days later he was 'as miserable in mind and Body, as Literary abuse, pecuniary embarrassment, and total enervation can make me'. Yet whatever its effect on Byron's debauchery and health, Brougham's review was good for his poetry. It caused 'rage and resistance and redress', he later told Shelley; and it strengthened his intention to abandon the sentimental poems he had been publishing, while adding edge to the satirical poem he had already begun.[11]

Nevertheless that rage and desire for redress were too late to affect his next publication. *Poems Original and Translated* was largely a second edition of *Hours of Idleness*. But as Byron had become reconciled to the new headmaster of Harrow through the good offices of Henry Drury, 'Childish Recollections' with its attack on Dr Butler as Pomposus was omitted. Also left out were the mildly amorous poems that had survived Byron's previous cull, and of their five replacements three poems looked back to his days at

---

* Professor McGann thinks they were probably written in 1803 when Byron was fifteen.[9]

Harrow and another was a feeble imitation of Macpherson's *Ossian*. Hence *Poems Original and Translated*, continuing the trend of its two predecessors, was the most insipid of Byron's four volumes of juvenilia, deserving the description by Hewson Clarke, a Cambridge enemy whose review of *Hours of Idleness* had come near to causing a duel, that it was a 'pretty little collection of namby-pamby verses' by a Lord who was now 'without his Bear, and is himself muzzled'.[12]

Byron's non-literary life was far from namby-pamby. He had at least two 'nymphs' or concubines in London, and the harem chief was evidently a Miss Caroline Cameron, whom Byron set up in Brompton. According to Hobhouse it was widely believed in Cambridge that he was going to marry her, a belief that was not shared by Byron. He sometimes dressed her as a boy to quell gossip; taken to Brighton thus dressed, she was introduced as his brother, Gordon. Just before and just after he parted from her in the summer, he wrote her three unmemorable poems. The tone of the last two is despondent, but the poet's depression was probably more the result of ill health and dissatisfaction with his mode of life than of grief at the end of the affair. At the theatre later in the year Miss Cameron went up to Scrope Davies, who had met her at Brighton, and launched a violent attack on Hobhouse, whom she presumably blamed for Byron's break with her. Scrope reported that she had been parading the lobby – a clear indication of her profession.[13]

Byron seems to have had two illegitimate children at this period. The first, born in 1807, was a boy whose mother died in childbirth or soon afterwards and to whom he wrote (but did not publish) a sentimental poem 'To My Son'. He probably provided for the child, but as he hailed him as 'dearest child of love', assured him that 'A father's heart is thine, my Boy!', and then, so far as is known, never saw him again, the poem does not make happy reading. His second illegitimate child was born to Lucinda or Lucy, who was one of his servants and lived to marry somebody else. Byron provided an annuity of £100 for mother and child, but it never occurred to him that what he later called 'the sad mishap' should lead to marriage. Timothy Shelley would have thoroughly approved.[14]

In all this Byron was not out of line with other young men of similar status. When studying law at Edinburgh, Boswell had a child by a servant girl and settled £10 a year on her, while Wordsworth had a daughter by Annette Vallon in France and returned to England without either of them. Nor, though he certainly indulged in excesses, was Byron much, if any, more debauched than other young men of his class. A lot of his dissipation in London occurred, he told Hobhouse, with 'other sensual Sinners' who formed 'a very sad set'. He seems unusually dissipated largely because he wrote so explicitly of his activities in letters and journals which, unlike those of most young men, have survived.[15]

Hobhouse was a natural recipient for such confidences, both as a friend and contemporary and – although Byron once contrasted his 'carnality' with Hobhouse's 'chastity' – as a frequent patron of prostitutes; like the good book-keeper he was, Hobhouse usually recorded both the occasion and the cost of such visits.* But Byron did not restrict his sexual boasting to appropriate correspondents. Despite having preserved his copy of *Fugitive Pieces*, the Reverend Becher probably did not relish receiving a caddish letter from Byron informing him that his young friend had been sacrificing 'rather too liberally' at the altar of his 'Paphian goddesses' and was nearly worn out with too much love.

For most of March Byron was ill, with laudanum as his sole support, suffering from a debility caused, he claimed, 'by too frequent connections'. That may have been part of the truth, but very probably he was suffering from a recurrence, or a new bout, of gonorrhoea. He recovered by the middle of April. A doctor later certified that he was a fit subject for a life insurance policy, being in good health and sober and temperate.[17]

Where Byron did differ from most of his contemporaries was that he was also worn down by debt. '*Entre nous*', he told Becher in the same letter, 'I am cursedly dipped'; his debts were over £13,000 before he went abroad. Yet his indebtedness incited rather than curbed his extravagance. He became even freer with the money he did not possess, tipping Harrow schoolboys, generously lending and giving money to friends, and resorting again to the money-lenders. By 1809 his mother thought ruin could only be avoided by his marrying a rich woman. 'Love matches is all nonsense', she feelingly told Hanson. 'Let him make use of the talents God has

---

* Byron later maintained that Hobhouse was 'more *carnivorously & carnally* sensual' than he was.[16]

given him'. Indeed Byron's father's sole talent had been the ability to marry heiresses who had money he could spend, but unfortunately neither Jack Byron nor God had endowed Byron with that aptitude.[18]

Not knowing any women of his own class in London – or, since he had forgotten or dropped Elizabeth Pigot and the girls of Southwell, anywhere else – and therefore largely confined to concubines, Byron had a low opinion of the female sex as a whole. 'His Lordship', as the poetaster Robert Montgomery put it, 'considered women in no spiritual light'. Again Byron was far from alone. In thinking that women in their purity, generosity, kindness and other qualities were superior to the other sex, it was Shelley who was unusual. Many dominant males in that age thought women existed to produce children and to satisfy the emotional and sexual needs of men; they were suspicious of clever women. Coleridge thought women should be 'characterless' and told his wife that not only in intellect and other matters was she 'inferior' to him but also in her 'sex'. Keats famously wrote that, to him, most women were like children to whom he would 'rather give a Sugar Plum than [his] time'. Byron did, nonetheless, take his low esteem further than most. Admittedly only half seriously, he complained to Hobhouse that one of his nymphs could read and write – 'unpardonable in a woman'. Hence he regarded marriage, he told Augusta, as the 'worst of evils'. According to Mrs Byron, there were tradesmen in Nottingham who would be ruined if her son did not pay them. Byron was then having his portrait expensively painted, but he remained unmarried and the tradesmen remained unpaid.[19]

In July 1808 he visited Cambridge to receive his degree. His opinion of the university was no higher than it had been when he was in residence. He told Dallas that the intellect of Cambridge graduates was as stagnant as the Cam and their pursuits limited to the 'Church – not of Christ, but of the nearest Benefice'. So his anxiety to obtain the degree is as hard to understand as Cambridge's willingness to confer it. Byron thought that the university could not avoid doing so. But as he had only been there for three full terms, a refusal would surely have been feasible, even though he was a Lord. In any case, unlike Hobhouse who received his degree three years later, he did not celebrate his achievement by hiring a prostitute for 19s. 6d., which was half the cost of booking a tennis court.[20]

*

Lord Grey's tenancy of Newstead ended in June 1808, and Byron went there from September to January. In a poem written when 'A Stranger [still] dwelt in the hall of my sires', he had noted that Grey had neglected the estate; but that neglect did not spoil his pleasure at returning to 'the land of my fathers'. Newstead should have been cheaper than London but, maintaining his carelessness about money, Byron decreed lavish improvements to a few rooms in the Abbey and invited his friends to stay, though not his mother. She was told that she would be the tenant when he was abroad – he had been talking of travelling abroad for the last two years – but was not to come until the refurnishing was completed.[21]

While Hobhouse was at Newstead with him, they attended the Infirmary Ball at Nottingham in October. There they met Jack Musters and his wife – Byron's Harrow love, Mary Chaworth – who invited them to dine at Annesley. Mary had already begun to realise that her mother and stepfather had been right about Musters not being a suitable husband for her. Once he had been stripped of the glamour provided by Chancery prohibitions and clandestine communications, she could see him as the boring foxhunter he was. The Annesley dinner renewed Byron's love for Mary and evidently kindled a love in her for him. If Byron was not yet the man of whom Stendhal wrote that he had never in his life seen 'anything more beautiful or more impressive', and on whose appearance Coleridge and Scott lavished similar praise, he was closer to it than to the fat bashful boy he had been five years earlier. Yet he was still so unnerved at the dinner, he told Hodgson, that he lost the nonchalance he had determined on and scarcely spoke, while the lady was 'almost as absurd as myself'. He was further upset by the entrance of the Musters' two-year-old daughter, who unsurprisingly looked like her father. On their way home Byron concealed from Hobhouse how deeply he had been affected, giving him a flippant account of the Musters' marriage. Consequently Hobhouse never believed that Mary Chaworth meant much to him.[22]

Instead Byron revealed some of his feelings to Hodgson and wrote two poems to Mary. The first, containing the lines, 'But near thee I can never stay;/My heart would soon again be thine', said that his heart was 'in all save hope, the same' as it had been before her marriage. The second poem written, he told Hodgson on being asked 'by a former flame' why he was quitting the country, ended with the stanza,

In flight I shall be securely wise,
Escaping from temptation's snare;
I cannot view my Paradise
Without the wish of dwelling there.

Despite publishing these two poems in the following year, Hobhouse remained obtuse on the subject of Mary Chaworth. Beau Brummell, the head, in Byron's phrase, of 'the dynasty of Dandies', knew better. Many years later he testified to 'Byron's never dying attachment to Mary Chaworth for I have frequently heard him romancing about her for hours'. Tom Moore thought the same. Byron himself told Shelley's cousin, Tom Medwin in Italy that had he married Mary Chaworth, 'perhaps the whole tenor of my life would have been different'.[23]

Hobhouse having left Newstead at the end of November, and Boatswain, his Newfoundland dog, having gone mad – oblivious to the danger of rabies Byron had wiped away the foam from the lips of the dying dog – Byron had no companion to raise his sprits. As well as writing an effusive epitaph for Boatswain, he built him a mausoleum and expressed a wish to be buried beside him. His bear and other animals and the ancient retainer, Joe Murray, as well as at least one pretty housemaid, were still at Newstead. Otherwise he was by himself. Living 'here . . . *alone*' suited his inclinations, but his moods fluctuated. He was 'a mighty scribbler', he told his sister, and as he was 'independent' he was happy as far 'as any person unfortunately enough to be born into this world can be said to be so'. Three days later, depressed by his debts, his 'Israelitish accounts' and Hanson's inability or disinclination to make progress over his Rochdale estate, which Catherine had earlier told Hanson had been 'shamefully neglected', he told his lawyer he supposed it would end in his 'marrying a *Golden Dolly* or blowing my brains out', two remedies which he considered very similar.[24]

His brains were still very much with him while he was writing his satire, *The British Bards*. He had begun it in London the previous October and had written some 400 lines before Brougham's attack on *Hours of Idleness* caused him to cast aside his first draft and start again. Although he wrote 20 lines on the day he read Brougham's review, he did not rush into print with his revenge, taking care not to risk a second setback for his 'poesy'. In resenting the tone of some of his critics and in wishing to retaliate, Byron was not being adolescent or especially sensitive or aggressive. His mild-mannered friend Francis Hodgson, who was eight years older and whose translation of Juvenal had similarly suffered from the attentions of the *Edinburgh* and other reviews, also penned a satire in reply, attacking 'But chiefly those anonymously wise,/Who skulk in darkness from detection's eyes,/And high on learning's chair affect to sit,/The self-raised arbiters of sense and wit.'[25]

Having added more lines at Newstead in the autumn and had the poem set in type at Newark, Byron showed it to Dallas in London, asking him to get it published without his name. As usual Dallas, while claiming that Byron knew his mind too well to think he could stoop to flatter, was lavish in his praise. He did, however, make some sensible suggestions, for example that Crabbe should be added to the few poets who were commended. He also took exception to the satire's title, and suggested a worse one; he even offered some lines by himself. Byron politely rejected both, but substituted a new title, *English Bards and Scotch Reviewers*, and continued to add lines of his own while the poem was going through the press. Longman's had refused the satire because of its 'asperity', and according to Byron some ten others had done the same, all thereby losing the chance to publish *Childe Harold's Pilgrimage* three years later. Nevertheless, another one, James Cawthorn, had accepted it.[26]

Byron was not solely concerned with his 'poesy'. He had long wanted to travel abroad. Britain was still at war with Napoleon, but he had anyway ruled out France and Italy as 'the common turnpike of coxcombs and virtuosos'. Accordingly in November 1808 he asked the Prime Minister, the Duke of Portland, to procure for him the permission of the East India Company 'to pass through their settlements'. Presumably he thought his position as a fellow peer and, more importantly, as a creditor of the Duke – Portland owed the Byron estate £1,000 and for some years had not even paid interest on the loan – entitled him to seek that favour. Portland did not agree, conveying in his reply that Byron had trespassed on his time and patience. In a dignified answer to the Prime Minister, Byron apologised if he had 'been guilty of any informality', without retreating from his belief that his original letter had been justified. He made a more telling rejoinder in his satire.[27]

His political ambitions were of much longer standing than his desire to go abroad. They dated from Harrow, if not from Aberdeen where he had talked of the House of Lords. Aged sixteen he had written of his intention to cut himself a path though life or perish in the attempt, and politics and oratory had long seemed the likeliest way to the 'greatness' that, he told his mother, lay before him. Accordingly, towards the end of 1808, he informed his guardian, Lord Carlisle, that he would be of age at the beginning of the next parliamentary session and intended to take his seat in the House of Lords. Their relationship had never been close: Byron justifiably complained that Carlisle's guardianship had been more 'nominal' than real. Carlisle, who had not wanted the job, had never invited his ward to stay at Castle Howard or taken any interest in his achievements. Even so, the least he could have done on receiving Byron's letter was to undertake to be present when Byron first went to the House of Lords or to have expressed regret that ill health or other commitments would unfortunately prevent him on that occasion from attending the House. Instead he merely sent Byron a cold letter explaining that a hereditary peer only had to take the oath and did not need an introduction, which was true but inadequate. And when asked to provide evidence that Byron's grandparents had been legally married in a private chapel in Cornwall – Carlisle's mother was a sister of Byron's grandfather – he was no more forthcoming. Very probably Carlisle did not have any helpful evidence, but again it was the frigidity of his response that caused understandable offence, leading Byron to take revenge in the poem he was writing.[28]

With Hanson being as sluggish as ever, Byron had to wait two months before the necessary evidence of his birth and ancestry had been produced. He would have gone to the House of Lords alone on 13 March had not Dallas, who happened to be passing down St James's Street, noticed his coach at his door and gone in to see him. A pale and agitated Byron invited his visitor to accompany him. Byron had no high opinion of their Lordships, regarding them as 'such a crew', he wrote earlier in the year, that it would 'be difficult to hold one's tongue among them'. He was not 'strongly in favour of either party', he told Hanson, a conservative Whig: 'on the one side we have the late underlings of Pitt, possessing all his ill fortune without his talents. . . ; on the other we have the ill-assorted fragments of a worn-out minority', a description of the parties which doubtless owed something to Brougham's savage attack in the Whig *Edinburgh Review*. All the same it was largely accurate.* Since the deaths of Pitt and Fox there had been, Canning and Castlereagh excepted, scarcely a front rank politician in either House. Except for the abolition of the slave trade, which was not a government measure, the so-called Ministry of All the Talents (which had made Hanson Solicitor to the Stamp Office) had been a failure even when Fox still lived, and it was succeeded by perhaps the two dimmest ministries of the nineteenth century. Byron described the first in his satire:

> Then, hapless Britain! be thy rulers blest,
> The senate's oracles, the people's jest!
> Still hear thy motley orators dispense
> The flowers of rhetoric, though not of sense,
> While Canning's colleagues hate him for his wit,
> And old Dame PORTLAND fills the place of PITT.

Nevertheless taking the oath in the House of Lords would have been something of an ordeal for almost any young man of twenty-one, and an agonising one for somebody of Byron's sensitivity and shyness, who was entering the chamber with no encouraging support.[30]

Apart from a short paragraph in Byron's Journal twelve years later, Dallas's account in his book on Byron is the only evidence of what happened next. According to him, Byron, looking both mortified and indignant, advanced to the table to take the oath, whereupon the Chancellor, Lord Eldon, welcomed him with a smile and an outstretched hand. But Byron merely 'made a stiff bow and put the tips of his fingers into a hand, the amiable offer of which demanded the whole of his'. According to Dallas, 'the Chancellor did not press a welcome so received, but resumed his seat, while Byron carelessly seated himself' on an opposition bench. Dallas who greatly admired Eldon was sorry to see this; Byron, who could not admire Eldon's political views or his sycophancy, explained to Dallas that, if he had shaken hands heartily, Eldon 'would have set me down for one of his party, but I will have nothing to do with

---

* Byron had good grounds for avoiding the words Whig and Tory. The ministerialists were called Tory by their opponents but not by themselves till well after Waterloo. The ministerialist or 'Tory' memorandum to the Prince Regent in 1812 said that 'the present administration is, as every administration in this country must necessarily be, a Whig administration.'[29]

any of them, on either side; I have taken my seat, and now I will go abroad'.

Probably Dallas's report is broadly true, but almost certainly exaggerated. For one thing Dallas would have had difficulty in discerning both mortification and indignation in Byron's 'countenance'. For another Eldon would have been unlikely to 'press' his welcome, whatever Byron had done. (According to Byron later, Eldon apologised for the delay, and Byron told him not to apologise: 'you did your *duty* – and you did *no more.*') The Chancellor was transacting business, and would not have interrupted it to hold an extensive conversation with a newcomer. For a third, even if Dallas could see that Byron only extended 'the tips of his fingers' into Eldon's hand, which is doubtful, that may not have been his intention but the result of his shyness, while his explanation of his conduct may well have been a rationalisation of his awkwardness. And for a fourth Byron in fact attended the Lords another seven times before he went abroad.[31]

Byron's satire was published a few days after his oath-taking. In it his opinion of contemporary poets was on a par with his opinion of contemporary politicians. Yet the 'asperity', which Longman's had complained of, was not just the consequence of Byron's rage at the *Edinburgh Review*. In his list of books that he had compiled well before Brougham's attack, he wrote that he had avoided mentioning English living poets because all of them would 'survive their productions'. Hence his satire criticised Coleridge in lines which in 1816 he labelled 'unjust', and even attacked Wordsworth, whom the year before he had praised in a review and whom he would certainly have spared now had he known of that poet's sympathy over Brougham's assault on *Hours of Idleness*.[32]

Particularly influenced by Gifford, whose inferior satires condemned everybody in sight, Byron's anger was much too all-embracing, as he himself soon realised; apart from his friend Hodgson and half a dozen other obscure practitioners, only Crabbe, Campbell, Rogers and Gifford escaped.* On the other hand, he was writing a satire, not a piece of academic literary criticism, and his attacks were not out of line with much

---

* Far less excusably, Jeffrey, though partly sheltering behind public opinion, came to a similar conclusion twenty years later. He thought Southey, Keats, Byron, Shelley, Wordsworth and Crabbe were all declining in reputation. Only Rogers and Campbell had 'withstood this rapid withering of the laurel'.[33]

contemporary criticism. In his Preface to the second edition Byron conceded that several of the writers censured in the poem unquestionably possessed 'considerable genius', but that did not save them. His likening of Jeffrey, the presumed target of his revenge, to Judge Jeffreys was ponderous; and the poem lacked form. Nevertheless it is a vigorous and amusing satire and a brilliant performance for a twenty-year-old. Furthermore, what Byron later called his 'indiscriminate acrimony' against contemporary writers did not stop him laughing at himself:

> I, too, can scrawl, and once upon a time
> I poured along the town a flood of rhyme,
> A schoolboy freak, unworthy praise or blame;
> I printed – older children do the same,
> 'Tis pleasant, sure, to see one's name in print;
> A Book's a Book, altho' there's nothing in't.

And again:

> Even I – least thinking of a thoughtless throng,
> Just skilled to know the right and chuse the wrong. . . .
> Whom every path of pleasure's flowery way
> Has lured in turn, and all have led astray.[34]

The poem, which was published after Byron had returned to Newstead, was well received: it was the first good satire since Charles Churchill's in the 1760s, and was greatly influenced by that writer. Byron was generally known to be its author. Learning of his success he came back to London to prepare a second edition, in which the poem was enlarged by a third. Its Juvenalian plan became more pronounced and the poem even fiercer. This time he himself supervised its passage through the press, resisting Dallas's pleas for occasional flashes of moderation, and adding some insults to Lord Elgin for wasting 'useless thousands' on his 'Phidian freaks', that is to say the Elgin marbles.[35]

He needed money to travel. Part of his difficulties were due to Hanson's inefficiency and procrastination. When Byron was abroad, Hanson did not answer any of his client's letters for a year; and his negligence over the Rochdale estate was continuous and extreme. Men as different as Hobhouse and Dallas urged Byron to replace or at least investigate Hanson, but he was too idle and ineffective ever to get rid of his idle man of affairs. 'I wish to have some conversation with you,' Byron wrote to him in January 1809, 'on the subject of raising the Newstead rents, which I hear may be done without distressing the tenantry'. Almost certainly, after years of neglect, the rents were too low. Other landlords raised theirs, often more than once, but at Newstead the rents remained as they were. Nearly two years later Catherine Byron told Hanson that ever since Byron had come of age the tenants had been expecting a rent increase and that it would be a pity to disappoint them. But 'disappointed' they continued to be.[36]

Byron's difficulties were aggravated by his own folly and generosity. At the same time as he was frantically trying to raise money to appease his creditors and to go abroad, he was giving £500 to Lady Falkland, the widow of a friend who had been killed in a drunken duel, and lending or giving money to the recently ordained Hodgson. He had also undertaken to provide money for Hobhouse to accompany him on his travels.

Scrope Davies was for long thought to have provided the loan which enabled Byron to leave the country, but the discovery in 1971 of some of Scrope's letters, which had lain in Barclay's Bank for well over a century, revealed that in June 1809 Scrope, a generous man, had not made or guaranteed a loan to Byron. He had in an earlier transaction, however, given a guarantee on Byron's behalf. Thus all the time Byron was abroad, Scrope was desperately worried that he would be called on to pay to the money-lenders the sum he had guaranteed but not lent. (Much later Scrope took over the debt and discharged it himself.) The generosity of the rake, Davies, was in strong contrast to the conduct of the pious Hodgson, who treated as gifts some subsequent contributions from Byron, which were unquestionably loans, and who refused to repay his estate after Byron's death.[37]

Byron gave a farewell party at Newstead for half a dozen friends, 'now and then increased by the presence of a neighbouring parson'. One of his guests, Wedderburn Webster, left in a huff; the dullest of Byron's friends, he was no loss. Byron had hired '*Monks'* dresses', and he had a fine cellar, into which heavy inroads were no doubt made. In consequence, fostered by his allusions to 'Paphian girls' and 'monks' and 'concubines and carnal companie,/And flaunting wassailers of high and low degree', in *Childe Harold's Pilgrimage*, the poem he began five months later, rumours later spread of blasphemous orgies, such as those associated with Medmenham

Abbey, also exaggerated, in the time of John Wilkes. Yet little untoward seems to have taken place at Newstead, other than dressing up and drinking. Matthews, who was struck by Byron's menagerie, among which the bear was prominent, was a homosexual. He would not have been entranced by Paphian girls or Byron's maids, who were probably the only females available; nor, presumably, would 'the neighbouring parson' have been an enthusiastic participant. The Newstead housekeeper, Nanny Smith, later maintained that Byron's friends were not licentious, and Hobhouse confirmed it, saying they did little more than 'drink heavily'.[38]

Not long before he left London Byron discovered that his valet Fletcher had taken his page, Robert Rushton, the son of one of his tenants, to a prostitute, despite his having been given strict instructions to watch over the boy's 'morals'. 'Did you ever hear anything so diabolical', Byron asked his mother, telling her that he was dismissing them both. His rage at Fletcher having taken his page to a whore has been attributed to his having made Rushton his catamite. Rushton was a good-looking lad, who slept in a bedroom next to his master's; and Byron was fond of him – in a will he made before he went abroad he left Rushton £25 a year for life. According to Lady Byron, Lady Caroline Lamb later alleged that Byron had admitted to her that he had 'corrupted' the boy. And there is a remark by Hobhouse which may be rather stronger evidence.

Even so, it is on the whole unlikely that Byron ever 'corrupted' Rushton. For him to have done that to the son of a tenant would have been far more dangerous than any of his other homosexual escapades. Tongues would surely have been busy, and he would have faced exile like William Beckford, Lord Leicester and other homosexuals involved in scandal. Indeed both his own and Rushton's lives would have been in danger. While other countries were becoming more liberal over homosexuality, England was becoming more draconian; the number of executions for sodomy was growing. Astonishingly, between 1805 and 1832, executions for murder outnumbered by less than six to one executions for sodomy. Further, when Byron discovered that Rushton had visited a prostitute, he sent him back to his father, which would have been crazily imprudent had he really corrupted the boy. So the corruption theory is probably wrong.[39]

Byron's frequent guilt over his own sexual activities partially shields him from the charge of hypocrisy when he criticises those of others, yet his rage was still ridiculous. He should have recalled that just before he wrote his letter to his mother he had written some new lines for the second edition of his satire:

> And every Brother Rake will smile to see
> That miracle, a Moralist in me!

Fortunately he soon recovered his senses. Both page and manservant were reinstated and went travelling with their employer. 'Robert, I take with me,' Byron told his mother, 'because like myself he seems to be a friendless animal'.[40]

Hanson finally managed to raise a loan of £6,000 from a Colonel Sawbridge, of which, however, only £2,000 was paid before Byron left the country. He missed the May Malta packet he had contracted to take, but eventually he and Hobhouse departed for Falmouth on 19 June. On their way they changed horses at an inn where William Beckford, described by Byron to Hodgson as 'the great Apostle of Paederasty' and the 'Martyr of prejudice', was staying. Beckford, the vastly rich author of the extraordinary Eastern fantasy *Vathek*, which Byron had evidently already read and admired, had in 1785 been driven out of England for a decade because of a homosexual scandal involving the young William Courtenay. Byron failed to see Beckford, but recorded that Courtenay was travelling 'only one stage *behind* him'. On receiving Byron's letter Hodgson, who had just sent his friend some pious poetic advice,

> Yet if pleasing change allure thee
> O'er the roughly swelling tide,
> May the one great Guide secure thee –
> Byron, ne'er forget thy Guide

may well have feared that forgetfulness had set in even before Byron had left.[41]

Despite being badly flea-bitten in Falmouth, and despite the presence of many Quakers (which might have been inhibiting), the travellers enjoyed themselves. To their surprise, the inhabitants of Falmouth, both male and female, were remarkably handsome. And an exchange of letters between Byron and Matthews in Cambridge suggests that not only Byron but, conceivably, Hobhouse, too, had homosexual encounters with youths. Byron's thoughts certainly turned in that direction. He would write a treatise, he told Henry

Drury, on 'Sodomy simplified or Paederasty proved to be praise-worthy from ancient authors and modern practice', while Hob-house, he added, hoped 'to indemnify himself in Turkey for a life of exemplary chastity at home by letting out his "fair bodye" to the 'whole Divan'.[42]

Naturally he did not favour his mother, to whom, as to Augusta, he had not paid a visit to say goodbye, with such confidences. Mrs Byron rightly thought he should not go abroad with 'his affairs in so unsettled a state' – and leaving Scrope Davies vulnerable – but she must have been cheered to hear from him that he left England without regrets and without wishing to revisit anything in it 'except yourself, and your present residence'. She would have been still more cheered if he had paid the bills for the expensive repairs and redecoration of part of her 'present residence'.[43]

Just before they left Falmouth, Byron sent some cheerful verses to Hodgson:

> Now at length we're off for Turkey,
> Lord knows when we shall come back.
> Breezes foul, and tempests murkey,
> May unship us in a crack.
> But since life at most a jest is,
> As Philosophers allow,
> Still to laugh by far the best is,
> Then laugh on – as I do now.
> Laugh at all things,
> Great and small things,
> Sick or well, at sea or shore,
> While we're quaffing
> Let's have laughing
> Who the Devil cares for more?
> Save good wine, and who would lack it,
> Even on board the Lisbon Packet?

Why were Byron and Hobhouse 'off for Turkey' on 'the Lisbon packet'? Hobhouse's presence is easily explained: he had quarrelled with his father and was in debt to Byron, who wanted a travelling companion. Byron's reasons are more complicated. Turkey was a long-favoured destination. He had read a Turkish history as a child and remained interested enough in the subject to read many others later. But the Lisbon packet was unintended. If Hanson had been able to raise money earlier, the travellers would have been off to Malta via Gibraltar.[44]

Byron had first expressed a wish to spend a couple of years abroad in February 1806. Although he told Elizabeth Pigot in October 1807 of an intended trip with his cousin, a naval captain, 'to the Mediterranean, or to the West Indies or to the Devil', his first specific mention of a journey to the East came a few months later when he told a Harrow friend of his intention of making a 'pilgrimage' to the eastern Mediterranean when he came of age in the following year. The pilgrimage was clearly not urgent, therefore, and Byron did not *have* to leave the country. Much the same was true at the end of 1808 when he told his mother and Hanson that he wanted to go abroad because, if he did not travel then, he never would, and that he had many other reasons for doing so: he might become a politician, and knowledge of other countries would help him; he wanted to learn about Asiatic policy; he had 'no pleasure in fashionable dissipation'; and it would be cheaper to travel abroad than to stay at home.[45]

'I am *dunned* from Morn till Twilight', he told Hanson in February 1809, 'money I must have or quit the country'. If he did not obtain his seat in the Lords immediately, he would sail for Sicily. The urgent need to leave was entirely due to his having no money, his exasperation arising from that and from the delay of his introduction to the Lords. In March in a 'very dismal letter' he told his mother he was 'ruined'. Early in April the urgency was still solely financial. Only later in that month did he strike a strong note of desperation. 'If the consequences of my leaving England were ten times as ruinous as you describe', he wrote to Hanson, 'I have no alternative, there are circumstances which render it absolutely indispensable, and quit the country I must immediately . . .'. Ten days later he was no longer desperate. He wished 'to do justice to his creditors', and was more fed up with Hanson than anything else. Only in a depressed letter from Albania seven months later did he partially revert to his not being able to live at home: 'I never will live in England if I can avoid it, *why* must remain secret, but the farther I proceed the less I regret quitting it'.[46]

And a secret it has remained. What were the circumstances, if any, which made it 'absolutely indispensable' for Byron to go abroad? If we dismiss straight away both any fear of the consequences of his satire – that is to say, one or two duels – and a wish to defraud his creditors, there seem to be five possible explanations. The first is financial. In 1808–9 and again in 1815 Byron did become worried to the point of being almost unhinged by debts, duns and moneylenders. The second (and currently the most popular) is the fear of exposure in some homosexual scandal, probably involving blackmail. The third is the reasons he gave in *Childe Harold's Pilgrimage* for the Childe's wish to leave. 'He felt the fullness of satiety:/Then loathed he in his native land to dwell. . . . And now Childe Harold was sore sick at heart. . . . With pleasure drugg'd he almost long'd for woe,/And e'en for change of scene would seek the shades below'. The fourth is his love for Mary Chaworth: he could not bear living at Newstead with her as a close but unattainable neighbour. The fifth is that there was no great secret: Byron merely wanted to travel and was fed up with England.[47]

His debts were serious enough to make him want to get away from England, but they were far from 'secret' and do not explain his apparent reluctance to return. The fear of a homosexual scandal is implausible for a number of reasons. Such a fear would have precipitated a hasty if not immediate departure; instead, Byron delayed for weeks while Hanson was his usual dilatory self. And had Byron been worried about a homosexual exposure he would hardly have risked promiscuous homosexual encounters with strangers at Falmouth. Finally, if homosexuality had been the cause of his fleeing England, he would surely have given another excuse for his need to leave instead of talking darkly about a 'secret' that he could not divulge. The third explanation amounts to no more than Byron's fits of melancholy; these are undoubted and presumably made him hope that he would be happier elsewhere, but they would hardly have made him desperate to leave, and again were anything but a secret. The fourth explanation is more plausible. While he was at Falmouth Byron composed yet another poem about Mary Chaworth, 'Stanzas to [Mrs Musters] on leaving England', in which he said

> And I must from this land begone
> Because I cannot love but one.

Indeed that was the refrain of the poem. Yet, although she almost certainly provided an additional incentive for his pilgrimage, Byron had been intending to go abroad well before he and Hobhouse went to dine at Annesley in October 1808; and Mrs Musters could scarcely have been the cause of that earlier intention. Hence the fifth explanation is probably the correct one. Byron was naturally restless, wanted to travel, lacked any close ties to keep him at home, was alarmed by his financial predicament, was frequently 'melancholy', knew that abroad he could live like a Lord but was too poor to do so at home, was in despair about Mrs Musters, was infuriated by Hanson's inactivity, and was generally weary of England. Rather than spell all that out in detail, he preferred to make a mystery and a secret out of his departure and exile.[48]

CHAPTER X

Post-University Blues II

Shelley 1811 (aged 18–19 years)

Unlike Byron, Shelley was not entirely alone in London – he had Hogg, Medwin and the Grove brothers with whom he had remained friends – he had not been 'left by his sire', or not yet, and there was no need for him to become 'half undone'. But, because of his father's stupidity and *amour propre* and because of his own arrogance, his expulsion had the effect of severing him from his family and half undoing him. A little common sense on either side would have ended the separation, but it was forthcoming from neither.[1]

Shelley and Hogg arrived in London on 26 March 1811, the day after their banishment from Oxford, no longer needing to pose as heroes. Even in a state of shock Shelley must have realised that his expulsion from Oxford was going to cause trouble at Field Place, and however much he wanted to continue his life with Hogg he should have been able to take the elementary precaution of getting his side of the story to his father and family first; or, better still, of going to Field Place himself.

He did neither. Instead, he took Hogg to see his male Grove cousins with whom they had a rather silent tea. Afterwards he woke up Medwin, whose Oxford career had been even shorter than his, at four o'clock in the morning to tell him breathlessly, 'I am expelled for atheism.' The next day he and Hogg looked for lodgings. Shelley was hard to please – one house was ruled out by the maid's nose, another by the landlady's voice – but eventually they settled on rooms in 15 Poland Street, off Oxford Street; the word Poland appealed to Shelley because of its revolutionary associations.*[3]

So Timothy Shelley first heard the news from University College.

---

* A better reason for choosing that street, had he known it, was that William Blake had lived there at number 28 in the 1780s. But Shelley had not then heard of Blake and probably never read him.[2]

His immediate reaction was to write to Hogg, cancelling his invitation to come to Field Place for Easter. Timothy was right to try to separate his son from Hogg, thus bringing the *folie à deux* to an end. His letter suggests that he held Hogg chiefly to blame for what had happened; if properly handled, therefore, he might have been open to persuasion from Shelley and have tried to induce his old college to lessen the punishment on his son. Indeed even Hogg thought afterwards that if Shelley's father 'had been taken the right way, things might have gone better'. Nevertheless Timothy's letter was ill judged: showing his displeasure with Hogg did nothing to attach his son to himself or to separate him from Hogg.

Still more ill judged was Shelley's belated letter to Field Place, in which he made no attempt to conciliate his father. Enclosing *The Necessity of Atheism*, he complained of 'the late tyrannical violent proceedings of Oxford', expressed not a glimmer of regret for anything he had done, and wholly ignored his letter to his father only a few weeks before in which he had undertaken not to expose his heretical opinions to the university authorities. Timothy had good reason to be angry, yet his reaction was characteristically inept. Elementary prudence demanded that he get his son back to Field Place as soon as possible. He should either have written a sympathetic letter telling Shelley how much his family wanted to see him at home, or have gone himself immediately to London. Instead, apart from his one letter to Hogg, he made no attempt to communicate with the delinquent couple. His attitude was one of hostile inactivity, doing nothing except discuss the matter with neighbours and employees.[4]

Hogg's father, John, was far shrewder. His friend and legal adviser, Robert Clarke, having made enquiries about what had happened at Oxford, discovered that 'the Pamphlet' was foolish but relatively harmless and that there was no danger of a criminal prosecution. Shelley had 'always been odd', he added, 'and suspected of insanity; but of great acquirements'. Recommending that Hogg senior write to his son 'telling him to come home', he added that if that did not work he, Clarke, would 'soon be at his elbow'.[5]

Meanwhile, undisturbed by their parents, the expelled couple occupied themselves in London much as they had in Oxford, writing and reading together in the morning and going out in the afternoon. Hogg says that on one walk they bought Byron's *English*

Bards and Scotch Reviewers which greatly pleased Shelley and was Shelley's first acquaintance with Byron's poetry. That cannot be right since, as has been seen, he had earlier plagiarised it in two poems in *St Irvyne*. And as *EBSR* had been published two years before, Hogg may be similarly mistaken in saying that Shelley first came across it in 1811.[6]

Timothy Shelley did not arrive in London till 4 or 5 April. He then wrote to John Hogg from the House of Commons, suggesting he came to London. Earlier he had sent a message to his son and Hogg 'directing' them to return to their respective homes, which had no effect. Nevertheless Timothy asked them both to dinner at Miller's Hotel on the 7th. Hogg's account of that occasion, at which the father of Shelley's friend Edward Graham was also present, is one of the most celebrated passages in his book. But, although he draws a cruelly funny caricature of Timothy's behaviour, he also, unintentionally, makes the squire of Field Place rather endearing and Shelley and himself unappealing. For Timothy to ask the errant pair to dinner was in itself a sign of friendly intent, and his attempt to convince them of error by reading passages from *Natural Theology* by Archdeacon Paley, whom he claimed to have provided with the book's arguments and whom he called 'Palley', was well intentioned, if pathetic in its naïvety and conceit.* After the wine had flowed, Timothy even made an overture to Hogg, asking him, when Shelley was out of the room, if his son was not 'rather wild'. Hogg agreed and suggested that he needed somebody to look after him; perhaps he should find 'a good wife'. Timothy carefully pondered this recommendation, which like his own question lends some support to Thornton Hunt's disclosure about Shelley's damaged health and its cause. Although Shelley at one moment rudely collapsed with laughter at something his father said, and although they were still far apart on the future, they seem to have got on rather better at the dinner than they did after it.[8]

Maybe thinking he had been too friendly at the dinner, or maybe just having a hangover, Timothy consulted William Whitton, his lawyer. The rigid and narrow-minded Whitton evidently frightened Timothy into being 'firm' by suggesting the danger, in reality non-existent, of a prosecution and highlighting the threat to the squire's

* Paley was an influential and enthusiastic apologist for England's barbarous criminal code, which would have recommended him to Timothy but not to his son if he knew of it. De Quincey thought Paley as a philosopher was 'a jest, the disgrace of the age'.[7]

social position and prestige. In consequence, Timothy wrote a letter to his 'dear boy' in which he pointed to the serious danger that hung over him and stressed that he himself had 'a duty to perform to his own character'. Above all, he added, 'my feelings as a Christian require from me a decided and firm conduct towards you'. After that unpromising start, the squire made his future aid and assistance dependent on his son going immediately to Field Place, not communicating with Hogg, placing himself under the instruction of a man appointed by his father and obeying every order of that gentleman 'for some considerable time'. If his son rejected these terms, Timothy had 'resolved to withdraw' himself from him, and leave him to 'the punishment and misery' that belonged to his heretical opinions. The letter ended with some overwrought rhetoric in which Timothy managed to cram into one sentence three mentions of 'wicked' and one of 'diabolical'.[9]

These parental demands were not in themselves unreasonable. As has been said, the squire was right to seek Shelley's divorce from Hogg, especially as he regarded Hogg – to some extent correctly – as the chief culprit. And his son's residence at Field Place under the guidance of a tutor – in default of a university – was similarly desirable. Yet Timothy's ultimatum was so dictatorially and offensively framed that it invited rejection. Unlike Dr Drury with Byron, and unlike John Hogg and Robert Clarke with Jefferson Hogg, Timothy could not understand that his son might be led, in Drury's words, by 'a silken string' but not 'by a cable'. Shelley was as firm as his father. With an irony which was probably missed by Timothy, he replied that, although it gave him pain to wound his father's 'sense of duty to [his] own character' and his 'feelings as a Christian', he refused assent to his father's proposals and affirmed that 'similar refusals [would] always be the fate of similar requests'.[10]

Having told Whitton that he was leaving 'this young lunatic to [his] management', Timothy went home in dudgeon. Such delegation of the 'management' of his son to his pig-headed lawyer was an illustration, if not a confession, of Timothy's inadequacy. Admittedly he was a frightened man. His brother-in-law Robert Parker, to whom Shelley had earlier sent a copy of *Zastrozzi*, and his nephew John Grove, both of whom had seen Shelley, sent him sensible letters. They suggested that, while his son was not yet ready to accept Timothy's terms, he appeared to be wavering and that a visit to Field Place would probably produce an acceptable arrangement. Timothy's response was to send the letters to Whitton with the comment: 'My answer was that I had placed the business in your hands to guard my character against prosecution in the courts'.[11]

Timothy was wounded as well as frightened. When Parker recorded that Shelley had made 'an expression of affection towards his mothers and sisters', the squire inserted the words 'never to me'. The absence of obedience was still more galling. In those days, of course, sons were expected to obey their fathers who, like General Tilney in *Northanger Abbey*, were 'accustomed to give the law' in their families. Yet, as he had shown at Eton and Oxford, Shelley had no respect for those in authority over him, and that included God and his father.* Timothy was understandably affronted by his eldest son's lack of any sense of filial duty, let alone piety. His other son, John, who was thirteen years younger than Bysshe and took much more after his father than his brother, used to say many years later: 'How could you expect my father to understand a boy like that?' 'The boy' was certainly beyond the squire's comprehension, but even by the standards of a patriarchal society Timothy was being an overmighty parent. His brother-in-law and nephew had both hinted that a softer approach was required; yet he continued his attempt to impose what Stockdale earlier called 'the most injudicious despotism' on Shelley, which even a much less rebellious son might well have resented.[13]

When Shelley forwarded counter-proposals which had been accepted by Hogg's father, Timothy's stance was again characteristically despotic. The proposals were that Hogg and Shelley would not 'obtrude' atheistical opinions on anybody, would return to their homes but maintain 'an unrestrained correspondence' and, when Hogg entered the law or another profession, 'Mr P. B. Shelley may be permitted to select that situation in life which may be consonant with his intentions, to which he may judge his abilities adequate'. The last item was pompously and provocatively phrased, but, as it was not immediately relevant, Timothy should surely have settled for such an agreement, even if it was not entirely satisfactory. Instead he wrote to Mr Clarke that Hogg's father was wrong to agree to 'the proposals'. Indeed, he asked, 'what right have these opinionated youngsters to do any such thing? Undutiful and

---

* In Blake's poem 'To Nobodaddy', God is the 'Daddy' who is yet 'Nobody'. Shelley would not have dissented from that, and would have included his own father.[12]

disrespectful to a degree!' At the same time he told Whitton that he had given nobody but him authority 'to relax from my letter'.[14]

In contrast John Hogg, seeing that the separation of the two boys was the principal objective, had made no attempt to impose unenforceable restrictions on their letter writing. He also used a sensible and moderate intermediary to deal with the matter. Consequently on 16 April Hogg was on his way home. Hogg senior thus achieved success by intelligent negotiations and concessions. Timothy Shelley achieved failure by refusing to negotiate and trying to demand, in the words of his own father, himself an atheist according to his grandson, 'unconditional submission'.[15]

Shelley was not ready to submit, unconditionally or otherwise. His normally dormant mother who had, probably wisely, intercepted one of his letters to his father, sent him money for his journey home. But he returned it and stayed where he was. Shelley behaved similarly when his father, thinking that travel would dispel 'the gloomy ideas' which tended to cause 'temporary insanity', offered him the chance of going to the Greek islands. Such a trip, one of the squire's best ideas, would have done Shelley at least as much good as it did Byron (who in Athens told his mother that 'there should be a law to set our young men abroad for a term'). Regrettably, Shelley's obsession with Hogg led him to refuse his father's offer. By thus treating his parents' olive branches in the same way as he treated their cudgels, he threw away an opportunity of reaching an amicable agreement with his family.[16]

Evidently wanting to free himself from the control that Timothy's financial power enabled him to exercise, Shelley, instead of making peace, extended the conflict. By such legal devices as strict settlements – vesting the legal ownership of a landed estate in trustees so that the apparent owner could not sell it, and constraining future owners with entails so that they could not sell it either – many landed families had maintained their estates and their political power intact since the days of the Commonwealth. When the eldest son came of age or was about to marry, he would agree with his father that the family estates should be entailed on his eldest son. In the next generation the same legal agreement was repeated. In consequence landed property was not parcelled out among members of the family, as in, say, France, but remained in the sole ownership of one heir. Eldest sons thus thrived, and so did the lawyers, while younger sons, widows and daughters were 'sacrificed', wrote Mary Wollstonecraft, 'to the eldest son'. The Dashwood girls in *Sense and Sensibility* are miserably treated by their half-brother and his appalling wife. And often, since a son was needed to cut off the entail, daughters were still worse off if their parents had no sons at all, for then the estate might be entailed on a distant male relative as is Mr Bennet's in *Pride and Prejudice*. 'How anybody', Mrs Bennet with five daughters to marry off lamented, 'could have the conscience to entail away an estate from one's daughters I can not understand, and all for the sake of Mr Collins too.' Such practices were the price of the aristocracy's worship of primogeniture and the continuity of great estates.[17]

Even those eldest sons who thought the system unjust to their siblings were induced to continue the entail by the threat that they would otherwise be kept penniless until their father's death. Godwin had denounced primogeniture and entails in *Political Justice*, and Godwin's disciple thought the system iniquitous. The day after Hogg left London, Shelley told Whitton that he was willing to resign the entail on that part of his grandfather's property which was entailed on him, provided that his father would divide it equally among his sisters and his mother (whom he added as an afterthought) and provided he was allowed an annuity of £100. Shelley was not, at this stage, attempting to give up all the money and land he probably would eventually inherit from his grandfather and father – he could not do that before Sir Bysshe had died and the contents of his will were known – but only that part of his grandfather's estate which was entailed on him. Nevertheless even that was a substantial sum – about £80,000. Shelley's proposal was looked on as an 'insult' by Whitton who sharply told the young man that he had no power to do anything of that kind until he was twenty-one. Yet he would be of age in a little over two years' time and could then jeopardise his father's and grandfather's hopes of establishing a landed dynasty in Sussex.[18]

That Shelley made his 'insulting' proposal suggests that in some moods, at least, he wanted to effect a break from his parents. To flaunt atheism was a rash act of defiance, but to tamper with the sacred rules of inheritance was mutiny; abjuring an entail was a far graver heresy than denying the existence of God. Not surprisingly, his son's plan gave Timothy the shock of his life, much worse than the news of the Oxford expulsion. Shelley's denial of his 'Maker', he told Whitton, abandonment of his parents, and wish to relinquish his fortune were 'sallies of Folly and Madness' which needed to be restrained. Even a landowner less insecure and conventional than Timothy would have been aghast at his son taking such an attitude and might well have had doubts about the soundness of his mind. When one employer paid his workers more than he needed to, his family decided he must have gone mad and tried to have him locked up. In the many years that strict settlements were in existence, Shelley, according to the authoritative historian of English land ownership, was the only man who on principle ever gave up or tried to give up his entail. In that, as in so much else, he was unique.[19]

Hogg's departure made Shelley feel 'a little solitary' in London. Sometimes he got on 'pretty well' by himself, he wrote; at others he shrank from his 'own company as it were that of a fiend'. His solitude was fleetingly mitigated by an invitation to breakfast from Leigh Hunt, to whom he had written from Oxford. Shelley was gratified to find that Hunt had a 'cultivated mind', and he hoped to rescue him from his 'damnable heresy from Reason' – Hunt was a deist. Luckily for himself he did not have the chance to do so, as Hunt did not at this time choose to cultivate him; only later was Hunt able to show himself to be almost as adept as Godwin at relieving Shelley of his money.[20]

Much more important in alleviating Shelley's 'most horrible' solitude were two sisters, daughters of John Westbrook, a retired taverner who had owned the profitable Mount Coffee House – coffee houses were in effect clubs – in Lower Grosvenor Street, Mayfair. Westbrook was a man of substance: he owned land and on his death his personal estate was £60,000. The elder of his two daughters, Eliza, was nearly twice the age of her sister, who was fifteen and a half and a fellow pupil of the Shelley girls in Clapham, where the Shelleys were still economising on the education of their children. In January shortly after his romance with Harriet Grove had been ended by the Groves, Shelley had asked Stockdale to send the younger Westbrook girl a copy of *St Irvyne*. He had never met her, but he was evidently excited by his sisters' talk of her being the acknowledged beauty of the school and probably also by her being called Harriet.[21]

Armed with a letter of introduction from his sister Mary, Shelley had in January followed up his gift of his novel by paying a call on the Westbrooks at their house in Chapel Street (now Aldford Street) off Park Lane, and was able to see Harriet for himself. This first meeting thus took place entirely on the initiative of Shelley and his sisters. Similarly the ensuing correspondence between Shelley and Harriet Westbrook was initiated by him not her. From then on Harriet Westbrook who, unlike her namesake, did not look at all like Shelley – there was therefore no narcissism in his feelings for her – took the place of Harriet Grove as his correspondent and as his chief target for conversion to his views. Initially horrified to learn that he 'was an atheist', she tried to shake his principles while refusing to listen to his arguments.[22]

In the nineteenth century Harriet Westbrook and her family came in for a good deal of posthumous denigration from Shelley apologists and keepers of the family flame. A number of letters and documents presumably favourable to Harriet were probably destroyed by Shelley's daughter-in-law, and other dubious means were used to blacken her reputation. 'Peacock', wrote Mark Twain, 'says Harriet wrote good letters, but apparently interested people had sagacity enough to mislay them in time'. The Shelley family exerted pressure on Shelley's authorised biographer, Edward Dowden, while Hogg had his own reasons – Harriet's rebuff of his clumsy attempts at seduction – for giving spiteful and sneering pictures of her and her sister Eliza.[23]

Nevertheless, there has always been unanimity about Harriet's beauty. When she walked in York in 1811, she attracted the admiration of all who saw her. Like Elizabeth Bennet's, her figure was 'light and pleasing'. She was short but graceful, and had regular and well-proportioned features. Shelley found her eyes 'radiant'. Peacock described her complexion as beautifully transparent: 'the tint of the blush rose shining through the lily'. Her hair was light brown, 'quite like a poet's dream', Hellen Shelley remembered. Hogg thought her 'radiant with youth, health and beauty and Bysshe's peculiar admiration'. She had a pleasant voice and was alert, intelligent and well-educated.[24]

In his letter saying 'this place is certainly a little solitary', Shelley told Hogg that Miss Westbrook – the eldest daughter was customarily thus designated – had at that moment called on him with her sister, adding that 'it certainly was very kind of her', an addition that was misleading. Shelley consistently underplayed to Hogg his affection for, and involvement with, Harriet. Almost beyond doubt, he had called again at the Westbrook house, which was quite near Poland Street, but without Hogg who, when he left London, had never seen Harriet. The Westbrook girls would not have visited Shelley two days after Hogg's departure, had he not invited them or his sisters asked them to do so. They would not have known where he was living, unless he had earlier visited them, or sent them a written invitation, or his sisters had told Harriet where he was. The Shelley girls used Harriet to deliver the pocket money which they hoarded for their brother.[25]

A week later Shelley told Hogg that his 'little friend, Harriet W. [had] gone back to her prison house'. Harriet's school friends would not speak to her and called her an 'abandoned wretch'. Except by his sister Hellen, she was 'universally hated'. Harriet, in her initial horror at hearing that Shelley was an atheist, and her school friends, in their execration of her for consorting with such an abandoned being, were of course behaving exactly like their elders if not betters.[26]

Shelley had soon followed her to Clapham, walking with her and her sister for two hours on the Common. Harriet was 'a most amiable girl', but her sister was 'really conceited, but very condescending'. He soon came to a more favourable opinion of Eliza, with whom he had taken the Sacrament, he told Hogg. Surprisingly he did not see anything odd in that. Shortly before, in the same letter he had written 'let this horrid Galilean rule the canaille . . .'. Yet here was Shelley himself joining the 'canaille'. Presumably the rabid unbeliever, deeply hostile to the Christian Church, did it to impress the Westbrooks. But as they knew his real views – and Shelley had extended his missionary activities to Eliza who was reading Voltaire – they can hardly have been much impressed except perhaps by his desire to please. A few lines after recounting his taking of the Sacrament, Shelley confessed that by encouraging Harriet to go down the road to unbelief he was 'perhaps inducing positive unhappiness'. He then wondered, however, whether trains of thought might influence 'a future state' (i.e. an after life), in which case he was doing her a service. Finally he broke off with the words, 'where am I gotten? – perhaps into another ridiculous argument'. And ridiculous it undoubtedly was.[27]

Evidently sensing that Harriet was becoming a rival, Hogg had told Shelley that he talked 'philosophically' about Harriet's kindness in calling upon him. Shelley replied that she was 'very charitable and good'. Two days later he sent Hogg another long letter in which he did not mention the Westbrooks, 'raved' (his word) against Christianity, and referred to Harriet Grove, which may have been an attempt to put Hogg off the scent of the other Harriet. Immediately afterwards in yet another letter to Hogg – Shelley was corresponding with the same frenetic intensity and lack of balance that he had shown at Christmas – he asked why it was that the moment he and Hogg separated he could hardly set bounds to his hatred of Christianity. A friend thought that 'over-study' had made him 'mad' on religious subjects; maybe so, but evidently Christianity also represented for him everything that was wrong with his family, England and the world. And solitude made him extreme, intolerant and resentful. His father would have put all that down to his 'temporary insanity'; and later, though admittedly in a slightly different context, Shelley himself referred to his 'madness' at Oxford; he might have added 'and London'. His hymns of hate against Christianity were no more rational now than they had been then.[28]

His 'poor little friend' had been ill, and he had been sent for. Her father had been civil, which for some reason Shelley thought strange, and her sister had been 'too civil by half' and begun 'talking about l'amour'. He had then stayed alone with Harriet till 12.30 while her father had a large party below. Harriet, certainly, and Eliza 'with some taming', would help to crush Christianity. They were 'both very clever', and Harriet was 'amiable'. Eliza's behaviour has been taken by some of Shelley's biographers to mean that she was playing the part of matchmaker. But the initiative constantly came from Shelley and at that stage, at least, he was not much of a match. While the heir to a baronetcy and a great deal of land would in normal circumstances be considered a marvellous catch, Shelley was not a normal heir to a baronetcy. The Westbrook girls had surely discovered from St Irvyne and his letters to Harriet, if not from his conversation, that he was opposed to the marriage bond; writing from the Westbrooks' house, where he was spending most of his time, he told Hogg that marriage was 'hateful detestable'. And to be the (probably temporary) mistress of a baronet's heir, especially one who wished to divest himself of his inheritance, was not an alluring prospect even for the daughter of a mere taverner – and John Westbrook was much more than that.[29]

Shelley met his father on two occasions in London that spring. One meeting was inadvertent. They ran into each other in a passage in the Groves' house. Shelley enquired after Timothy's health, to which the squire's only response was to look 'as black as a thundercloud' and say 'Your most humble servant'. Timothy evidently believed that what he called his son's 'solitary confinement' would financially and emotionally starve him into submission. 'I hear he is woefully melancholy', he told Whitton without regret, ignoring the possibility that Shelley might get money from other members of his family, as he did, and diminish his solitude by involving himself with a young woman, which also is what happened. Yet Shelley did want to go home.[30]

The other meeting was at dinner at Norfolk House. The Duke, known as 'the jockey' or 'Jockey of Norfolk – a man of some size' as Byron called him, had not been put off by Shelley's 'atheism': he still planned to bring Timothy's son into Parliament at the next election, when he would be of age, as member for Horsham, a borough over which he had gained full control by paying £91,000 for the Ingrams' property there. Accordingly he advised the eighteen-year-old youth to turn his thoughts immediately towards politics, a suitable career for a man of his ability and station in life. Sharing Byron's view, expressed in *Hints from Horace* shortly before this, of the mediocrity of Britain's rulers, the Duke considered them also to be mostly indolent or devoid of talent; consequently Shelley's chances of success would be high.[31]

Shelley's thoughts had in fact been turned to politics for some time, as his poems and his support for Peter Finnerty and Sir Francis Burdett demonstrated; and he liked the Duke who, like himself, had consistently opposed the Peninsular War and had supported Burdett against the government at the Commons in 1810. In addition Shelley had visited the House of Commons several times with his father, which had given him an even lower opinion of its inmates than Norfolk and Byron. According to Hogg, he regarded MPs as 'wretched beings' and 'animals'. If recently that had attracted him to Parliament, now it repelled him. Norfolk's attempted persuasion, he told his cousin, was intended to shackle his mind and make him a mere follower of the Duke. Admittedly those who represented pocket boroughs were often largely in the pocket of their patron, as of course was Timothy Shelley. Yet that had not put Shelley off when, only a few weeks before, he had told

Leigh Hunt that he expected to succeed his father in Parliament – which he could only have done under the patronage of the Duke.[32]

Shelley's rejection of Norfolk's overtures is another illustration of how far he had travelled in a short time. Whereas previously a political career had seemed natural to a young man not at war with his family, now the conformity it would impose on him to the Duke in Parliament and to his father outside it made the prospect intolerable. His political and personal independence would be lost, and there could be no question of his resigning the entail. He therefore abandoned all thought of a parliamentary career, and decided to become a surgeon.

Although his great-grandfather had been a quack doctor, medicine was hardly a traditional profession in the Shelley family. But, unlike politics, it did not involve shackles or patronage; nor was he too young to start on it straight away – John Keats, who was three years younger, had already embarked on a medical career. Shelley went on hospital rounds with his cousin John Grove, who was a surgeon, and attended a course of lectures on anatomy with John's brother, Charles, who was a medical student. His medical ambition, which was serious while it lasted – until July, about as long as Southey's had lasted in 1794 – was probably fuelled by his own medical problems, real or imagined, as well as by his desire to heal other people and his need for an income.[33]

His rounds of St Bartholomew's Hospital made him familiar, he told Medwin later, with death in all its forms and, quoting from *Paradise Lost*, that in it 'were laid/Numbers of all diseas'd, all maladies/Of ghastly spasm or racking torture, qualms/Of heart-sick agony, all feverous kinds. . . .' And there, he told Medwin, he 'expected it would have been his fate to breathe his last'. As the hospital contained a ward for those suffering from venereal disease, one of the maladies of 'racking torture' he became familiar with must have been syphilis; and that, if Thornton Hunt was right about his health having been 'seriously and not transiently injured' by a venereal disease, or even if he just thought it had been injured, would have been a particular source of 'heart-sick agony'.[34]

Presumably influenced by these experiences and by his hatred of Christianity, Shelley wrote in June his poem *Zeinab and Kathema* in which war and syphilis figure:

> Unquiet death and premature decay,
>   Youth tottering on the crutches of old age,

And ere the noon of manhood's riper day
    Pangs that no art of medicine can assuage,
Madness and passion ever mingling flames,
And souls that well become such miserable frames –

The poem's targets also include God, whose 'blind ire' has defiled the world; Christians who are 'murderous' and worship gold; England, where 'wealth' alone prospers and 'famine, disease and crime' are everywhere; and prostitution, into which the heroine had been driven. Having then waged war against it, she had been executed. Finding her gibbeted body on a heath, the hero commits suicide.[35]

Shelley had a fever for a fortnight in April. Of course his 'fever' may well have been just that and nothing more serious. But it could have been a psychosomatic venereal illness or a real one caused by a visit to a prostitute – Richard Holmes thinks an encounter with a prostitute took place at Oxford or when Shelley was living in Poland Street. That, as we have seen though, might not have been his first such encounter. His horror at his initial adventure – 'the venom'd melody' – and its consequences would not necessarily have stopped him from repeating it. Finally his ravings in his letters make it not unlikely that he was troubled by worries about his health. In *Zoonomia* which Shelley ordered in 1812, the most eminent physician of the late eighteenth century, Erasmus Darwin, wrote that it was 'a very common insanity' among young men to believe that they were 'infected with the venereal disease when they only deserved it'.[36]

The seven weeks that Shelley spent in London did much to determine the course of his life. Leaving for Sussex on 10 May he went, not to Field Place where his father at first would not have him, but to the Cuckfield house of his uncle John Pilfold, who had commanded a frigate and won promotion at Trafalgar. The friendly Captain, whom Shelley thought had 'behaved very nobly' to him, soon persuaded his brother-in-law, whom he did not admire, not only to receive his son but to promise him £200 a year and let him live where he wanted. These were much the same terms as Shelley's cousin, John Grove, had persuaded Timothy to offer in London, but the squire had almost immediately repudiated that agreement. This one, though not cordial, lasted a little longer.[37]

At Field Place Shelley's favourite sister Elizabeth was ill with scarlet fever, and when she recovered she was not friendly and not receptive to his views. A few years later Benjamin Robert Haydon, the painter, was profoundly shaken by Shelley's opinions on God, Christianity and marriage. So young girls like Elizabeth Shelley and Harriet Westbrook were not being schoolgirlish, over-religious or unduly conventional in being similarly shocked. But Elizabeth's defection, her siding with her father rather than with her brother, who had such strong feelings for her and to whom she had been so close, was a painful blow to Shelley.[38]

Admittedly Shelley thought his sister was no more of a Christian than he was, but even to a non-Christian his views on marriage, which were strongly disputed by Hogg, would have been enough to cause offence. As Catherine Byron had found, married women then had few rights. Unless the bride's parents ensured that her property remained in the hands of trustees, her husband had full control of it; and by the standards of the twenty-first century and by Shelley's standards at the time, the position of most wives was heavily subordinate. Shelley's 'anti-matrimonialism' stemmed in part, no doubt, both from his sympathy for downtrodden wives and from his distaste for the Christian marriage service. Yet his remark to Hogg that he 'could not endure the bare idea of marriage even if he had no arguments' suggests deeper reasons: he had surely derived much of his hatred of the institution chiefly from seeing it in operation at Field Place. Evidently there was something eerie in the atmosphere of that household both then and for many years afterwards, which was noticed by later observers, and which affected Shelley and his sisters, though in different ways. Timothy Shelley's despotism was extreme and lasted until his death. Yet, unlike their brother but like their mother, Shelley's sisters did not challenge it. Mary Wollstonecraft would not have been surprised. The mother of Shelley's second wife believed that girls were 'taught slavishly to submit to their parents' as a preparation for 'the slavery of marriage'.[39]

Yet Shelley's detestation of the marriage tie seems to have stemmed not just from observing his parents but from a dread or dislike of living alone with a woman, something which he was to try to avoid in both his marriages. He believed that laws – marriage ones and others – were necessary for ordinary human beings because human nature was corrupt, but for those like Hogg and himself who were 'men of honour', 'beings capable of exalted notions of virtue', and 'who felt the passions of soft tenderness', they were pernicious. So, although Shelley denied he was an aristocrat or any sort of 'crat', his anti-matrimonialism had temporarily and illogically forced him into embracing the idea of a secular 'elect'; he believed in an aristocracy not of birth but of morals. Unfortunately, however, the moral aristocrat had got it wrong. Since many even of these exalted beings would have strayed from a union without the marriage bond, as indeed did Shelley himself even with one, the predicament of the female would have been even worse within the moral elect than outside it. The right way to improve her position was to reform the laws of property, not to abolish marriage.[40]

While accepting her husband's general attitude to the quarrel with their eldest son, in her treatment of him Elizabeth Shelley was far less hostile than the squire. Thinking his mother 'rational' and tolerant and praising her 'liberality', Shelley naturally far preferred her to his father whom he disliked and despised. Nevertheless, his feelings for her were not warm. When the family received an anonymous letter accusing Elizabeth Shelley, who was then forty-eight, of adultery with Shelley's young friend and contemporary, Fergus Graham, her son's reaction was to send Graham two humorous (but unfunny) poems, in which he called his father 'old Killjoy', a coward and a cuckold, and likened his mother to Ninon de Lenclos, a seventeenth-century French beauty who was reputed to have seduced a priest when she was eighty.[41]

Much earlier, when she was a mere fifty-six, Ninon had had to assuage the passion of an insistent lover by confiding to him that he was her natural son. Leaving aside the possibility that Shelley equated his mother with that famous courtesan because he had unconscious incestuous feelings for her, the comparison does not demonstrate much filial love for Elizabeth Shelley. And her son's poem was even more malevolent than it seems if, as is probable, he also wrote the anonymous letter which gave rise to it. As the letter arrived shortly after Shelley had come to Field Place, he could easily have arranged its posting from Cuckfield; later his father was chary of opening letters in case his son was using a disguised script; and nobody else is likely to have made such a far-fetched allegation. His object would have been to sow dissension in the family that was aligned against him or simply to make mischief.[42]

According to his mood, Shelley sometimes teased and tantalised

Hogg by sending him poems about love, hinting that they had been inspired by Harriet, when they had in fact been written well before he had met her; at other times he implied that there was nothing between Harriet and himself. He was still trying to promote Hogg's suit with his sister Elizabeth and to convert her to his own views on marriage, which she sarcastically dubbed 'the honourable advice of a brother;' at the same time Shelley was also trying to discourage Hogg's pursuit of his sister. While he and Hogg were 'inseparable', he told his friend, his sister was no longer worthy of him since Hogg deserved 'a perfect being'. Imperfect though Elizabeth undoubtedly and fortunately was, she retained her good sense, telling Shelley that those whom she had seen and who had seen her had 'some excuse for their folly' in loving her; Hogg had none. Her reproach, 'you and your mad friend Hogg', was a statement of fact as well as an insult. Confirming it by being mad enough not to be put off by Elizabeth's offhand dismissal of his love, Hogg persuaded Shelley to invite him to Field Place. But his surreptitious visit, which Shelley's mother was aware of, was hardly worth the trouble. Elizabeth resolutely refused to see him. All he got was a 'peep' at her through the windows of Warnham church. Even a peep, though, would have been enough to confirm that Elizabeth looked just like her brother. So the otherwise abortive visit did not cure Hogg of his fixation; if anything it strengthened it.[43]

Elizabeth was not the only member of the family to refer to madness. In a letter to Hogg, Shelley talked about his own. After a passage about suicide – 'wherefore should we linger?' – Shelley asked himself, 'why do I write madly? ... Why are you and my sister ever in my mind ... I am going to take the sacrament ... in spite of my melancholy reflections the idea rather amuses me.' Three days later he admitted he had been mad. He then sent Hogg a poem which he described as a mélange of madness, implying that he had just written it, though it had been written a year before. He could find 'an excuse of [Hogg's] madness', because he himself was 'often mad'.[44]

Shelley, who had long had a recurring fantasy of adopting and educating a little girl, asked a friend at Field Place to assist in his plan to bring up two five-year-old girls in solitude without religion. He intended to watch over them as if he were their own father, so that he could eventually discover what the impressions of the world were 'upon the mind when it has been veiled from human prejudice'. Had Shelley read more than a smattering of Herodotus at Eton, that bizarre experiment would not have been contemplated. Herodotus records that, anxious to discover which of the many human languages was the original one, a man left a baby to grow up with a flock of sheep. Returning to it a few years later, he was disappointed to find that the only sounds made by the child were 'baa-baa'. Shelley was saved from similar disillusionment by his friend voicing the weighty objection that the girls' chastity would be later endangered, thus persuading him of the folly of his scheme.[45]

Hogg was not Shelley's only correspondent. Before he left London he had 'arranged a correspondence' with the Misses Westbrook; and to keep his relationship with Harriet secret from his family their letters were sent not to Field Place but to Pilfold House. That caution reduces the significance of the only extant letter of this correspondence. In it Eliza Westbrook adjured Shelley not to tell his sister Mary, or indeed any of his family, about his intimacy with the Westbrooks – for particular reasons which she would explain when they met. This has been taken by many to show that Eliza Westbrook was attempting to entrap Shelley into marriage with her sister. That is of course plausible. But as Eliza, who was not a fool and knew that Shelley was not one either, could hardly have failed to recognise the possible implication of what she was saying, an innocent interpretation is more probable. The point of the admonition may have been to remind Shelley not to tell Mary, who was still at Clapham, anything that might make Harriet's position at the school even more difficult than it currently was. And it was already, Eliza's letter said, so uncomfortable that her father had decided that she should not return there again after the end of the term.[46]

Shelley's third major correspondent was Elizabeth Hitchener, a local schoolmistress whom he had met at the Pilfolds' – one of their daughters was at her school. Miss Hitchener, whose father was a retired smuggler and currently a publican in Brighton, was tall, angular and dark-skinned; she seems to have lacked all physical attraction, but became an innocent victim of Shelley's proselytising zeal and his taste for triangular relationships. After arguments at the Pilfolds', he embarked on a correspondence to convert her to his views on Christianity and the deity. 'Am I being prolix?' he asked her. He certainly was, but Miss Hitchener seems – only drafts of her letters survive – to have been still more so. One passage in her first letter, containing few commas, took 197 words to reach a semi-colon. As he had to both the Harriets, Shelley sent her books, including his 'most favourite poem', Southey's pretentious epic *The Curse of Kehama*. He talked much about adopting 'reason' in philosophy, but he was slow to adopt it elsewhere.[47]

Even the joys of proselytising were not enough to lighten the gloom of Field Place or calm Shelley's disturbed mental state. His mother had become less friendly – understandably so, if she suspected his authorship of the letter and knew of his poems to Graham. She talked to him only about the weather. His sister Elizabeth was alienated and his father hostile. So almost anywhere else would be an improvement on Sussex, and he solicited an invitation from his cousin Thomas Grove to visit his 10,000-acre farm in Wales. As well as getting away from his family, which both his father and Whitton also favoured, such a trip carried two other possible advantages. The Westbrooks had an estate not far away, to which Mr Westbrook had invited him, and he might also be able to visit Hogg, now learning law in York. He would go to Wales on foot, he told Miss Hitchener, in order to observe the manners of 'the peasantry'. In fact he went by coach.[48]

Shelley also told Miss Hitchener that he would visit her in London on his way to Wales, but did not, attributing his failure to 'pressing & urgent business'. He almost certainly spent most of his time with Harriet Westbrook, but at least some of his 'occupation' seems to have been far from urgent. At a time when the country was undergoing an economic crisis occasioned both by Napoleon's Orders in Council, which disrupted British trade with the continent, and by deteriorating relations with America, the Prince Regent had given a fête at Carlton House, where 'wealth' had been extravagantly flaunted in a way that not only Shelley but many others found offensive, even though it cost much less than the £120,000 mentioned by the poet. He wrote a 50-line satirical poem, which has not survived – fortunately, if four lines remembered by the Grove family are any guide:

> By the mossy brink,
> With me the Prince shall sit and think;
> Shall muse in visioned Regency,
> Rapt in bright dreams of dawning Royalty.

He spent some of his time in London throwing copies of it into rich people's carriages instead of visiting his proselyte.[49]

Wales and Cwm Elan, four miles down the Elan valley from Rhayader, were a disappointment. According to the Grove family tradition, Shelley on his visit in the following year delighted in the countryside and was out early and late. But this time, having described the scenery as 'most divine', he went on to say, quoting Hamlet, that it was 'all very dull stale, flat and unprofitable – indeed this place is a great bore.' Cwm Elan House and village are now under a reservoir, but the Welsh Hills are still there, and one thing that the scenery is not is 'flat'. Not surprisingly, it is mountainous, craggy, black and dramatic, which was probably depressing to a youth already in a melancholy state.[50]

Also depressing were his health and the lack of company. He had 'a short but violent nervous illness', and he did not see 'a soul'; all was 'gloomy and desolate'. He had only two things to cheer him up: his correspondence with Hogg and the prospect of seeing the Westbrooks. He told Hogg that Harriet had sent him Amelia Opie's novel *Adeline Mowbray, or The Mother and Daughter*. If Hogg had read the book, he would have realised that the Shelley–Harriet relationship was approaching a crisis. Amelia Opie, the wife of the painter, had fallen out with Godwin and more so with Mary Wollstonecraft, and in her novel she satirised their theoretical opposition to marriage, illustrating in both that book and her earlier novel *Father and Daughter* the pains and penalties of illicit love and unmarried motherhood: social ostracism and financial destitution for the mother and cruelty for her children. Her novel could only have been relevant and recommended to Shelley by Harriet, had he already – in the family tradition – proposed an elopement.[51]

Shelley's health soon improved, assisted no doubt by the thought of life with Harriet.* A 'nervous illness' had a wider meaning then that it does today, including, according to the contemporary writer, Dr Thomas Trotter, 'cramps and spasms', to which Shelley was later much prone, in the stomach, bowels, kidneys and elsewhere. Furthermore the most celebrated surgeon in Europe, Sir

---

* Medical writers from Galen in the second century onwards had recommended sex as a remedy for melancholy. For Shelley the mere prospect of it may have been therapeutic.[52]

Astley Cooper, confided in lectures, which were heard by Keats, that if 'Medical Men cannot ascertain a disease, they call it nervous'. In any case the description that Shelley later gave of himself at this time:

> Then would I stretch my languid frame
> Beneath the wild wood's gloomiest shade
> And try to quench the ceaseless flame
> That on my withered vitals preyed

suggests more than a nervous illness. Even so, much of the pain may have been caused by his fear that he was destined for an early death brought about by a venereal disease. But if he felt that, how, it may well be asked, could he even contemplate carrying off a young girl? The answer is that he was probably advised by his cousin John Grove that his disease (if he had ever had it) was no longer infectious, that it had been satisfactorily arrested, and that in any case it would not affect his wife or mistress. At that time doctors often authorised their patients to continue conjugal relations despite their infection.[53]

Shelley kept his relationship with Harriet a profound secret from Medwin and everyone else except Hogg. And even to Hogg, he did not tell the whole truth because of his peculiar relationship with him. Hence his claim to Hogg that if he knew 'anything about Love', he was 'not in love'.* In fact he did not know much about it and pretty plainly was in love.

Harriet's father, Shelley assured his friend on 3 August, two days after Harriet's sixteenth birthday, had 'persecuted her in a most horrible way' by trying to compel her to go to school. Whatever had made Mr Westbrook change his mind about sending Harriet back to Clapham – he may have thought that school was the safest place for her – to tell a daughter just turned sixteen that she must stay at school was hardly persecution, horrible or otherwise, even if her contemporaries were going to be nasty to her. Evidently to Shelley, however, all schools were 'prison houses' like Syon House and Eton, with Harriet being subjected to 'Shelley-baits'. Similarly

---

* Four months later he was evidently recalling his own feelings at this time, when he reflected to Hogg how easy was 'the transition to the wildest reveries of ungrateful desire!' 'Passion' would urge 'love to its extreme consummation' for 'sensation [was] something terribly strong'. Hogg had been 'terribly intoxicated with passion', and so now, no doubt, was Shelley. But he was not going to admit it to Hogg or even himself.[55]

all fathers were tyrants; Mr Westbrook had become like God and Timothy Shelley.[56]

Shelley told Hogg that he had recommended resistance; to which Harriet had rejoined that resistance would be useless but that 'she would fly with me and throw herself on my protection'. We have only Shelley's word for that, and it is improbable. As the prospect of being sent back to school was unpalatable but not intolerable, Harriet did not need 'protection'. Nor was Shelley well placed to provide it. If Harriet needed to be protected, it was from, not by, an impecunious heir to a baronetcy who did not believe in the marriage tie. Three years later, after Shelley's second elopement, the second wronged and resentful father called him a 'pretended protector' of his daughter and stepdaughter. And with Harriet, too, Shelley was surely her pretended protector.[57]

No doubt, though, he made himself believe that his protection was genuine and needed. In love with Harriet, he wanted love's 'extreme consummation'. But he had a chivalrous nature, and even in his unstable mental condition he must have realised that to carry off a girl barely sixteen without marrying her was an action hard to defend. He needed an excuse to give to the world, to Hogg and to himself – but not to Miss Hitchener. Although he had failed to call on her in London, he had not, despite the distractions of his pursuit of Harriet and his correspondence with Hogg, neglected his impressive indoctrination of another disciple. Having established that religion was 'bad for man', he moved on to politics and morality. If he were a moral legislator, he told her, he would propose to his 'followers that they should arrive at the perfection of morality'. He was shocked that, in London, theatres had been converted 'from schools of morality into places for being the inculcation of abandonment of every moral principle whilst the haughty aristocrat, and the commercial monopolist' united in sanctioning 'depravities'. She would 'always occupy', he had assured her, 'a most exalted place in [his] warmest esteem', and he now saw 'the impropriety' of dining with her or even seeing her. In this high moral atmosphere any mention of Harriet might well have confused his pupil.[58]

The day after his nineteenth birthday an excited Shelley returned to London and paid a quick visit to Sussex, where he borrowed £25 from T. C. Medwin, Tom's father. He did not tell him what it was for, but T. C. Medwin would have known that the loan would not please Timothy. Harriet was still undecided, and it took Shelley another fortnight to persuade her to accept him. While Harriet was havering, Shelley continued to exhibit his ambisexuality or some degree of sexual derangement, writing in one letter to Hogg, '*Your noble and exalted friendship, the prosecution of your happiness, can alone engross my impassioned interest*' – an unusual declaration to a youth from another youth who was hoping to elope with a sixteen-year-old girl. But it was not an aberration. On the following day Shelley told Hogg that, while his own projected elopement 'engrossed' his thoughts and time, it did not so wholly occupy them 'but that you & your interest still is predominant'.[59]

A few days later, on 25 August, Shelley and Charles Grove went in a hackney-coach to a small coffee house in Mount Street near the Westbrook household in Chapel Street. They ordered breakfast, but Harriet was late. Inevitably worried that she had changed her mind or had been intercepted by Mr Westbrook, Shelley calmed his nerves by flinging across the room the shells of the oysters they had been eating. When Harriet eventually arrived on foot, the three of them left in the coach for a hostelry in the City where they spent the day until Shelley and Harriet took the evening stagecoach to Edinburgh. On leaving, Shelley gave his cousin a misleading and insulting letter to his father, demanding his belongings, and requested Grove to post it next day. Timothy had discovered that something was going on and asked Whitton to investigate, but he was too late.[60]

The proximity of Shelley's rendezvous with Harriet to the Westbrooks' house has been adduced as evidence that her father condoned her elopement. But, as Charles Grove was also present when Shelley and Harriet met in Mount Street, the meeting would not have seemed suspicious to other people; and Mr Westbrook's involvement is altogether improbable. Both Shelley and Harriet were very young – Shelley was nineteen and three weeks old and Harriet sixteen and two weeks – and Mr Westbrook, an intelligent and cautious man, would surely not have risked letting his daughter run off with a man who declared that he did not believe in marriage. Hogg maintained, indeed, that Mr Westbrook was 'exceedingly angry' with his daughter.[61]

And no doubt he was. In fact, though, while Shelley was trying to persuade Harriet to elope with him, he had belatedly become converted to matrimony. Maybe he was influenced by Amelia

Opie's novel that Harriet had sent him; more probably he had come to see that Harriet would agree to an elopement only if it was to lead to a wedding. In any case, although he remained 'convinced of the unholiness of the act' of marriage, he had at last realised that dispensing with the marriage bond entailed a disproportionate sacrifice for the woman: 'she who [was] most loved, [would be] treated worse by a misjudging world'.[62]

Two months later, Shelley gave Miss Hitchener his version of why he had married Harriet: he claimed that she had become 'violently attached' to him, had talked much of suicide, and he 'being much affected' by her predicament had agreed to unite his fate with hers. Had all that been so, Shelley would not have had to spend two anxious weeks in London, waiting for Harriet to agree to the elopement; and the truth was very different. It was he not Harriet who had become 'violently attached'; the elopement and his conversion to matrimony were the outcome of a protracted courtship, lasting from January to August 1811, during which time he had made virtually all the running. While waiting for Harriet in the coffee house and evidently thinking of his grandfather who certainly never eloped out of pity, Shelley said to his cousin: 'Grove, this is a *Shelley* business'.[63]

The five months which comprised Shelley's expulsion from Oxford and his elopement with Harriet were decisive for the rest of his short life. They ruled out a fairly conventional land-owning and parliamentary career; consequently, Shelley was a politician *man-qué*. Though deeply concerned with politics and social reform or revolution, his involvement could merely be literary. Those months also perpetuated an estrangement from his family and set in stone the views that he had formed at Eton and Oxford of the prevailing morality, religion and politics of England. In addition they may well have had a considerable influence on his future mental and physical health. The period was for him one of loneliness, rejection, unhappiness and depression, but the end of it gave hope of a happy life with a beautiful and charming young girl.[64]

Byron's post-university period was also one of unhappiness, dissatisfaction and frustration. He was always acutely conscious of his age – in a Memorandum written on his way back from his Grand Tour in 1811 he recorded that he was 'aged 23 years and five months & some days' – and was all the more so in the years between childhood and manhood. As he 'bid adieu to youth', he felt that his 'spring of life [had] quickly fled'; he was similarly conscious of the fleeting hour of love, which was as 'transient as every faithless kiss'. These feelings helped to breed depression and misanthropy, which Dallas noticed and which Byron expressed in his inscription on Boatswain's tomb and elsewhere. Yet, like Shelley, Byron emerged from his post-university interval with brighter prospects: his satire had been a success and he was getting away from England. If only Shelley had accepted his father's offer of a trip to the Greek islands, he could have done so too.[65]

CHAPTER XI

Poetic Madness

Citing Socrates, who believed that provided it came 'as the gift of heaven . . . madness [was] a nobler thing than sober sense', A. E. Housman in the 1930s thought madness could be an asset for a poet, and instanced Blake, Cowper, Collins, and Smart.

Blake claimed to be 'under the direction of Messengers from Heaven, Daily and Nightly', and said he could praise 'the Grandest Poem that This World Contains' because he was only 'the Secretary': 'the Authors are in Eternity'. Southey considered him clearly 'insane'. Yet to Coleridge he was 'a man of Genius' and 'a Mystic', who made Coleridge himself seem mired in 'common-place common-sense'. Blake was never in a madhouse, and rather than being mad he was an eccentric genius who evidently suffered from manic depression. Cowper did spend time in an asylum and twice tried to hang himself. A Calvinist, he believed that he was one of God's elect for damnation; he also believed that in a dream God had commanded him to commit suicide, and that his failure to do so was his unforgivable sin. There is not much doubt therefore about his bouts of insanity.[1]

Little is known about Collins, who with Gray was the most admired lyric poet in the later eighteenth century. But he is said to have run whining like a dog about Chichester Cathedral, and he too may have been what would be popularly called insane – Byron thought both Cowper and Collins 'mad'. Christopher Smart wrote his greatest poem in a madhouse, but apart from heavy drinking and dirty linen the charge against him was his habit of kneeling down in the street and inviting other people to pray with him – something that might nowadays be held up in some quarters as an example to us all. He may merely have suffered from cyclothymia or mood disorders.[2]

Housman's examples demonstrate the difficulty of identifying madness. Even contemporaries differ on people's insanity, and over generations or centuries the meanings of words change. When

Socrates talked about 'madness [coming] from God' he was referring less to insanity than to high emotion, mood changes and divine inspiration, which Schiller called 'the momentary and passing madness that is found in all creators'; in the same spirit Shelley thought Plato's 'praise of poetic madness' in *Phaedrus* 'a wonderful passage'. In the eighteenth century, 'madness' was a broad category with many meanings, and in the early nineteenth century Thomas Beddoes, eminent physician, author and father of the poet who admired Shelley, considered 'mad' a word which could 'mean almost everything and nothing'. Opinions and fashions also change. Dr Johnson thought that 'many a man [was] mad in certain instances'; the father of Charles Darwin went further, asserting that 'everybody [was] insane at some time'. And in 1821 the *Literary Gazette* reviewing Shelley's *Adonais* had no doubt that 'any man, who insults the common order of society, and denies the being of God, is essentially mad'. Today the words 'mad' and 'insane' are scarcely in the medical vocabulary, though they remain in the lay one.[3]

In 1813 Byron told his future wife, Annabella Milbanke, that poets 'rarely' went '*mad*', but were generally very 'near' it; after she had left him, he drew her attention to Shakespeare's lines:

> The lunatic, the lover, and the poet
> Are of imagination all compact.

And he told Lady Melbourne that but for writing 'rhyme' he believed he 'should very often go mad'. A decade later Lady Blessington records him saying that 'we of the craft are all crazy, but I more than the rest'. Lady Blessington knew Byron much less well than she made out, and with her he often indulged in the Regency pastime of 'bamming' and 'humming', i.e. bamboozling, humbugging or leg pulling; and as her book contains much invention and much culled from other books, it is an untrustworthy record of Byron's conversation.* But her account of that one rings true, as does this one: 'I assure you,' said he, 'I often think myself not in my right senses, and this is perhaps the only opinion I have in common with Lady Byron . . .'.[4]

Shelley, too, often referred to himself as 'mad', and he also used that word about Byron. After spending the summer of 1816 with him in Geneva, Byron was 'as mad as the winds', Shelley told

---

* At the time it was aptly nicknamed *Imaginary Conversations* after Landor's book of that name.

Peacock, later telling him that 'the spirit' in which the last canto of *Childe Harold's Pilgrimage* was written was, 'if insane, the most wicked & mischievous insanity'. At much the same time, however, Shelley addressed a more temperate poetic fragment to Byron:

> O mighty mind, in whose deep stream this age
> Shakes like a reed in the unheeding storm,
> Why dost thou rule not thine own sacred rage . . .

Byron was more charitable about Shelley, only once going so far as to call him 'crazy against religion and morality'. Neither poet, though, thought that he himself or his friend should be dispatched to an asylum. Nor, of course, when Wordsworth wrote

> We poets in our youth begin in gladness;
> But thereof come in the end despondency and madness.

did he think that all poets should be locked up. None of them was avowing or alleging clinical insanity; they were using the words 'mad' and 'madness' in the loose contemporary sense of an eccentric mental or emotional condition or extravagant behaviour.[5]

Yet a poet or anybody else can be affected by mental illness without being insane. Kay Redfield Jamison's recent study of the subject found that, of the thirty-six leading poets born in the century after 1705, one half (among them Keats) suffered from mood disorders or cyclothymia, and thirteen (among them Cowper, Chatterton, Blake, Coleridge, Shelley, Byron and Clare) suffered from manic depression. If that startling verdict is anywhere near right, it lends some force to Macaulay's remark that perhaps nobody could be a poet 'without a certain unsoundness of mind'.[6]

Manic-depressive illness tends to run in families. It is not a dementing disease, and, as its name implies, it is strongly cyclical. Its symptoms, which usually do not appear until the late teens or early twenties, include in the depressive phase 'apathy, lethargy, hopelessness . . . a loss of pleasure in normally pleasurable events' and thoughts of suicide and death. In the manic or hypomanic phase the 'mood is generally elevated and expansive (or not infrequently paranoid and irritable)'; also characteristic of hypomania are an exaggerated self-esteem, over-optimism, 'hypersexuality, inappropriate laughter and joking . . . excessive involvement in pleasurable activities with lack of concern for painful consequences', such as indulging in spending sprees and giving away money which the donor does not possess.[7]

Dr Jamison thinks the evidence from other studies also points to a strong relationship 'between mood disorders and creativity', arguing that there is 'a compelling association, not to say overlap', between the artistic and the manic-depressive temperament. The 'opposite moods and energies, often interlaced', of manic depression when joined with poetic or artistic genius 'can become', she believes, 'a powerful crucible for imagination and experience'. In the early twentieth century the psychologist William James, who himself, like his brother Henry, suffered from serious depression and mood swings, thought much the same: 'when a superior intellect and a psychopathic temperament coalesce . . . in the same individual, we have the best possible condition for the kind of effective genius that gets into the biographical dictionaries. Such men do not remain mere critics . . . their ideas possess them, they inflict them for better or worse upon their companions or their age'.[8]

But they are not likely to get into the biographical dictionaries if their careers lie in occupations which impose a demanding routine. Manic depression is clearly less debilitating for a poet than for, say, a doctor, a lawyer or a politician. Indeed probably only one leading British statesman has been a manic-depressive: in 1767 the elder Pitt was described by Lord Lyttleton as having been 'disabled by dejection of spirits almost approaching to insane melancholy'. Edmund Burke, whom Gibbon called 'the most eloquent madman' that he ever knew, also suffered from melancholy, but he held only minor office for a short time and was almost as much a writer as a politician. Since in his view 'measured lines [were] not necessary to constitute' a poet, Thomas Moore thought that 'if Burke and Bacon were not poets, [he] did not know what poesy meant'.[9]

Poets and other artists are not similarly disbarred by melancholy, which may indeed help their creativity. But whatever the artistic uses of manic depression, they carry a heavy cost. The illness often kills or destroys. Its melancholic phase leads to near-intolerable suffering, and its manic phase can be almost equally unsettling. Consequently, however talented and brilliant they may be, sufferers need an extraordinary degree of self-control to maintain the quality of their work and remarkable self-discipline to keep their lives on a roughly even keel. Seventeen years after Shelley's death but many years before modern research into mental problems, his widow described how 'the weight of thought and feeling burdened him heavily; you read his sufferings in his attenuated frame, while you perceived the mastery he held over them in his animated countenance and brilliant eyes'.[10]

Diagnosis of such a disease in people long since dead is difficult and hazardous. Not only did doctors in past centuries use medical terms more loosely than they do today, the type of neurosis from which people suffer does not remain constant. Another difficulty – or so it seems to a layman – is that many, if not most, people have periods of depression and cheerfulness; and drawing the line between commonplace mood swings caused by external circumstances, and pathological ones, that are innate, is not easy. Finally, there is almost an instinctive reluctance to look at great poets or anybody else through a biological glass darkly. Yet, if Socrates was right in saying that 'the men of old who gave names to things saw no disgrace or reproach in madness', there can be no reproach in manic depression which is not even madness. Most manic-depressives are fully sane. In any case there has now been too much research into these matters for it to be easily ignored.[11]

Byron first wrote about his melancholia when he was at Harrow, but his depressions then generally had good cause, such as his dread of staying or being about to stay with his mother at Burgage Manor; and in one vacation from Cambridge he told Augusta, who had noticed a change in him, that he could not pretend to possess 'that *Gaieté de Coeur* which formerly distinguished' him. A year later he considered himself 'destined never to be happy'. That of course would accord with the first signs of manic depression usually appearing in late adolescence.[12]

Yet Dallas thought Byron's frequent 'depression of spirits' was chiefly caused by his 'peculiar position of isolation' rather than 'any gloomy tendency received from nature'. Byron had indeed, many objective reasons for melancholy. His lameness had made him acutely self-conscious, and his mother's taunts about him being 'a lame brat', he wrote in his destroyed memoirs, had caused him horror and humiliation. Although he was fond of his mother, they quarrelled ferociously and were better apart. He had no father, about which he wrote mawkishly in 'Childish Recollections':

> Can Rank, or ev'n a Guardian's name supply,
> The love which glistens in a Father's eye?

That Jack Byron's 'eye' would ever have glistened with paternal love is an improbable thought unless his son had made some money; all the same Byron had reason to regret the lack of a father and family. He had been abused as a boy – 'his passions', wrote Moore, had 'forestalled the future' – and latterly he had scarcely had a home. He had very few friends. His bad foot hampered him from being a man of action. Unlike many landowners, he could not immerse himself in shooting and hunting. Earlier he had enjoyed shooting, although he despised those of his neighbours who thought of little else; latterly, however, probably influenced by Pope's opposition to killing animals, he had come to 'hate all field sports'.[13]

He thus had no apparent occupation ahead of him other than writing poetry, which at this stage he could not envisage as a possible career.* Even much later Byron wrote in *Beppo*: 'One hates an author that's all author', much preferring those 'Who think of something else besides the pen'. He had had an unhappy infatuation with Mary Chaworth and may have been disturbed by his bisexuality or at least by its possible dangers. His great abilities easily exposed the massive hypocrisies of the time and made him dissatisfied with what he saw around him, while what Dallas called his 'impiety' prevented him gaining any comfort from Christianity; Moore thought one of the causes of his melancholy was his 'sceptical views of religion'. Byron himself considered his doubting of immortality 'a disease of the mind', attributing it to his disgust with Calvinism and having been 'cudgelled to church' in Aberdeen. Moreover, like Cowper, he often believed that he was a 'damned soul': and like Childe Harold, 'life-abhoring gloom/ Wrote on his faded brow curst Cain's unresting doom.' In addition, his chronic indebtedness, which was largely caused by his financial stupidity and carelessness, was by itself good cause for melancholy. And finally he was usually on a diet which made him, he said, lighter and livelier but was so severe that Dallas thought it was more like 'starving'. No wonder Aeschylus' *Prometheus* was 'always so much in [his] head', for not only was Byron fascinated by Prometheus' story and fate, but also, as he wrote of that Titan, he himself habitually had 'ceaseless vultures' gnawing his stomach.[15]

While Dallas with good reason pointed to Byron's isolation – 'he felt himself ALONE' – John Galt, a talented novelist who first met

---

* He did not, though go as far as T. S. Eliot, who regarded 'poetry [as] not a career, but a mug's game.'[14]

him in Gibraltar in August 1809, pointed with even better reason to what he called a 'hereditary sullenness of humour'. There was certainly much mental instability in the family. On the Byron side his grandfather once had a disease 'that deprived him of his reason', and his father may well have committed suicide. On the Gordon side both his grandfather and his great-grandfather killed themselves. And there were on both sides many other indications of instability – the Byrons had a double dose of Berkeley blood, and his mother had a violent temperament. Byron himself believed his 'depression of spirits' to be 'constitutional'. He told his mistress Teresa Guiccioli that his 'melancholy was something temperamental', which he had inherited from his mother's family, and that it was 'not constant'. He also believed it ridiculous to deny that we 'inherit our passions as well as the gout, or any other disorder'.[16]

Byron's fits of depression and mood swings were noticed not only by his friends but by people who did not know him well, such as the British Ambassador in Constantinople and Lady Hester Stanhope in Athens, as well as by Dallas and Galt. Writing of the third canto of *Childe Harold* Sir Walter Scott, Byron's favourite novelist, thought that there was 'something dreadful in reflecting that one gifted so much above his fellow creatures should thus labour under some strange mental malady' that destroyed his 'peace of mind'. Dr Millingen, who was with Byron in Greece in 1823–24, wrote that only somebody who had lived with him could believe that a man's temper could assume so many shapes. It might 'literally be said' that 'at different hours of the day he metamorphosed himself into four or more individuals, each possessed of the most opposite qualities'.[17]

Byron touched on his metamorphoses in his poetry. In 1813, J. W. Ward, whom he liked and who reviewed poetry in the *Quarterly Review*, thought these lines, which Byron added in 1811, near the beginning *Childe Harold's Pilgrimage* were a pretty accurate self-portrait:

> Yet oft-times in his maddest mirthful mood
> Strange pangs would flash along Childe Harold's brow,
> As if the memory of some deadly feud
> Or disappointed passion lurk'd below:
> But this none knew, nor haply car'd to know;
> For his was not that open, artless soul
> That feels relief by bidding sorrow flow . . .

A few years later Byron was more explicit:

> The heart is like the sky, a part of heaven,
>   But changes night and day too, like the sky;
> Now o'er it clouds and thunder must be driven,
>   And darkness and destruction as on high:
> But when it hath been scorch'd, and pierced and riven,
>   Its storms expire in water-drops; the eye
> Pours forth at last the heart's-blood turn'd to tears,
> Which make the English climate of our years.[18]

From his Cambridge days onwards, wherever he happened to be, 'the climate' of his mind and moods was always 'English'. Both daily and seasonally his state of mind fluctuated wildly between high spirits (or violent irritation) and deep melancholy, or just feeling 'rather hippish' (low-spirited) as he called his mood in *Beppo*. Having in a late canto of *Don Juan* distinguished 'want of heart' from 'mobility/ A thing of temperament and not of art', he added a note defining mobility as 'an excessive susceptibility of immediate impressions – at the same time without *losing* the past; and is, though sometimes apparently useful to the possessor, a most painful and unhappy attribute'. That was an acutely self-aware and accurate diagnosis of his own condition, which, poetically, was 'sometimes apparently useful to the possessor'. Save when his marriage was breaking up, Byron was rarely called mad except by himself and Shelley, although James Holmes, who painted him, thought that 'at times [he] gave the appearance of a touch of insanity'; and he clearly was not mad. But this inevitably superficial look at the evidence points to him having been afflicted with manic depression.[19]

Shelley had far less mental instability in his forebears than Byron. Against the sheaf of suicides and other abnormalities in earlier Byrons and Gordons, the Shelley family could field only a lunatic great-uncle together with a grandfather who had a dash of insanity. And Shelley never ascribed his melancholy to his ancestry. Although the tragedies of his life occurred in his later years, even in 1811 he had, like Byron, good reason for depression. He had been persecuted at both his schools. Syon House had been so awful for him that he never again talked about it to Medwin and mentioned it to Hogg only when they passed its gates. At Eton he had had the prolonged and terrifying experience of being hunted by a mob in full cry. And he neither liked nor respected his father. 'A Cat in

Distress', a poem which is often thought to date from 1804 or earlier but was probably written between late 1809 and early 1811, contains the lines:

> Some a living require,
> And others desire
> An old fellow out of the way,
> And which is the best
> I leave to be guessed
> For I cannot pretend to say.

The 'old fellow' evidently refers to Timothy Shelley wanting Sir Bysshe out of the way, but it probably also reflects Shelley's own exasperation with his father.[20]

He certainly did not want his ineffectual mother out of the way, though he had no great love for her. But he loved Field Place and his sisters, and was now cut off from both his home and his family. He had been rejected by Harriet Grove because of his rejection of Christianity. Obviously he could gain no consolation from religion, though he could gain some from his anti-Christian missionary activities.* He had been expelled from Oxford and, having spurned Norfolk's offer, now had no chance of pursuing a political career as a Member of Parliament. He had abandoned his second-choice career: medicine. His financial position was precarious, and so was his health. Almost certainly he had worries, justified or not, about being infected with a venereal disease. He may also have been worried or confused by some of his sexual feelings. But it was not just his personal troubles that affected his health. Shelley was a refutation of Dr Johnson's flawed dictum that 'public affairs vex no man'. And the England of 1809–11 contained much to vex him. 'Old Corruption' was rampant. The Duke of York's mistress had been bribed by those who wanted army commissions or favours. The press was subsided and prosecuted. The government was nondescript. Economic conditions were good for the rich and miserable for the poor. In Italy in 1819, a friend of the Shelleys feared that the political state of England was 'very injurious to his health'. That was also true of his earlier years. As an article on the

---

* Religion provided consolation for some, but was a source of madness for others. The leading physician, scientist, inventor and poet, Erasmus Darwin, maintained that Methodist preachers 'frequently' frightened people into madness and suicide; and criticising Methodist 'nonsense, melancholy and madness', Sydney Smith complained in 1808 that 'their piety end[ed] in Bedlam'. A table of the causes of insanity in Bedlam compiled two years later did indeed show that 'Religion and Methodism' accounted for 10 per cent of the inmates.[21]

penal reformer, Sir Samuel Romilly, in Leigh Hunt's *Examiner* pointed out in 1813, many things will 'disturb and agonise [the] feelings' of a benevolent man. Shelley was unquestionably benevolent, and his dislike or hatred of almost every feature of public life in Church and state irritated and depressed him. No wonder he was often what his father called 'woefully melancholy'.[22]

At the same time much of his melancholy was innate. His friends and contemporaries who became his biographers had no doubt that his temperament was unsettled. Medwin found Shelley's moods 'most disturbing to witness' – they caused an utter 'prostration of spirits'. Hogg called him 'fugitive, volatile' and 'of morbid sensibility', adding that his 'natural melancholy' had been heightened by much vexation and disappointment. Like Byron, Shelley suffered from what the American Dr Benjamin Rust called in 1812 'tristimania' (a mania of sadness), which he thought more accurate a word than the one then in common use, 'hypochondriasis', and by which he meant agitated forms of depression. Shelley's melancholy was certainly agitated. In poems composed during his two visits to Wales in 1811 and 1812 he wrote of himself as being in the earlier year a 'maniac-sufferer', and of his 'misery' and his

> time of woe,
> When even tears refused to flow.[23]

Often, as in 1811, his depression was associated with ill health. When he was well in Italy, his widow later wrote, 'his spirits were buoyant and youthful to an extraordinary degree'; but 'ill health and continual pain preyed upon his powers', and together with solitude 'weighed upon his spirits'. Writing of his life in England, Hogg was more cynical about Shelley's psychosomatic illnesses, claiming that whenever he was hard pressed, 'his poetical imagination invented a touching fable of a delicate and dangerous state of health', though in fact his health was 'robust'. Hogg surely exaggerated the element of intention in Shelley's illnesses. If his 'physical sufferings' did not produce his 'mental ones', Medwin said, they tended to aggravate them. And sometimes, no doubt, cause and effect were reversed, as they evidently were in 1811. Depression and illness went together. 'The Retrospect: Cwm Elan 1812', a poem which contrasts his happiness at Cwm Elan on his second visit – 'every gloomy feeling gone' – because Harriet was with him, with his 'overwhelming woe' when he was there alone in

1811, indicates that he had physical as well as mental troubles in the earlier year:

> The sunken Eye, the withering mien,
> Sad traces of the unuttered pain
> That froze my heart and burned my brain.[24]

Shelley was unquestionably subject to mood swings. Medwin thought that at one moment he looked 'forty and the next eighteen'. The year before he died Shelley told Claire Clairmont that his health was 'still characterised by irritability & depression; or moments of almost supernatural elevation of spirits'. And according to Hogg he frequently talked of suicide 'with fervid melancholy fancies'. In his immensely detailed, scholarly biography Newman Ivey White conceded that Shelley had 'what modern psychologists would undoubtedly call a manic-depressive psychology'; but he did not think anything was to be gained by giving the various manifestations of that temperament the 'type name' of manic depression. Since much of Shelley's depression seems not to have been pathological, but caused either by ill health of one sort or another or by disasters in his life which would have depressed even a normally cheerful and insensitive man, that seems reasonable. Furthermore Shelley's moods seem not wholly to fit the manic depression pattern. Finally manic depression is a genetic disease, and there is little sign of that in Shelley's genes. The contrast between the tempestuous Catherine Gordon and the possibly suicidal and certainly unreliable Jack Byron on the one hand and the undeviatingly conventional and wholly ordinary Timothy and Elizabeth Shelley on the other is stark. So the probability is that Shelley was not a manic-depressive.[25]

Yet his behaviour was often decidedly odd. Many people thought him mad or near it. At Syon House he had 'a violent and extremely excitable temper', and was considered at times 'to be almost upon the borders of insanity'. His sobriquet at Eton, 'Mad Shelley', can be disregarded because of the agonising provocation to which he was continually subjected. However, Shelley's paranoid story of his father having wanted to send him to a madhouse and being prevented by Dr Lind cannot be similarly ignored. At Oxford, as has been seen, Elizabeth Grant believed him to have been 'half-crazy', and John Hogg's legal adviser discovered that he had been 'suspected of insanity'. Both John and Charles Grove thought his mind '*unhinged* and strange at times'. His father called him a 'young lunatic', and later in 1811 after one of Shelley's visits to Field Place Timothy told Whitton that, had Shelley stayed in Sussex, he 'would have sworn in Especial Constables around me'. Certainly Shelley's rages were terrifying. Merle saw one of them, when Shelley's 'countenance underwent a fearful change', and said he would never forget it, while Shelley himself wrote in 1814 of 'the excess of my madness' at Oxford. Peacock kept Shelley's rages out of his *Memoirs of Shelley*, but in private conversation he was less discreet about his friend's 'violent fits of passion'.[26]

'At least between the ages of twenty and twenty-three', thought Newman Ivey White, 'Shelley was on the verge of insanity as it is ordinarily recognised.' The only striking aspect of his judgement is the choice of twenty for the beginning of that period, for when Shelley was eighteen and nineteen he was surely just as near the verge. In the 1850s Leigh Hunt and Peacock, the two closest friends who long survived him, declined to write his biography in large part, presumably, because they did not want to damage his reputation by revealing his faults. Tom Medwin, who knew Shelley well both early and late in his life, was less scrupulous and more candid. He was unreliable on facts and dates, but he greatly liked and admired Shelley; and only ten years after his death he would not have lightly written that 'insanity hung as by a hair suspended over the head of Shelley'.[27]

Medwin went on to say that almost all Shelley's and Byron's 'finest things were written under the effects of a temporary derangement'. Medwin exaggerated. But Shelley did have the poetic madness praised by Socrates. As for the other sort of madness he was, wrote Hunt, 'one of those great and rare spirits, who, by a combination of the extremes of intellectual perceptiveness and nervous sensibility, may be said, instead of being the madmen that ordinary judgements would pronounce them, to possess reason itself in excess'. Although Hunt's convoluted remarks suggest some unease on the subject, they can be accepted. 'Reason', Shelley wrote in *A Defence of Poetry*, 'is to imagination . . . as the shadow to the substance'. Of him that was true in life as well as in poetry. Neither his reason nor any other 'shadow' could control his volatile excitable imagination. But while he may sometimes have been on the verge of insanity, he remained like Blake just on the right side of it.[28]

CHAPTER XII

Byron's Grand Tour

Byron 1809–11 (aged 21–23 years)

Under the command of Captain Kidd, dubbed by Byron 'our gallant or rather gallows Commander', Byron and Hobhouse sailed from Falmouth to Portugal. They were supported by Byron's valet, Fletcher, Old Joe Murray, Robert Rushton and a German servant, Friese, who was an 'experimental traveller'. The voyage took under five days, but the sea was rough and both of them were seasick. They had a beautiful view of Lisbon from its harbour: 'Her image floating on that noble tide', wrote Byron. That, however, was almost the only beauty they allowed the city. They found the Portuguese women ugly, Lisbon dirty, and the conduct of its inhabitants despicable.[1]

Such adverse reactions may well have owed something to Whig hostility to the war. The rising of the Spanish people against Napoleon might have been expected to appeal to the Whig love of freedom. Sheridan, breaking with most of his party on the issue, told the Commons that Britain should 'strike a bold stroke for the rescue of the world' and let Spain know that we were 'resolved . . . to stand up for the salvation of Europe'. Napoleon, he pointed out, was there not contending, as he was elsewhere in Europe, against 'princes without dignity and ministers without wisdom' but against a united people. According to Wilberforce, Sheridan was drunk at the time. If so, Sheridan drunk was better than his party sober, and neither his eloquence nor the Spanish rising affected Whig attitudes to the war, which continued to be captious, unpatriotic and defeatist. Like the Prince Regent; some Whigs probably even feared that the popular insurgency in Spain would put dangerous ideas into the heads of English plebeians.[2]

Even so, whether or not the visitors were right about the women, they were certainly right about the filth. An officer, then serving in Portugal, Colonel Roberts, bears out their criticisms. 'The Portuguese, by some odd whims infected', he wrote, 'Have Cloacina's temple quite rejected.' Walkers in the city were in constant danger, as in Edinburgh's old town, of having chamberpots emptied over their heads. In addition, again in Roberts's words: 'It is a fact well known, the Portuguese/ Cherish voluptuously both lice and fleas'. Yet, as the travellers naturally consorted almost exclusively with English officers, many of whom, as Colonel Roberts admitted, 'scandalously' abused Portuguese hospitality, they inevitably gained a one-sided picture of the English occupation.[3]

Four days after their arrival Byron and Hobhouse cheered themselves up by an excursion to Cintra,* a village fifteen miles away which Byron thought perhaps 'the most beautiful' in the world, making 'amends' for Lisbon. The name of Cintra had first impinged on English consciousness less than a year earlier. After Sir Arthur Wellesley, soon to be Duke of Wellington, had heavily defeated General Junot at the battle of Vimiero, some earlier ineptitude by 'old Dame Portland's' government had caused the British Army, in comic opera fashion, to be commanded within twenty-four hours by three different generals, the last two of whom, Sir Harry Burrard and Sir Huw Dalrymple, threw away some of the fruits of Wellesley's victory. By the Convention of Cintra the defeated French were allowed to return home in British ships with their arms and their plunder. Wellesley justifiably complained of 'Dowager Dalrymple and Betty Burrard haggling with [the French] over inadmissible terms and losing a glorious opportunity'. But, as he could not get rid of his successors and as neither of them was fit to command an army against the French, he realised that even such an incompetent removal of Junot's army from Portugal was valuable.

A court of inquiry in England cleared all the commanders of blame. Though thus exonerated, Dalrymple and Burrard were, fortunately, never given another command, while Wellesley, who had been blameless as well as exonerated, returned to the Peninsula.[4]

In England Byron had apparently been uninterested in the war – unlike his fellow poet Walter Savage Landor who wanted the Spaniards to spare not a single Frenchman, and unlike Wordsworth who in his pamphlet *The Convention of Cintra* had condemned the

---

* They stayed the night at Lawrence's Hotel. Later it became almost derelict while retaining a plaque saying 'Pousade do Lord Byron'. It has now been well restored and turned into an excellent hotel by a cheerful and enterprising Dutch couple.

French for their 'pillage, sacrilege and murder' in Portugal. But later Byron was savagely critical both of the generals (including, mistakenly, Wellesley) and of the Convention – 'Britannia sickens, Cintra! at thy name'. In stanzas in the end deleted from *Childe Harold's Pilgrimage*, a poem which, according to a Cintra tradition, he began while he was there but which in fact he began shortly afterwards in Albania, he wrote of the furore the Convention caused in England, and of the generals' vindication: 'And as they spared our foes so spared we them.' Byron was both milder and pithier than Wordsworth who wrote of the 'generals [being] blind . . . to the interests of their country' and of their 'infatuation' and 'absurdity'.[5]

At the Palace of Sefeais in Cintra the tourists thought they had seen the place where the Convention was signed, but despite its name it had been negotiated at Torres Vedras and signed in Lisbon. They were better occupied climbing a high crag to see the 'toppling convent', *Nossa Señora da Pena*, a visit which produced a fine Gibbonian couplet:

> Deep in yon cave Honorius long did dwell,
> In hope to merit Heaven by making earth a Hell.

Byron also saw, this time by himself, the Palace and Monastery of Mafra, ten miles north of Cintra, where

> . . . the Babylonian whore [had] built
> A dome, where flaunts she in such glorious sheen,
> That men forget the blood which she hath spilt,
> And bow the knee to Pomp that loves to varnish guilt.

There he conversed in Latin with the monks, one of whom asked him if there were any books in England. Neither he nor Hobhouse was impressed by the priests of Portugal or anywhere else, and in his second canto Byron wrote a stanza as anti-clerical as anything Shelley ever produced:

> Churchman and votary alike despised
> Foul Superstition! howsoe'er disguised,
> Idol, saint, virgin, prophet, crescent, cross,
> For whatsoever symbol thou art prized
> Thou sacerdotal gain but general loss!
> Who from true worship's gold can separate thy dross?[6]

Together Byron and Hobhouse visited Monserrate, near Cintra, the Palace where 'the great Beckford' had spent two years of his exile, while retaining his seat in Parliament. Now deserted and denuded of the expensive furniture he had bought, it was nominated by Byron as 'the first and sweetest spot of this kingdom'.* Three stanzas of *Childe Harold's Pilgrimage* were originally devoted to Beckford, but as Byron, like Beckford's hero in *Vathek*, was 'not over-fond of resisting temptation', he sensibly cut out the one that spoke of Beckford's 'unhallowed thirst of nameless crime'. That stanza was perhaps as much a guilty reminder to himself of the dangers of pederasty in England as a hypocritical outburst against desires to which he himself was prone.[7]

Though well aware of the public anger at the Convention in England – with some poetic exaggeration Wordsworth claimed that 'the tidings of this event' had 'spread . . . like an earthquake which rocks the ground under our feet' – Byron evidently did not know that it had caused similar outrage in Portugal and that in consequence the Portuguese were in 1809 not feeling particularly grateful to the British. Indeed, although the French Army was by far the more rapacious and had massacred the men, women and children of Evora, General Junot had been 'much liked' in Lisbon, Hobhouse noted in his diary. The Portuguese did not see a vast difference between the two occupations; they felt, as *The Times* put it, not that they had 'recovered their liberty, but had been consigned over to new masters'.[8]

Had the travellers been properly aware of local resentments, they would have been less jaundiced about the Portuguese. Hobhouse alleged that many married women 'were prostitutes for pay which they share with their husbands', adding that 'avarice [was] the reigning passion of the Portuguese', while Byron later described them as 'paltry slaves . . . Who lick yet loath the hand that waves the sword'. Portugal, he added, was a land 'where law secures not life' and Englishmen were 'butchered' daily, a claim which was partly based on personal experience: after dining with J. W. Ward and going to the theatre he and Hobhouse had been 'attacked . . . by four men'. Although his claim had some other factual basis, too, it was exaggerated, and ignored the provocation of much English behaviour.[9]

---

* Like the 'toppling convent', it has been obliterated by a barbarous nineteenth-century edifice seemingly constructed in a Moorish delirium.

Nevertheless, even with diarrhoea and mosquito bites, Byron professed himself 'very happy' in Portugal and 'infinitely amused' with his 'pilgrimage' so far. He had swum across the Tagus from Old Lisbon to the magnificent and still standing Torre de Belém, a distance of some two kilometres, which Hobhouse, probably wrongly, thought a 'more perilous' feat than his famous passage of the Hellespont. He had been seasick but not homesick. Delighted to be free of the tribulations of England, he had no intention of returning home unless compelled to do so.[10]

But it was time to move on; his 'pilgrimage' was to the East. Sending old Joe Murray and most of their retinue by sea to Gibraltar, Byron and Hobhouse rode the more than 300 miles to Seville, attended only by Robert Rushton and a Portuguese servant. Presumably they used the saddles which Byron had bought from J. W. Ward for £30, a sum that was evidently excessive. Although Ward had seen, he later claimed, that Byron 'was a person of no common mind', he contentedly admitted that he had cheated him 'extremely'.* Byron and (probably) Hobhouse wore staff uniforms and had 'orders from the Government', sensible precautions since, according to Hobhouse, 'emissaries of the Junta' tried but failed to seize their horses at Albuera. That village was shortly to be the scene of a bloody and incompetent English victory – Wellington was not there – of which Byron aptly wrote, 'Oh, Albuera! glorious field of grief . . .'; Wellington's verdict was similar: 'another such battle would ruin us'.[12]

The Spanish roads were good, 'very far superior to the best British roads', Byron assured his mother, so that they could travel seventy miles a day 'without fatigue or annoyance'. But the signs of war were all around them, and 'the barbarities on both sides' (i.e. the French and the Spanish) shocking. Byron said little then about the scenery – 'the Sierra Morena [is] a very sufficient mountain' – but a fragment that he later wrote as a possible preface to *Don Juan* suggests that an incident in the mountains helped to inspire that poem: peasant girls dancing to the musical accompaniment of a

---

* Ward did not cheat Byron because he was hard up. Creevey later said of him that he was 'in a state of lingering existence under the frightful pressure of £120,000 a year'. When Ward became Lord Dudley and Ward, his habit of talking to himself in two different voices led to the saying that it was only 'Lord Dudley conversing with Lord Ward'. And on his becoming Secretary of State for Foreign Affairs in Canning's government, somebody said of him that 'les affaires lui ont été étrangères'.[11]

Portuguese servant belonging to two foreign travellers, with French prisoners looking and listening from behind bars, and a Spanish gentleman telling his story to an elderly audience.[13]

Wellesley had entered Spain less than three weeks before the travellers and on 27–28 July was fighting the battle of Talavera while they were in Seville. Both at the time and later Byron was scornful of Wellesley's campaign. Some of his scorn was justified. His line in *Childe Harold*, 'The Grave shall bear the chiefest prize away', was a near-echo of Wellington's remark to his brother that never had there been such a 'murderous battle'. Byron was not far from the truth, either, when he told his mother that in England they would call it 'a victory, a pretty victory! 200 officers and 5,000 men killed all English. . . .' All the same the French casualties were even heavier than the English losses, and Talavera was an English victory, even if, as Shelley's would-be patron, the Duke of Norfolk, told the House of Lords, its results were not 'the proper usual consequence of a victory'. By the time Wellesley got back to Portugal, he had lost one-third of his army; and a few months later the French entered Seville.[14]

Owing to 'the Grand Junta being settled here', Hobhouse recorded, Seville had '30,000 more than ordinary inhabitants', so he, Byron and their servants ended up 'all 4 in one little room' in the house of two attractive Spanish ladies. From them, Byron soon found that 'reserve [was] not the characteristic of . . . Spanish Belles', who were 'form'd for all the witching arts of love'. The night before he left, one of them, who was shortly to be married, invited Byron to 'come to bed to' her, an invitation made all the more enticing, presumably, by Byron's own overcrowded bedroom. But the lady wanted his ring as well, which he refused to give her. The resulting discord was perhaps part of the reason why Byron did not precede her future husband to her bed. Although a few months later he wrote in *Childe Harold* that 'Brisk confidence still best with woman copes', another part of it may have been that never having made love to a lady of his own class – in that very limited sense he was still a virgin – Byron got stage fright.* In any case he accepted a three-foot lock of the lady's hair† while rejecting the

---

* A dozen years later Byron recalled to Sir Walter Scott the 'tremulous anxiety with which one sometimes makes love to a beautiful woman of our own degree', whereas 'we attack a fresh-coloured housemaid' without remorse.[16]
† Hair was considered to have a particular sentimental value in the nineteenth century and gifts of it were frequently not only between the sexes but between people of the same sex.

rest of her. Keeping quiet about the ring to his mother, he cheerfully told her that his 'virtue' had induced him to decline the lady's invitation, an assertion which may have raised Catherine's eyebrows.[15]

Before they left Seville they tried to see the British Minister Plenipotentiary to the Spanish Junta, John Hookham Frere, but he was having dinner. Byron referred to him accurately enough in his prose as 'bewildered Frere' and as 'blundering Frere' in a deleted line of *Childe Harold*. Despite his lack of any military experience, the inefficient Frere had been injudiciously meddlesome and had given poor advice to Sir John Moore, who had succeeded Wellesley, Burrard and Dalrymple as the British Commander-in-Chief. Luckily, Moore, the son of the author of *Zeluco*, the novel which had so influenced Byron as a boy, disregarded most of Frere's advice and misleading information. Even so, he was forced to retreat to Corunna where his army escaped but he was killed. Byron later came to like Frere, who had a vital influence on his later poetry; Frere's poem *Whistlecraft*, published in 1817, revealed to him the possibilities of the stanza form, *ottava rima*, so paving the way for *Don Juan*.[18]

On their two-day journey to Cadiz 'through a beautiful country', Byron and Hobhouse stopped at Jerez de la Frontera, where they met 'a great merchant' who, like Byron, was a Gordon. One of the two biggest sherry producers, Jacob Arthur Gordon Smythe 'was extremely polite', Byron told his mother, 'and favoured me with the inspection of his vaults and cellars, so that I quaffed at the Fountain Head'. The 'I's were characteristic. Referring to a stanza added to *Childe Harold's Pilgrimage* at the last moment, Byron told Dallas that 'anything [was] better than I I I I always I'. But in his graphic letters to his mother on his pilgrimage he invariably wrote 'I' not 'we', and he did not even mention 'my companion Mr Hobhouse' until they were in Albania. Even odder, a dogged but uninitiated reader of the 1813 version of Hobhouse's long-winded book on their travels would have to pass on to page 439 before he discovered that the author's fellow traveller was Byron. Byron is mentioned by name only twice more before he and Hobhouse part on page 1047. In a revised version of his book published forty years later, Hobhouse is much less sparing in his use of Byron's name.[19]

Shelley's widow, Mary, asked Byron for a lock of his hair which she kept in her dressing case until her death, together with the hair of her children, her mother and Shelley.[17]

Cadiz was 'a complete Cythera', Byron told Hodgson; in *Childe Harold* he has Aphrodite fleeing there from Paphos: 'And Venus . . . fix'd her shrine within these walls of white'. But despite the presence of Venus, despite his being evidently as attractive to the women of Cadiz as he had been to those of Seville, and despite his surmise that the Virgin Mary was 'the only virgin' there, Byron had no occasion to summon his 'virtue' to ward off the 'respectable' ladies of Cadiz. That partly accounts for his lavish praise of them. He was almost always most lyrical about his women and boys, as with Mary Chaworth and John Edleston, when the relationship remained 'pure'. In Cadiz, said Hobhouse, Byron 'contrived to fall in love at short notice' – as though that was not a fairly common happening – with the daughter of Admiral Cordova. She offered to teach him the language, but because of the very short time he was in Cadiz their intimacy was largely confined to sitting together at the theatre, and his attending her home to the Admiral's mansion.[20]

While staying in Cadiz the tourists went to see what Hobhouse called 'a bull feast'. Byron was struck by its taking place on a Sunday but, having already attacked Sabbatarianism in England –

> Suppressors of our Vice! . . .
> By whose decrees, our sinful souls to save
> No Sunday tankards foam, no barbers shave;
> And beer undrawn, and beards unmown, display
> Your holy rev'rence for the Sabbath-day

– he realised that all countries had their Sunday 'fooleries'.* And, as with war, he was both enthralled and appalled by the 'ungentle sport'. In a dozen or so stanzas of *Childe Harold* he gives a wonderfully vivid picture of the scene and the drama until what should have been its climax – the contest between the single matador and the bull – is unaccountably truncated. Byron noted, as

---

* At the height of the invasion scare in 1804 fervent Sabbatarians had persuaded many Volunteers to refuse to attend drill on Sunday, as if, wrote the *Annual Review*, 'a special interposition of Providence' would prevent an invasion on the Sabbath. But Byron was chiefly satirising the recently formed Society for the Suppression of Vice. Its predecessor, the Proclamation Society, formed by Wilberforce to enforce George III's 1787 Proclamation against Vice and Immorality, which had been 'no more minded in Town', Horace Walpole remarked, 'than St Swithin's day', had done little. But since then nearly two decades of the new conservative moralism had brought a real change to the moralistic weather, and the new Society was much more active – at least against the pleasures of the poor. 'Any cruelty may be practised to gorge the stomachs of the rich,' wrote Sydney Smith, 'none to enliven the holidays of the poor'. He thought it should be renamed 'A Society for suppressing the vices of persons whose income does not exceed £500 per annum'. In other words the 'Suppressors of Our Vice' were a prime example of the cant and hypocrisy of early nineteenth-century England that Byron later subjected to merciless scorn and ridicule.[21]

have other observers, that at the bullfight the Spanish 'female eye' does not shrink from the blood and gore, 'nor ev'n affects to mourn'. In contrast both he and his companion were seen to shudder and grow pale at the sight of the 'tortur'd' and 'mangled' horses. Still, unlike D. H. Lawrence a century later, they did not stump angrily out: they saw several fights, and they did not profess themselves shocked by the cruelty of the sport. Hobhouse merely observed that an Englishman could be 'much pleased' by the sight of two men beating themselves to pieces, but was disgusted by the spectacle of horses with their bowels trailing on the ground.*[22]

Maybe, nevertheless, the travellers, like some Spanish ladies, found the bullfighting sexually exciting, for after a visit to the theatre they had, recorded Hobhouse, 'a peep into the seraglio, dancing bad'. Probably that only means that they saw a ballet of that name, and the dancing was bad. All the same, Byron's poetry suggests that his 'virtue' may have been in abeyance in Cadiz – Hobhouse's certainly was. In *Childe Harold* the shrine of Venus contained brothels:

> Ah, Vice! How soft are thy voluptuous ways!
> While boyish blood is mantling who can 'scape
> The fascination of thy magic gaze?

And in *Don Juan* the next man chosen to be eaten after the shipwreck was the 'fattest', the master's mate, who was spared only because he had caught a venereal disease from the ladies of Cadiz. Byron caught nothing in Cadiz; so that part of the poem was not autobiographical. But it was founded on fact. While Byron was in the opera box with the Admiral's daughter, Hobhouse sought and found a whore from whom he caught a bad dose of gonorrhoea.[24]

Byron and Hobhouse spent only four full days in Cadiz before sailing to Gibraltar in the frigate *Hyperion*. Arriving next day Byron immediately became depressed. Again that was not just the onset of his 'melancholy'. Although Coleridge had spent five pleasant days there in 1804, Gibraltar is at the best of times a dreary place and it must have seemed particularly so after the joys of Cadiz. Hobhouse described their two rooms as 'very buggy looking and dirty like the rest of this stinking hotel'. Their servants did not reach Gibraltar for another week, which induced worrying conjectures. The delay,

---

* Bullfighting had only recently been restored by the Junta. In 1805 Charles IV had decreed its 'absolute prohibition' partly on humanitarian grounds but chiefly because it wasted the time of agricultural and other workers.[23]

however, had merely been caused by their captain, 'a wretch [and] a detestable Scot', according to Hobhouse, having left over a week late. Byron then sent both Joe Murray and Rushton home, thinking that one was too old and the other too young for the East. Boys were not safe in Turkey, he informed his mother, and he told Rushton's father to deduct £25 a year from his rent for the boy's education.[25]

While dining with Lady Westmoreland in nearby Algeciras, the tourists met General Castaños, who the year before had beaten the French at Bailén. Their two subsequent attempts to dine with the General were not wholly successful. The first time contrary winds prevented them landing, and on the second occasion they arrived too late – a difficult thing to do in Spain – and the last course was already on the table. Even so, the General was good humoured and polite. Byron's wish to see more of him probably stemmed not merely from boredom – he thought 'Gibraltar the dirtiest most detestable spot in existence' – but from dissatisfaction with his lack of an occupation.[26]

'The pleasure of visiting an army', Lady Caroline Lamb's brother wrote a year later from Spain, 'except for a soldier [he was a soldier] I can never understand'. Byron might have said the same. Unlike Hobhouse, he did not mind the discomfort, but being a mere tourist, a spectator of a struggle in which many of his contemporaries were engaged, must have been galling, especially as he had worn an army staff uniform when travelling. Like Shelley he had already conceived a hatred of war – Childe Harold 'loath'd the bravo's trade, and laugh'd at martial wight' (prowess) – but unlike Shelley he was also fascinated by it. Even at Cambridge he had told Long that he hoped to 'raise a corps of cavalry' and see some military service, but found a life 'exclusively devoted to Carnage' repugnant. Yet, like John Donne and other seventeenth-century poets, he did not regard writing poetry as a full-time occupation, repeatedly asserting he had given it up; and recently politics and the House of Lords had not seemed particularly alluring.[27]

So his 'desire for fame' and his 'hope for posterity's praise', which he had confided in verse to the Reverend Becher three years earlier, might be best achieved in the army; and even though he did not then have what shortly before his death he called 'the unmanageable delirium of my military fever', his subsequent exploits in Italy and Greece make it likely that he was tempted by a military career while he was in the Peninsula. The young man who only two years earlier had asked:

> Can I sing of the deeds which my Fathers have done,
> And raise my loud harp to the fame of my sires?
> For glories like theirs, oh, how faint is my tone!
> For Heroes' exploits how unequal my fires!

can hardly have failed to think that he should be fighting, not touring, in Spain. And although he did not know it, there was already a poetic precedent: Landor had recently enlisted in the Spanish Army; but unlike Shelley, who read aloud Landor's epic *Gebir* with such 'tiresome pertinacity' that Hogg once threw the book out of the window, Byron never thought much of Landor's poetry. On his way back to England two years later with his 'affairs' seeming 'desperate', he intended to adjust them, he told Hanson, by joining one of the armies, aiming to get an 'appointment on Lord Wellington's or General Graham's supernumerary staff', which he had been told would be easy enough. That was just a passing whim; in 1809 he was probably more serious, and his depression in Gibraltar deepened because he was a mere civilian.[28]

Byron's lack of military experience would not have been an obstacle to changing that status: in 1812 the memoir-writer Captain Gronow entered the army as an officer 'without any military education whatever', and Shelley's cousin, Tom Medwin, did the same. Nor, probably, would his lameness have been a barrier. Maybe the complicating presence of Hobhouse, together with his own equivocal attitude to British involvement in the Peninsula and his long-felt urge to travel, overcame any military ambitions. He 'should have joined the Army', he told his mother from Gibraltar, before weakly adding that they had 'no time to lose before getting up the Mediterranean and Archipelago'. So the nearest Byron got to becoming a British soldier was to pay a Gibraltar tailor 50 dollars for 'a most superb uniform as a court dress'.[29]

The eponymous hero of *Childe Harold's Pilgrimage* did not land at Gibraltar, and no doubt Byron wished he had done the same. Instead, he had to endure it for over a fortnight – three days more than he had spent in Spain. They then embarked on the Townsend packet for Malta. Among the other passengers, noted Hobhouse, was 'Mr Gault, a Scotsman', whom a year later he suspected of being 'deranged'. In later life Galt was a businessman, who suffered many business failures, and a writer, highly praised by Coleridge as being 'in the first rank of contemporary novelists'. He wrote *The Member*, the first political novel in English, and in 1830, he produced what a later critic termed a 'so-called Life of Byron'. In 1809, however, Galt was, according to his biographer, a nervous, lonely, 'touchy' and disappointed young man, and, according to himself, 'in indifferent health' being 'afflicted with a nervous dejection'. As he was, too, both a snob and an inverted one, Galt was temperamentally less inclined to admire than resent a man nine years his junior, who was already a fairly successful poet and, as a man of rank, the possessor of all the apparent advantages of breeding that he himself lacked. Much the same was true of Galt twenty years later when he wrote his book on Byron. He had just emerged from a debtors' prison, and had read in the books published since Byron's death that the poet had sometimes been less than effusive in his references to his future biographer.[30]

Galt, who had first seen Byron in the garrison library, recounted in his 'so-called Life' of him that, while Hobhouse quickly made himself one of the passengers, his companion 'held himself aloof'. Byron had much to think about. Fortuitous and brief though his visit to the Peninsula had been, both his early and his later poetry prove that it left an indelible mark upon him. Iberia's scenery, its monks, its people – particularly the women – its social conditions and habits all had an abiding effect on a young man who had read widely but had lived in a limited circle in England.[31]

Typically Galt alleged in his biography that Byron had passed through Spain, 'without feeling any sympathy with the spirit which then animated that nation'. Even a cursory glance at the first canto of *Childe Harold's Pilgrimage*, over 40 per cent of which is devoted to the war, would be enough to demolish that charge. Hating the folly, futility and bloodshed of war, Byron saw it as the sport of 'tyrants', in which 'thousands fall to deck some single name'. Shelley expressed the same sentiment in one of his 'Margaret Nicholson' poems: 'oppressors of mankind. . . . For you how many a mother weeps her son'. In Spain Byron conceived a lasting hatred of invaders and unequivocally supported Spanish resistance to the French aggression. In his room at Harrow he had had a bust of Napoleon, whom he admired then and later, though only on the continent; he did not want him in England. But now, because of what he had learned in Spain and Portugal, he characterised

Napoleon as 'Gaul's Vulture', a 'bloated Chief', and 'the Scourger of the world'. Though not hopeful of the outcome, he urged 'ye sons of Spain [to] awake! Advance', and in lines added after his return to England, to win 'for Spain her well asserted right' to freedom. In those more optimistic stanzas – in the intervening two years the war had gone worse for France – Byron was scathing of the Spanish upper classes for letting down those they should have been defending,

> Here all was noble, save Nobility;
> None hugged a Conqueror's chain, save fallen Chivalry!

and admiring of their 'vassals' who 'fight for freedom who were never free . . . [and] combat when their chieftains flee'. He was 'enamoured' of Spain, which was the first oppressed country to arouse his sympathy.[32]

In the eleven days the ship took to reach Sardinia, the 'aloof' Byron spent only one night in the cabin with Galt and the other passengers. 'His Lordship affected', Galt later complained, 'more aristocracy than befitted his years or the occasion'. The touchy Galt was doubtless on the lookout for slights real or imagined; here, though, he was accurate. A dozen years later, according to Lady Blessington, the poet himself remarked that Galt's 'manner had not deference enough for my then aristocratic taste'; Lady Blessington was a friend of Galt's, and probably the words quoted are hers not Byron's. Still, a few weeks after their voyage with Galt, Hobhouse recorded that his companion had given him 'a lecture about not caring enough for the English nobility'. Byron was certainly over-conscious of his rank, yet as his friendships with John Jackson and others showed, his snobbery was variable and intermittent. He liked 'low life'. But on board ship he had some reason not to mix with the other passengers. He was eating and drinking very little, and he was writing 'The Girl of Cadiz', his rollicking tribute to the ladies of Spain and to Miss Cordova in particular.[33]

At Cagliari Galt thought Byron extravagant in his thanks for the British Ambassador's hospitality; Hobhouse considered 'the manners of the women very licentious, so much so that there are no common whores'; and Byron made no comment on the place in prose or verse. The ship left the next day and made a similarly brief stop at Agrigento, which Byron and Hobhouse saw by moonlight, something that Byron always remembered, and where they were the only two passengers allowed to land. They arrived in Malta two days later. According to Galt, Byron and Hobhouse did not go ashore straight away, because they were expecting a salute. If so, their expectation was less bizarrely presumptuous than it seems today. The *Regulations and Instructions Relating to His Majesty's Service at Sea*, established by His Majesty in Council (1808), laid down that, if a 'Nobleman' visited a ship, he might on leaving it be saluted with thirteen guns. In any case the Governor, Sir Alexander Ball, whom Coleridge, when his secretary, had thought 'a very extraordinary man – indeed a great man' and who had been one of Nelson's best captains and a close friend, invited them the next day to a 'family' dinner and, when they could not find anywhere to stay, 'gave [them] a house for nothing'.[34]

Byron was 'very popular with all the ladies', Hobhouse wrote, 'as he is very handsome, amusing and generous', though too general in his attentions. In fact Byron's attentions to one lady were highly particular. Constance Spencer Smith was 'a very extraordinary woman whom you have doubtless heard of', he told his mother; she had had a number of adventures, including a dramatic escape from the French, and had incurred the enmity of Napoleon, but, he continued, her character had never been impeached and she was not yet twenty-five. An Austrian, who was in fact of doubtful reputation and a year or so older than she let on, she was unhappily married to John Spencer Smith, the former Minister to the Sublime Porte and the brother of the other Sidney Smith, the defender of Acre. Both Byron and Hobhouse considered her very pretty, though Hobhouse thought her arms fat. While finding her 'very eccentric', Byron fell deeply in love and challenged an ADC, who had evidently made some remark about her, to a duel. Although Galt sniffed that Byron merely 'affected a passion for her, [for] it was only Platonic', Byron's poems to and about 'Florence' (though not his admiring but tepid stanzas on her in *Childe Harold* by which time his passion had subsided) as well as his subsequent letters show that the affair was far from platonic. Still his claim when writing of Mrs Spencer Smith in *Childe Harold* that he 'was not unskilful in the spoiler's art' was a delusion. He had not yet practised that art, and the affair was unconsummated. Even so, Mrs Spencer Smith, unlike the lady in Seville, was able to relieve Byron of his ring. As the ADC whom he had challenged was 'explanatory' of his offence, and Mrs Spencer Smith was 'chaste' and left for Cadiz, Byron escaped, he told Henry Drury and Scrope Davies, both 'murder and adultery'. It seemed at the time, though, that adultery had only been postponed. The two agreed to meet again in Malta in twelve months' time.[35]

The attractions of 'Florence', which made Byron 'view [his] parting here with dread', and those of Malta's inhabitants, who were 'hospitable and pleasant', were not the only reasons for the tourists lingering on the island for three weeks. They could not make up their minds where to go next. Byron bought an Arabic grammar for a dollar and they took lessons in that language, which suggests they were aiming to go to Syria or Egypt. Yet in his book Hobhouse does not mention either country. Instead he claims that, having hesitated between Smyrna and European Turkey, they decided in favour of the latter through an 'accident': the Governor of Malta provided them with a passage on a warship. That is transparently wrong. They would not suddenly have decided to go to Albania, where, as Byron said, very few Englishmen had ever been because 'of the savage character of the natives', unless they had been asked or persuaded to do so; nor would Sir Alexander Ball have offered them a passage there out of a mere accident. In any case, a fortnight earlier he had advised them to go to Smyrna. Like Hobhouse, Byron was misleading about their decision. 'Circumstances, of little consequence to mention, led Mr Hobhouse and myself into [Albania]', he afterwards wrote, 'before we visited any other part of the Ottoman dominions'. In fact the 'circumstances' were probably of too great 'consequence' for Byron 'to mention'.[36]

Since Bonaparte's extinction of the Venetian Republic in 1797, the control of the Ionian islands, its former colony, had several times changed hands. As the chief British strategic concern was that those hands should not be French, some Englishmen, most notably Admiral Collingwood, decided, after the Treaty of Tilsit had awarded the islands to Napoleon in 1807, that it was time they changed hands again. For them to be securely British, not only did they have to be captured, but friendly relations had to be maintained with the ruler of neighbouring Albania, the murderous warlord, Ali Pacha, who himself coveted the islands. Though nominally subject to the Porte, Ali Pacha, like Mehemet Ali, his fellow Albanian in Egypt, was virtually independent of Constantinople and had greatly extended his dominions to include Epirus and much of present-day Greece – his son Veli was Pacha of the Morea. Earlier in the year Britain had sent Captain Leake to Ali Pacha with guns and ammunition for use against the French and, to keep him cooperative, Britain had indicated that two of the Ionian islands would be his when Britain had conquered them, an undertaking which had been prompted by French offers to him of the coastal town of Parga. Ali did not know that Britain was not going to keep that promise, but he had his suspicions and was anyway an uncertain ally; hence, as a British invasion of the islands was imminent, any opportunity of pleasing him should be taken.[37]

The scheme to flatter the famously bisexual Ali Pacha by sending a handsome young Lord to him was formulated by the former British Consul for the Ionian islands, Spiridion Foresti, and his son George. A brave and entertaining man of Greek descent with an English education, Foresti, who was in correspondence with Ali Pacha and involved in the British plan to capture the islands, must have pleased Byron by his criticism of Lord Elgin for defacing 'many fine columns in Athens' and still more by introducing him, in Hobhouse's words, to 'la célèbre Mrs Spencer Smith'. Byron and Hobhouse were probably themselves flattered to be used as emissaries; and since the Governor of Malta, who had for long favoured an active British strategy in the Mediterranean, offered them a passage to Preveza in a warship, he too, must have come round to the idea. Accordingly on 21 September they sailed for Albania in the brig *Spider*. The British invasion force was only three days behind them.[38]

Ten days later Byron and Hobhouse landed briefly at Patras in order to 'put foot on the Morea' and do some pistol shooting; in the distance they saw Missolonghi. After another two days they disembarked at Preveza in the rain. Byron wrote in *Childe Harold*:

> The scene was savage, but the scene was new;
> This made the ceaseless toil of travel sweet,

In reality Preveza, which had been almost destroyed since Ali Pacha captured it from the French ten years earlier, was the least 'sweet' part of their travels. They were so disheartened by the dreary town, Hobhouse admitted, that they were inclined to return to Patras. In Ali Pacha's palace they were told that one of the rooms was 'for the *boys*'; and three days later they heard, Hobhouse recorded in his diary, that Ali Pacha 'had a *scintum perineum* from making like

Phaedo the most of his youth'. 'Scintum perineum' is very bad Latin, but it seems to have been a symptom of secondary syphilis, evidently caught by having been the passive partner in homosexual intercourse. In his book Hobhouse merely said that Ali had 'a disorder which is considered incurable'.[39]

As well as Fletcher, now their only servant, and a Greek interpreter, Byron and Hobhouse took four Albanian soldiers on the next stage of their journey to guard their convoy of ten horses, whose cargo included three beds and two bedsteads. After passing through 'a country of the most picturesque beauty', they shared a room at a hostel with a priest and four Turks who had been sent to Corfu by Ali Pacha, generally known in his dominions as 'the Vizier'. Each of the ten people in the room slept 'with a pistol under his pillow and yet no fear from intrusion from without'.

In Ioannina, now in north-west Greece, Ali had given orders that Hobhouse and Byron be provided for; he also provided them with an escort for the journey to Tepelenë where he was waging a *'petite guerre'*. The travellers complied, but in their own time, first spending six days in what Byron called 'the capital of the Pachalick', a prosperous city of over 30,000 inhabitants.* As well as meeting two of Ali's grandsons whose 'painted complexions [were] like rouged dowagers' and who were, Byron told his mother, 'the prettiest little animals I ever saw', they dined with the British Resident, Captain Leake,† described by Nelson as 'an officer of distinguished merit'. Leake, a scholar and geographer as well as a soldier and diplomat who knew Greece better than any other foreigner, now had a cold and was cold in manner, presumably out of uncertainty as to what Byron and Hobhouse were doing and worry that they would trespass on his territory.[41]

Travel in Albania was even more difficult than usual as it was both the rainy season and Ramadan. Near Zitza, on their way to meet Ali Pacha, Byron with Fletcher and some of the escort became separated from Hobhouse; they lost their way and were caught in a thunderstorm for nine hours. In a lyric of 72 lines written, he said,

---

* Ioannina, though it is still a thriving and attractive town, is no longer what Byron called it: 'the primal city of the land'. When some years later Bishop Phillpotts showed a country clergyman's wife the view of the sea at Torquay, 'Ah my Lord,' she gasped, 'it reminds one so much of Switzerland'. 'Precisely', said the Bishop, 'except that there we have the mountains without the sea, and here we have the sea without the mountains'. Unlike Torquay, Ioannina with its lake encircled by mountains is like Switzerland.[40]

† Four years before, Coleridge in a fit of despair had agreed to accompany Leake on a mission to seek corn for Malta in the Crimea, but luckily for him the mission fell through.

during the storm, after lamenting that 'Our guides are gone, our hope is lost', Byron's thoughts turned to 'Sweet Florence' who had 'still the power to keep my bosom warm'. When he had recovered from these physical and emotional experiences, Byron found Zitza's position the most beautiful he had ever seen, 'always excepting Cintra', and later devoted five stanzas in *Childe Harold* to it. The 'situation' of 'monastic Zitza' is still 'beautiful', 'the convent's white walls' still 'glisten fair on high', and still 'Ne city's towers pollute the lovely view', of 'nature's volcanic amphitheatre'.[42]

It took them a further week to reach their destination, Tepelenë, in the mountains of what is now southern Albania. Tepelenë reminded Byron of the Scottish Highlands, as did the Albanian Highlanders. In the Vizier's palace they were given 'a good apartment' and a 'bad dinner'. The next day they were received by their host. Ali Pacha, a man of great power and prestige, was insistent on the trappings as well as the reality of dominance; even the British Ambassador in Constantinople, no doubt with his tongue in his cheek, addressed him in such terms as 'Most High, Magnificent and Powerful Prince'. The premier landowner and brigand in Greece, Ali was charming and ruthless, clever and illiterate, sybaritic and violent, polished and barbaric. Similarly his court and palace gave a thin coating of luxurious splendour to a regime of ferocious extortion and cruel despotism, all of which was a heady mixture for two impressionable young men in their early twenties. For Byron, his stay at Ali Pacha's palace was one of the most memorable episodes of his life.[43]

'In marble-pav'd pavilion', he wrote in *Childe Harold*,

> Ali reclin'd, a man of war and woes;
> Yet in his lineaments ye cannot trace,
> While Gentleness her milder radiance throws
> Along that aged venerable face,
> The deeds that lurk beneath, and stain him with disgrace.

In fact Ali, who was short – about Hobhouse's height – and fat with a white beard, stood to receive them, which Byron thought was a compliment to his rank; much more probably it stemmed from Ali thinking that they had been sent by the British government. That did not inhibit him from looking, Hobhouse thought, 'a little leeringly at Byron'. Affable and good humoured, Ali told his guests he regarded them as his children; he treated them as such, sending them fruit and sweetmeats after dinner. During the audience they were served by 'four or five young persons very magnificently dressed' who had 'their hair flowing halfway down their backs'. Ali, who, a French general noted, 'is almost exclusively given up to Socratic pleasures, and for this purpose keeps up a seraglio of youths from among whom he selects his confidants and even his principal officers', complimented his handsome guest on his birth, his small ears, curling hair and little white hands, and was clearly making sexual advances.[44]

On each of the next two days they visited Ali again. On the first occasion he congratulated them on the British capture of four of the Ionian islands, and was no doubt expecting his reward. Byron was over-impressed by the Vizier's claim that he preferred 'the English interest' and abhorred the French 'as he himself told me', when in fact Ali had recently been in alliance with Napoleon and, like most contemporary rulers, always preferred what he believed to be the winning side. Yet Byron and Hobhouse kept their heads: they were not taken in by Ali Pacha in the way that so many intellectuals allowed themselves to be deceived into supporting twentieth-century dictators. Ali, Byron told his mother shortly after they had left Tepelenë, was 'a remorseless tyrant, guilty of the most horrible cruelties . . . Toasting rebels etc. etc.'[45]

At both their second and third conversations, they talked of war and travelling, politics and England, and at the third one the visitors asked leave to take their Albanian attendant with them. This was granted, and Ali gave orders that at the various stages of their journey they should be provided with as many guards as were necessary.[46]

Byron's response to Ali's advances and their visit was to write these lines in *Childe Harold's Pilgrimage*, half of which were not published:

> But from the chambers came the mingling din,
> As page and slave anon were passing out and in.

> Here woman's voice is never heard: . . .
> For boyish minions of unhallowed love
> The shameless torch of wild desire is lit,
> Caressed, preferred even to woman's self above,
> Whose forms for Nature's gentler errors fit
> All frailties mote excuse save that which they commit. . . .
> It is not that yon hoary lengthening beard
> Delights to mingle with the lip of youth. . . .

Childe Harold with that chief held colloquy
Yet what they spake it boots not to repeat;
Converse may little charm strange ear or eye;
Albeit he rested in that spacious seat
Of Moslem luxury the choice retreat
Of sated Grandeur from the city's noise:
And were it humbler it in sooth were sweet;
But Peace abhorreth artificial joys,
And Pleasure, leagued with Pomp, the zest of both destroys.[47]

These lines are suggestive enough, but did Byron (and Hobhouse) make a more immediate response to Ali's approaches? A distinguished American critic, Cecil Y. Lang, claims that the episode in Canto IX of *Don Juan*, in which Catherine the Great takes Juan as her lover, is a disguised account of what happened between Ali Pacha and Byron (and Hobhouse). In other words Byron and Hobhouse were the pathics (passive partners) of the Vizier, and Byron's joke at Falmouth that Hobhouse hoped to make up for his chastity in England 'by letting out his 'fair bodye' to the whole Divan' was an anticipation of what happened at Tepelenë. Undoubtedly there were, as Hobhouse later wrote, 'monstrous sensualities' at Ali's court, and almost certainly, as Hobhouse implied by a Latin quotation from Suetonius, there were 'swarms of catamites' in the palace. But there is no hint anywhere that either Byron or Hobhouse was ever the passive participant in homosexual activity or that they ever liked any males other than youths. Moreover knowing, as they did, that Ali suffered from a sexually transmitted disease, it is well nigh inconceivable that they would have subjected themselves to the attentions of a fat sixty-year-old syphilitic.[48]

Yet Byron's lines do hint that something sexually illicit took place at Tepelenë. In his 'Addition to the Preface' which he wrote for the fourth edition of *Childe Harold* he referred to a page in a book on chivalry. That page describes how a lady, when visited by a chevalier, told the most beautiful of her maidens to 'go at once and lie with this Chevalier and serve him if need be'. Byron's specific citation of that passage gives a far more plausible clue to what happened at Tepelenë than any amount of ingenious detective work on *Don Juan*. Ali Pacha did not sodomise Byron and Hobhouse, but he sent them two of his most beautiful youths.[49]

In lines he added to *English Bards and Scotch Reviewers* but subsequently altered, Byron had claimed to be finished with scribbling:

> And quite content, shall no more interpose
> To stun mankind with poems or prose.

That contentment did not last long. Byron's urge to dramatise his experiences in the Peninsula and Albania would anyway have been strong, if not irresistible, but was doubtless made all the stronger by his realisation that, having failed to join Wellington's army in Spain, 'poesy' was now the only 'passage to [that] Grandeur' that five years before he had told his mother he would 'carve' for himself. Accordingly back in Ioannina after, this time, only a four-day journey from Tepelenë, Byron started *Childe Harold's Pilgrimage, A Romaunt*, which Hobhouse termed 'a long poem in the Spenserian stanza', so-called because the Elizabethan poet had not only used but invented it.

Shortly after he had spent the summer of 1816 in Geneva with Byron, who was then writing the third canto of *Childe Harold*, still, of course, in the Spenserian stanza, Shelley, too, chose it for his poem *Laon and Cythna*. He did so, he told his readers, largely because he was enticed 'by the brilliancy and magnificence of sound which a mind that has been nourished upon musical thoughts can produce by a just and harmonious arrangement of the pauses of this measure'. Byron, though, evidently chose it in 1809 merely because he was greatly impressed by extracts from *The Faerie Queene* which he had read in an anthology he had with him, and partly because James Beattie, whom Byron quoted in his preface to *Childe Harold*, had used it for his poem *The Minstrel*. Although subsequent events showed that it was not the ideal verse form for him, it was almost certainly the best available for his purposes at the time, and certainly better than the heroic couplet, which he had used in *English Bards*, was to use again, less successfully, in his next two long poems, *Hints from Horace* and *The Curse of Minerva*, and for which he later said he had 'not the cunning'.[50]

Although his poem is (amongst other things) about his travels, Byron never mentions Hobhouse in it. Like his letters to his mother it is about 'I' not 'we'. Yet *Childe Harold* features not only the poet or narrator but also an anti-hero, Childe Harold. Byron repudiated the idea that he was Harold who, he claimed, was 'the child of imagination' and a 'most unamiable personage'; he told Dallas that he would greatly dislike Harold's character being identified with his. Certainly Harold, in the poem which the young Keats called an 'enchanting tale, the tale of pleasing woe', is not the whole of Byron, but he is part of him. In 1809 Byron did not know, or even suspect, that he suffered from an hereditary illness. He knew only too well, however, that he frequently suffered from melancholia, and Harold is Byron in his melancholy moods and depressive states. The early stanzas of the opening canto of his poem give a very depressed account of Harold (Byron) in England – he 'spent his days in riot most uncouth' and 'through Sin's long labyrinth had run' – described in archaic Spenserian language. Byron has been much criticised for using these archaisms, although in so doing he was clearly ridiculing – amongst others – Scott and Southey, and his model, Spenser, had similarly used words that in his day were archaic.

At much the same time as Byron began *Childe Harold*, which has its defects but is never boring, Hobhouse persuaded him to burn what Byron called a very exact journal of every circumstance of his life. Byron later said that Hobhouse had thus robbed the world of a treat. Fifteen years later Hobhouse robbed the world of a much greater one. Proving himself the most calamitous literary executor of all time, he was chiefly responsible for the burning of Byron's Memoirs after his death.[51]

Ali Pacha, Albania and the Albanians, and the Peninsular War made a lasting impact on Byron. Of course Greece made an even greater impact, but whereas the Peninsula and Albania took less than four months, the rest of the pilgrimage lasted more than a year and a half and its effects were less concentrated. So, unlike Childe Harold who had 'many a mountain-path to tread,/And many a varied shore to sail along', but like Don Juan, of whom Byron says

> I shall not be particular in stating
> His journey, we've so many tours of late,

we shall now 'get o'er the ground at a great rate'.[52]

On their way back to Preveza where, they recorded, Leake 'did not ask us to dinner', Byron noted the smallness of the bay near Actium where 'Antony lost the world'. Because of the danger of robbers the travellers attempted the next stage of their journey by sea. But after the ineptitude of the Turkish sailors had nearly sunk

the ship and drowned the passengers, robbers seemed less dangerous than sailors, especially as they had been given a guard of thirty-
seven Albanian soldiers. So they went largely by land to Missolonghi, where the British Consul – English-born consuls were rare –
mistook Byron for a new ambassador and addressed him in French.
On the way Byron wrote another poem about Constance Spencer
Smith, 'Stanzas written in passing the Ambracian Gulf'.[53]

From Patras Byron asked Hanson to see that the rents at
Newstead were raised or at least regularly paid. He did not wish 'to
oppress the rascals' but he had to 'live, as the saying is'. True
enough, but he hardly had to buy what he told his mother were
'very magnifique Albanian dresses' which cost fifty guineas each.[54]

On their way to Athens the Grand Tourists stayed for over a
week at Vostitza with Andras Londros, who, though not yet twenty
and a Greek, was the Governor of the district. There Hobhouse and
Byron went out to shoot woodcock. They found none, but Byron
shot and wounded an eagle, which he tried and failed to save. In
consequence he resolved never to shoot another bird. Londros, who
had the face and figure of a chimpanzee, turned out to be a strong
Greek nationalist, and his passionate recital of a Greek version of
the 'Marseillaise' inspired both of the travellers to make translations
of it, Byron's beginning 'Sons of the Greeks, arise'. Londros had
shown them that, however far below the surface, there was a Greek
sense of nationhood. Just a few days later, having crossed the Gulf
of Corinth to Delphi, Byron inserted into stanzas of *Childe Harold*
about Spain's struggle against Napoleon and the attractions of
Spanish women a hymn to Parnassus 'whom I now survey . . .
soaring snow-clad through thy native sky'. After hearing Andras
Londros, he can hardly have avoided at least partly linking Greek
and Spanish nationalism, and thinking that the Greeks might in
time emulate the Spaniards. Shortly afterwards he wrote that there
was a 'fire still sparkling in each eye' which burned for the country's
lost liberty, even though he certainly did not then think that Greece
would win her independence.[55]

On Christmas morning the travellers saw 'a more glorious prospect', in Byron's opinion, than even Cintra or Constantinople, as
'the plain of Athens, . . . the Aegean and the Acropolis, burst upon
the eye at once'. In Athens they lodged with the mother of three
attractive daughters, the widow Macri, to whom the English Consul

usually directed British visitors – her husband had been an earlier English vice-consul. Byron wrote only two short letters in Athens but he finished Canto I of *Childe Harold* on 30 December, and evidently began Canto II immediately afterwards.[56]

Unlike Ioannina, Athens was little more than a large village, containing about 10,000 people in some 1,300 houses; Hobhouse, who, though short, was a fast walker, could walk round it in 47 minutes. Ioannina was also superior, Byron wrote later, 'in the wealth, refinement, learning, and dialect of its inhabitants'. Apart therefore from its situation and climate, there was little in early nineteenth-century Athens to console a traveller for the loss of Greece's 'shatter'd splendour' which had been vanquished by 'Time and Fate'. Having suffered 'war and wasting fire', Athens, Byron wrote in his second canto, was now under

> the dread sceptre and dominion dire
> Of men who never felt the sacred glow
> That thoughts of thee and thine on polish'd breasts bestow.[57]

And religion could not bring solace for the transitoriness of human life and greatness. In a note (later suppressed) appended to some irreligious stanzas, Byron remarked that when people saw that religions fight and succeed one another, they might begin to think that as only one of them can be right, most of them may be wrong. Religion, he further noted, had had less effect in making people 'love their neighbours, than inducing that cordial Christian abhorrence between sectaries and schismatics'. In a stanza based on Lucretius, who evidently appealed as much to him as to Shelley, Byron affirmed that there was no future life and 'peace awaits us on the shores of Acheron'. In addition to death being the end, and human life, greatness and empires all being transient, the stone monuments and embodiments of former greatness seemed scarcely less impermanent.[58]

A war which Hobhouse called 'more than civil' had been raging in Athens over 'my Lord Elgin's pursuits in Greece'. This diplomatic war was between Britain and France over Greek sculpture or, as Byron put it, 'over the privilege of plundering the Parthenon'. When appointed Ambassador in Constantinople in 1799, Elgin had decided to improve the taste and artistic appreciation of Britain by having drawings and plaster casts made of the sculptures in Athens, and to that end he engaged a considerable staff – had he been less mean he could have had the young J. M. W. Turner among them.

Nelson's victory of the Nile and Sir Sidney Smith's defence of Acre, followed by Bonaparte's return to France, which made Britain the dominant power in the eastern Mediterranean, enabled Elgin to defeat the French in Athens. Gradually and without prior intent, his staff began taking not just plaster casts but statues and pieces of the Parthenon as well.[59]

In London Byron had adopted the (temporarily) fashionable and ignorant view that Elgin's sculptures were overrated and greatly inferior to the Graeco-Roman statues that had long been admired. As has been seen, he had attacked Elgin in *English Bards* for bringing back 'Mis-shapen monuments and maimed antiquities', adding in a cruel footnote that 'Lord Elgin would fain persuade us that all the figures, with and without noses, in his stoneshop, are the works of Phidias! "Credat Judaeus!"' (Elgin's nose had been largely eaten away by syphilis).

In Athens Byron had good contacts with both sides of the 'more than civil war'. Soon after his arrival he was visited by Lusieri who was the artist employed by Elgin to make drawings and paintings of sculptures and buildings and who was still living in Athens though Elgin himself had left Constantinople early in 1803. Byron saw a great deal of the talented Lusieri and had a love affair with his brother-in-law, Nicolo Giraud. His relations with the other side were also close if less intimate. He became friends with the long serving and widely respected French Consul M. Fauvel and a French merchant 'of respectability', M. Roque, who was the uncle of the three Macri daughters. Yet his renunciation of the opinion that the sculptures were not much good did not curb his enmity to Elgin. As early as 3 January he was writing of Lusieri as 'the agent of devastation', and he denounced Elgin in *Childe Harold*.

> The last, the worst, dull spoiler, who was he?
> Blush, Caledonia! Such thy son could be! . . .
> Cold as the crags upon his native coast,
> His mind as barren and his heart as hard. . . .

He was even more stridently and humourlessly hostile in later poems.[60]

Byron's attitude would have been understandable had he remained in England. Hobhouse initially talked of 'my Lord Elgin's rapacity' but later came to a more balanced view. The buildings were already in a sorry state, and the one thing certain about the marbles is that if Elgin had left them in Athens they would not have survived there. Elgin was not an attractive character, but if he and, in Byron's words, 'ye classic Thieves of each degree' had not 'pilfered' the Parthenon, the marbles would have been pilfered by the French, appropriated in small quantities by other travellers who might not have preserved them, or been progressively vandalised by travellers and the Turkish Army, as was already occurring daily. So, however distasteful Elgin's methods, his apparent vandalism was in the circumstances of the time a great public service not just to England but to art. John Galt, who was with Byron and Hobhouse when they saw that two large pieces of sculpture had fallen off the Parthenon since their last visit and who was not above doing a little plundering himself, understood that point. But Byron, who prided himself on his cynical realism, never conceded it, preferring to continue with often mere vulgar abuse of Elgin and all his works.[61]

During their ten weeks in Athens, Byron told Henry Drury, they 'topographised Attica', singling out 'the Sunian Promontory' and the plain of Marathon which was offered to Byron. Unlike Coleridge, who believed he would 'walk over the plain of Marathon without taking more interest in it than in any other plain of similar features', Byron was considerably affected by Marathon, but could not afford the mere £900 needed to buy it. For unexplained reasons he did not accompany Hobhouse for a five-day visit to Negroponte which occasioned Hobhouse's first mention in his book of his travelling companion by name:

Lord Byron was unexpectedly detained at Athens; so that any additional defects in the narrative of this short tour must be attributed to the absence of my companion, who, to quickness of observation and ingenuity of remark, united that gay good humour which keeps alive the attention under the pressure of fatigue and softens the aspect of every difficulty and danger.

John Galt, whose ego had perhaps been assuaged by Byron and Hobhouse calling on him two days after his arrival in Athens and then riding with him on several trips, also testified to Byron being an exceptionally amusing companion.[62]

As recently as the middle of November Byron had written of 'fair Florence' that he 'would not lose thee for a world'. Two months later in Athens, however, 'The spell is broke, the charm is flown'. As well as 'life's fitful power', the spell breakers were the girls living in the house in which he lodged. According to a traveller, who stayed with the widow Macri two years after Byron, it was considered 'a sort of duty for English travellers to fall in love with one of the daughters'. If Teresa, the youngest who was twelve, was the model for Byron's poem 'Maid of Athens, ere we part', Byron did perhaps do his 'duty', though Galt was sceptical, believing Byron's passion to be 'equally innocent and poetical'. And if Galt's description of Teresa as a 'pale and pensive looking girl with regular Grecian features' is accurate, she sounds very different from 'Spain's dark-glancing daughters' whom Byron extolled in *Childe Harold* and not at all like his sort of woman. From Constantinople he light-heartedly wrote to Drury that he was 'dying for love of three girls at Athens', two of whom had promised to accompany him to England. He did put them into the Sultan's harem in *Don Juan*, but that was as far as the affair probably went. Their mother was disappointed. She was 'mad enough to imagine', Byron told Hobhouse, that he 'was going to marry the girl'. But he had 'better amusement', by which he probably meant boys in general, and Nicolo Giraud in particular.[63]

Happy in Athens, where Byron found the climate 'a perpetual spring', he and Hobhouse were surprised to be offered a passage to Smyrna by a naval captain, but accepted it. They stayed in Smyrna for five weeks with the hospitable British Consul-General, Francis Wherry, the interior of whose house, Hobhouse thought, was worthy of London. Commercially Smyrna was the most 'consider-able city of the Turkish Empire', but because of frequent earth-quakes and other calamities, that was its only distinction. Soon, therefore, the tourists journeyed to Ephesus, but Ephesus, too, was a disappointment. One of the Seven Wonders of the World, the Temple of Diana, had almost entirely disappeared, and jackals howled in the ruins. With nobody living in what had been Ephesus, and only four Christians living even in the vicinity, St Paul, Byron pointed out, had no call 'to epistolise the present brood of Ephesians'. In Smyrna he was depressed, still having received no money from Hanson, and told his mother that he did not have the courage to write her (or anybody else) a long letter. He did, however, finish the second canto of *Childe Harold*. Offered a passage to Constantinople on a frigate, HMS *Salsette*, on its way to fetch the British Ambassador, Robert Adair, the travellers were keen to accept. Byron had had his usual effect on the ladies. 'B tells me', recorded Hobhouse, that the Consul's wife 'actually cut off a lock of his hair. I saw', Hobhouse went on, 'her cry at parting – pretty well at 56 years at least.'[64]

After a day's sailing the *Salsette* anchored at Tenedos just south of the Dardanelles. No warship was allowed to enter the straits without permission from the Turks, and only one British ship of war was allowed through them at a time. This Ottoman caution was understandable. After war had broken out between Turkey and Russia in 1806, Britain, frightened by the prospect of a Franco-Turkish alliance and anxious to support her ally Russia, had declared war on Turkey. A British fleet under Sir Sidney Smith then forced the Dardanelles and destroyed a Turkish squadron before anchoring at Constantinople. When it withdrew shortly afterwards, the British fleet in turn suffered heavy damage. Britain's declaration of war and attack were singularly ill-timed. For one thing Napoleon and Russia shortly afterwards made peace at Tilsit with the result that Britain soon found herself in the ridiculous position of being at war with both the belligerents, Turkey and Russia. For another, 1807 was the year in which Napoleon wrote: 'I find that providence has decreed that the Turkish Empire cannot survive any longer'. Seeing himself as providence, Napoleon was unlikely to make a prolonged alliance with a doomed power. Thus Britain clearly had to make peace with Constantinople and, with the help of Ali Pacha, Robert Adair had eventually negotiated and signed the Treaty of the Dardanelles in January 1809.[65]

While waiting for permission from the Porte, Byron and Hobhouse landed every day and visited the Troad. Byron enjoyed himself reading Pope's translation of the *Iliad* on what, contrary to the fashionable opinion of the day, he rightly believed to be the site of the Trojan war. Even more did he enjoy swimming the Hellespont at the second attempt. It took him one hour ten minutes, five minutes more than Lieutenant Ekenhead of the Marines who had entered the water at the same time and to whom he presented a gold watch. Unlike Leander's, Byron's swim was a single not a return journey, but it was an emulation of a legendary hero and a considerable feat – especially by a man with a deformity – of which he was immensely proud. It earned him his second mention by name in Hobhouse's book.[66]

His successful swim revived Byron's letter writing. It was an exploit of which he took 'care to boast', he told his mother. She, Henry Drury, Hodgson and even Dallas, to whom he expressed regret that he had had 'no mistress to comfort [him] at landing', all learned of his feat in long letters from Constantinople. And while still on the way there he wrote, 'Written after swimming from Sestos to Abydos May 9, 1810'. In Constantinople he and Hobhouse for the first fortnight dined at the Ambassador's table where they met the First Secretary, Stratford Canning, who had played for Eton against Byron in the 1805 cricket match and had not forgotten the impression made by his appearance. He later wrote of his agreeable recollection of Byron: 'Good . . . and varied conversation'. On other occasions the travellers kept less exalted company. At 'a wine house' Hobhouse saw, he wrote in his diary, 'a boy dancing in a style indescribably beastly'. Hobhouse preferred taking his pleasures sadly. Two days later he records going 'with Byron and a party' to similar 'wine houses' and seeing 'two old and ugly boys' dance. After the performance, when Hobhouse asked if these boys would not be hanged in England, a janissary told them, 'Oh yes, directly. De Turk take and bugger dem d'ye see?' Probably the party did not ape 'De Turk', but if they did they were in good company. Casanova evidently had a homosexual experience in Constantinople.[67]

In Constantinople Byron did at last receive a remittance from Hanson. He was further cheered by a ride round the city's walls. He had never 'beheld a work of nature or art', he told his mother, equal to what he had seen there. At the end of the same letter Byron, the moralist, reappeared. He would not allow his Newstead tenants a privilege he did not permit himself, 'that of debauching each other's daughters'. (He only debauched his own housemaids.) Byron was probably right in thinking that the man in question should marry the girl he had 'debauched', but the recrudescence of 'That miracle, a Moralist in me' showed how young in some ways he was. His moralising did not accord either with his own behaviour or with his other – often brilliant – letters written at much the same time. 'I am tolerably sick of vice which I have tried in its agreeable varieties', he told Hodgson before adding, perhaps in deference to Hodgson's earlier poetic advice, 'and mean on my return to cut all my dissolute acquaintance'. In less of a reforming mood he informed Drury that in England the vices in fashion were 'whoring and drinking, in Turkey sodomy and smoking, we prefer a girl and a bottle, they a pipe and a pathic'.[68]

A month before his letter to his mother proscribing immorality at

Newstead, Byron had exhibited his immaturity in public. Invited by the Ambassador with other Englishmen to join his procession when he took leave of a high Turkish official, Byron and Hobhouse duly arrived in their regimentals. But when Byron found that his peerage gave him no precedence and he would have to walk behind Stratford Canning, he refused, flounced off and sulked for three days. Yet only eighteen months earlier he had told his tutor at Trinity that the man who 'assumed a false Consequence from *title* only' was '*very low* in the *Scale* of *human beings*'. Even after he had been appeased by a special invitation from Robert Adair to dine on the King's birthday, he still had not learned his lesson. When further invited by Adair to attend his ritual departure from the Sultan, and warned that again he would have no precedence, he did not accept the invitation until he had contacted the highest authority on protocol. When that gentleman ruled against him, Byron in a letter of apology to the Ambassador did admit that he had been wrong and undertook to atone, cheerfully misquoting Shakespeare, by following 'not only your excellency "but your servant or your maid, your ox or your ass, or anything that is yours"'. He kept that undertaking. During the almost interminable ceremonies Byron shone in his staff uniform, 'delighting', according to Stafford Canning who was critical of his earlier behaviour, 'those who were nearest to him by his well-bred cheerfulness and good humoured wit'.[69]

His preceding ill-bred conduct, or what Moore called his 'jealous pride of rank', had a number of causes. His remembrance of poverty in Aberdeen, the knowledge that he was an abnormally poor peer, the indifference of his 'noble' guardian, and his awareness of his mother's vulgarity combined to make him almost as socially insecure as Timothy Shelley. Moreover in that age there was an often obsessive preoccupation with social status, with precedence, with decorations – Lord Elgin delayed the departure from England of his ship to Constantinople while he applied to fill a vacancy in the Order of the Thistle – and with mounting the peerage ladder from Baron to Viscount or Earl to Marquess. Even so, if Byron could see through the cant of the age, he should have been able to do the same with its snobbery, thereby following the advice of Lord Chesterfield, whom he had read but evidently not digested: 'Never be proud of your rank or birth', Chesterfield admonished his son, 'but be as proud as you please of your character.'*[70]

Another cause of Byron making a fool of himself over precedence was his depression. On the ship taking him home, Robert Adair thought Byron was 'labouring under great dejection of spirits'. Presumably he was in the depressed phase of his manic depression, but that was probably accentuated by other trouble. Galt thought he had detected a deterioration in Byron's character, brought on by his money worries. Although Hanson had not sent a letter with the remittance, the news of his affairs was bad. His mother was desperately worried by the threat of creditors stripping Newstead to recover their money. In addition he was bored in Constantinople. The Turks did not mix with foreigners, so his company was mainly English. He had intended to continue *Childe Harold*, but then gave up the idea; idleness always lowered his spirits. And finally he did not know where to go to next. He told Drury that his stay depended on his 'caprice', that he was 'quicksilver' and could 'say nothing positively', none of which would have surprised Elizabeth Pigot, who wrote that he never knew 'his own mind for ten minutes together'.[72]

Hobhouse, meanwhile, was returning home. His keeping of the accounts produced the calculation that he owed Byron nearly £900, which he thought was enough, especially as he could not repay it. Byron dismissed the idea, but Hobhouse doubtless reckoned it was time to get on with his life. Before he left England, Byron had told Augusta that he could not 'bear the company of his best friend above a month'. He now told his mother that a year's experience of Hobhouse had made him sick of travelling companions. To Scrope Davies he was even less complimentary: though he liked Hobhouse and always would, 'that amiable soul' would never be anything but the 'Sow's Ear'; Byron did at least add that he himself had nothing to recommend him as a companion. A year is a very long time for

---

* In *Mazeppa* written in 1818 Byron reiterated the view he had expressed to his Cambridge tutor.

> A count of far and high descent . . .
> As if from heaven he had been sent:
> He had such wealth in blood and ore . . .
> And o'er his pedigree would pore,
> Until by some confusion led,
> Which almost look'd like want of head,
> He thought their merits were his own.[71]

two friends to spend in close and often isolated proximity. Hobhouse's prissiness must often have been irritating, and he was often exasperated by Byron's continual changes of mind. Yet they seem to have got on fairly well together. The division of labour was simple. The plodding Hobhouse did most of the work – not only reconnoitring and keeping the books but making the arrangements and doing the research which bored his companion – while Byron supplied most of the jokes and the gaiety as well as the money. They both left Constantinople with the returning Ambassador on the *Salsette*; Byron disembarked at Cape Sunium near Athens three days later, while Hobhouse continued his journey to England. 'Took leave, *non sine lacrymis*', recorded Hobhouse on 17 July, 'of this singular young person.'[73]

In Athens, a place which he thought he preferred to any other, Byron returned to the Macris' house where he met Lord Sligo with whom in London he 'had supped with seven whores, a bawd and a ballet-master'.[74] Despite being 'sick of travelling companions', he told his mother, though Hobhouse had not been 'a bad one', he could not prevent Sligo with his vast entourage – they had '29 horses in all' – accompanying him to the Morea. At Corinth, however, he separated from the Marquess and went on to Patras, where he had some business with the Consul, before going south to Tripolitza to see Veli Pacha, the ruler of the Morea and the son of Ali. The son was even more pressing in his attentions than the father had been, honouring him with a 'number of squeezes and speeches' and presenting him with 'a very pretty horse'.[75]

On his way to Patras Byron had found a very pretty youth, 'my dearly-beloved Eustathio', he told Hobhouse, whom he had met on an earlier trip. The youth had shocked Byron's valet, Fletcher, by 'riding with a *parasol* ... to save his complexion', though that seems one of his more sensible actions: after all, English officers went into battle in the Peninsula holding umbrellas. The two of them 'travelled much-enamoured',* but after some tantrums and embraces 'enough to have ruined the character of a county in

---

* Byron's affair with Eustathio was the sort of thing Hobhouse had in mind when he noted that Moore in his biography had no idea of the 'real reason' why Byron preferred having no Englishman 'constantly near him'. Yet Hobhouse's comment was at least partly the product of pique: he had just read Moore's remark that as a travelling companion he had become 'a chain and a burden'. And in fact Fletcher was with Byron for six months after Hobhouse had gone and only left then because he had to take important 'Scotch papers home'.[76]

England', Byron sent Eustathio home because of his whims and *'epileptic* fits' which, since Hobhouse was told to tell Matthews about them, evidently had a homosexual connotation.[77]

Back in Athens Byron was 'most auspiciously settled' in a Capuchin 'convent'. With Fletcher and the rest of his suite he had moved from the Macris, partly because the mother wanted him to marry or buy her youngest daughter at a time when Byron was not very heterosexually inclined or was otherwise engaged, and partly because the company at the monastery, where Galt had stayed, was highly congenial. Life there was something of a reversion to his Harrow days. For, as well as a hotel, the monastery or convent was a school consisting of six 'regatzi' or 'sylphs', of whom his favourite was Nicolo Giraud, who was teaching him Italian and wanted to live and die with him. Byron had spent most of the day, he told Hobhouse, 'in conjugating' the Greek verb meaning to embrace or kiss. 'Progress [was] rapid.'[78]

There was no question of him conjugating Pitt's niece, the six-foot-tall Lady Hester Stanhope, who arrived in Athens with her travelling companion Michael Bruce. She claimed to have given Hobhouse 'a good set down' in Malta, and wanted similarly 'to argufy' with Byron, who despised 'the sex too much to squabble with her'. Nevertheless he evidently affronted her – she was easily offended – by pleading urgent business at Patras and leaving Athens shortly after she and Bruce had arrived. For, while she was in Athens, she and Bruce were very polite, inviting Byron to accompany them to Constantinople where she created trouble for Stratford Canning; but in her memoirs she 'saw nothing in [Byron] but a well-bred man, like many others', and thought 'he had a great deal of vice in his looks'. Earlier in his diary Hobhouse had characterised her as 'a violent vulgar woman' and 'a masculine lady who says she would as soon live with packhorses as women'. She ended up living in Syria, convinced that she was destined to be Queen of Jerusalem.[79]

If Lady Hester thought that Byron left Athens because of her arrival, she was right. In Patras where he had fled with Nicolo Giraud, he complained of Athens being infested with English people, but 'they' (evidently Stanhope and Bruce) were 'moving, Dio benedetto!' He and Nicolo caught a fever in Patras. In a note to his second canto Byron wrote that his two Albanian servants had saved his life by threatening to cut the throat of his physician if

Byron did not recover by a certain date, thus frightening him away. In fact there were two physicians, 'assassins' Byron called them, but he still recovered. He was not too ill to compose an amusing epitaph, a parody of Pope's lines on the Duke of Buckingham:

> Here victor of a fever and it's friends,
> Physicians and their art, his lordship *mends.**[80]

Nor was he too ill to complain to his mother that in the fifteen months he had been away he still had heard nothing about his financial state from Hanson, who had been negligent, culpable and uncivil. So much so that Byron told Hobhouse to ask him if he was insane. He also complained to Hanson himself. When that 'most dilatory of mortals' did finally put pen to paper, Byron had returned to Athens. Your letter 'tells me I am ruined', he replied. Nevertheless, not even 'the Devil' would make him do what Hanson wanted, which was to sell Newstead. In fact common sense should have been enough to make him sell it. He could not afford to keep it up, and its sale would have solved his financial problems. As well as berating Hanson and romping with the schoolboys, Byron enjoyed himself riding regularly and revisiting places he had seen with Hobhouse. On one expedition to Cape Sunium with Lusieri and other friends, the party was lucky not to be captured by pirates. Byron was saved from the pirates, as from his physicians, by his Albanians, whose presence led the pirates to believe that he was well guarded.[81]

Byron exaggerated when he told his mother that he wrote to 'nobody but yourself', but until Hobhouse left him Mrs Byron was his only regular correspondent. He wrote one thoroughly unkind letter telling her that his only tie to England was Newstead without including her. But otherwise he was a dutiful son, demonstrating that underneath their quarrels when they were together there was a strong affection. He was already a good letter writer when he left England; on his Grand Tour he became a wonderful one, sending vivid, entertaining letters to his mother and some of his friends, adjusting their content to the correspondent he was addressing. Whereas in England he had insensitively inflicted his sexual boasting on the Reverend Becher, he now never mentioned his boys

---

* Fourteen years later at Missolonghi there were more physicians and, regrettably, no Albanian servants to frighten them away. So his lordship did not 'mend'.

to the pious Hodgson, confining that subject matter to his letters to Hobhouse and Drury (though he, too, was a clergyman).* Indeed he evidently kept something back even from them, telling his Journal a few years later, 'H. doesn't know what I was about the year after he left the Levant; nor does anyone. . . ' though what that can have been is hard to imagine.[83]

If Byron's 'epistolising' flowered while he was abroad, his poetry after he had finished the second canto of *Childe Harold* did not. Although he revised *Childe Harold* in early 1811, he wrote very little in the eleven months following 28 March 1810. Indeed in Turkey he told Drury and Dallas that he had 'renounced scribbling', and in Athens in January 1811 he told his mother that he had 'done with authorship'. In Constantinople his abandonment of scribbling was probably the result of boredom and depression. In Athens it was because he was cheerful: he had no cause to seek emotional relief by writing poetry.[84]

Yet one of his early poems said that he had been ruled by his muse 'through infancy's days', and now after a few months' abdication she resumed her sway. In less than a fortnight at the beginning of March 1811 he wrote *Hints from Horace*, which was 'an Imitation' of Horace's Epistle 'Ad Pisones de Arte Poetica' and was intended to be a sequel to *English Bards*. In contrast to *Childe Harold*, *Hints* acknowledged Hobhouse's presence in Greece as Byron's companion: it addressed him, though not by name; the poem would also be dedicated to him, Byron told his friend. Like Tennyson, Swinburne, Thackeray and other writers, Byron had 'hated' Horace at school, and there are still traces in *Hints* of his continuing resentment at Harrow's relentless classical diet, which was enough to give anyone 'a well-founded horror of hexameters'. His *Hints* was an act of homage to Horace, but it was also an act of arrogance. For, when Horace wrote his *Ars Poetica* he was, after Virgil, the leading writer of the day and thus well qualified to advise others how to write, whereas Byron, a mere poetic novice, had no such status or qualification. Yet the arrogance was not premeditated: Byron would not have embarked on the poem had he not come across a copy of Horace in the convent library, and probably would not have finished it but 'for lack of other argument'.[85]

---

* Henry Drury did not at all object, but his biographer thought Byron's letters were written 'without much regard to the propriety usually preserved in a correspondence with a divine'.[82]

Like Horace, he included some witty lines of quasi-autobiography:

> Rough with his elders with his equals rash,
> Civil to sharpers, prodigal of cash;
> Constant to nought – save hazard and a whore,
> Yet cursing both – for both have made him sore.

But, though intended to be a sequel to *English Bards*, it is mostly a dull poem, in which Byron ignored his own advice to 'ye bards':

> Command your audience or to smile or weep,
> Whiche'er may please you – any thing but sleep.

He then wrote some 60 lines of *The Curse of Minerva* which is even more vitriolic than *Childe Harold* about Elgin and Scotland – 'A land of meanness, sophistry and mist'. This was probably more an emulation of Charles Churchill's attack on Scotland in *Prophecy of Famine: A Scots Pastoral* and the product of his lingering resentment against the *Edinburgh Review* than the exposure of a deeply felt antagonism to the land of his birth.* But in any case, since Byron was himself a Scot, he had to allow a few Scotsmen, 'the letter'd and the brave', exemption from the general damnation of their country. He continued *The Curse* in England but, apart from its fine opening lines which he later used in *The Corsair*, that poem is even worse than his Horace. Fortunately *Hints* did not appear in his lifetime, even though he wanted it published in 1811–12 and again in 1821, and *The Curse* appeared only in pirated editions.[87]

Byron's burst of activity in March enabled him to tell Hobhouse on his way home that he had written some 4,000 lines 'on [his] travels', an output which by his later standards was low. During his working life of sixteen years he published some 80,000 lines of verse or an average of 14 lines a day over the entire time. On his travels, by contrast, even including the lines that were not published during his life he averaged a mere six lines a day.[88]

In Athens this time his prose was better than his poetry. He wrote

---

* In *Don Juan* Byron recalled that

> And though, as you remember, in a fit
> Of wrath and rhyme, when juvenile and curly
> I railed at Scots to shew my wrath and wit,
> Which must be own'd was sensitive and surly. . . .[86]

some long notes to *Childe Harold*, suggesting in one of them that people knew more than enough about the ancient Greeks. The younger men of Europe, he thought, 'devote much of their time to the study of the Greek writers and history, which could be more usefully spent in mastering their own'. That sensible view of education, which was not adopted by the English public schools for the next century and a half, led Byron to reflect that, while boys and men studied the language and harangues of the Athenian demagogues, 'the real or supposed descendants of these sturdy republicans' were in the present day left languishing in tyranny although only a very slight effort was needed 'to shake off their chains'.[89]

On an early draft of stanza 73 of his second canto, written probably in 1810, which asked several questions about who would free Greece, Byron has several times scribbled 'Byron'. That was then sheer fantasy. In 1810 it was no more likely that he would play any part in making Greece independent than it was that the young Miss Catherine Gordon shrieking 'Oh my Birron, Oh my Birron!' in the Edinburgh theatre would marry a man called Byron. In 1810 Byron did not even believe in the possibility of an independent Greece. Later his agreeable social life in Athens with enlightened foreigners as well as Greeks and also his own reflections led him to change his mind about the possibility of Greek freedom. He now scoffed at those who attacked the Greeks all the time. He still considered independence to be out of the question, but he thought the Greeks could become subjects rather than slaves. And he now believed that foreign intervention would be necessary.[90]

Because of the subjection of Greece to the Turks, Byron had considered the country during his first stay in Athens to be 'no lightsome land of social mirth'. Now, however, Greece had a good deal of social mirth for him. Many English people were then in Athens, but he did not regard them as 'infesting' the place like Lady Hester Stanhope. He was on dining terms with all, and had disputes with none of them. He went to balls 'and had had a variety of fooleries with the females of Athens'. He had had so many trysts with boys that he was 'almost tired of them'. He also had non-sexual friendships with Fauvel and Lusieri as well as with five learned Danes and Germans. His appetite for travel was satiated, and he was 'tranquil and as contented as I suppose one can be in any situation'. All in all, the months of his second stay in Athens were probably the happiest time of his life.[91]

He told Hobhouse that he was off to Mount Sion, Damascus and Cairo. Yet he was short of money and had no travelling companion. In any case, however beckoning was the East and however pleasant were Athens and Greece, his financial affairs compelled a return to England. So, after giving 'two English gentlemen', who had escaped from France, money to return to England, Byron returned himself, parting friends with all the English and French. He had, however, been too friendly with 'a number of Greek and Turkish women' and was 'clapped'. Leaving on 22 April he had with him Nicolo Giraud and was near to having Teresa Macri as well, but her mother demanded too high a price for her. Also on the ship were Lusieri and some of Elgin's marbles.[92]

In the Lazaretto on Manoel Island at Malta, where all arrivals from the East were quarantined for eighteen days, Byron caught a tertian fever (malaria) and had to be treated by a regimental surgeon for that, as well as for his gonorrhoea and his 'haemor-rhoids'. Once out of quarantine he met at the Governor's palace Constance Spencer Smith who, undeterred by his previous failure to keep their engagement, had returned to the island in the hope of seeing him. Byron was depressed, the sirocco was blowing, his passion for her was long over, he had a lot of explaining to do, he still had his malaria and was no doubt additionally inhibited by his clap. The meeting was therefore difficult but conclusive. The lady sailed away up the Adriatic, and he still had not made love to a woman of his own class.[93]

While in Malta Byron wrote himself a memorandum, which revealed 'the gloomy wanderer', Childe Harold, the anti-hero of one of the poems packed in his trunk, writing in prose: at twenty-three the best of life was over; his leg would get worse as he aged; he grew 'selfish and misanthropical'; his affairs were 'gloomy'; neither maid nor youth delighted him; he had outlived all his appetites; and had even outlived 'the vanity of authorship'. Fortunately the last claim, at least, was exaggerated. He was not so gloomy and misanthropical as to make a bonfire of his vanities; the manuscripts stayed safe in his trunk. Indeed four days later Byron wrote a cheerful doggerel, 'Farewell to Malta', in which he hailed the: 'Triumphant sons of truest blue!/ While either Adriatic shore,/ And fallen chiefs, and fleets no more,/ And nightly smiles, and daily dinners,/ Proclaim you war and women's winners.'[94]

Byron left Malta on the *Volage* frigate without 'Fair Florence', without Nicolo, who was to be educated there, and without Lusieri and the marbles (except some of Hobhouse's), but with a letter from the Italian painter to be delivered to Elgin. The voyage took six weeks which, with his 'affairs' at home seeming 'desperate enough', would in any event have been tedious. But in addition he was still ill with his fever, piles and gonorrhoea. Telling his mother from the ship about his indifference to his return, he had the grace to assure her that she was not 'comprised within that apathy'. Shortly before he landed he got rid of his malaria, but he arrived back in England with the other two complaints, on an entirely vegetable diet, and as depressed as when he had left the country just over two years before. He soon had good reason for even greater depression.[95]

But while Byron's time abroad did not cure his melancholy – probably that could only have been done by the modern drug lithium which might well have 'cured' him of poetry as well – in other ways it was enormously beneficial to him. According to Shelley's admirer Trelawny, Byron told him that if he was a poet 'it was the air of Greece' which had made him one. There was some poetic licence there from Byron, if not from Trelawny. Aside from his juvenilia, he had written *English Bards* without the air of Greece and much of the first canto of *Childe Harold* in what was then Albania. Yet Greece had undoubtedly inspired him poetically, whereas Turkey had not.[96]

Greece had also stimulated his homosexual feelings, or at least allowed him to give them full play. But while his tour did not 'cure' him of his bisexuality any more than of his depression, his hetero–homosexual balance markedly shifted on his return. Whereas in Greece he had been predominantly homosexual, in England he became predominantly, if not wholly, heterosexual. Neither in England nor in Italy – except possibly in Venice in the winter of 1818–19 – is there evidence of any homosexual affairs. Indeed his excesses in Greece seem to have got homosexuality almost out of his system. Only when he returned to Greece at the end of his life were his homosexual inclinations fully revived; and then his failure to satisfy them was a contributory factor in depressing his spirits and hastening his death.[97]

As he told his mother from Athens, he had greatly benefited from 'looking at mankind instead of reading about them', as well as from not 'staying at home with all the narrow prejudices of an Islander'.

And although that partly meant merely that he had no particular desire to live expensively in the cold of England rather than cheaply in the warmth of foreign countries, he had become genuinely broad and cosmopolitan in his outlook. If his prejudices had ever been narrow, they were so no longer; as he was himself, they were fully mature. His weeks in Spain and Portugal and his proximity to the war had strengthened his 'detestation of *licensed Murder*' and what he had seen there and in Greece had intensified his love of freedom and his hatred of oppression. He had become a philhellene and felt himself 'a citizen of the world'.[98]

CHAPTER XIII

Return and Luddism

Byron: 1811–12 (aged 23 years)

On landing at Sheerness after just over two years' absence, Byron's first priority was to see to the publication of his poems, his second to meet his friends, his third to 'repair his irreparable affairs' and his fourth to see his mother and Newstead.[1]

From Greece he had derided Dallas's insensitive egotism, telling Hodgson that Dallas had been blind to Sheridan's enormous losses, when his Drury Lane Theatre was destroyed by fire, and solely concerned with the fate of the manuscript of his second-rate farce. Nevertheless, on his way home, Byron had written to Dallas mentioning his satire *Hints from Horace*. Although he had added that he would not inflict it on him, his distant kinsman, sniffing that he was once more on to a good thing, hurried round to Reddish's Hotel, where Byron was staying. Byron gave him his satire to read, and when Dallas, understandably 'disappointed' with its quality, asked next morning if Byron had really not written anything else, Byron, according to Dallas, replied that he had written 'nothing worth troubling [him] with' before eventually handing him *Childe Harold's Pilgrimage*.

The word 'Pilgrimage' has a pretentious ring to it now, but originally a pilgrimage was merely a journey made by someone who went on a journey or was a wanderer. Two hundred years ago 'pilgrimage' was much more commonly used than it is today; describing his tour of Italy in his *Memoirs* Gibbon uses it on successive pages. Byron was certainly a wanderer, and his pilgrimage was, as Professor Stuart Curran has pointed out, 'a religious quest, [which] visits literally dozens of shrines'; Hazlitt claimed that the poem turned the universe 'into a stately mausoleum'. In any case, even if the title of Byron's cantos had been pretentious, Dallas would have been the last man to find that objectionable. After consulting Waller Wright, a former Consul-General of the Ionian Islands, he told Byron that *Childe Harold* was 'one of the most delightful poems' he had ever read, though he thought 'some

262

alterations and omissions [were] indispensable'. Even then, according to Dallas, its author needed much convincing that the poem should be published.[2]

From the beginning Byron was 'very fond of' *Hints from Horace* – his intention was to publish it before *Childe Harold*, but he was dissuaded by Dallas – and nine years later he thought it one of the two 'best things' he had written. But if he greatly overrated the merits of his new satire, he did not correspondingly belittle those of *Childe Harold*, although he did tell Dallas the 'one person' who had read it had found 'much to condemn'.* Yet in Athens earlier in the year Byron had extensively revised *Childe Harold* and had added some long prose notes. All that was not done just for his own edification; he clearly had every intention of publishing *Childe Harold*. Furthermore both from Malta and from his frigate he had written about his new satire to Cawthorn, the publisher of *English Bards*; and on his return, contrary to the impression given by Dallas, he had immediately sent Cawthorn the manuscript. Had he not planned to publish *Childe Harold*, there would, therefore, have been no urgency in bringing in Dallas, whom Hobhouse called 'Dull ass' or 'Damn'd ass'. So if, beyond showing becoming modesty about his ambitious poem, Byron gave Dallas the impression that he did not want it published, he was 'humming' or 'bamming' that conceited and easily bamboozled man, as is strongly indicated by his assurance to Dallas, when he gave him his satire, that 'he had never had the least idea of writing' about his travels. Alternatively Dallas in his book invented or exaggerated Byron's diffidence about *Childe Harold* in order to appropriate spurious credit for having achieved the publication of the most popular poem of the day.[4]

William Miller, who was Lord Elgin's bookseller, rejected *Childe Harold* because of its religious scepticism and its attack on Elgin, and Longman's were ruled out because of their rejection of *English Bards*. So Byron let Dallas take it to John Murray, who had earlier expressed interest in publishing Byron's collected poems. Dallas told Murray that he had been given the poem by Byron and expected 'a very liberal agreement' for it. After consulting his chief

---

* Neither Dallas nor Byron ever disclosed who the 'one person' was. The obvious suspect is Hobhouse, who was a poor literary critic. Byron told him in Ioannina that he had started the poem; and as the two of them were alone together a great deal, one would expect Byron to have shown it to his companion. Yet there is no mention in Hobhouse's diary of his having read it. And in Byron's letters to Hobhouse on 31 August 1811, the words, 'In the poem which I wrote abroad', and 'at the close of the first canto which treats of Spain . . .' suggest that Hobhouse did not know the poem. So the question remains open.[3]

reader, the sour and second-rate William Gifford, who was also editor of the Tory *Quarterly Review* and one of the few poets praised by Byron in *English Bards*, Murray agreed to publish it and to give Dallas half the profits. Like his temporary partner in profit, Murray wanted the poem toned down and substantial alterations made.[5]

The evening Byron arrived in London Scrope Davies called on him, 'drunk' but 'very friendly' and with a new set of jokes. The financial pressures he had been under, because of the crucial guarantee he had given on Byron's behalf, were evidently forgotten, and they dined together the next day. Hobhouse had had to join the militia as the price for his father paying off his debts; he was stationed at Dover, and meeting halfway he and Byron spent two days together at Sittingbourne. Byron had only to journey from London to Harrow to stay with Henry Drury. He also met Hodgson, who unlike Drury had been a good correspondent, but, as their meeting was interrupted, Hodgson 'prolonged' it by a verse letter, urging him to 'Spread, like a flame, my Byron, through the land/That natural warmth no scoundrel can withstand.'[6]

Byron's acute financial difficulties were the main cause of his return from Greece, and on the voyage home after even briefly considering procuring an appointment on Wellington's staff, he had 'made up his mind to bear the ills of Poverty'. Yet there was no need for him to bear those 'ills'. Although he owed a lot of money and, unlike Hobhouse, had nobody to pay up for him, he could have paid his debts and made himself moderately well-off simply by selling Newstead. And even if obstinate folly prevented him taking Hanson's good advice and selling his dilapidated Abbey, he could still have diminished his debts.[7]

Byron knew that money was to be made from poetry. His unpublished preface to *Hints from Horace* claimed that he had been provoked into showing how easy it was 'to say ill-natured things and to sell it also'. No law said that Dallas not the author should profit from the sale of *Childe Harold*, as even the pushy and grasping Dallas should have had the decency to explain to Byron. Dallas was sufficiently self-centred, however, to avoid any prickings of conscience on that score.[8]

Other people's consciences are often odd; other periods' ethics are even odder. In a postscript to *Hints* Byron indignantly denied that he had 'written *English Bards* for money'. Earlier in that poem he had attacked Scott for selling *Marmion* 'for just half a crown a line'

> [Since] when the sons of song descend to trade
> Their bays are sear, their former laurels fade.

Scott later explained that such a charge was unjustified, and Byron then expressed regret for his earlier 'wholesale Assertions' whose 'ghosts' now 'haunted' him. Yet he and others thought not merely that 'sons of song' should not 'descend to trade' but that gentlemen should not descend to taking money from tradesmen. 'I have been anxious', wrote Jeffrey, 'to keep clear of any tradesman-like concern in the [Edinburgh] *Review*', and he therefore confined himself 'to intercourse with gentlemen only'. So Byron, rather than accept a substantial sum of money that he had earned from one tradesman, that is to say a bookseller (as publishers were then called), preferred to leave other tradesmen unpaid and himself in debt. Indeed he got himself even further into debt by his feckless extravagance in ordering a new carriage. Another feature of the period's ethics, of course, was that gentlemen did not have to hurry to pay their bills. That tradesmen could wait was an almost universal 'gentlemanly' view, one that was shared by Shelley who left various bills unpaid.[9]

Catherine Byron was much more sensible, thinking her son should have had a lot of money from 'the bookseller' of *English Bards*. Catherine had been ill, and in July had murmured to her maid how strange it would be if she were to die before her son came back. It was indeed strange, and also unnecessary. But Byron's preoccupation with his poems, his visits to friends, his pressing creditors, Hanson's usual dilatoriness and his own dawdling had kept him from Newstead. Evidently feeling guilty for not having visited his mother, he wrote to tell her, after he had been back for a week, that he was detained only by the need to sign papers and was reluctant to stay in town, adding in a postscript that she should consider Newstead as her home, not his. In view of the way she had defended his interests while he had been away – there had once been four bailiffs in the house because he had not paid the bills for his expensive renovating – and her refusal to make herself financially independent by buying the annuity that Byron had suggested, that was no more than she deserved.[10]

She did not tell him that she had long been unwell, and still he lingered in London until summoned by her doctor on 1 August. Not having enough money for the journey, he had to draw on Hanson for £40. He was too late. Learning on the way that his mother was dead, he was assailed by grief and guilt. His mother had been the chief recipient of his letters for the last two years and those letters show his understanding that she was an intelligent, well-informed woman. When they were together, their relations had usually been less good. During their worst period in his later Harrow and earlier Cambridge years, he had called her in a letter to John Pigot 'Mrs Byron Furiosa' – he had read Ariosto's *Orlando Furioso* – and, worse, he called her his 'amiable Alecto', the most awful of the three Furies.* He had even written a mock 'Epitaph on Mrs [Byron]', beginning

> Prone to take Fire, yet not of melting Stuff,
> Here lies what once was woman, that's enough.
> Such were her vocal powers, her temper such,
> That all who knew them both exclaimed 'too much!'[12]

Catherine Byron's rages were indeed fearsome, exhibiting all the mental instability of the Gordons. But she had been much put upon by her husband and by her son, both of whom she treated a great deal better than they treated her. Yet John Galt was sure from what he had heard Byron say of Catherine that his 'filial love' had been beyond the ordinary. And now, sitting by her body, Byron belatedly exclaimed to her maid: 'Oh, Mrs By, I had had but one friend in the world, and she is gone!' Yet even as he had 'shun[ned]' saying goodbye to her when he went abroad, he did not attend her funeral, boxing with Rushton instead. Although that failure was due to what Galt called 'the integrity of his affection' and not to callous disregard, it was deplorably self-indulgent. As Moore charitably put it, Byron behaved with 'a degree of eccentricity and indecorum' which might have led superficial observers to question 'the sensibility of his nature'.[13]

Before his mother was buried, Byron heard that his friend Charles Skinner Matthews had been drowned in the River Cam. 'In ability, who was like Matthews?' he wondered to Scrope Davies. And when

---

* In one sense that was unintentionally apt since a function of the Furies was to hear complaints against children's insolence to parents, but as Alecto, like the other Furies, was a crone with bloodshot eyes, dogs' heads, bats' wings, and snakes for hair, it was not in other ways complimentary.[11]

he told Scrope in the same letter that 'some curse hangs over me and mine', he spoke truer than he knew. A few days later he learned that John Wingfield, one of his Harrow 'juniors and favourites', who had appeared in 'Childish Recollections' as the 'best and dearest of my friends', had died of a fever, while serving with the Coldstream Guards in Portugal. Yet another death was that of his Harrow friend and contemporary, Hargreaves Hanson, the son of his solicitor.[14]

Byron had for weeks been waiting for that solicitor to accompany him to his estate in Lancashire, where he expected to be 'busy and savage' with everyone. But the man he understandably called 'everlasting Hanson' and 'the most dilatory [man] in the world' procrastinated as usual. When they did eventually go in October, Byron, despite the desperate state of his finances – and his frequent talk of needing to marry somebody 'inclined to barter money for rank', claimed not to have gone 'within ken of a coalpit', leaving that task to the ineffective Hanson, while himself staying nearby at a 'pleasant country seat . . . full of the fair and fashionable sex'; yet his host noted that he was there 'on business'. On his return he learned that John Edleston had died in May 'of a consumption'. Thus in just over two months he had suffered the loss of his mother and four young friends. When Hodgson exhorted him to be 'cheerful' and to 'banish care', Byron sent him his 'Epistle to a Friend', in which cheerfulness not care was banished. After sadly recalling his dinner with Mary Musters, he ended this deeply gloomy poem with an unfavourable caricature of himself which anticipated the Byronic heroes of his later Turkish tales:

> Thou hear'st of one, whose deepening crimes
> Suit with the sablest of the times,
> Of one, whom love nor pity sways . . .

So adverse was his self-portrait that Hodgson later cut out the last few lines of the poem, noting that 'the poor dear Lord *meant* nothing of this'.[15]

Having told Byron that *Childe Harold* was 'delightful', Dallas immediately devoted considerable effort to making it less so. His chief objections were to what he called Byron's 'sceptical stanzas'. He had no worries about the attack on 'the Babylonian whore'; the papacy was fair game. But he sought to make the rest of Christianity a protected species. Despite, though, the strong pleas of

Murray as well as Dallas, Byron insisted on preserving his free-thinking stanzas. He only agreed to one change, removing this stanza, which would certainly have shocked many readers,

> Frown not upon me, churlish Priest! That I
> Look not for Life, where life may never be,
> I am no sneerer at thy phantasy –
> Thou pitiest me, alas! I envy thee,
> Thou bold Discoverer in an unknown sea
> Of happy isles and happier tenants there –
> I ask thee not to prove a Sadduccee;
> Still dream of Paradise thou know'st not where,
> Which if it be, thy sins will never let thee share.

and replacing it with one which left open the possibility of an after life. Having pleased Dallas by that substitution, Byron pleased himself by inserting next to it a stanza in which he dreamed he might meet again a dead person –

> Whose love and life together fled
> Having left me here to love and live in vain

– which would have horrified Dallas had he known it concerned a former chorister. But Byron assured him, falsely if understandably, that it did not allude to 'any male friend'.[16]

Dallas and Murray had better luck with minor amendments and with some of the stanzas on Cintra. These needed to be changed, as the war had gone better since Byron wrote them, even though Shelley dismissed England's successes as 'barren victories' and a 'prodigal waste of human blood'. But they should not have been omitted. For instance the following lines required improvement, not erasure:

> Convention is the dwarfy demon styled
> That foiled the knights in Marialva's dome
> Of brains (if brains they had) he them beguiled,
> And turned a nation's shallow joy to gloom
> For well I wot, when first the news did come
> That Vimiera's field by Gaul was lost,
> For paragraph ne paper scarce had room,
> Such Paeans teemed for our triumphant host,
> In Courier, Chronicle, and eke Morning Post.
>
> But when Convention sent his handy work
> Pens, tongues, feet, hands, combined in wild uproar;

Mayor, Aldermen, laid down the uplifted fork
The Bench of Bishops half forgot to snore; . . .

More positively, Dallas was partly responsible for Byron's inclusion of a note praising the Duke of Wellington. Byron was reluctant to put his name to the poem. Naturally nervous that its autobiographical nature might expose him to the sort of attack that his preface to *Hours of Idleness* had helped to provoke from Brougham, he favoured anonymity, but he was persuaded by Dallas to make clear his authorship of *Childe Harold*. Dallas attributed Byron's compliance with his wishes, limited though it was, to the poet's knowing 'how sincerely' Dallas loved him.[17]

Much more important to the poem than the importunities of Dallas and Murray were the deaths of Byron's mother and his friends. 'All thou couldst have of mine, Stern Death! Thou hast,' Byron wrote towards the end of the second canto: 'The parent, friend, and now the more than friend'. That last phrase referred, of course, to Edleston. Although Byron had not expected to see him again, it was Edleston's death which most affected him.[18]

As *Childe Harold* was a contemporary record of Byron's life, he was bound to mention in it the loss of his friends and his mother; he needed furthermore an escape for his feelings which only the writing of poetry could provide. But the combination of these events and other pressures altered the balance of the poem. The manuscript of *Childe Harold* that Byron brought back from Greece comprised, in the words of Jerome J. McGann, 'about equal parts of ironic raillery and sarcasm and of romantic melancholy'. Indeed a tenth of the first canto was 'buffooning' or satirical. The alterations made in England drastically changed those proportions, much reducing the satire and increasing the melancholy. Professor McGann has powerfully argued that, so far from spoiling the poem, those alterations changed it from a 'derivative personal travelogue' into 'the revolutionary confessional poem which so decisively influenced Romantic and post-Romantic art'.[19]

This is doubtless true. But while Byron's emotionally charged changes played a key role in the unprecedented success of *Childe Harold* in 1812, they also played a large part in the later decline of its reputation, which has only recently recovered. In a later canto of his poem, Byron apostrophised 'Man' as 'Thou pendulum between a smile and a tear'. If he had not removed most of the smiles from the first two cantos, scarcely ever showing Harold 'in his maddest mirthful mood', while multiplying the tears by dwelling on the deaths of his friends, not only would he, at least to some readers' taste, have published a much more attractive poem, he might well have set his poetic career on a different and preferable path. But just as Dallas, Gifford and Murray later hated *Don Juan*, they hated anything in the original version of *Childe Harold* that anticipated it.[20]

Byron had lost four friends, but he was making new ones. After the second edition of *English Bards* revealed that Byron was its author, Thomas Moore had sent him a challenge because of his derisive comments about Moore's quarrel with Jeffrey in 1806. In the *Edinburgh Review* Jeffrey had been even ruder about Moore's poems than Brougham was about Byron's, accusing him of aiming 'to impose corruption upon his readers' and of being 'the most licentious of modern versifiers'; his poetry was 'a public nuisance'. Moore challenged Jeffrey, but their duel was aborted by the police, who had been warned by one of Moore's friends. The rumour soon spread that their pistols had not been loaded, though that was contradicted by the seconds who had loaded them. It was because Byron had given 'the lie direct' to what Moore and the seconds had said that Moore had sought to challenge him. Cawthorn had sent his letter unopened to Hodgson, who, suspecting it was a challenge, did not forward it to Byron.[21]

Having heard that Byron had returned to England, Moore wrote again in later October, saying that because of his recent marriage his circumstances had changed, and this time he was seeking 'intimacy' and a 'satisfactory explanation', not issuing a challenge. Although saying that his attack had been directed against Jeffrey, not Moore, Byron was initially guarded in his response, but Scrope Davies, whom he consulted, thought 'friendship' not 'fighting' was 'the most likely result', and after an exchange of letters Byron agreed to meet Moore for dinner at the house of Samuel Rogers. Thomas Campbell, who like Rogers had been praised in *English Bards*, was also present. Except, according to Rogers, for Byron refusing the fish, the mutton and the wine, and eating only potatoes – which was in accordance with the 'entire vegetable diet' he had in June told his mother he was following – the evening was a success.* He and Moore got on so well that, when a few months

* In his *Table-Talk*, Rogers tells the well-known story of how 'Some days after, meeting Hobhouse', he had asked how long Byron would 'persevere in his present diet', and

later Byron was involved 'in a similar business', he asked Moore, who settled the matter, to act for him.[23]

Spared two duels, Byron helped to save an acquaintance, Robert Bland, whom he had favourably mentioned in *English Bards*, from another. On Byron's return, Hodgson had resumed his rhyming and his prose efforts to convert his friend to Christian orthodoxy, to which Byron responded in prose and verse, repudiating 'immortality' and 'any revealed religion'. Hodgson also sought to spur him to energetic activity in the House of Lords: 'O'erthrow the bulwarks that corruption rears,/And from proverbial dullness rescue half thy peers'. Unfortunately, in pursuit of the first objective as well as the second, Hodgson had to rely on precept not example. In the middle of November Byron reported that, at a dinner for Rogers and Moore, Hodgson 'of course was drunk and sensibilitous'.* A clergyman, minor poet and former Harrow master, Bland had placed his 'whore' in Hodgson's care while he was abroad. Hodgson's care took the form of asking the whore to marry him. She turned him down, preferring 'an officer of Dragoons'. So Hodgson lost his virtue and the girl, though he escaped a possible duel. On his return Bland challenged the dragoon, but Byron who thought dinners 'preferable to duels' with difficulty secured a peaceful outcome. The remorseful Hodgson, Byron told Hobhouse, 'gets drunk and cries', and all the trouble had been over 'a bitch not worth a bank-token'. Bland had caught, he added, 'a gonorrhoea, a clerical & creditable distemper', and Byron conjectured from Hodgson's querulousness that he must have 'a syphilis'. But the future Provost of Eton seems to have been uninfected.[25]

Hodgson's political encouragement of Byron involved no such

Hobhouse had replied: 'Just as long as you continue to notice it.' Rogers added that he had later discovered that after leaving his house Byron had gone to a club 'and eaten a hearty meat-supper'. Alluding to Cyril Connolly's claim that 'imprisoned in every fat man a thin one is wildly signalling to be let out', the penetrating scholar and critic, Gilbert Highet, thought that the reverse was sometimes true and that inside a thin man like Byron 'there was a fat man roaring to be set free'. Unquestionably Byron did sometimes, after a period on a spartan diet, break his fast with a large meal; according to Hogg, Shelley, who a few months later also adopted a strict vegetarian regime, similarly lapsed from it at least once, eating 'an enormous round of boiled beef' in the Lake District. Yet Rogers's story is not true as it stands, since Hobhouse and Rogers did not then know each other. Furthermore the dinner was in early November and Hobhouse was in Ireland till February; and anyway Moore maintained that Byron had made 'a rather hearty dinner' out of the potatoes.[22]
* Hodgson's reforming efforts were also hampered by his debt to Byron. According to Hobhouse, Byron used to say of Hodgson's religious advice: 'As soon as he pays me my £1,200, I'll listen to him.'[24]

embarrassment; it was merely otiose. 'I wish parliament were assembled, that I may hear, and perhaps some day be heard', Byron told him on 8 December. His first mention of the serious trouble in his own county came a week later: 'Riots in Notts, breaking of frames & heads, & out-manoeuvring the military'. Byron already knew where he stood:

> The starv'd mechanic breaks his rusting loom,
> And desperate mans him 'gainst the common doom.[26]

He was leaving town, he told Hobhouse, 'for Notts, where the weavers are in arms and breaking of frames, Hodgson thinks *his frame* will be broken among the rest – I hope not'. As Newstead was close to the hub of the violence, Hodgson's concern was not entirely groundless, but he and Byron's other guest, William Harness, remained unscratched throughout their Christmas holiday.[27]

Like Hodgson, Harness was ordained in 1812. Two years younger than Byron and like him lame, at Harrow he had been one of the smaller boys whom Byron had protected from bullies. Harness recalled much later that, not surprisingly, 'nothing in the shape of riot or excess occurred when I was there . . . Byron was retouching', Harness continued, 'the stanzas of *Childe Harold*'. Hodgson was working on the *Monthly Review*, which he edited, and 'I was reading for my degree'. Harness, like Hodgson, was to combine a career in the Church with literary pursuits. He edited Shakespeare and, less happily, wrote *The Wrath of Cain*, a refutation of Byron's drama. In that essay Harness asserted the literal truth of the book of Genesis, which he deemed 'a plain relation of events that actually occurred', a view that in 1822 was already old-fashioned and obscurantist, and one that even some of the Fathers of the early Church had found untenable.[*28]

According to Harness, the talk at Newstead was usually of 'poets and poetry'. Occasionally, however, it 'rose into very serious discussions on religion' when Hodgson and Harness tried to dislodge Byron's 'miserable prejudice' that the principles of Christianity were identical to 'the extreme dogmas of Calvinism'. The duty of disabusing Byron of this error fell chiefly on Hodgson whose contribution of 'judicious zeal and affectionate earnestness (often speaking with tears in his eyes)' was much admired by Harness. In

---

* Harness's acceptance of the literal truth of Genesis entailed believing, *inter* a great deal of *alia*, that Abraham had himself circumcised at the age of ninety-nine (Genesis 17:24–6).

view of Hodgson's earlier crying on a matter far removed from Calvin, Byron may have found his tears less affecting, especially as Hodgson's earnestness had to contend with Byron's affection for a new housemaid, Susan Vaughan. 'I am principally occupied with a fresh face and a very pretty one too', he told Hobhouse on Christmas Day, 'a Welsh girl whom I lately added to the bevy, and of whom I am tolerably enamoured for the present'.[29]

Byron was understating the intensity of his latest attachment. Although 'the present' lasted only till the end of January, the break was caused not by his eye roving elsewhere but by his page, Robert Rushton, telling him tales of Susan's indiscretions. Byron was quite deeply affected, asking Hodgson never again to mention a woman to him and writing three poems complaining of Susan's alleged betrayal.

> Again deceived! again betrayed!
> In manhood as in youth
> The dupe of every smiling maid
> That 'ever lied like truth'.[30]

Although Byron left no record of having investigated the frame-breaking in his county during his three weeks at Newstead, the absence of written proof is not necessarily significant, since a short letter to Hobhouse and two business communications are all that survive of his visit to Nottinghamshire. And despite the snow, his duties as host, the proofs of *Childe Harold*, and the lures of Susan Vaughan, he had ample opportunity to find out what was going on. With Newstead being near the centre of the troubles, his old friend the Reverend J. T. Becher, who was playing an intermittently enlightened part in trying to pacify the county, could easily have briefed him.

Two months later, in the House of Lords, Byron said that he had seen the conditions under which the rioters suffered, and earlier he had said the same thing in a letter to Lord Holland. More important, his speech then showed that unlike nearly everybody else in the Lords or the Commons he knew what he was talking about. Almost certainly, therefore, his assertion that he had seen the reality on the ground was true, even though at that time he had little reason to expect that the troubles on his doorstep would be the subject of his first venture in Parliament.[31]

The disturbances in the Nottinghamshire hosiery (stocking-making) and lace trades, which soon came to be called Luddite, had begun in February 1811 and subsided in April, while Byron was still in Greece. The harvest failed in 1811, and violence, more widespread and more systematic than before, broke out again in November, lasting until early February 1812. By then about a thousand stocking frames had been broken in the East Midlands. Attacks on the machines used in the West Yorkshire woollen trade began as those in Nottinghamshire were ending, and machine-breaking then spread to the cotton industry in Lancashire and Cheshire.[32]

In the absence of legal trade unions, violence against machines or men was normally the only bargaining weapon that workers possessed. Hence machine-breaking was common, not usually because of any blanket hostility to machines, but because it was the workers' most effective way of controlling the labour market without violence to persons. Mere withdrawal of labour left the way open to employment of other workers, who could be deterred only by threatened or actual violence. A destroyed machine could not be worked by scab labour or anybody else. The possibility of machine-breaking, moreover, like arson in agriculture, was something an employer would bear in mind. The government's view that machinery was always beneficial to the workers involved was not shared by many of the public or even by the greatest economist of the time, David Ricardo. Writing during the Luddite era, Ricardo conceded that machinery was often 'very injurious to the labouring class' and believed their hostility to it to be reasonable and 'conformable to the correct principles of political economy'.[33]

The technology of the hosiery trade changed little between the sixteenth and eighteenth centuries. Shortly after 1800, however, a wider machine had been evolved which could be used by unskilled labour to produce inferior goods at a lower price. Its introduction did not immediately lead to disputes, yet it exacerbated the troubles eight years later. The hosiery industry in Nottinghamshire had been in decline for many years, and its workers' living conditions had long been deteriorating. In addition there were many abuses, including 'truck' (payment in goods not money), to which the reputable employers were as much opposed as the stockingers. In other words the industry badly needed regulation, and did not get it, a failure that produced violence.[34]

In Nottinghamshire 'Luddism' was not the instinctive reaction of

Shelley's grandfather, Sir Bysshe Shelley. He founded the family fortunes by extreme miserliness and two elopements with heiresses. He was not sympathetic to his grandson's elopement with a non-heiress.

William Whitton, lawyer to Shelley's father, Timothy. Stiff-necked, complacent and narrow-minded, he was the worst possible choice to deal with Shelley after his expulsion from Oxford university.

Shelley's cottage on Chestnut Hill, Keswick, where he lived with his wife, Harriet Westbrook, with whom he eloped, and sister-in-law, Eliza, for three months in 1811. His chemical experiments aroused the hostility of his landlord and neighbours, but he was able to meet Robert Southey who lived in Keswick.

ORIGINAL POETRY;

BY

VICTOR AND CAZIRE.

CALL IT NOT VAIN:—THEY DO NOT ERR,
WHO SAY, THAT, WHEN THE POET DIES,
MUTE NATURE MOURNS HER WORSHIPPER.
Lay of the Last Minstrel.

WORTHING:
PRINTED BY C. AND W. PHILLIPS,
FOR THE AUTHORS;
AND SOLD BY J. J. STOCKDALE, 41, PALL-MALL,
AND ALL OTHER BOOKSELLERS.
1810.

POSTHUMOUS FRAGMENTS

OF

MARGARET NICHOLSON;

BEING POEMS FOUND AMONGST THE PAPERS OF THAT
NOTED FEMALE WHO ATTEMPTED THE LIFE
OF THE KING IN 1786.

EDITED BY

JOHN FITZVICTOR.

OXFORD:
PRINTED AND SOLD BY J. MUNDAY.
1810.

Shelley's first two published volumes of poetry. The first had to be withdrawn because of plagiarism; the second was a failure.

(*Left*) 15 Poland Street, London, where Shelley lived with Hogg after their expulsion from Oxford. Shelley chose the house because of the revolutionary associations of 'Poland'. (*Right*) 23 Chapel Street, London, the home of the Westbrook family. It was frequently visited by Shelley in 1811.

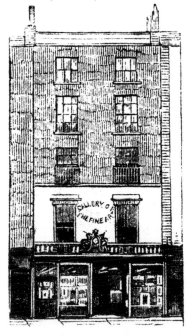

(*Left*) 60 George Street, Edinburgh, where Shelley and his wife honeymooned in 1811 for a month, during which they were joined by Hogg. (*Right*) 7 Lower Sackville Street, Dublin, where Shelley, Harriet and Eliza lived in 1812.

(*Left*) Thomas Jefferson Hogg, Shelley's biographer and his closest friend at Oxford. He fell in love with both Shelley's eldest sister, Elizabeth, and Shelley's wife, Harriet. (*Right*) Thomas Love Peacock, satirical novelist, essayist and poet. He became a close friend of Shelley and wrote reliable *Memoirs* of him.

(*Left*) William Godwin, relentless sponger and author of *Political Justice* (1793), the book which influenced Shelley more than any other. (*Right*) Thomas Moore, an Irish poet who challenged Byron to a duel but then became his friend and biographer

The 16th-century Belem Tower, Lisbon, where Byron landed
after swimming the river Tagus from Old Lisbon.

The building which was then the Buenos Aires Hotel,
where Byron and Hobhouse stayed in Lisbon.

The 18th-century façade of the Mafra Palace and Monastery in Portugal. One of the monks asked Byron if there were any books in England.

The hotel where Byron and Hobhouse stayed in Cintra, the village which Byron thought 'the most beautiful, perhaps, in the world'.

Mary Chaworth. Byron fell in love with her when he was at school at Harrow, but she was two years older and already committed to her future husband. She remained in Byron's memory and imagination.

Teresa Macri, daughter of the widow Macri with whom Byron and Hobhouse lodged in Athens. Byron's poem beginning 'Maid of Athens, ere we part' was addressed to Teresa, whose mother, Byron wrote, was mad enough to think he would marry her.

Ioannina, the capital of Ali Pacha, the murderous warlord who ruled northern Greece and Albania. Ioannina was superior to Athens, not only in size, Byron wrote, but in 'wealth, refinement [and] learning'.

Now the Ali Pacha Museum in Ioannina. Ali Pacha was killed there by the Turks in 1822.

blindly ignorant people lashing out violently at the first hint of trouble. For one thing the violence of the 'Luddites' was highly selective: only the machines of unpopular employers were attacked, and only certain machines were destroyed. For another, they had first tried peaceful methods. They had sought redress from their employers, from the local magistrates and from Parliament. Many of the employers were sympathetic and supported the workers' efforts. But, as they never could get the agreement of all their number, the intervention of an outside body was necessary for any regulation to be binding and successful. An appeal to Parliament did not initially seem to be the forlorn hope that it turned out to be. Parliament was not prevented from intervening in industry; it frequently intervened on behalf of the employers. For those who believed the rhetoric about the British constitution there was no reason why Parliament should not intervene in proper cases on behalf of the workers. And so far as Nottinghamshire was concerned it was not a case just of intervening on behalf of the workers; since many of the hosiers supported many of the workers' demands, it was a case of intervening to help the whole industry. But Parliament and the government were too addicted to *laissez-faire* to heed the appeals of the stockingers.[35]

In 1810, twenty-six banks had failed, and many people went bankrupt. By 1811 conditions were lamentable virtually everywhere. As Byron wrote in November

> The idle merchant on the useless quay,
> Droops o'er the bales no bark may bear away.

Napoleon's continental system and Britain's retaliatory Orders in Council had cut down trade with Europe. The American Non-Intercourse Act, which was the United States's retaliation against the Orders in Council and which became operational from February 1811, wrecked trade with the United States. British exports to America in 1811 were less than one-fifth of what they had been in 1810. Probably each of the three countries was most damaged by the measures taken by its own government. In England a junior minister thought Britain and France were like two men who had put their heads in a bucket of water and were trying to see who could keep his head submerged the longer.[36]

Between 1809 and the Luddite outbreaks, wages fell by one-third; to add to the vexations the English harvest failed in each of those years, and in 1811 and 1812 the continental crops failed also. Hence while wages were falling the cost of food was rising, and food rioting was more general than machine-breaking. All the witnesses before a parliamentary committee agreed that distress in the working class was greater than at any previous time. The general decline in trade came on top of the endemic fragility of the stocking frame industry. By the end of January 1812 nearly half of the population of Nottingham was living on the poor rates.[37]

The most unusual feature of the machine-breaking that broke out in 1811–12 in the East Midlands, Yorkshire and Lancashire was its scale. Bands of up to seventy men attacked machinery in Notting-hamshire, while 150 men attacked Rawfolds Mill in Yorkshire, the central incident in Charlotte Brontë's *Shirley*. Even more striking was the force deployed by the government. The strength of the army used against the machine breakers or Luddites was some 12,000 men, considerably more than the number Wellesley had taken to Portugal in 1808. When the militia are included – Mary Chaworth's husband Jack Musters was an active colonel in the Nottingham Militia – the government forces numbered 35,000.[*][39]

Even if the militia are ignored, the Luddites were faced with a force some six times as large as had ever previously been used for such a purpose. Even so the army had considerable difficulty in putting down the disorder. If 'General Ned Ludd' was less formidable than Napoleon, he was more effective than some of Napoleon's marshals in tying down British troops. Indeed before the end of the summer of 1812 Wellington had to send four regiments back to England because of a shortage of horses caused by the mobilisation of cavalry to put down the industrial unrest in the north.[40]

No wonder news of the workers being 'reduced to starvation' and of soldiers being sent to Nottingham reached Shelley in Keswick, and no wonder he thought that 'curses should light on them for their motives' if they destroyed any of its people.[41]

---

* The government had brought 50,000 men to London to maintain order in 1810, nearly double the number of *British* soldiers that Wellington had at Waterloo.[38]

CHAPTER XIV

Marriage and Exile

Shelley: 1811 (aged 19 years)

On the day (25 August 1811) that Shelley left London, eloping with Harriet Westbrook to Edinburgh, he had met a family acquaintance at the City hostelry. Far from being abashed by the encounter he had borrowed £10 from him. Still short of cash, he sent a note to Hogg when the coach reached York, telling him that he was with Harriet and asking him to send £10 to Edinburgh.

On the coach Shelley fell into conversation with a friendly young Scottish lawyer who told him how they could get married in Edinburgh, and having arrived there on the morning of Wednesday the 28th he quickly engineered a wedding, probably on the following day. As he and Harriet were minors, that entailed two witnesses falsely affirming that Harriet had resided in Edinburgh for six weeks and that she and Shelley were both 'of legal age', as well as the clergyman breaking the laws of his church – seven years later he was transported for similar transgressions – but for the time being the ceremony was good enough.* Shelley and Harriet also quickly found excellent lodgings in the newly built George Street, the landlord agreeing to finance them until funds arrived, in return for the newly-weds treating him and his friends to a supper in honour of the occasion.[1]

The marriage lasted barely three years. The private part of the honeymoon was relatively even shorter. Shelley's request for £10 when he passed through York had contained no invitation to Hogg

---

* Oddly, neither Shelley nor the Scottish lawyer seems to have been aware that unless a church wedding was essential, which it certainly was not for Shelley, none of this subterfuge was necessary. He could have married Harriet easily and openly, as did many English elopers, at the Old Blacksmith's Shop at Gretna Green on the Scottish border or elsewhere in Scotland. Jane Austen was better informed. In *Pride and Prejudice*, published two years later, Lydia Bennet implies that she is eloping to Gretna Green to marry Wickham – though in fact they stayed in London. To avoid a breach of promise suit in 1820, the great advocate Lord Erskine, whom Byron found brilliant but inordinately egotistical, ran off from London at the age of seventy in female clothing to marry his long-established mistress and housekeeper at Gretna Green. Fifty years earlier, though for different reasons, he had similarly eloped and married at Gretna Green.[2]

to join him and Harriet. But Hogg, who had been hoping to go on a walking tour with his friend, evidently considered a honeymoon a collective enterprise and arrived in Edinburgh a few days after the wedding. In his book he camouflages – skilfully enough to deceive his biographer and others – his blatant gatecrashing by saying that in his letter accompanying the £10 he had 'promised to be with' Shelley almost as soon as his letter.[3]

In any case his appearance in Edinburgh was 'hailed triumphantly', he tells us, 'by the new-married pair'. That is easily credible since, even if Shelley did not fully share Oscar Wilde's view that 'in married life three is company and two is none', he certainly preferred three to two, even on honeymoons; he needed a buffer or a cushion between himself and his wife or lover. And if Harriet found the speedy arrival of a reinforcement for their married bliss surprising, she kept her doubts to herself. Not only did Shelley welcome Hogg's gatecrashing, he extended it. As soon as his friend reached George Street, Shelley told him: 'We will never part again. You must have a bed in the house', though even Hogg, who was never one for self-effacement, would have been content with a bed a mile or two away from the honeymooners. Shelley had of course no intention of sharing the bed with Hogg – he regarded physical homosexual relations as 'detestable' and, if he was thinking of anybody sharing Hogg's bed, it would have been Harriet, not him – but his response to his friend's arrival was at least as strange as Hogg's assumption that the solution to his holiday problem was to honeymoon with the Shelleys. The reactions of both of them show that the love affair and marriage of Shelley and Harriet had not obliterated the earlier love affair of Hogg and Shelley.[4]

For Hogg, seeing the 'lovely young bride . . . bright, blooming, radiant with youth, health and beauty' caused love at virtually first sight; just how much that instant love was precipitated by Harriet being Shelley's wife as well as by her natural attractions can only be conjectured. In his book Hogg satirises Harriet's reluctance to descend Arthur's Seat in the wind for fear of showing her ankles, but he does not add that her excess of modesty was probably caused by her wishing to escape his lascivious glances. In any case Hogg soon discovered that Harriet was not just a beauty. He corrects those 'reckless or ill-informed biographers' who alleged that she was not a fit companion for Shelley because she was 'illiterate'. On the contrary, Hogg says, she had been 'well-educated' and was 'exceedingly well read'. Having in Edinburgh only indicated it, in York Hogg made a declaration of his love to Harriet, who forbade any repetition and decided in a thoroughly adult way not to tell Shelley in case such intelligence impaired his friendship with Hogg.[5]

The trio's forenoons were devoted to study. Shelley was translating the writer whom Hogg typically calls 'the immortal Buffon',* while Harriet was translating a contemporary novel from the French. She translated two volumes of the novel 'exactly and correctly' in a neat 'legible feminine hand'. Sadly both her manuscript and Shelley's have been lost. In the afternoons, after dinner, the trio went for long walks, returning only at dusk. Shelley later complained of what he called 'the filth and commerce of Edinburgh'; he considered commerce even more 'contemptible' than 'vile aristocracy'. Certainly parts of the old town were renowned for their dirt and stink, but there would have been nothing of that sort in George Street, which Hogg found 'spacious, noble and well built'; and Shelley cannot have been much affected by the city's commerce, which was anyway hardly a matter for complaint. Contrary to the impression he gave, Edinburgh in 1811 was one of the most beautiful cities in Europe, but the young bridegroom, Hogg correctly says, was not interested in architecture or pictures at this time; even Arthur's Seat, which Boswell at much the same age called 'that lofty romantic mountain' and to which he 'bowed thrice', had no effect on Shelley. So 'the Athens of the North' left as little trace on his poetry as, after a very much longer sojourn, the definitely non-Athenian Aberdeen left on Byron's.[6]

In his book Hogg enjoys himself caricaturing the reigning Presbyterianism of the Scottish capital, making Edinburgh seem a modern version of Calvin's Geneva. When he and Shelley decided to sample a service in the kirk, Harriet sensibly declined to go on the grounds that what Hogg calls 'the wearisome performance' would give her a headache. The prayers, the loud music and the lengthy preaching with its threats of everlasting punishment did not give Shelley a headache, but they made him 'the picture of perfect wretchedness'. On another occasion, refusing to be dissuaded by Harriet, Hogg and Shelley decided to go to 'the Catechism' which, it

---

* As a member of the Académie Française, Buffon who died in 1788 was one of the 'forty immortals'. He was an agnostic, which would have appealed to Shelley, but when attacked by the Roman Church he temporised, telling a colleague, 'it is better to be humble than hung', which would not have appealed to his translator. He was perhaps the most influential naturalist since Aristotle, his de l'Histoire naturelle running to forty-four volumes. How much of it Shelley hoped to translate is not known.[7]

was ordained, 'children and domestics must attend'. After the conductor of the proceedings had asked a number of questions in, not surprisingly, a Scottish accent, 'Shelley burst into a shrieking laugh, and rushed wildly out of doors.' Understandably Harriet, who was in some ways the most mature of the three, had little sympathy for their 'sufferings'. They had, after all, behaved like children, if not domestics.[8]

In the evenings after brewing tea they listened, according to Hogg, to Harriet reading aloud. Though she read very well with a remarkably clear articulation and Hogg remained attentive, Shelley, he claims, sometimes went to sleep – much to Harriet's irritation. Hogg was writing nearly fifty years after the event and his cameo of Harriet relentlessly reading for hours every evening as Shelley went to sleep is most likely the result of bad memory or malice.[9]

At the end of six weeks, according to Hogg (though in fact they were in Edinburgh for only a month), his work in a conveyancer's office required his return to York; and in order that, in Shelley's phrase, they might remain with him 'for ever', the bride and groom went too. Only the generosity of his Uncle Pilfold, who had been subsidising them in Edinburgh, enabled them to leave George Street. They travelled in a post chaise for Harriet's benefit, and she read aloud for much of the way. On arrival they discovered that in Hogg's protracted absence his landlady had let her entire house to another family. After a search in the rain and the twilight they ended up in dingy lodgings in a poverty-stricken house.[10]

Shelley had had no word from his father. As soon as Timothy received his son's letter of 25 August, posted by Charles Grove (which, as we have seen, boorishly demanded his belongings), he had hastened to London to consult Whitton, his solicitor. He would have liked to disinherit his son, but Whitton showed him that the entails ruled that out, much as they had ruled out Shelley disinheriting himself. So, after two meetings with the Westbrooks, Timothy had to content himself with cutting off his son's allowance of £50 a quarter, the next instalment of which was due on 1 September; Mr Westbrook similarly agreed not to finance his daughter.[11]

As before, Timothy also decided not to answer his son's letters, though if he was silent to Shelley he was so talkative to his friends that echoes of his gossiping reached Whitton, who advised him to keep quiet except to his wife. Timothy wrote to advise Hogg's father that he had learned that Hogg had joined Shelley and 'a young female' in Edinburgh, ending with the gloomy reflection that only God could know what would 'be the End of all this Disobedience'. Hogg senior was not unduly worried, expecting shortage of money to ensure his son's early return to York.[12]

Shelley, too, badly needed money, for which the obvious source was his father. Yet in his necessarily one-sided correspondence with Timothy he once again demonstrated his frequent inability to grasp reality. When he went to Oxford, his father had told him that he would pay for bastards but would not forgive a *mésalliance*. Harriet, as De Quincey later put it, was 'respectably connected', but her family was not 'in a rank corresponding to Shelley's'. Timothy, who had had for years to put up with his father's demotic behaviour in Horsham, was inevitably dismayed by his son's marriage to the daughter of a coffee-house owner, even if he was rich. Inevitably a parvenu like Timothy Shelley was even less likely to overlook such a *mésalliance* than more socially secure land-owners. Having just about established his family's respectability despite his father, he saw his son now endangering that hard-won accolade.[13]

In addition Shelley had practised deceit on his family, attempting to conceal both his elopement and his destination. If, therefore, he was to persuade his father to resume supplies, he needed to appease Timothy's natural resentment at the way he had been treated. Yet in his letters there was a divorce between his end and his means of achieving it. A few weeks later Shelley told the Duke of Norfolk that his letters to his father had been 'calculated to make his [father's] considerations of [his] proceedings less severe'. They read more, though, as if they were designed to do the opposite. Instead of trying to please or at least conciliate Timothy, Shelley went out of his way to affront him.[14]

Five days after his gratuitously aggressive London letter, Shelley sent a polite request for £50. But his claim that he knew nobody more certain to help him 'when in distress' than his father was so palpably insincere that its sarcasm could not have escaped Timothy. His third letter, written a fortnight later, again asking for money, admitted that he had 'perhaps acted with impoliteness', but lectured his father on the uselessness of anger and on the Christian duty of 'forbearance and forgiveness'. Some ten days later he admitted to being married, but this letter was even more patronising and reproving than its predecessor. It is Timothy who has erred, not Shelley; in consequence his father is lectured on his 'duty' to the God whose worship he professes, and is told to 'judge not, lest you be judged'. And just in case he has not been sufficiently offensive, Shelley casually mentions parricide: '. . . if my crime were even deadlier than parricide, forgiveness is your duty'. Timothy, he adds, was lower 'in real virtue [than] the libertine atheist'. Shelley always knew that what he wanted to do was right – unlike Byron, who often knew what *he* wanted to do was wrong, even though he, like Macbeth, went on and did it: as he had written in 1809, he was 'Just skilled to know the right and chuse the wrong . . .' So, to Shelley, the sinner now was not the youth who had committed the offence but the man who refused to forgive it. And in one important sense he was right. Having acceded to the arguments of Harriet and Mrs Opie's novel, he had married Harriet; he had not turned her into a 'fallen woman'.[15]

At York Shelley decided that in married life three were not enough. He sought an additional recruit in the angular shape of Elizabeth Hitchener.

In his first embarrassed letter from York explaining his marriage and regretting 'the equivocality of [his] conduct', he merely asked Miss Hitchener to pay him a visit; now that he was married, Harriet would not see any 'impropriety' in their 'intercourse'. Miss Hitchener quickly replied that she longed to be introduced to Harriet, who 'would have a Sister's affection, for are you not the Brother of my soul'; still, for the present, her situation prevented her accepting his invitation. Shelley 'instantly' replied: 'My dearest friend I will dare to say I *love*, . . . nor do I risk the supposition that the lump of organised matter which enshrines *thy* soul excites the love which that soul *dare* claim'. Had Shelley had more humour, he would have realised that his intended compliment to his correspondent's spirituality would read more like an insult to her body. 'Henceforth', he continued, 'will I be your's . . .'. He was leaving York that night to see 'that mistaken man', his father. Likening himself to 'the God of the Jews', he was no respecter of persons. Then digressing into philosophy, everything was connected, he told her, and there was a train of events; so the turn which his 'mind [had] taken originated from the conquest of England by William of Normandy'. Adopting Miss Hitchener's pretentious expression, he assured her that he loved her more than any relation he possessed; 'you are the sister of my soul, its dearest sister . . .'. When he came into his estate, it would be shared with, amongst others, Hogg and herself. Hogg and he already considered, he went on, their 'property as common, that the day will arrive when we shall do the same, is the wish of my soul whose consummation I most eagerly anticipate'. (That may not have been the only 'consummation' he antici-pated.) 'Sister of my soul adieu,' he finished, 'With I hope eternal love your Percy Shelley'.

When he wrote that letter, Shelley had been married for less than two months and had met Miss Hitchener, at the most, twice in his life.[16]

During the fortnight that he was in York, in even deeper need of money, he wrote three more letters to his father and one to his grandfather, asking him for money. As himself a veteran eloper, Sir Bysshe might have had some sympathy with the novice effort of his grandson, even though Shelley's letter was inappropriately truculent and self-important. Sir Bysshe had twice, however, chosen heiresses whose birth was higher than his; if his grandson had been similarly prudent, there would have been no objection. But, as Harriet was of lower birth and not an heiress, Sir Bysshe was deaf to his grandson's appeal.[17]

Timothy did at last send on his son's belongings, but instead of thanking him, Shelley, who had heard that Timothy had forbidden his name to be mentioned at Field Place, abused him for not having written as well. His own letters were becoming increasingly hysterical. Learning that Timothy had foolishly told Hogg's father that it would not surprise him if Shelley left 'his lady' on Hogg's hands, Shelley told the squire that such a charge was 'a cowardly, base, contemptible expedient of persecution'. Becoming more and more furious, he alleged that after his expulsion for atheism, Timothy had wished that he had been killed in Spain; he even hinted that if his father had not been a coward he would have had his son murdered. He finished with this outburst: 'I shall take the first opportunity of seeing you – if *you* will not hear my name, I will pronounce it. Think not I am an insect whom injuries destroy – had I money enough I would meet you in London, & hollow in your ears Bysshe, Bysshe, Bysshe – aye Bysshe till you're deaf' [unsigned].[18]

Whitton had called one of Shelley's Edinburgh letters 'an

extraordinary production', which showed 'how lost' were 'his feelings' to his father, mother and sisters. This letter was even more extraordinary. Shelley's allegation that his father wanted him murdered and his own talk of 'parricide' suggest that it was he who had murderous fantasies. The letter must have enhanced Timothy's doubts about its writer's sanity, doubts which would have been further aggravated had he seen Shelley's letters to Miss Hitchener.[19]

Not content with his policy of silence to his son, which fuelled Shelley's fears of rejection and abandonment, Timothy had not restored his allowance. 'To be profoundly angry', Captain Pilfold told his nephew, 'is all very well, but to stop supplies is a great deal too bad'. It was also pointless: Shelley could not unmarry Harriet. But Timothy was too eaten up with anger that his parental authority had been flouted and with fear that his social standing had been jeopardised to make the best of what he regarded as a bad situation; so as usual he merely made matters worse.[20]

Yet Shelley was as irrational as his father. Admittedly he seems to have written almost no poems at this time, and his letters to Timothy and to Miss Hitchener were to some extent substitutes for poetry. In them he was dramatising his feelings and cutting a figure. Three years before he had told an Eton friend that, after reading 'Novels and Romances all day', in the evening he fancied himself 'a Character'. His threat to deafen Timothy by 'hollowing' Bysshe in his ear derived from Shakespeare's Hotspur vowing to 'hollo Mortimer' in the ear of King Henry – a phrase also misquoted by Byron earlier that year in his *Hints from Horace*. Mortimer was Richard II's designated heir whom Henry IV had left to starve on 'barren mountains' – a rather harsher fate than that currently being suffered by Shelley and Harriet. According to Hogg, Shelley was 'the creature . . . of his irresistible imagination'. Elizabeth Hitchener, too, was largely the creature of that imagination: her real self bore little relation to the near-perfect woman invented by the young poet. In his letters to her, both he and Miss Hitchener were partly invented characters, fantasies living in a novel as much as in real life.[21]

Even so, at least when corresponding with his father, Shelley should have had the wit to subdue his imagination and either divest himself of his 'characters' or adopt a more serviceable one for himself. Instead of behaving as his father's stern preceptor denouncing his dim pupil's failure to live up to the highest standards of a religion, which he himself despised, he should have portrayed himself as a misguided innocent throwing himself upon his father's protection. But evidently his hatred of his father and, presumably, his feelings of rejection, first aroused by his banishment to Syon House, blinded him to everything else. So he, too, pursued a self-defeating course.

Shortly after his 'Bysshe, Bysshe, Bysshe' letter to his father, Shelley set off by himself for Sussex, leaving his wife behind with Hogg in their 'dismal' and 'dingy' lodgings. Thus, although he had only recently upbraided his father for saying that he might leave his wife on Hogg's hands, Shelley proceeded, temporarily at least, to do exactly that. As soon as Hogg's parents learned what had happened, John Hogg wrote to Shelley's father expressing their disquiet, and Mrs Hogg wrote to Harriet to say that it was 'very imprudent' for Harriet to be left alone with Hogg and offering to help. Harriet wrote 'a very civil answer, much in the style of a gentlewoman', thanking her for her kindness but 'declining her services for the present.'

As Shelley must have been at least as aware as his friend's parents of Hogg's proclivities, and much more aware than them both of Harriet's considerable attractions and of Hogg's susceptibility to them, he cannot have failed to know just how 'imprudent' it was to leave Hogg alone with his wife. Before the elopement Shelley had been at pains to conceal from Hogg his true feelings for Harriet; during the honeymoon he must have noticed that Hogg was drawn to his bride. Yet for ten days he left her at Hogg's mercy. Presumably he had some hope that, while he was away, they would have sexual relations or at least make progress towards having them. Such a suspicion is strengthened by his having 'spoken slightly' to Hogg, both before and after York, of 'the monopoly of exclusive cohabitation', by his having told Byron's doctor five years later that he had done all he could to induce Harriet to love Hogg in return and by his subsequent encouragement of similar behaviour between Hogg and his second wife.[22]

Throughout the honeymoon Shelley got on well with Harriet; a poem he wrote in York sang her praises:

> Yes! though the landscape's beauties flee
> My Harriet makes it spring to me. . . .

And each pure feeling shall combine
To tell its Harriet 'I am thine!

Yet, within a few days of its beginning, he insisted that a male friend, with whom he had an intense relationship, should join him and his wife in their lodgings. Not long afterwards he wrote a love letter to another woman (though in view of her physical unattractiveness he evidently saw her as a surrogate mother as much as a potential mistress) and invited her to visit them. Then he left his wife alone with his male friend. All in all it was an unusual honeymoon.[23]

After three days and two nights 'on the outside of a coach' Shelley arrived at his uncle's house. Captain Pilfold, who was a 'most generous fellow', was on bad terms with Timothy – he told T. C. Medwin, who had recently been displaced as Norfolk's steward, that 'Dukes ... can be as fawning and as mean as a Shelley, their purposes once served they cast you off' – and that hostility doubtless did not diminish his generosity to Timothy's son. At Cuckfield, Shelley had his third meeting with 'the sister of [his] soul'.

His visit to Field Place, where his father told him that financial arrangements were in the hands of Whitton, was less successful. Admittedly, Timothy's decision to deal with Shelley through a stuffy, unsympathetic solicitor would have angered an heir more dutiful and less prone to rage than his eldest son, but Shelley's reaction was madder than his letters. He became so angry that he frightened not only his father but, Timothy wrote, 'his mother and sister exceedingly [so that] now if they hear a dog bark they run upstairs'. His father thought Shelley's mind was 'perturbed' and 'disordered' and he was 'such a pupil of Godwin' that he was unlikely to be persuaded that he owed any obedience to his parents. [24]

The day after this scene, Trafalgar Day, the squire sent a rude letter to his brother-in-law, written in the third person, 'apprising' the Captain of Shelley's 'irrational notions' and telling him that everything had been placed in Whitton's hands, 'that no other person may interfere'. Shelley then sent an even more offensive, if not mad, letter to his mother, enlarging on what he had evidently raved about at Field Place: her allegedly illicit relations with Shelley's friend, Fergus Graham (for which there was no foundation except the anonymous letter mentioned earlier that had probably been written by Shelley himself) and her allegedly impure motives 'for so violently so persecutingly desiring to unite' his sister

Elizabeth to 'the music master Graham'. One critic has speculated that Shelley's verbal violence – later he wrote to Miss Hitchener of Mrs Shelley's 'depravity' – stemmed from a quasi-incestuous affection for his mother. Be that as it may, the one benefit of Timothy's abdication in favour of Whitton was that Shelley's letter was sent on to the solicitor, so that his mother never saw what Whitton justifiably called his 'harsh and unfeeling sentiments'. Whitton likened one letter that Shelley sent him to that of 'a mad viper'.[25]

Yet, on a visit to his grandfather, 'the youngster', Timothy affectionately commented to Whitton, 'behaved very well'. And Shelley told T. C. Medwin, who, like Pilfold, had fallen out with the squire – probably because of his loan to Shelley before the elopement – that he wished to 'take the precaution of being re-married' and wanted to settle £700 a year on Harriet 'in case of my death'.*[26]

Shelley returned to York after Whitton had both refused to see him and pompously informed him in a letter that he would not get any money until he acted 'more consonant' with his duty to his father and considered his 'injured feelings'. Unfortunately Whitton, like his client, could not get it into his head that Shelley was indeed a 'youngster' and so should not be treated as a fully adult delinquent. The youngster's Sussex visit had been abortive; for the time being, his fund raising had failed. All he had achieved was a worsening of his relations with his family. But he did not give up. He seldom did. Acting on the recommendation of Charles Grove, he wrote a well judged letter to the Duke of Norfolk, asking for his help in inducing his father to allow him a sufficient income. Charles Grove's advice was good. 'The Jockey' clearly liked Shelley, and he thought Timothy was mishandling their quarrel. 'Mr Shelley, you can't do it', he had told the squire a few days before.[27]

By the time Shelley returned to York on about 24 October their 'destinies', Hogg maintained, had been 'entirely changed'. He attributed this change to the arrival of Harriet's sister Eliza, who, he asserted, had 'superseded' Shelley and ruled in his stead, at least when she was not brushing her hair. This, according to Hogg, she did for sixteen hours a day. Shelley 'became nothing', Hogg

---

* In the event, though, he did not remarry Harriet till 1814 and never did settle £700 on her, which he anyway did not have.

asserted, and he himself 'very much less than nothing'. In Shelley's absence there had indeed been a change in the household, but not for the reason given by Hogg. The true reason was Hogg's attempted seduction of Harriet, which she had successfully resisted and strongly resented. And that had bred Hogg's reciprocal resentment.[28]

Eliza had been going to travel north with Shelley, but after Hogg's failed seduction Harriet had summoned her sister to bolster her defences. Arriving with some much-needed money, Eliza was inevitably hostile to Hogg. Consequently she earned his immediate hatred then and his unremitting malice fifty years later when he wrote his book.* Hogg's hostility to Eliza, who had 'superseded' him, not Shelley, as the third member of Shelley's threesome and whom he designated 'a barmaid by origin', was not at that time shared by Shelley. Eliza, he told Elizabeth Hitchener, was 'a woman rather superior to the generality'. Shelley, as has been seen, hankered after having more than one woman in the house, as he had had among his sisters at Field Place. Hogg's tampering with the documents, his direct lies and false innuendoes make this the most dishonest section of his biography, reducing it to little more than forgery and fiction.[30]

Shelley cannot have failed to notice the change in the atmosphere at York. But, much as Harriet had stopped Hogg from writing to Shelley in Sussex confessing his sins because she feared 'its effect on [his] mind at such a distance' – an interesting revelation of her worries about Shelley's mental balance – she was reluctant to tell her husband the full story of Hogg's 'unworthiness'. Her hints alarmed Shelley 'vaguely', but enough for him to take Hogg for a long walk, during which Hogg was persuaded to confess 'the secret of his unfaithfulness'. Three days afterwards, at the beginning of November, the Shelleys decamped with Eliza. Characteristically Hogg claims to have been invited to go with them, but that was a lie. The whole point of their departure from York was to escape from him.[31]

Leaving behind a largely illegible and unintelligible note which seemed to indicate Richmond as their destination, the trio had made pursuit by Hogg impossible. Probably on their journey Shelley

---

* Hogg in his book is also, as Humbert Wolfe points out in his Introduction to the twentieth-century edition of it, consistently 'slighting' of Harriet's character. 'Anticipating the poor girl's suicide', Wolfe adds, Hogg seeks to 'muddy the waters' by claiming that she constantly talked of taking her life.[29]

wrote a fragment of verse which referred to Hogg as 'a mind with radiant genius fraught', but only later did he reveal to him their whereabouts: not Richmond but Keswick. During their long conversation in York, Shelley had pardoned Hogg, telling him that only his vices not himself were the object of his hatred – though that can have given Hogg only limited comfort. There now ensued yet another intense correspondence, while Shelley was at the same time giving a commentary on it to Miss Hitchener in a similarly intense exchange of letters. 'Virtue', he told her, had lost a defender; 'vice [had] gained a proselyte'.[32]

Hogg was distraught at the separation, threatening suicide, not very seriously, unless Harriet forgave him. He had a double role: the spurned lover of Harriet and the deserted non-carnal lover of Shelley, who was himself almost equally upset by the separation and Hogg's fall from grace. He, too, had a double role: the protector of Harriet, on whom 'Nature [had] exhausted the profusion of her loveliness', and the lover of Hogg, to whom he strangely wrote: 'Tell me that it t'was another, & I will adore you as the first of men, and as now I love you as the dearest to me. . . . I am half mad', he went on, 'I am wretchedly miserable. . . . Ah! how I have loved you. I was even ashamed to tell you how!'[33]

Shelley's abhorrence of Hogg's behaviour does not dispel the suspicion that he had expected something of the sort to happen while he was in Sussex. His censure of Hogg was grounded not on his friend having tried to make love to Harriet, but on Harriet's opposition to it, and on Hogg's persistence and dishonesty. Hogg had tried to overcome Harriet's objections by using 'arguments of detestable sophistry'. For example, 'there is no injury to him who knows it not'. Hogg in other words had been selfish which, according to Shelley's philosophy of love, was unforgivable. He had been motivated not by love which, Shelley told Miss Hitchener, 'seeks the good of its object first', but by lust which seeks only its own gratification. Had love been dominant and Harriet willing, Shelley told his friend, he would have had no objection; he was often inclined to think that 'the Godwinian plan' – no sexual monopoly – was 'best'. In those circumstances Hogg could have had 'the possession of Harriet's person'; he would have been 'welcome to even this'. But with Hogg lust had ruled, Harriet was not willing, and they must 'not sport with the feelings of others'.[34]

Hogg could seldom understand anybody's point of view but his own, and he went on making what Shelley called 'his supplications' for a reunion. Shelley was adamant that that was impossible. The past was not the only problem after all; the future was a bigger one. Hogg said he could never cease to love Harriet and to her annoyance continued to flatter her in letters. In 'Passion: To the [Woody Nightshade]', a poem written at Keswick, Shelley called passion:

> Prime source of all that's lovely, good and great
> Debasing man below the meanest brute . . .

If Hogg was allowed back, plainly he would try again, and Shelley was not prepared to 'barter Harriet's happiness for [Hogg's] short-lived pleasure'. After three weeks of endless letter writing, during which Hogg, no more seriously than his threat of suicide, challenged his friend to a duel, Shelley became bored. 'I do not love him now', he informed Miss Hitchener; and after telling Hogg that the very sight of his letters cast his wife into a gloom and that he could not 'consent to the destruction of Harriet's peace', he did not write again for a year.[35]

He continued, however, to find Miss Hitchener's letters 'an exhaustless mine of pleasure'. 'Your friendship', he told her, 'seems to have generated a passion to which fifty such fleeting inadequate existences as these appear to be but the drop in the bucket too trivial for account – with you! I cannot submit to perish like the flower of the field, I cannot consent that the same shroud which shall moulder around these perishing frames shall enwrap the vital spirit which has produced sanctified (may I say eternized) a friendship such as ours'. 'You are', he told her in another letter, 'as my better genius, the judge of my marriage, the guide of my actions . . .'[36]

In 'The Retrospect: Cwm Elan 1812', written a few months later Shelley wrote:

> when peaceful love
> Flings rapture's colours o'er the grove,
> When mountain, meadow, wood and stream
> With unalloying glory gleam
> [They] to the spirit's ear and eye
> Are unison and harmony.

Yet in his relations with women Shelley sought not harmony but narcissistic unison. He even made a verb out of the word, writing to Miss Hitchener, 'you who understand my motives to action which I flatter myself unisonize with your own, you . . . I will dare to say I love . . .'. Shelley sought himself or his own likeness in a woman. He had the beauty and love of Harriet who, like Catherine Morland in *Northanger Abbey*, listened to him 'with all the civility and deference of the young female mind', but he wanted his intellect as well and thought he saw it in Miss Hitchener whom he scarcely knew. Inevitably, when she later came to stay with him and Harriet, she turned out a very different being from the one he had imagined. According to Hogg she had traces of a beard, and she also had more serious non-physical imperfections. So the relationship ended in disaster. Shelley thought Mary Godwin, his second wife, embodied the features he most loved in himself, but soon found she lacked other things. Once again disillusionment followed. Since nobody was like him, his quest was bound to fail. The achievement of 'harmony' is difficult enough. 'Unison' is both impossible and undesirable.[37]

Shelley's quest and his inevitable disappointment were presumably less the fault of his theory of love than the result of his feminine streak and his bisexual trait. Calling Miss Hitchener 'thou reciprocity of thought', he told her that everything, including the body, which related 'simply to this clayformed dungeon [was] comparatively despicable, and in a state of perfectible society could not be made the subjects of either Virtue or Vice'. Still odder, even allowing for its echoes of Plato, whom Shelley vastly admired and whose *Symposium* he later translated, was his assertion to a woman (Miss Hitchener) that the differences between men and women were 'detestable distinctions [which] will surely be abolished in a future state of being'.* Certainly his enthusiasm to, and for, Miss

---

* Shelley's androgynous inclinations and his feeling that the ideal union was between identities not opposites may have partly stemmed from some anatomical abnormality, as the Maniac seems to suggest in Shelley's 1818–19 poem *Julian and Maddalo*:

> Thou wilt admire how I could e'er address
> Such features to love's work . . . this taunt, though true,
> (For indeed nature nor in form nor hue
> Bestowed on me her choicest workmanship)
> Shall not be thy defence . . . for since thy lip
> Met mine first, years long past, since thine eye kindled
> With soft fire under mine, I have not dwindled . . .

Whatever the truth about Shelley, that was not Byron's problem. When his tomb was opened in 1938, the churchwarden recorded that Byron's 'sexual organ showed quite abnormal development'. Yet what was once said about Wordsworth may by analogy apply to the

Hitchener had little connection with the present state of being or the real world.[39]

In real life Shelley's letter to the Duke of Norfolk proved productive. 'The Jockey' responded with a civil though not encouraging letter which indicated doubts about Shelley's recent conduct. Yet he discussed the matter with Timothy, and when he discovered that Shelley at Keswick was only fifteen miles away from Greystoke, his Gothicised northern seat which boasted the biggest park in England, he invited Shelley, Harriet and Eliza to stay on 1 December. They must have made a good impression, as their visit was extended from four to eight days, even though Shelley was argumentative and did not conceal his views. He afterwards complained of being 'fatigued with aristocratic insipidity', but that said less about the company at Greystoke than about his tendency to complain about anybody who was different from him or did not agree with his increasingly democratic views. Two of the other five guests were not aristocrats and, though the Jockey himself had many faults, 'insipidity' was not one of them. Later two of the guests, William Calvert, a friend of Wordsworth, and his wife, were kind and very helpful to him during the rest of the stay at Keswick.[40]

The thought should surely have crossed Timothy Shelley's mind that, if his eldest son and his daughter-in-law were good enough to stay with his patron, the premier Duke of England, they were good enough to be accepted at Field Place. But Timothy had earlier told Whitton that 'the young man' had both to 'manifest to the world his abhorrence of [his] monstrous opinions' and to demonstrate 'a contrite heart' before he could 'receive him upon his knees'. Not only did he not receive the newly-weds at Field Place, neither he nor his cold, supine wife ever even saw their beautiful daughter-in-law.[41]

Elizabeth Shelley may have been alienated by her son's outbursts over the Graham non-affair, and Timothy may have feared that Shelley would convert his young sisters to atheism. In view of Shelley's passion for proselytism, that was a danger, and at this time he did in fact write a secret letter to the youngest sister, Hellen: 'Show this letter to no one'. It was to be delivered to her by his

churchwarden. When some Wordsworthians were deploring the poet's confession that he got drunk at Cambridge, the novelist Joseph Shorthouse commented that in all probability 'Wordsworth's standard of intoxication was miserably low'.[38]

father's huntsman, who delivered it to Timothy instead. All the same, the squire could easily have safeguarded his daughters from his son's missionary compulsions by keeping the girls away from Field Place when Shelley and Harriet were there.[42]

Probably influenced by Harriet keeping ducal company, Mr Westbrook decided to give her an allowance of £200 a year; and after Shelley, on the Duke's advice, had written him an unusually conciliatory letter and had received a stiff and far from conciliatory reply, Timothy followed suit in January. In view of Shelley's occasional carelessness over bills, the squire's graceless taunt that he did so to prevent his son 'cheating strangers' did have some point.[43]

Shelley's landlord, a Mr Dare, wanted him, Harriet and Eliza to leave their Keswick house. Their neighbours had been alarmed by 'odd things' they had seen at night. Shelley had made some experiments with hydrogen gas which had created a 'vivid flame'. He was also engaged in less anodyne activities. He had been further radicalised by the industrial unrest in the North and by seeing the plight of the poor at first hand, which for somebody of his benevolence and sensitivity was a searing experience. 'I have beheld scenes of misery,' he told Elizabeth Hitchener. 'The manufacturers [i.e. workers] are reduced to starvation [and] the military are gone to Nottingham.' All this made politics rather than religion Shelley's dominant concern. He was still interested in discussing such subjects as the immortality of the soul, in which he believed, but politics now came first. Had it done so when he was at Oxford, he would probably not have written *The Necessity of Atheism* or suffered expulsion, and he would have accepted the Duke of Norfolk's invitation to become MP for Horsham at the next election. But, having cut himself off from a parliamentary career, he could now be only a paper politician. The people, not Parliament, were his audience. He was writing essays to be published in the summer, and was hoping soon to publish his newer poems with a preface to show his political intentions.[44]

Mr Dare was dissatisfied both with Shelley's explanation and his tenancy, but he did not insist on his departure; that was a relief to his tenant, who was hoping soon to meet the Lake poets. The Southey and Coleridge families lived at Greta Hall, a large house that looked down on Keswick. Wordsworth did not live there and anyway had quarrelled with Coleridge, who himself, as so often, was away. Hence Shelley only saw Southey, whom he first met with the Calverts. But Southey was kind to the young poet. Not only was Shelley like Southey's 'own ghost' in holding the opinions the older man himself had held twenty years earlier, he had been expelled from Oxford for writing a pamphlet as Southey had been expelled from Westminster School. More weirdly, Shelley was like the young Southey in physical appearance as well. In his complacent way Southey assumed that as he grew older Shelley would become like him, but he detected traces of genius in the young man and thought that Shelley would become 'an honour to his name and his country'.[45]

On his side Shelley had long admired Southey's poetry. Later Hogg referred to his 'terrible epics'; at the time Walter Scott privately criticised their 'absurdities'; and Byron had publicly appealed to 'the Balladmonger Southey' to stop 'verseward plod-[ding] thy weary way' with annual epics which 'cram the creaking shelves'. Yet Shelley had a taste for them, which is hard to understand today. He had known much of *Thalaba* by heart, while *The Curse of Kehama*, of which Byron was at this time writing that 'X plus Y is at least as amusing . . . & much more intelligible', had been his favourite poem. And on meeting their author he found him to have 'all that characterises the poet'. Earlier he had told Miss Hitchener that he was shocked by what he called Southey's 'tergiversation', that is to say his change from being a hater to a 'votary' of 'Bigotry, Tyranny and Law'. Politically Southey was indeed deeply reactionary, but socially he was enlightened. Like the other Lake poets and Sir Walter Scott, he was opposed to the political economists of the day and to *laissez-faire*. He was eloquent on the sufferings of the poor. He thought children employed in factories were 'white slaves' and boy chimney sweeps 'the British negroes', and later he was strongly in favour of factory legislation. As his political opponent Hazlitt said of him, 'once a philanthropist, always a philanthropist'. In admiring his poetry and deploring his stance on public affairs, therefore, Shelley got things the wrong way round: Southey was a better economist than he was poet.[46]

Southey liked his young visitor. He gave him the run of his library, ensuring that he read Berkeley in the hope of converting him. And after much 'talking with Southey', Shelley found him 'a great man', whose patience he must, however, have sometimes tried. Once, when Southey was reading *Kehama* aloud to him,

Shelley disappeared under the table overcome with sleep. Although slumber reflected a more accurate assessment of the merits of the poem than his earlier enthusiasm, it was not polite. On another occasion, when his host was eating some of his wife's tea cakes, Shelley burst out, 'why! Good God, Southey ... it is awful, horrible, to see such a man as you are greedily devouring this nasty stuff!' Mrs Southey, who was present, was understandably affronted, but she was soon mollified when Shelley, after a close inspection, began eating her cakes as greedily as her husband.[47]

Despite Southey's many kindnesses, Shelley's enthusiasm for a friend, as often happened with him, did not last. By the time he left Keswick, he doubted if Southey was even 'amiable in his *private* character'. Yet, although the older man later became the enemy of Shelley (and Byron), they were, when they parted in 1812, still on friendly terms. Some twenty years later Coleridge regretted that he had not been there, and that Shelley 'fell in with Southey instead'. Coleridge thought he 'could have done him good' and would have 'laughed at his atheism'. That is very possible; yet Southey had sensibly told Shelley not to call himself an atheist since he believed that the universe was God. In any case Coleridge would not have converted him from Godwinism. Shelley's discovery with 'inconceivable emotions' at Keswick that, contrary to what he had thought, Godwin was not on 'the list of the honourable dead', was his last disaster of the year.[48]

Godwin, who was born in 1756, followed his father as a Dissenting minister. A Tory and a very strict Calvinist, who came, like Byron, to believe he was damned, he later confessed that both his schoolmaster and his fellow pupils pronounced him 'the most self-conceited, self sufficient animal that ever lived'. His various Dissenting flocks liked him little better: four congregations rejected him in four years, and he failed to be ordained. During that time he gave up Toryism for Whiggism and discarded Calvinism first for deism, then for Socinianism, before abandoning the ministry for writing and journalism. Nevertheless, he continued on occasion to call himself the 'Rev. William Godwin'.[49]

Deeming the French constitution of 1791 'the most glorious fabric ever raised by human integrity since the creation of man' and favouring its imitation in Britain, he published in 1793 *An Enquiry Concerning Political Justice and its Influence on General Virtue and*

Happiness. By that time he had become an atheist. In *Political Justice*, a logical exposition of anarchism, Godwin sought to flatten and lay waste the political landscape. Government was an evil. Monarchy was the grave of human virtue. The Church was a system of blind submission and abject hypocrisy. Law was a pernicious institution. All punishment was unjust and inappropriate; hence all criminal law should be abolished. The system of property was iniquitous, and aristocracy, which profited from it, was founded in falsehood. Abstracted from the individuals of which it was composed, society was nothing. Not only were marriage and cohabitation evil; so to some degree was all cooperation.*[51]

Godwin's aims were therefore comprehensively revolutionary. But although he led his followers to the water, he would not let them drink. He set out ambitious revolutionary ends, while withholding the means of attaining them; the only methods he countenanced were so conservatively passive that they amounted to no means at all. He did not seek immediate revolution; he was content to wait for years. There must be no violence. So important was it not to inflame the people that even associations for reform were deprecated. The only revolution a philanthropist could support was a change in sentiments and dispositions. As reason was infallible and truth omnipotent, a steady progress towards universal illumination was inevitable. In time the whole species would become reasonable and virtuous.[52]

In this emerging utopia, crime and war would end, equality would be unchallenged, and only half an hour's manual labour a day would be needed. Everybody would be a philanthropist, and would, perhaps, be immortal. And this prodigious reformation would unquestionably occur because of 'necessity', a notion which was both plagiarism and, more important, a distortion of Hume. Godwin turned Hume's scepticism into dogmatic determinism, transforming 'necessity' into a secular equivalent of Calvin's doctrine of predestination, but with a happy ending. His book was a conscious imitation of the Gospel, an atheistic bible in which 'the tidings of liberty and equality [were] tidings of good will to all orders of men'. Man would return to the Garden of Eden, and

---

* Even orchestras were suspect; it would be preferable for one man to play the whole piece. Similarly actors could not be expected to repeat words written by another. So theatres, too, would have to go.[50]

paradise would be regained, with immortality on earth not in heaven. Regrettably, Godwin failed to explain why man had ever left Eden or why paradise had been lost; and without such an explanation he could provide no convincing reason why man should ever return to paradise. But that difficulty was ignored. Past, present and future were bound together 'as links of an indissoluble chain' and, although the past had been wretched like the present, the future would be glorious. That his prediction (made only four years earlier) that the progress of 'liberty, humanity and science' was likely 'to render despotism, cruelty, and ignorance subjects of historical interest' had already been falsified by the September massacres and other events did not discomfit Godwin. He remained confident of a radiant future. 'Necessity' ensured it.*[54]

Earlier in the century David Hume had pointed out, in a book which was 'a favourite' of Shelley's at Oxford, that 'all plans of government, which suppose great reformation in the manners of mankind, are plainly imaginary'; and *Political Justice* supposed a complete reformation. It was what Wordsworth later called 'a work/Of false imagination, placed beyond/ The limits of experience and of truth'. Yet for a short time some very intelligent people greeted it with enthusiasm. Godwin thus enjoyed fame and what Hazlitt termed 'a sultry and unwholesome popularity', but only in a limited circle and not for long. He was one of the targets of the conservative counter-attack of the later 1790s, his fame becoming something akin to infamy. Ironically, as his popularity plummeted because of his reputation as a dangerous revolutionary, Godwin's radicalism also waned, though his quietism did not. In successive editions of *Political Justice* Godwin, who conceded that he was 'bold and adventurous in opinions, not in life', retreated from his most extreme positions, removing some of their most glaring silliness. De Quincey, a little unfairly, regarded the second edition as a travesty of the first, and while applauding Godwin's honesty Coleridge told him that he was 'all too persuadable a man'.[55]

---

* Peacock satirised 'necessity' in his 1816 novel *Headlong Hall*. 'Who fished you out of the water?' said Squire Headlong. 'What is that to the purpose?' said Mr Cranium. 'The whole process of the action was mechanical and necessary. The application of the poker necessitated the ignition of the powder: the ignition necessitated the explosion: the explosion necessitated my sudden fright, which necessitated my sudden jump, which, from a necessity equally powerful, was in a curvilinear ascent. . . . I was, by the necessity of gravitation, attracted . . . into the water beneath . . . and he could no more help jumping into the water than I could help falling into it.'[53]

In *Political Justice* Godwin downgraded the importance of sensual pleasure. Acceptance of 'the doctrine of necessity' should enable men to be 'superior to the tumult of passion'. Sexual intercourse was 'a very trivial object'; reasonable men would 'propagate their species', not because of the pleasure 'annexed to this action but because it [was] right the species should be propagated'. Nevertheless Godwin and the radical feminist author who had replied to Burke's *Reflections* and vindicated *The Rights of Women*, Mary Wollstonecraft, became lovers and, because they practised what she called Godwin's 'chance medley system' of birth control, which was ineffective, they found they were propagating when it was not right or at least not convenient to do so. Marriage, Godwin had informed his readers, was 'a system of fraud'; for him 'to engross one woman to myself' was 'the most odious of monopolies'. Yet, whatever Godwin's defects of character and common sense, he usually had enough wit not to allow his philosophic writings to influence his conduct. Accordingly he and Mary married, an apostasy from Godwinism which shocked some of their friends, and thus became, on 30 August 1797, the parents of a legitimate daughter Mary Wollstonecraft Godwin, the future Mrs Shelley. But influenced, Godwin wrote, 'by ideas of decorum' which overrode her advanced views on the sexes, Mary Wollstonecraft – unlike Catherine Byron nine years before – had engaged only a female midwife and, very possibly through no fault of the midwife, died a few days later.[56]

After a period of odium, Godwin married again and sank from public view. In 1802 Sydney Smith, who disliked his philosophy, wrote in the *Edinburgh Review*, 'we hear no more of Mr Godwin'. As well as his fame, the philosopher's creative powers were in decline or, more probably, he realised that his philosophy had reached a dead end. In his 1799 novel *St Leon*, which was later praised by Byron, Godwin pronounced in favour of marriage and concluded that 'true wisdom will recommend to us individual attachments', both of which had been condemned by his earlier 'wisdom'. Rather than continue his retreat from the untenable ground of the first edition of *Political Justice*, Godwin abandoned philosophical speculation, becoming once again a high-class hack. He had long venerated Burke and frequented Whig dinner tables, and he had recently been converted from atheism to deism by Coleridge. As he later admitted, he was a republican in principle but a Whig in practice, a position which accorded with his timorous nature and was likely, in time, to bring aid to his increasingly shaky finances.[57]

Believing Godwin to be long since dead, Shelley was unaware of this precipitate decline. To him he was still the philosopher-author of *Political Justice*. His friend Peacock later noticed Shelley's weakness for bad books and how prone he was to be decisively influenced by them. Godwin's book is surely the supreme example of that failing. Even in the heyday of the French Revolution few intelligent people had taken *Political Justice* seriously for long. They had been briefly bewitched when it was 'bliss . . . In that dawn to be alive'. But for Shelley still to be bewitched by it twenty years later is extraordinary. By then not even Godwin was a Godwinian. Besides, Shelley's avid reading of Hume at Oxford should have given him immunity from Godwinism; instead, he became an addict. *Political Justice* had more influence on him than any other book he ever read.[58]

And, unluckily, either the copy of it that Dr Lind lent him or the one he subsequently bought seems to have been the first edition; certainly that edition, which contained the full farrago of Godwinian absurdities, was the one Shelley preferred. His addiction to abstract ideas and his reluctance to accept the real world were thus fortified by his absorption in *Political Justice*, where reality seldom intruded. In December he had contemplated what became his first mature long poem, the Godwinian *Queen Mab*. 'By anticipation' it was to be 'a picture of . . . a perfect state of society'. Both he and Harriet thought it might land him in jail. He put it aside, though, when Ireland, the publication of his essays and shorter poems, and 'a tale' explaining the failure of the French Revolution became higher priorities.[59]

But now he had the even higher priority of paying personal tribute to Godwin. Informing him of his 'reverence and admiration', Shelley expressed the firm belief that the philosopher was 'still planning the welfare of humankind'. In fact Godwin at this time was mainly occupied with his own welfare. He was trying to save his and his wife's bookshop business, which was chronically in debt and facing bankruptcy. Shelley begged for an answer, and Godwin immediately gave him one, though he complained that the 'generalising character' of Shelley's letter rendered it 'deficient in interest'. Perhaps he was encouraged that even in his decline he could inspire such an enthusiastic disciple. Alternatively, although Shelley had said nothing about his material circumstances, the philosopher may have smelt money. Shelley's second letter removed any doubts on that score. While again giving lavish praise to Godwin, providing some not scrupulously accurate details of his own past life, and criticising his father, Shelley revealed that he was 'the Son of a man of fortune' and the 'heir by entail to an estate of £6,000' a year. That again produced an immediate reply, in which Godwin expressed a 'deep and earnest interest in [Shelley's] welfare' and questioned his remarks about his father. Unaware that however passive Godwin was in politics he was an activist in borrowing money and a persistent and brazen sponger, Shelley was surprised and delighted to receive 'so prompt and so kind an answer'.[60]

His flattering and exciting new correspondent did not cause him to neglect Miss Hitchener. Despite a terrible headache and a nervous attack which had necessitated 'a quantity of laudanum', he wrote her three lengthy letters in the first half of January. Eliza Westbrook was 'a very amiable girl', but Shelley sought a larger entourage. He wanted Miss Hitchener not just to visit but 'to *live* with us'. He hoped, he told her, '*never* to part with you again'; Harriet was above 'the littleness of jealousy'. Shelley did nevertheless add that anybody who got hold of his letter would think he was 'a Bedlamite', adding that his 'reputation for madness' was too well established for that to matter.[61]

In another letter he told his 'fellow labourer', to whom he would be 'devoted . . . till annihilation', that like Godwin he was opposed to popular insurrections and revolutions, though if any did take place he would 'take the side of the People'. He desired 'to establish on a lasting basis the happiness of human-kind'. Human-kind had apparently some way to go, however, before achieving that state. The countryside at Keswick was lovely, but 'the people [were] detestable', and industry was deforming 'the loveliness of Nature with human taint'. Shelley's origins in a Sussex land-owning family, while not checking his scorn of the 'imbecility of aristocracy', also did not prevent him from despising commerce and industry. 'Commerce springs', he wrote a year later in *Queen Mab*, from 'selfishness' and was a 'venal interchange . . . beneath whose poison-breathing shade' no virtue dared to spring. Like Southey, he was becoming aware of the industrial evils of the time.[62]

In the same letter he enclosed 78 lines of a poem with the

Godwinian title 'A Tale of Society as it is: From Facts, 1811'. The result of his having observed the hardships of the poor, it concerned two people whom he did not detest: an old crippled woman and her son who, having been torn away from her and 'compelled' to fight 'the tyrant's foes', had been badly wounded and returned with his health ruined.

> And now cold charity's unwelcome dole
> Was insufficient to support the pair,
> And they would perish rather than would bear
> The law's stern slavery and the insolent stare
> With which law loves to rend the poor man's soul

The English Poor Law was unique and much admired by foreign visitors. By the public provision of relief for the poor, it cushioned hardship and, except in London and the large towns, usually prevented destitution. Canning believed that it had also prevented revolution. Yet, as its administration was often harsh and arrogant, Shelley's 'cold charity' was fair comment. What followed was less fair. The 'dole' that was provided was seldom if ever 'unwelcome', though obviously second-best to profitable employment.[63]

Having less faith than Canning in the Poor Law's efficacy as a preventative, Southey told Shelley that a revolution in England was '*inevitable*'. And in another poem written at Keswick, 'The Crisis', the young poet denounced 'Despots', 'Falsehood', 'Corruption' and all the other appurtenances of tyranny, before looking forward rather unconvincingly to a brighter future:

> Then may we hope the consummating hour
> Dreadfully, sweetly, swiftly is arriving
> When light from darkness, peace from desolation
> Bursts unresisted, –
>
> Then mid the gloom of doubt and fear and anguish
> The votaries of virtue may raise their eyes to Heaven,
> And confident watch till the renovating day-star
> Gild the horizon.

In his later poetry Shelley sometimes used similar images, 'a Shape arrayed in mail' or 'a glorious Phantom', to suggest that despite all appearances to the contrary Utopia might soon be here.[64]

But despite his sympathy for the misery of the poor in England and his hatred of 'the existing establishment of every kind', Shelley's chief preoccupation was now with Ireland. In his third letter he told his 'dearest friend, the partner of my thoughts', that he, together with Harriet and Eliza Westbrook, was seriously thinking of going there immediately. The Southeys and virtually everybody at Keswick were opposed to their trip, as was Captain Pilford. So, too, was Godwin, who was knowledgeable about Ireland and even more opposed to political activity there than anywhere else. Shelley, however, was determined to go; he was convinced that he would 'have success' and that failure was impossible.[65]

His visit to the Duke of Norfolk at Greystoke probably had much to do with his new interest in Ireland. The Duke, a lapsed Catholic and according to Shelley a deist, had long been a strong supporter of Catholic emancipation. Since 1793 Irish Catholics had been allowed to vote if they were otherwise qualified, but they could not sit in Parliament or hold high military, civil or judicial office. The Duke's friend, the Prince of Wales, who early in the following year was to gain the full powers of Regency, had formerly been sympathetic to Irish claims, but it was now widely assumed that he was about to let the Irish down. Ironically he had begun to turn against them just at the time when Irish disabilities had become even more indefensible than before. From 1807 onwards Britain was fighting in defence of Roman Catholics in Spain and Portugal while denying full rights to her own Catholics at home. As Thomas Moore put it: 'While prais'd at distance, but at home forbid,/Rebels in Cork are patriots at Madrid'.[66]

Even so, Shelley's insistence on going to Ireland is surprising. Admittedly, he thought that Ireland was part of 'the crisis' to which he referred in his poem of that title and which he told Miss Hitchener was 'a great crisis in opinions'. Presumably, though, England with its troubles on his doorstep – food riots and Luddite disturbances – was also part of that great crisis. Yet, for some reason, Shelley decided that Ireland rather than England was the proper place for his first (and effectively last) active and practical attempt to accomplish particular and immediate political reforms, as opposed to his subsequent endeavours to lay the foundations of a future social revolution. He probably thought that the disqualification of Catholics and hostility to the 1801 Union with England made Ireland a more fertile field. Probably, too, his belief that an Irish mission would not be without danger – 'everybody is not killed that goes to Dublin', he told Miss Hitchener – was another enticement. In any case he had already written much of *An Address to the Irish People*, which was to be printed cheaply and widely circulated. He also planned other pamphlets 'to shake Catholicism at its basis and to induce Quakerish and Socinian principles of politics'. Yet he did realise that a frontal attack on the Christian religion 'would do no good to the vulgar just now'.[67]

Before Shelley, Harriet and Eliza Westbrook left for Ireland, Shelley and Harriet had an odd exchange with the sister of Shelley's soul and suffered an odd incident at Keswick. Elizabeth Hitchener had gathered from Harriet that she was pregnant. Shelley soon disabused her. That 'was a piece of good fortune' he 'could' not expect – a curious remark for a newly married man to make especially as he added that he hoped to have a large family. Harriet, too, told Miss Hitchener that she did not 'expect' to be pregnant for 'some time, years perhaps', which is an equally curious remark for a newly married wife to make. In the event, the Shelleys did not have their first child till nearly two years after their wedding. Since they had no reason to practise birth control, which in any case his language here seems to rule out, and since he could only expect the arrival of 'a little stranger . . . at some distance', their sexual practices were evidently not such as to make conception probable. That presumably was due to Shelley's ill health. Maybe, justifiably or not, he was not sure that he might not infect Harriet.[68]

On 28 January 1812 the *Cumberland Pacquet* recorded that in the last fortnight several attempts at robbery had been made in the neighbourhood of Keswick. One of them was at Shelley's house. 'Mr Shelley being alarmed by an unusual noise . . . went to the door; was knocked down by some ruffians, and had remained senseless for a time, when Mr Dare, hearing the disturbance rushed out of the house, [whereupon] the villains fled immediately'. Shelley told Elizabeth Hitchener a week after the incident that he considered it 'a complete casual occurrence . . . the man evidently wanted to rifle my pocket; my falling within the house defeated his intention'. That looks straightforward. But at the time the residents of Keswick believed that the attack was an illusion of Shelley's. Certainly he had been taking laudanum, but in a letter written three days before the incident he had said he was quite recovered. On the other hand, in a letter to Miss Hitchener a week later, Harriet wrote that Shelley was much better than he had been for some time and expressed the hope that 'as he gets strong he will outgrow his nervous complaints', which can be read either way. Shelley's explanation that the ruffian had been foiled by his having fallen inside the house is not plausible. Still, on balance the incident was probably not an illusion.[69]

On 2 February the party left Whitehaven, which Shelley thought a 'miserable manufacturing seaport town', for their Irish adventure.[70]

CHAPTER XV

Maiden Speeches

Shelley: 1812 (aged 19 years)
Byron: 1812 (aged 23 & 24 years)

Shelley and Byron had of course both performed at 'speeches' at Eton and Harrow – Shelley in 1810 and Byron in 1804 and 1805. And Shelley had spoken at a debating society in London. But they made their maiden speeches in public on successive days in 1812: Byron, on the Luddite disturbances, in the House of Lords on 27 February and Shelley on the urgent need for drastic reform in Ireland, at a large meeting in Dublin on 28 February.

England had long misgoverned Ireland, treating her more as a neglected colony than as one half of a dual monarchy. The penal laws had made the Irish Catholic, in Burke's phrase, 'a foreigner in his own land', and only 5 per cent of that land remained in Catholic hands. With no English-style Poor Law to cushion their poverty, the Irish peasants lived in conditions even worse than those in France.[1]

The Irish rebellion of 1798, an Irish landlord told the Prince of Wales, had been caused by 'immediate and local outrage in the feelings of the lower classes'. In that rebellion, with many atrocities committed by both sides – the English Viceroy, Lord Cornwallis, remarked of his own troops that 'murder [appeared] to be their favourite pastime' – about 30,000 people lost their lives. 1798 had convinced Pitt that only union with Britain could break the political monopoly of the Irish Protestants, but for that union to be genuine there had to be Catholic emancipation as well. Without the removal of Catholic disabilities, Cornwallis pointed out, England would be making a union 'with a party in Ireland' instead of with 'the Irish nation'. Nevertheless, because of George III's veto of Catholic emancipation, which had forced the resignation of Pitt, that was the only union permitted.[2]

By the time the Shelley trio arrived in the country conditions had scarcely improved. Their 'most tedious' journey from Whitehaven to Dublin had taken nine days. After being detained for some time on the Isle of Man they had been driven by a storm to the north of Ireland, which fatigued Harriet and Eliza. On his voyage to Ireland a decade earlier, much the same had happened to Southey, whose house Shelley had just passed for the last time 'without one sting'. On his brief visit, Southey found Dublin 'a magnificent city', as indeed it was, and had been impressed by the width of its streets. He had been less impressed by its inhabitants, thinking to 'civilise' them would be difficult, as the Irishman, like 'a true savage', was too idle to work to better himself.[3]

Shelley, who took rooms in Sackville Street (now O'Connell Street), Dublin's widest thoroughfare, formed before long an even lower view of the 'Irish *mob*', but initially he was optimistic about the people of Ireland and the chances of effecting an improvement. The object of his *Address* to them, which he had written at Keswick and revised in Dublin where it was printed cheaply and shoddily, was to 'awaken . . . the Irish poor' to the evils of their present state and suggest 'rational means of remedy – Catholic Emancipation, and a Repeal of the Union Act, (the latter, the most successful engine that England ever wielded over the misery of fallen Ireland,) . . .'. Hence Shelley had 'wilfully vulgarised its language', he told Godwin, to suit 'the taste and comprehension of the Irish peasantry who have been too long brutalised by vice and ignorance'. Although that was doubtless his intention, it was not the result. Shelley's ideas were greatly influenced by Tom Paine as well as by Godwin, but he had none of Paine's genius for expressing them in vivid, sharp and easily understood language. Consequently, in virtually every respect, his pamphlet was ill suited to its intended audience.[4]

It was far too long – 22 pages of small print and some 12,000 words. And almost from its beginning, despite what he had told Miss Hitchener about not offending 'the vulgar' over religion, Shelley ignored the susceptibilities of his hoped-for readers. As he was not a Protestant nor a Catholic, he wrote, he was better able to judge between them, which was bound to excite the hostility of any Irish 'peasant' who, in Shelley's words, 'attentively read [his] address'. For, though Shelley's prose at this time was much influenced by French Revolutionary ideas, he was not mindful of what as Godwin's erstwhile hero, Robespierre, had explained to his fellow revolutionaries in 1793: while 'atheism is aristocratic, the idea of a Great Being who watches over oppressed innocence and punishes triumphant wickedness is altogether popular'; Robespierre had even added Voltaire's well-known words that 'if God did not exist it would be necessary to invent Him'. That was surely even truer of Ireland in 1812 than of France twenty years before.[5]

Yet Shelley further offended his target readers by telling them that the gates of heaven were open to people of every religion, which was not the general view in a country where, as Byron had written in November, 'jarring sects convulse a sister isle'. Shelley then embarked on an irrelevant disquisition about the early years of Christianity and the quarrel between the Roman and Greek churches, which led on to an attack on the Massacre of St Bartholomew's Eve and on the monstrous 'vices of Monks and Nuns in their Convents'. In the unlikely event of any member of the Irish poor having got so far, he would then have found himself patronised by being told 'to think for your children and your children's children'. 'Be calm, mild, deliberate, patient', Shelley told him, and 'recollect you can in no measure more effectually forward the cause of reform than by employing your leisure time in reasoning, or the cultivation of your minds'.[6]

Shelley's pamphlet was more of a sermon, albeit a Godwinian one, than a political statement. The Irish poor were instructed to stop purchasing 'drunkenness and ill-health' and to relieve the pains of their fellow sufferers. In a surreal passage Shelley enjoined them to: 'Let your children lisp of Freedom in the cradle – let your death-bed be the school for fresh exertions – let every street of the city, and field of the country, be connected with thoughts, which liberty has made holy'. Scarcely more realistic was the view he confided to the poor that 'the increase of virtue and wisdom' would lead people to find out 'that force and oppression [were] wrong and false', which would in time 'prevent government from severity'.[7]

The weakness of the *Address* lay in its misjudgement of its hoped-for readers and its objective. It contained virtually nothing to appeal to the taste or the comprehension of the Irish peasantry; otherwise much of what it said was sensible and well expressed. Shelley left no doubt in any reader's mind that repeal of the Union and enactment of Catholic emancipation were essential, even though, he emphasised, emancipation would not benefit the mass of the Catholic population. He was equally firm that these objectives must be achieved by non-violent methods. While he was wise in Godwinian style to stress, however repetitively, the importance of renouncing violence, the danger of violent insurrection was vastly exaggerated by Godwin. Memories of the horrors of 1798 and the ignominious failure of Emmet's rising five years later made another rebellion highly unlikely. Furthermore, although the government no longer had in Ireland the 70,000 British regular soldiers it had had in 1798 – twice as many as ever fought on the continent against Napoleon – its military strength remained substantial.[8]

The Address came back from the printers on 24 February. Since the Irish poor certainly could not afford it, cheap though it was, and few others would want to buy it, its distribution presented a problem. But Shelley believed it had been solved, telling Miss Hitchener three days later that 400 of his pamphlets 'disseminating the doctrines of Philanthropy and Freedom' had already been sent into the world. Despite his repeated admonitions to the Irish poor not to drink, and despite strict sobriety as well as determination being needed to start let alone get through his address, sixty public houses had been chosen as points of distribution. The 'blundering honest' David Hill (or Healy), who later returned to England with Shelley, was engaged to help with its dissemination. Thinking everything was proceeding well, Shelley maintained that his pamphlet had 'excited a sensation of wonder'. Almost certainly, though, that was as much a delusion as his claim at Oxford that *Margaret Nicholson* had sold 'wonderfully', although his publishers thought she 'was almost still-born'. Some of the remaining 1,100 copies were got rid of by Shelley and Harriet giving them to passers-by or by throwing them down from their balcony, which amused Harriet, particularly as 'Percy [looked] so grave' while doing so. Shelley was evidently surprised that no prosecution had been 'yet attempted', but the authorities, like the poor, had probably not read his address.[9]

However risible were Shelley'a attempts to boost the circulation of his pamphlet and however misjudged was much of its contents, he had a firm grasp of Irish politics which he demonstrated in both his maiden speech and another pamphlet. The object of the 'Aggregate Meeting of the Catholics of Ireland', at which he spoke, was to assert once again the Catholics' right to emancipation and to send a petition to that effect to the Prince Regent. The gathering was very large and distinguished; Catholics were not permitted to hold political meetings of representatives or delegates – hence the

Aggregate Meeting. The audience had previously heard Daniel O'Connell, who was even then the leading Irish radical, and a number of other speakers, yet Shelley addressed it for over an hour. Even in the age of long speeches and even longer sermons that was something of an imposition upon his audience and showed, at the very least, unusual self-confidence in a young man of nineteen. He was after all an outsider, who had only been in the country for a few days and who had no qualifications other than goodwill to speak on Ireland. That he was well received testifies both to the good manners of the Irish and to the quality of his speech.[10]

It and he left little impression, however, on the two government spies who attended the meeting. Only one of them gave him even the barest mention; the other evidently reported part of his speech but attributed it to another young man. But there were three reports in the papers, all of them favourable. Shelley evidently gave some account of himself and his background, explained that he had come to Ireland solely to help its people, and then launched into an attack on the evils England had inflicted on Ireland, which were outrages that made him blush for his country. He particularly singled out the Union, the penal code and the state of representation. Although none of these reports indicates that there was any vocal opposition to any of his speech, Shelley told Miss Hitchener a fortnight afterwards that his speech had been 'misinterpreted'; he had been hissed when he 'spoke of *religion*, tho' in terms of respect', but applauded when he 'avowed [his] mission'. Assuming that on religion he expressed in his speech the same sentiments that he had in his *Address* and did again in his second pamphlet, *Proposals for an Association of Philanthropists*, which appeared a few days afterwards, the hissing is readily understandable. Support of religious toleration was popular, but talk of 'the extermination of the eyeless monster bigotry, whose throne has tottered for two hundred years' and the assertion that 'the purest religion is that of Charity' would not have appealed to all of even the most sophisticated listeners. Indeed in speaking of religion at all, let alone in those terms, Shelley badly misjudged his audience. He was seemingly incapable of understanding how strongly many people felt on the subject and how far away their views were from his. All the same his speech was a success.[11]

Yet he soon began to realise that his pamphlets had not caused 'a sensation of wonder' and that his success so far from being certain was virtually out of the question. His disillusionment had a number of causes. He did not admire either the rich or the poor of Dublin. He thought the latter had been reduced through no fault of theirs to 'one mass of animated filth'; 'intemperance and hard labour [had] reduced them to machines.' He compared their intellects to those of oysters, though to individuals he was his usual charitable self. To the rich he was not charitable; they had ground their fellow beings 'into worse than annihilation'.[12]

Godwin had given him a letter of introduction to John Philpott Curran, whose speeches had provided valuable material for Shelley's *Address*. A brilliant orator, barrister and author of the apophthegm often shortened to 'the price of liberty is eternal vigilance', Curran had defended the leaders of the 1798 rebellion. His involvement in the 1803 rebellion was more tenuous; it was limited to Robert Emmet having been in love with his daughter. But that would have appealed to Shelley who, during his Irish visit, wrote two poems to Emmet after apparently visiting his tomb:

> Not the scrolls of a court could emblazon thy fame
> Like the silence that reigns in the palace of thee,
> Like the whispers that pass of thy dearly loved name,
> Like the tears of the good, like the groans of the free.

Yet, despite Shelley several times calling at his house, Curran, who had suffered from Godwin's financial importunities and may have thought that Godwin's protégé was of the same ilk, made no effort to see him for over a month. Shelley expressed his irritation by telling Miss Hitchener that he did not like Curran 'for accepting the office of Master of the Rolls', though Curran had in fact accepted it six years before from the Whig Ministry of All The Talents. A strong opponent of the Union with England, he spoke of 'Ireland, like a bastinadoed Elephant, kneeling to receive the paltry rider'. He himself, however, did not do much kneeling.[13]

When Curran did at last return Shelley's calls and twice had him to dinner, the relationship did not prosper. Shelley conceded that the lawyer was 'a man of great abilities', but he was otherwise not impressed. Although Curran was a renowned conversationalist and a famous wit, the serious and thoughtful Shelley found, according to Hogg, 'the unceasing jests, perpetual farce, and profane and filthy ribaldry of the comic Master of the Rolls . . . wearisome, puerile, and worse'. He said much the same to Godwin, though putting his criticism far more mildly. He was perhaps still offended by Curran's earlier offhand treatment, but, as later he often talked of 'the withering and perverted spirit of comedy', he would probably anyway have found the Irishman's jokes tedious and inappropriate. In contrast, when Byron, who like Shelley was sensitive to Irish wrongs, met Curran the following year, he was 'delighted . . . with his humour' and thought him 'a man of a million' and a '*Machine* of Imagination'.[14]

Nor did Shelley like Lord Fingal, who had presided at the Aggregate Meeting, or '*any* of the Catholic aristocracy', thinking their intolerance only equalled by 'the hardy wickedness' of the Prince Regent. For Shelley everybody tended to be either hero or villain, though heroes often became villains. And, apart from Harriet and for the time being Eliza Westwood, he now disliked or disapproved of virtually everybody, while almost the only people he currently admired, Godwin and Elizabeth Hitchener, were in their very different ways wholly unworthy of his extravagant adulation. He kept up his correspondence with both of them throughout his stay in Ireland, although only that with Miss Hitchener provided much comfort.[15]

In his letters to Miss Hitchener, whom he had still only seen three times in his life, she remained the creature of his imagination rather than her real self. He had 'entreated' her to join his circle and come to Ireland with them. But he now accepted that that was impracticable. Instead they would meet 'in Wales, and *never part again*'. His writing would then be 'enlightened with the emanation of [her] genius, and invigorated by the deductions of [her] reason'.[16]

In the meantime, he addressed her in blank verse:

> The Ocean rolls between us.
> 					O thou Ocean . . .
> . . . and with each wave whose echoings die . . .
> Shall die a moment too – one of those moments
> Which part my friend and me.

And having heard that 'a new Republic' had been set up in Mexico, he sent her a 'short tribute to its success'. As no republic was set up in Mexico till nearly two years later, Shelley may have meant Venezuela.

> Cotopaxi! Bid the sound
> 			Through thy sister mountains ring
> Till each valley smile around

At the blissful welcoming,
And O! thou stern Ocean-deep
Whose eternal billows sweep
Shores where thousands wake to weep
Whilst they curse some villain King,
On the winds that fan thy breast
Bear thou news of freedom's rest.

Cotopaxi is a volcano in Ecuador and hence nowhere near Mexico and quite far from Venezuela. The poet's geography was thus as random as his history, but the poem is one of his best of this period, and his view that republicanism was spreading in Latin America and that soon no province would recognise the sovereignty of Spain was prescient and accurate. Otherwise, however, he displayed an idealisation of that continent similar in its ignorance to that of Byron a few years late when he contemplated emigrating to Venezuela.[17]

While looking forward to living in 'eternal union' with Elizabeth Hitchener, Shelley saw himself in 'a relation of pupilage' to William Godwin. Yet his relationship and correspondence with his London master was only slightly more real than that with his Sussex schoolmistress. For Shelley saw himself as the pupil of the Godwin of 1793, the radical philosopher who, as has been seen, was a very different being from the virtually Whig Godwin of 1812, whom Walter Scott had criticised for his 'most unfeeling prolixity' and who ran an unsuccessful bookshop and juvenile library in Clerkenwell.[18]

This Godwin disapproved not only of political activity but of youthful authorship, which he regarded as 'detrimental to the cause of general happiness'. The pupil was therefore doubly at odds with his master. In his defence of wanting to publish what he wrote, Shelley explained that, as he was 'constitutionally nervous' and already often fatigued, he could not hope to live as long as Godwin. Also his *Address* could not, as Godwin alleged, 'widen the breach between the Kingdoms', since he attempted to convey to the Irish poor the sentiments of philanthropy. He would only publish things that would 'conduce to virtue', which ensured that any influence he had would be 'to good'. Godwin was far from convinced, considering that there was no necessary connection between writing and publishing and that to do both merely led to 'a series of retractions'. Shelley was undoubtedly presumptuous in seeking to reform the world in general and Ireland in particular at the age of nineteen. But Godwin had been thirty-four when he published *Political Justice*, and even then he had in successive editions made a series of retreats or retractions. So neither his experience nor his book was a good argument for delayed authorship.[19]

A greater disagreement was over political activity. Shelley's second Irish pamphlet advocated the formation of 'An Association' which would have 'for its immediate object, Catholic Emancipation and the Repeal of the Act of Union', as well as the 'annihilation or palliation of whatever moral or political evil' it was 'within the compass of human power to assuage or eradicate'. As has been seen, Godwin so disliked associations of any kind that he was even suspicious of orchestras and 'theatrical exhibitions' because they involved 'an absurd and vicious co-operation'. Hence Shelley's proposal was anathema to him. His views and Shelley's, Godwin told his disciple, were 'decisively at issue'. Shelley's association would either be ineffective or have 'no very remote tendency to light again the flames of rebellion and war'. And to add to these misdemeanours, owing to Shelley having used the post instead of 'some other conveyance', his letter and its enclosures had cost Godwin £1 1s. 8d. The Irish circumstances of the time did indeed make Shelley's proposal ineffective, and an English youth was not a suitable sponsor of it. But in itself it was an intelligent and feasible idea; something of the sort eventually achieved Catholic emancipation. Shelley was much more in the right, therefore, than the former philosopher.[20]

Shelley began his reply by deferentially telling Godwin that 'when you reprove me, reason speaks. I acquiesce in her decisions'. Yet his acquiescence was limited. He pointed out to Godwin that in the twenty years since *Political Justice* had been published, it had had no effect. 'Vice and misery' had not vanished from the earth. Furthermore he conceived his proposal for a Philanthropic Association to be fully in accordance with *Political Justice* – which it plainly was not. And as to the *Address*, it had been designed for 'the Irish mob' whose conditions could not be worse. Finally he did not think his *Address* could possibly lead to violence, as he had taken great pains to insist on 'pacific measures' – which indeed he had. But that did not satisfy Godwin, who was opposed to any kind of political action.[21]

Aghast at his disciple's heretical belittlement of the sacred text of

Political Justice and alarmed by 'the impotence of [his previous] expostulations on so momentous a topic', Godwin was prepared to make one more effort to save Shelley and the Irish people from 'the calamities' with which his disciple's proposals were 'fraught'. The claim that Shelley's ineffective pamphlets could engender calamities was yet another Godwinian absurdity; they were highly unlikely to engender anything at all. But Godwin repeated that he had made 'a main pillar' of his doctrines 'a hostility to associations' and, trying to counter Shelley's thrust that *Political Justice* had had no effect, he told his pupil that if he could see from 'the pinnacle of ages' the last twenty years would 'shrink to an invisible point'. 'Shelley, you are preparing a scene of blood!' he unwarrantably and melodramatically added, before recommending his wayward disciple's immediate return to London.[22]

This correspondence should surely have led Shelley to reappraise his allegiance to Godwin and Godwinism. But that necessary reassessment was precluded by his having embraced Godwinism with the same quasi-religious fervour as he had espoused 'atheism' at Oxford. Nevertheless, his 'pupilage' to Godwin did not entail unswerving obedience. Admittedly he now confessed error to his mentor; he also withdrew his pamphlets from circulation and prepared to leave Dublin. But except for the admission of error, those decisions owed little to Godwin's rebukes and adjurations. Much as his professed dislike of Lord Fingal and the Irish aristocracy, whom he had scarcely met, was an effect rather than a cause of his disillusionment with Ireland, Shelley's decision to leave the country was the result of his gradual realisation that his schemes were impractical and his mission a failure, not of a conversion to Godwin's irrational prejudice against associations. That had had some reason in the days of the French Revolution, but now associations clearly did not necessarily lead to violence, and they were almost the only route to reform. If they were ruled out, things would remain as they were and reform would be almost out of the question. Even Godwin perceived that Shelley was 'but half a convert' to his arguments, which was probably an overestimate.[23]

A week before he received Godwin's last letter, Shelley had expressed doubts to Miss Hitchener that 'the Association' would be established, adding that he was 'sick' of Dublin and longed to be with her. Four days later in another letter to her he confided that his hopes of the Association daily grew fainter, even as his 'perceptions of its necessity' grew in strength. Miss Hitchener had already enjoined them to leave the city.[24]

Quite apart from the failure of his Association, Shelley had reasons to be sick of Dublin. Irish Catholicism was far stronger than he had thought at Keswick; he had no chance of inculcating Socinian or Quakerish opinions. Above all there was the terrible plight of the Dublin poor, whose condition made his 'blood boil to madness'. He tried to help individuals but without much success. One woman's crime was stealing a penny loaf. She was drunken, and so there was nothing that he or anybody could do to save her from 'ultimate ruin and starvation'. 'The rich grind the poor into abjectness', he commented, '& then complain that they are abject'.[25]

There were not many compensations for all this, though the Shelleys did make some friends in Dublin, most notably John Lawless or 'Honest John' as he was known. Shelley called him a 'valuable man'. Lawless was an advanced radical of whom an observer later said that he would have been a good official 'under the French republic'. A competent journalist, he wrote a most flattering article on Shelley and his speech, and was also something of a historian. Shelley hoped to establish a newspaper with him and tried to assist him in the publication of a history of Ireland. On his next visit to the country Shelley stayed with Lawless, but they later quarrelled. 'Honest John' was evidently a misnomer. According to Harriet in 1813, Lawless's behaviour had been 'so dishonest that Mr Shelley [would] not do anything for him as present' – maybe he had also been dishonest the previous year, and Shelley had 'pouched' him to procure that laudatory article. Catherine Nugent was another friend made in Dublin, though more Harriet's than Shelley's; she later called Harriet 'an amiable and unaffected person – very young and very pleasing'. Miss Nugent, too, was a radical, a philanthropic furrier's assistant, who after the 1798 rebellion, Harriet told Miss Hitchener, had visited all the prisons to give their inmates courage and hope.[26]

Towards the end of February the Shelleys, Harriet informed Miss Hitchener, had 'forsworn meat and adopted the Pithagorean [sic] system', as it was then called; the word 'vegetarian' did not come into use for another thirty years. After a fortnight of the Pythagorean system, Harriet reported that she and Shelley did not find themselves any the worse for it; indeed they thought it the best thing in the world. In a pamphlet written a few months later,

Shelley attributed much of the ills of the world to the eating of flesh and the drinking of fermented liquors. Indeed he associated the fall of man and 'the allegory of Adam and Eve' with the resort to 'unnatural diet'. But in Dublin his motives for never taking 'any substance into the stomach that once had life' and for drinking only distilled water seem to have been more humanitarian and medical than ideological. He did not try to impose vegetarianism on other people. Confirming a dinner invitation to Miss Nugent, Harriet assured her that 'a murdered chicken had been prepared for her repast'.

In London Byron had been for some months under a similar Pythagorean regime. He had 'left off wine entirely', he told Hobhouse, describing himself to Hodgson in December as 'a leguminous-eating Ascetic'. A decade later, according to Lady Blessington, he told her that animal food engendered the appetite of the animal fed upon; if he did say that, he was 'humming' or 'mystifying' her. Like Shelley's initially, his reasons for adopting a vegetarian diet were not ideological, but intellectual, aesthetic and medical. If he took normal meals, he contended, he lost all power over his intellectual faculties; furthermore he was proud of looking thin, and eating a lot made him feel ill. He may well have been an anorexic.[27]

Despite Dublin's lack of attraction, the Shelley party were in no hurry to leave. Although at the Aggregate Meeting the government's spies had shown little interest in Shelley, he had evidently come under government scrutiny. Another John Stockdale, a Dublin printer, was ready to publish some of Shelley's poems. A former associate of Peter Finnerty, the journalist whom Shelley had tried to help when he was at Oxford, Stockdale, who had himself been imprisoned, must have seemed a congenial spirit to the young poet, but he had changed sides and was now a government informer. Furthermore Shelley had sent to Miss Hitchener a box containing a letter from Harriet, the remaining copies of his pamphlets, and his *Declaration of Rights*, a broadsheet which he had had printed at the same time as his second pamphlet. A Customs official at Holyhead was sufficiently alarmed by the box to send samples of its contents to the Home Secretary, Richard Ryder. As the *Declaration*, which was only four pages long, was modelled on the Declarations of Rights issued during the French Revolution, and as the government was already on the alert because of the

Luddite troubles, the official's alarm is easy to understand. Nevertheless, on 4 April the trio departed from Ireland without trouble.[28]

On their way home, after thirty-six hours on board ship without food, they all made a temporary return to an unnatural diet. 'Percy and my sister', wrote Harriet, had 'suffered so much by the voyage, and were so much weakened by the vegetable system', that a continuation of it might have led them to 'a premature grave'. The end of Shelley's mission to convert the Irish to peace, freedom and religion was far from premature. He had left Dublin, he said, 'because I had done all that I could do. . . .' And that was very little. But if Shelley had proved much less than a St Augustine, a St Patrick or a Martin Luther for Ireland, the Irish had wrought something of a conversion in him. He had earlier made the painful discovery that he was very different from the rest of his family, but he had not learned that he was very different from everybody else as well. Ireland taught him that he was. It also taught him that men were not rational beings, let alone philanthropists. His Irish stay was thus an education in politics. That had still some way to go, but at least he now understood that politics was much more complicated than he had thought at Keswick.

His weeks in Ireland were his equivalent of the Grand Tour. 'The use of travelling', wrote Dr Johnson, who had got as far as the Hebrides, 'is to regulate imagination by reality, and instead of thinking how things may be, to see them as they are'. Shelley seldom managed to do that but, like Byron in Greece, he had learned a great deal in Dublin from seeing another country and different manners. Despite being four years younger, he already had an outlook that was in some respects similar to Byron's but, because he had no experience of foreign countries, he could for the time being at least be a citizen of the world only in aspiration. After Dublin he realised that he could not single-handedly reform the world; nevertheless he was still determined to do what he could to improve it.[29]

'Nottinghamshire is in a sad state', Byron reported to Hobhouse after his return to London in January. Yet, apart from sending troops, the government had done and said nothing to suggest that the troubles in his county would provide an occasion for him 'to try a speech'. At the beginning of February 'the Catholic question' looked more likely to provide such an opportunity, and only the government's introduction of a bill to make frame-breaking a capital offence removed Byron's uncertainty. He got in touch with Lord Holland to ask for advice and documents, to which Holland as the Recorder of Nottingham had access. At the same time, Byron 'from all that fell under my own observations during my Christmas visit to Newstead' stressed to Holland the need for *'conciliatory'* measures.[30]

Conciliation was not an idea that entered the heads of the ministry. A number of people understood the nature of the trouble, but cabinet ministers were not among them. They were incapable of appreciating the connection between distress and violence. Hence they were not concerned with what had given rise to the disorders, only with their results. Indeed they were not greatly interested even in those. Although *The Times* commented that the disturbances and the movement of troops gave the 'appearance of a state of war', the Cabinet did not discuss the issue until the end of January; it then approved the Home Secretary's two draft bills which were to be rushed through Parliament. Not for the first or the last time the procrastination of a weak government had produced not careful deliberation but ill-considered drastic action – against the advice of the most capable people on the spot; and as so often in the previous century, repression was the ministry's only aim and the gallows its favourite resource.[31]

'Old Dame' Portland's ministry had been broken by failure and by Canning's understandable insistence that Castlereagh's disastrous tenure of the War Office be ended. Its successor, lacking both men, was even more mediocre, but against the odds it survived, partly because the Whig leaders were too indolent and vain, when given the opportunity of office, to make the effort needed to take it. Sydney Smith did the new Prime Minister, Spencer Perceval, an injustice when he implied there was nothing to be said for him except that he was 'faithful to Mrs Perceval and kind to the Master Percevals'. Perceval was indeed a narrow-minded ultra-Protestant reactionary, but he was also courageous and a good though long-winded speaker. Nevertheless the government was at least as uninspiring as the opposition. Perhaps its most distinguished feature was that, in a Cabinet of ten, three of the highest ranking ministers

– Perceval himself, Eldon, whom Shelley abhorred, and Westmor-
land, whom Byron thought 'certainly silly' – had eloped, and unlike
Shelley, had got married at Gretna Green or nearby.[32]

Byron had no enthusiasm for either party, as he had told Hanson
in 1809, but after he had taken the oath he had sat on the
opposition benches and there he remained. A few years earlier his
enemy, Henry Brougham, who became a radical Whig, had had a
similar attitude. Had the Tories made him a good offer, he would
probably have become a ministerialist. Though they let him slip
through their fingers, the Tories were ready to offer a *carrière
ouverte aux talents* to aspiring politicians who lacked birth and
resources. In contrast, the Whigs, said Charles Lamb, were 'all
cousins', a claim which was echoed by Brougham from outside the
Whig magic circle and confirmed by Grenville from inside it when,
referring to the appointment of a Whig leader in the Commons, he
wrote that Grey, the party leader, had no cause for offence if he was
'desired to recommend his wife's uncle instead of his sister's
husband'.[33]

Moreover in the Commons, at least, the Whigs were ineptly led
and badly divided. 'Nothing', a leading Whig told Grey in February
1809, 'could keep the present ministers in their places a week but
the state of the opposition'. Except for Timothy Shelley and a few
other die-hards, the Whigs were of like mind in supporting Catholic
emancipation; they were united on virtually nothing else. Whiggism
was described by Brougham in 1812 as 'the re-establishment of the
ancient intercourse between the Whigs and the people'. Yet for
some years both before and after 1812 the Whigs and the people
were separated, if not divorced. Partly because the great Whig
families had too many pocket boroughs and sinecures of their own
to summon enthusiasm for their abolition – the Duke of Norfolk,
who was 'by far the best of the English noblemen', Shelley told Miss
Hitchener, 'desires and votes for reform but has not virtue enough'
to get rid of his own boroughs – and partly because they were
scared of increased popular participation in politics, the Whigs were
unable to embrace the popular causes or advocate measures to
alleviate economic distress and political exclusion. So while *vis-à-vis*
the Tories the Whigs were themselves, politically though not
socially, underdogs they were scarcely more on the side of the real
underdogs than were the government. They were slightly more
liberal and less obscurantist than the ministerialists, yet the

resemblances of the two parties were far greater than their differences, and there was no reason to suppose that in office the Whigs would be any less incompetent than their opponents.[34]

In one respect, indeed, they would certainly have been much worse. Their antipathy to the war prevented them being an alternative government and gave the Prince Regent good reason, when the restrictions on the Regency ended in February 1812, not to turn out his Tory ministers and install in their place those who had been his Whig friends and comrades.[35]

The bill to make frame-breaking a capital offence was introduced into the House of Commons on 14 February, by which time Nottinghamshire frame-breaking had ended; all its stages were completed within a week, and it was sent up to the Lords. In the Commons opposition to it was half-hearted, the government winning the single substantive division, 94–17. Only one eccentric backbencher stressed the workers' 'unprecedented distresses', complained of the government seeking to 'hang up the people for outrages into which their own mal-administration had driven them', and criticised ministers for their 'total indifference . . . to the suffering of . . . their miserable fellow subjects'. In contrast, making the most hardline speech in support of the government, the very conservative Whig, William Lamb, whose wife Caroline was shortly to have a very public affair with Byron, did not think it right to enquire into disputes between masters and workmen, since such enquiries tended to influence workmen into thinking they had rights which had been infringed. He believed 'the atrocity' of machine-breaking to be 'as deep as any offence against property could be' and to call for the severest punishment. 'The terror of death' would operate powerfully on the public mind. As Lord Melbourne and Home Secretary at the end of the 'Swing riots' of 1830, Lamb, who seems from his private correspondence to have been something of a small-scale sadist, helped to carry those sentiments into ferocious effect.[36]

'Wretched as the state of representation is in England', Tom Paine wrote in *Rights of Man*, 'it is manhood compared with what is called the House of Lords; and so little is this nick-named house regarded that the people scarcely inquire at any time what it is doing'. For once Burke did not greatly differ from Paine. In 1793 he singled out the House of Lords as 'the feeblest part of the constitution', and in the intervening years it had done nothing to upset that judgement, its debates being pompously pedestrian and attendance low. An observer nevertheless found it 'impossible not to admire the peers; so truly noble-looking and finely dressed, with their stars, garters, etc. etc.'; compared to them he found the Commons 'like trash'. George III had recently come near to opening Parliament with the salutation 'My Lords and Peacocks'. Though relatively sane at the time, the King was clearly confused: it was the Lords not the Commons who were the peacocks.[37]

Their Lordships did, however, retain just enough vigour to defeat any reforming measure that passed the House of Commons. Whether it was the slave trade, the criminal law, the penal laws against Catholics, parliamentary reform, or the protection of child chimney sweeps – the Lords were invariably against any ameliora-tion of the current position. Sydney Smith may have been right in thinking that in trying to hold up parliamentary reform in 1832 the Lords were like Mrs Partington trying to push away the Atlantic Ocean with her mop. Yet in lesser matters the Lords succeeded in sweeping back reform. In 1810, for instance, they defeated by 31 votes to 11 a bill to abolish capital punishment for stealing five shillings' worth of goods in a shop; the attack on this dangerous proposal was led by the Lord Chief Justice, Lord Ellenborough, whose religious faith was described by Shelley as 'bloody, barbar-ous and intolerant', and by the Lord Chancellor, Lord Eldon, of whose cant and sycophancy Shelley memorably wrote:

> Next came Fraud, and he had on,
> Like Eldon, an ermined gown;
> His big tears, for he wept well,
> Turned to mill-stones as they fell.

These legal luminaries were supported by the Archbishop of Canterbury and six bishops; not a single prelate supported the bill.[38]

The Lords continued for a number of years to defeat all attempts to civilise the penal code, but with the House of Commons still mired in the reaction against the French Revolution and almost equally hostile to change, only occasionally were their Lordships called upon to stifle other attempts at improvement. Yet the atmosphere of 'the nick-named house' was itself stifling; it discour-aged able peers like Lord Grey, who to his dismay had to go there in 1807 on the death of his father, and infected them with indolence. 'What a place to speak in!' Grey told his wife after making his maiden speech. 'It was like speaking in a vault by the glimmering of a sepulchral lamp to the dead.' Admittedly some three-quarters of the ministry customarily sat in the Upper House, but such ministers were often mediocrities, and in February 1812 they were nearly all nonentities. Putting it at its lowest, therefore, the Regency House of Lords was not a forum in which an ambitious young politician of outstanding abilities and radical views was likely to prosper.[39]

Had Byron's main concern been to launch a conventional political career by gaining the esteem of his peers, he would have attuned his speech to his audience. He would have politely asserted his Whig credentials, mildly criticised the government for proposing the death penalty for frame-breaking, demonstrated his upper-class orthodoxy by attacking the mob and calling for severe punishment of its violence; and then after expressing his sense of honour at having been able to address their Lordships and his gratitude for their having listened to him he would have sat down. Such a speech would have been wholly out of character. Byron did not admire his audience, and ingratiation was not his aim. He knew from the debates in the Commons that his views on the disturbances differed markedly from those of his Whig colleagues, let alone the government, and he was not prepared to modify them to further his political career. The chief Whig objection was to the government's failure to institute an inquiry before introducing the bill, whereas Byron, as he told Holland, considered the workmen 'as a much injured body of men sacrificed to ye views of certain individuals who have enriched themselves by those practices which have deprived the frameworkers of employment'. Byron added that he feared Holland would think him 'half a framebreaker myself'.[40]

Opening the Second Reading debate in the Lords on 27 February, Lord Liverpool, the Secretary of State for War, said that 'the chief difficulty' for the authorities 'was the difficulty of detection under the existing applicable law'. He foresaw that many would think that to make the law more Draconian by turning frame-breaking into a capital offence would make detection still more difficult, yet he himself believed without offering reason or evidence that 'the operating dread of the severer punishment would be attended with beneficial results'. A few years before, Liverpool had been a last-ditch defender of the slave trade.[41]

Byron, who had largely memorised his speech and had only a list of twenty-two headings for notes, was next. He began by mentioning his connection with 'the suffering county' and stressing the extent and seriousness of the disturbances which had 'arisen from circumstances of the most unparalleled distress'. The misery was so widespread that the military had been useless, though 'several notorious delinquents had been detected', men guilty 'of the capital crime of poverty'. Improved machines had thrown many out of work, but these produced inferior goods which were not marketable at home.

> The rejected workmen in the blindness of their ignorance, instead of rejoicing at these improvements so beneficial to mankind, conceived themselves to be sacrificed to improvements in mechanism. In the foolishness of their hearts they imagined that the maintenance and well-being of the industrious poor was an object of greater consequence than the enrichment of a few individuals by any improvement in the implements of trade which threw the workmen out of employment and rendered the labourer unworthy of his hire.*[43]

When British commerce was prospering, Byron conceded, the adoption of the enlarged machinery could be beneficial to both master and servant, but when as in 1812 manufactures were 'rotting in warehouses, without a prospect of exportation', the larger frames merely aggravated distress. He contrasted the treatment of the well-off with that of the poor. While 'the exalted offender' could find means of baffling the law, 'new snares of death' were devised 'for the wretched mechanic, who is famished into guilt'.

The government had shown its inefficiency and its imbecility in the methods it had adopted to try to quell the disturbances. The military had been placed 'in situations where they can only be made ridiculous. As the sword is the worst argument that can be used, so should it be the last'. Had the government tried to discover the grievances of the men and their masters, and had 'proper meetings been held in the earlier stages' of the riots, means could have been devised, Byron believed, to restore 'tranquillity to the country'. As it was, the country suffered 'from the double injustice of an idle military and a starving population'.

---

* Shortly after the defeat of the Armada Queen Elizabeth refused Lord Hamsdon's request, on behalf of the Reverend William Lee, for a patent or monopoly for his stocking frame machine with the words: 'My Lord, I have too much love for my poor people who obtain their bread by the employment of knitting, to give my money to forward an invention that will tend to their ruin by depriving them of employment, and thus make them beggars.'[42]

All this had been happening within 130 miles of London, Byron went on, and yet this was the first time the House had been officially apprised of the disturbances. The government and the country had been enjoying 'our foreign triumphs in the midst of domestic calamity. But all the cities you have taken, all the armies which have retreated before your leaders, are but paltry subjects of self-congratulation, if your land divides against itself, and your dragoons and your executioners must be let loose against your fellow-citizens'. The government dismissed the rioters as 'a mob, desperate, dangerous and ignorant'. But were they aware, Byron asked, 'of our obligations to the mob? It is the mob that have enabled you to defy all the world, and can also defy you when neglect and famine have driven them to despair.'

The government acted with 'alacrity' to help its 'distrest allies', but left 'the distressed of your own country to the care of Providence or – the parish'. 'I have traversed', Byron continued, 'the seat of war in the peninsula, I have been in some of the most oppressed provinces of Turkey, but never under the most despotic of infidel governments did I behold such squalid wretchedness as I have seen since my return in the very heart of a Christian country.'

That led him to his peroration:

Setting aside the palpable injustice and the certain inefficacy of the Bill, are there not capital punishments sufficient in your statutes? Is there not blood enough upon your penal code that more must be poured forth to ascend to Heaven and testify against you? How will you carry the Bill into effect? Can you commit a whole country to their own prisons? Will you erect a gibbet in every field and hang up men like scarecrows? or will you proceed (as you must to bring this measure into effect) by decimation, place the county under martial law; depopulate and lay waste all around you? and restore Sherwood forest as an acceptable gift to the crown, in its former condition of a royal chase and an asylum for outlaws? Are these the remedies for a starving and desperate populace? Will the famished wretch who has braved your bayonets, be appalled by your gibbets? When death is a relief, and the only relief it appears that you will afford him, will he be dragooned into tranquillity? Will that which could not be effected by your grenadiers, be accomplished by your executioners?

If you proceed by the forms of law, where is your evidence? Those who have refused to impeach their accomplices, when transportation only was the punishment, will hardly be tempted to witness against them when death is the penalty. With all due deference to the noble lords opposite, I think a little investigation, some previous enquiry would induce even them to change their purpose. That most favourite state measure, so marvellously efficacious in many and recent instances, *temporising*, would not be without its advantages in this. When a proposal is made to emancipate or relieve, you hesitate, you deliberate for years, you temporise and tamper with the minds of men; but a death-bill must be passed offhand, without a thought of the consequences. Sure I am from what I have heard, and from what I have seen, that to pass the Bill under all the existing circumstances, without enquiry, without deliberation, would only be to add injustice to irritation, and barbarity to neglect. The framers of such a bill must be content to inherit the honours of that Athenian lawgiver whose edicts were said to be written not in ink but in blood.

But suppose it past, suppose one of these men, as I have seen them, meagre with famine, sullen with despair, careless of a life, – which your lordships are perhaps about to value at something less than the price of a stocking-frame – suppose this man surrounded by the children for whom he is unable to procure bread at the hazard of his existence, about to be torn for ever from a family which he lately supported in peaceful industry, and which it is not his fault that he can no longer so support, suppose this man, and there are ten thousand such from whom you may select your victims, dragged into court, to be tried for this new offence, by this new law; still, there are two things wanting to convict and condemn him; and these are, in my opinion, twelve butchers for a Jury, and a Jeffreys for a Judge.[44]

The rest of the short debate was banal, ministers making little attempt to answer their critics before easily winning the vote by 32 to 17. Three days later, however, according to the report of the debates, an extraordinary thing happened. An amendment which removed the death penalty from the bill was moved by Lord Grosvenor and 'agreed to'. If that had really occurred, it would have been notable as the only recorded occasion in the nineteenth century when the Lords agreed to be more liberal to human beings than the Commons. Sadly the House of Lords Journals show that Grosvenor's alleged amendment was never moved or at least not agreed to. And the Commons Journals are similarly conclusive in showing that no such amendment ever came back to the Commons.[45]

Judged merely as a piece of prose, Byron's maiden speech was probably the best oration made in the House of Lords in the nineteenth century.* Clearly, however, speeches should not be judged just as prose but also on their manner of delivery and their effect on their audience. Two opposition leaders, Holland and Grenville, had words of praise for Byron during the debate. Such public congratulations are almost obligatory after a maiden speech, but Byron himself was pleased with his reception. Dallas – and it is an illustration of Byron's isolation at that time that the dull and unctuous Dallas was the only one of his friends there to hear him – reported that Byron was 'glowing with success' when he left the chamber and thought that he had provided 'the best advertisement for *Childe Harold's Pilgrimage*'. Afterwards Byron told Hodgson that Holland had said that he would beat them all if he persevered and Grenville had compared the construction of some of his sentences to Burke's. In addition he had had many marvellous eulogies from the 'ministerial – yea ministerial!' side as well as the opposition.[47]

Yet private congratulations on such an occasion are not necessarily any more sincere than public ones. Holland gave his real opinion many years later. 'Byron's speech was full of fancy, wit and invective, but not exempt from affectation, nor well-reasoned, nor at all suited to our common notions of Parliamentary eloquence'. Only the claim that the speech was not 'well-reasoned', which evidently meant that Holland did not agree with it, seems unfounded. Other contemporaries had the same impression. Indeed, Byron himself wrote that he 'spoke very violent sentences with a sort of modest impudence, abused everything and everybody, and put the Lord Chancellor very much out of humour, and if I may believe what I hear, have not lost any character by the experiment – As to my delivery, loud and fluent enough, perhaps a little theatrical . . .'. The chief difference between Byron's verdict and Holland's arose from Byron having taken the 'eulogies' at their face value; hence his implausible belief that his audience had actually

---

* It did not have much competition. The House of Lords has seldom been the home of great oratory; apart from anything else, very few great orators have ever sat in it. In the eighteenth century Chatham made some great speeches on the American issue – 'My Lords, you can not conquer America.' The most notable Lords speech of the nineteenth century was probably that of Brougham winding up for the government on the Reform Bill in 1831. That speech does not read well, however, and if the story is true that Brougham sank to his knees on the Woolsack to deliver his peroration he must have looked ridiculous and probably sounded it too.[46]

appreciated 'everything and everybody' being 'abused' and had not resented a new young peer speaking 'very violent sentences' in an impudent and theatrical manner.[48]

In conversation Byron had a fine melodious voice; yet Tom Moore, who never heard him speak in the Lords, assumed that in his speech he had used 'the same chanting tone that disfigured his recitation of poetry'.* That is probable. When Byron rehearsed his speech 'he altered', according to Dallas, 'the natural tone of his voice . . . into a formal drawl and he prepared his features for a part – it was a youth declaiming a task'. Byron later claimed that neither House had ever struck him with more awe or respect than 'the same number of Turks in Divan or of Methodists in a barn would have done', but making his maiden speech he was inevitably and admittedly nervous, so that his performance was probably even more theatrical than the rehearsal or his poetry recitals. If so, that would accord with Holland's criticism that his speech flouted contemporary 'notions of parliamentary eloquence': the style of speaking in both Houses was more conversational than declamatory. All the same, as most people's opinion of a speech is chiefly determined by its content, it was what Byron said rather than the way he said it which would have chiefly offended his peers; even Dallas conceded that his speech 'produced a considerable effect'. The radical Sir Francis Burdett, who came over from the Commons to hear him, told him that it was 'the best speech by a Lord since the "Lord knows when"', probably, Byron added, 'from a fellow feeling in the sentiments'. Byron drew the correct inference then, but failed to draw it when his speech was praised by people who shared none of his sentiments.[50]

Byron's views were so profoundly sensible that even if he had been a far older man and had spoken in a conversational style they would still have shocked the great majority of his listeners. In his maiden speech he was years ahead of his time, whereas in 1812 and throughout the nineteenth century their Lordships were years behind theirs.† Conversion of his audience was therefore never a

---

* This seems to have been common. Hazlitt was intrigued by the 'chaunt' with which both Coleridge and Wordsworth read their poetry, and Haydon records Keats reciting poetry 'in his usual half chant' or 'with a tremulous under tone'.[49]

† The social reformer, the seventh Lord Shaftesbury, when translated from the Commons to the Lords in mid-century, felt that he might as well be in 'the Pampas or Timbuctoo', where the rule was 'know nothing, see nothing, hear nothing'. Later he felt that 'wealth and luxury and indulgence and sloth . . . loathed [him] and showed their loathing accordingly'.[51]

realistic possibility – as Byron may well have realised. Otherwise he probably would not have denounced the bloody code or reminded the House of their obligations to 'the mob'. Such heresies were at least as provocative to the Lords as John Wilkes's words to the Commons when he commended the 'wonderful, comprehensive mind' of the Lord Protector, Oliver Cromwell.[52]

If, as Byron later claimed, he was thinking 'rather of the *public without* than the persons within – knowing (as we all know) that Cicero himself and probably the Messiah could never have alter'd the vote of a single Lord of the Bedchamber or Bishop', his speech was well judged. It was extensively reported in Nottinghamshire, Yorkshire and Lancashire newspapers. More probably, however, Byron was aiming 'within' as well as 'without'. And his audience 'within' was 'dull' and self-satisfied. As he later told Hobhouse, '*our* house is not animating like the hounds of the Commons, when in full cry. Tis but cold hunting at best in the Lords.' Yet when he spoke there Byron was always in full cry after some seemingly animated prey. Hence his speeches did not appeal to the great majority of their Lordships, who regarded their House more as a temple than a hunt.[53]

Yet, however badly Byron misjudged the only political arena open to him – as Shelley misjudged his Dublin audience on religion – the facts and argument of his speech were correct save for one small error. He implied that the 'improved frames' which produced inferior goods in greater quantities than had formerly been possible had been introduced very recently, whereas they had been in use since about 1803 – a misapprehension which was widely shared. In every other respect his analysis of the situation and his attack on the bill were justified. Holland later agreed with the government that the bill had proved 'effective in putting down the evil', the reason presumably, for his allegation that Byron's speech had not been 'well-reasoned'. In fact, as Byron predicted, the bill proved ineffective.[54]

Nobody was sentenced to death at Nottingham Assizes for the violence in that county. As a result of his good sense and relative leniency the judge, Bailey, was barred from further Luddite trials. His successors did what was expected of them, and twenty-seven people were hanged at Lancaster, Chester and York; Shelley and Harriet wanted to contribute to a fund for the families of the seventeen hanged at York, who had been very poorly defended by a negligent Brougham. The hangman's haul included, however, a number who had committed quite different offences, ranging from murder through administering unlawful oaths to food rioting – one woman was hanged for stealing potatoes. Few of those who were slowly strangled according to law (which was at that time what hanging usually meant) died because of the frame-breaking Act. Nor was the Act much of a deterrent. Frame-breaking had stopped in Nottinghamshire before the bill was introduced, and its enactment did not prevent some minor recurrences at the end of the year. Luddism flowed and ebbed more according to the degree of distress and the despair of redress than the severity of the possible penalty.[55]

Byron was not alone in thinking that the government had a responsibility to alleviate the distress of the poor. Yet the attitude of the government and of almost all of Parliament was that nothing could or should be done to help the distressed. All that any government could do, ministers believed, was to put down the disturbances. Parliament and the government thus worshipped the laws of supply and demand, while they profaned the law of cause and effect. Crudely and crassly they dealt with effects; causes they ignored – the rich 'goad' the poor 'to famine', wrote Shelley, 'and hang them if they steal a loaf'. Luddism was a crime and, as in the eighteenth century, the only proper reaction to crime was to send for the hangman. In his 'Ode to the Framers of the Frame Bill', which he sent for anonymous publication in the *Morning Chronicle* at the beginning of March, Byron savagely but not unfairly pilloried the government's attitude:

> The rascals, perhaps, may betake them to robbing,
> The dogs to be sure have got nothing to eat –
> So if we can hang them for breaking a bobbin,
> 'T will save all the government's money and meat:
> Men are more easily made than machinery –
> Stockings fetch better prices than lives –
> Gibbets on Sherwood will *heighten* the scenery,
> Showing how Commerce, *how* Liberty thrives.

Two months earlier in a letter to Miss Hitchener, Shelley had expressed a similar attitude. Assailing 'the imbecility of aristocracy', he gasped at the contrast between 'plate & balls & tables & kings' and the 'famine-wasted inhabitants' of Nottingham. While the rich revelled, 'the groans of the wretched' went unheeded. That, however, was before his expedition to Dublin. His exposure to the

Irish 'mob' bred a more aloof attitude to the Luddite disturbances. Writing to Miss Nugent in May, he feared that 'hunger [was] the only excitement of our English riotings' and thought it likely that any change they produced would 'be devoid of principle & method'. Nevertheless, he still hoped that 'a just indignation' would prevail against 'that crowned coward & villain', the Prince Regent.[56]

A few days after Byron's speech, Cantos I and II of *Childe Harold's Pilgrimage* were published. In 1812 and in subsequent editions the poem looked very different from how it does in modern collections of Byron's poems. As well as the two cantos, there were Byron's notes, a number of additional poems – fourteen in the first edition and thirty in the tenth – and a long appendix on modern Greek or Romaic authors, much of it in Romaic. The book was therefore a substantial volume. In the tenth edition, for instance, the two cantos of *Childe Harold* occupy 118 pages out of a total of 302.[57]

Samuel Rogers, to whom Byron had sent the printed sheets of the poem before it was published, thought that 'in spite of all its beauty' it would 'never please the public'. In fact it was an immediate and sensational success. The first edition of 500 copies was sold out in three days, and 4,500 copies were sold in six months. Even in a poetry-reading age the reasons for such an astonishing success are not altogether plain. Indeed what Rogers told his sister before publication might well have proved correct: readers would 'dislike the querulous repining tone that pervades it, and the dissolute character of the hero'. Moreover religious scepticism and hostility to the war, which were still conspicuous in *Childe Harold* despite the changes pressed by Dallas and Murray, were abhorrent to many potential readers and would in any other poem have brought heavy censure from Tory critics. But, as this one was published by John Murray, who also published the Tory *Quarterly Review*, whose editor, William Gifford, had advised Murray to accept it, the Tory guns were largely masked. And so far from Byron's 'repining tone' and Harold's 'dissolute character' putting off readers, they proved a strong attraction. The earlier stanzas about Harold having 'spent his days in riot most uncouth' with 'concubines and carnal companie', having 'felt the fullness of satiety' and run 'through Sin's long labyrinth', and being 'sore sick at heart' since 'none did love him' etc., which were largely satirical in intent, were taken seriously by readers and gave the author an attractively sad, romantic image.[58]

The poem had additional advantages. Because of the war, the upper classes had been starved of travel, and *Childe Harold* with its fine descriptive passages gave them the chance to enjoy it vicariously. Also because of the seemingly permanent state of war, Harold's dejection and disillusionment could be easily understood and widely shared. Byron modestly attributed much of his poem's success to his 'being a Lord'. Hard though it is to overestimate the snobbery of Regency England, that remark managed to do so. All the same, while Byron's lordly and condescending Preface to *Hours of Idleness* had provoked inverted snobs like Brougham to attack his poetry, his 'being a Lord' now made him seem even more romantic, thus contributing to *Childe Harold*'s success. Moreover, Byron, with what the Duchess of Devonshire called his 'pale, sickly, but handsome countenance', was on the spot and was lionised by fashionable London. Four years later he was shunned by the same people, but in 1812 his social and his poetic success fed on each other. He became 'the universal talk of the town'. Finally, and most importantly, although Cantos I and II were not poetry of the highest class, they were anything but boring, and the best long poem that had been published for many years; *The Prelude* had been written, but was not published till long afterwards.[59]

Byron's celebrated remark a few years later, 'I awoke one morning and found myself famous', was justified. The instantaneous acclaim which greeted *Childe Harold* has been compared to the English publication of Rousseau's *Confessions*, but by then Rousseau was already famous. A closer parallel is probably the publication of the twenty-two-year-old Dostoevsky's first novel *Poor Folk*. The Russian critic, Belinsky, said there had been no other example in Russian literature 'of fame so quickly won'. Even so, Dostoevsky's novel, which like Byron's *Childe Harold* was a book vastly inferior to his later productions, did not have the spectacular impact of Byron's poem.[60]

Byron later became famous not just in England; he was one of the most famous Britons of the nineteenth century. In March 1812, however, the fame to which he 'awoke' was confined to a small circle. After all, the first edition was only 500 copies. And the book was expensive: it cost 30 shillings, and as it was sold in board or paper wrappers it had to be rebound at the cost of another 20 shillings to prevent it from soon falling to pieces. Subsequent editions were less expensive but not cheap. At that time some stockingers in Nottinghamshire were being paid seven shillings a week, and even the lucky ones got only 14s. 6d. Not of course that the very poor could have afforded *Childe Harold's Pilgrimage*. But it was not only prohibitively expensive for the poor, it was too dear for any but the very well off. So, when the Duchess of Devonshire said the poem was 'on every table', she meant the tables of her friends and acquaintances, mostly the very rich.[61]

Shelley never did awake to find himself famous. Although still only nineteen, he was about to begin the work he had mooted to Miss Hitchener in December: his first long poem, the usually underrated *Queen Mab*. But in common with his earlier poetry it did not win him public renown. Indeed four years later in another long poem, *Laon and Cythna*, he was still not sure that his 'fame' ever would 'cleave its natal gloom'. Like Byron, he sometimes had infamy heaped on him by his contemporaries but, unlike Byron, only in a very limited circle did he ever gain respect and recognition during his lifetime. Not until after his death did Shelley's 'fame', as he put it in the same poem,

> become
> A star among the stars of mortal night.[62]

Epilogue

Although Shelley and Byron did not meet in person until 1816, they did in a sense meet in verse some years earlier. In a letter to Miss Hitchener in January 1812, Shelley included 'a few stanzas which may amuse you'. These originated from *The Devil's Thoughts*, a poem which Coleridge and Southey had published in London in September 1799. Southey later described how it was composed: 'There while the one was shaving/ Would he the song begin;/ And the other when he heard it at breakfast,/ In ready accord join in'.[1]

Southey, who was the shaver, wrote only the first three verses; Coleridge wrote the other fourteen. Echoing, though in a milder tone, their earlier radical politics, the poem was a gentle satire on the current state of the country. The Devil visits England and finds there many things to his liking. As its mode of composition suggests, *The Devil's Thoughts* was a light-hearted affair. Published anonymously in the *Morning Post*, it was a great success, helping to revive the fortunes of that paper. Oddly, the verses were widely attributed to Richard Porson, the distinguished classical scholar. Professor Porson was a radical Whig and he did have some satirical ability, but he had nothing to do with *The Devil's Thoughts*. Maybe Porson who, as we saw at Cambridge, was outstandingly drunken, claimed authorship when intoxicated, and the claim stuck.[2]

Shelley was never under that delusion. Evidently Southey showed him the poem at Keswick, together with some stanzas he had subsequently added. Shelley similarly expanded (and altered) the 99 lines he had sent to Miss Hitchener and called the finished product 'The Devil's Walk'. Although he derived the idea of his poem, some of its targets and even some of its language from Coleridge and Southey, his versification was much looser than theirs. And while not so good humoured as *The Devil's Thoughts*, his poem was much less savage than his later great satires: *Peter Bell the Third* and *The Mask of Anarchy*.[3]

A year later, in December 1813, Byron, too, wrote a poem, 'The Devil's Drive', about a Satanic jaunt to Britain. In doing so, he was not in any way influenced by the poetic prestige of Coleridge and Southey. He was one of the many who thought the 1799 poem had been written by Porson. Nor was he influenced by Porson's prestige as a classical scholar. 'Of all the disgusting brutes – sulky – abusive – and intolerable – Porson', wrote Byron, 'was the most bestial . . .'. Nevertheless that did not put him off the idea, which like Shelley he found attractive, of looking at England through the eyes of the Devil, and he subtitled his poem 'a sequel to Porson's "The Devil's Walk";' thereby getting wrong the title of the original poem and inadvertently giving it the one Shelley had chosen for his version.[4]

Byron did not think very highly of his own effort. Calling his poem 'a wild, rambling, unfinished rhapsody', he never published it. Like Shelley's poem, Byron's 'sequel' is in much freer verse than Coleridge and Southey's original. Instead of the heroic couplets of his previous satires, 'The Devil's Drive' is in rhymed stanzas of verying length. Sportive and humorous, it points in content as well as form to his later satires, *Beppo* and *Don Juan*.[5]

When Shelley sent Miss Hitchener his first attempt at the poem, he told her that he 'was once rather fond of the Devil'. And fond of him he remained. The Devil appears in some of his best later poems. Byron had a similar weakness for Lucifer; His Satanic Majesty is prominent in *Cain*, *The Vision of Judgment* and elsewhere.[6]

A poetic penchant for the Devil was not all that the two poets shared; they both chose a number of the same victims for their satire and the Devil's admiration. Inevitably the royal family was a prime target. Shelley concentrated on 'a brainless King' and on the Prince Regent's gluttony, his 'princely paunch' and 'each brawny haunch';* Byron on the Regent's 'Haram so hoary' and on the absurdity of the Duke of Cumberland with his sleazy past being made a Field Marshal.[8]

The rich and the Church were also in the firing line. Shelley wrote of the wealthy:

> For they thrive well, whose garb of gore
> Is Satan's choicest livery,
> And they thrive well, who from the poor

---

* Shelley's emphasis on the Regent's greed was probably stimulated by the price of wheat being at its highest ever in 1812 and by food riots in Devon where he was living.[7]

Have snatched the bread of penury,
And heap the houseless wanderer's store
On the rank trial of luxury.

In his poem Byron scoffed at 'a new barouche, and an ancient peer', whom the Devil bade to 'be true to his club . . . his brothel and his beer'. On religion Shelley took aim at the evangelicals and the bishops while Byron tilted at the Methodists' emphasis on faith rather than works.[9]

Shelley attacked the war in Spain, 'where ruin ploughs her gory way', and the blood spilt in Ireland in 1798. Byron, who was writing only two months after the battle of Leipzig, in which the Russians and the Prussians defeated Napoleon and some 100,000 men were killed or wounded, portrayed the Devil perching 'on a Mountain of Slain';

Then he gazed with delight from its growing height,
Nor seldom on earth had he seen such a sight,
    Nor his work done half so well:
For the field ran so red with the blood of the dead,
    That it blushed like the waves of Hell!
Then loudly and wildly and long laughed he:
'Methinks they have little need here of *Me*.'[10]

Both poets also attacked politics and politicians. Shelley's Devil was sure that 'a Statesman' would be his 'unchanging lover'. Visiting both Houses of Parliament, Byron's Devil thought that 'to hear' the peers 'were flat', but he was so 'shocked' by the strong language of the Lord Chief Justice that 'quoth he "I must go/ For I find we have much better manners below"'. In the Commons the Devil was more at home:

He had been there many a day;
And many a vote and soul and job he
Had bid for and carried away in the Lobby.[11]

Not only their Devils but Shelley and Byron themselves were opposed to virtually all the institutions of Church and state and to the major war that was being waged by the state with the support of the Church. That combination of oppositions was not common in any class. Among old Etonians and old Harrovians it was rare, if not unique. The early life of Byron and Shelley had thus not merely made them the poets they were; it had made them heretics or rebels as well. This shared dislike of so much that almost all their contemporaries unquestioningly accepted, and most of them revered, provided a strong foundation for their future friendship.

Abbreviations

AR	Annual Register
BJ	The *Byron Journal*
BL	British Library
Blessington	*Lady Blessington's Conversations with Lord Byron*, ed. E. J. Lovell, Jr. 1969
BLJ	*Byron's Letters and Journals*, ed. Leslie A. Marchand. 13 vols. 1973–94
CHP	*Childe Harold's Pilgrimage*
CMP	*Lord Byron: The Complete Miscellaneous Prose*, ed. Andrew Nicholson. 1991
Conversations	*Medwin's Conversations with Lord Byron*, ed. E. J. Lovell, Jr. 1966
CPW	*Lord Byron: The Complete Poetical Works*, ed. Jerome J. McGann. 7 vols. 1980–93
DNB	*Dictionary of National Biography*
E & M, II	*The Poems of Shelley*, ed. K. Everest and G. Matthews. Vol. II. 2000
EBSR	*English Bards and Scotch Reviewers, A Satire.* 1809
ER	*Edinburgh Review*
Esdaile	*Percy Bysshe Shelley: The Esdaile Notebook*, ed. K. N. Cameron. 1964
Gisborne	*Maria Gisborne and Edward E. Williams, Shelley's Friends. Their Journals and Letters*, ed. Frederick L. Jones. 1951
GM	*The Gentleman's Magazine*
Harrow	*A History of Harrow School* by Christopher Tyerman. 2000
HC	*The House of Commons 1790–1820*, ed. R. G. Thorne. 5 vols. 1986
Hutchinson	*Shelley: Poetical Works*, ed. Thomas Hutchinson. 1971

HVSV	*His Very Self and Voice. Collected Conversations of Lord Byron*, ed. E. J. Lovell Jr. 1980
Jeaffreson	*The Real Lord Byron*. 1884
Jeaffreson, I & II	*The Real Shelley*. 2 vols. 1885
Journal	*The Journal of Thomas Moore*, ed. Wilfred S. Dowden. 6 vols. 1938
K–SJ	*The Keats–Shelley Journal*
K–SMB	*The Keats–Shelley Memorial Bulletin*
K–SR	*The Keats–Shelley Review*
L & J	*The Works of Lord Byron. Letters and Journals*, ed. R. E. Prothero. 6 vols. 1898–1901
LBAR	*Lord Byron's Accounts Rendered* by Doris Langley Moore. 1974
Letters	*The Letters of Percy Bysshe Shelley*, ed. F. L. Jones. 2 vols. 1964
LLB	*The Late Lord Byron*, by Doris Langley Moore. 1961
LRB	*The London Review of Books*
M & E, I	*The Poems of Shelley*, ed. G. Matthews and K. Everest. Vol. I. 1989
Marchand	*Byron, A Biography*, by Leslie A. Marchand. 3 vols. 1957
Medwin	*Medwin's Revised Life of Shelley*, ed. H. B. Forman. 1913
MLN	*Modern Language Notes*
MLQ	*Modern Language Quarterly*
Moore	*The Works of Lord Byron: With his Letters and Journals and his Life*, by Thomas Moore, Esq. 17 vols. 1847
Moore, *Letters*	*The Letters of Thomas Moore*, ed. Wilfred S. Dowden. 2 vols. 1964
NBSR	*Newstead Byron Society Review*
P & P	*Past and Present*
PD	*Parliamentary Debates*
PH	*Parliamentary History*
PMLA	*Publications of the Modern Language Association*
Poetry	*The Works of Lord Byron. Poetry*, ed. E. H. Coleridge. 7 vols. 1898–1904
PR	*Parliamentary Register*

Prose	*Shelley's Prose*, ed. D. L. Clarke. 1988
Prose Works, 1	*The Prose Works of Percy Bysshe Shelley*, Vol. I, ed. E. B. Murray. 1993
QR	*Quarterly Review*
R & F	*The Complete Poetry of Percy Bysshe Shelley*, Vol. I, ed. D. H. Reiman and N. Fraistat. 2000
R & P	*Shelley: Poetry and Prose*, eds D. H. Reiman and S. B. Powers 1977
Raizis I	*Lord Byron Byronism – Liberalism – Philhellenism*, ed. M. B. Raizis, 1988
Raizis II	*Byron and the Mediterranean World*, ed. M. B. Raizis, 1995
Recollections	*Recollections of the Last Days of Shelley and Byron*, by E. J. Trelawny. 1858
Records	*Records of Shelley, Byron and the Author*, by E. J. Trelawny. 1887
S & C	*Shelley and his Circle 1773–1826*, ed. K. N. Cameron, D. L. Reiman et al. 8 vols. 1961–86
SH	*Social History*
Smith	The works of the Rev. Sydney Smith, 3 vols. 1840
ST	*State Trials*

Notes

Introduction
Pages 1 to 11

1 Byron: *EBSR*, l. 299; *CPW*, I, pp. 238, 258, 404; McGann: *Fiery Dust* (1968), p. 9; Knatchbull-Hugessen: *Diplomat in Peace and War* (1949), p. ix; Moore, II, pp. 132–3; Shelley: *A Defence of Poetry*, in R & P, p. 508; Moore, II, pp. 132–3.

2 *Letters*, I, p. 504; *Poetry*, IV, p. 342; Paulson: *Representations of Revolution* (1983), p. 252; Berlin: *The Roots of Romanticism* (1999), pp. 6–12; Hough: *The Romantic Poets* (1967), p. 7; Schenk: *The Mind of the European Romantics* (1966), pp. xxii–iii, 3; Raisanovsky: *The Emergence of Romanticism* (1992), p. 69; Harris: *Romanticism and the Social Order 1780–1830* (1969), pp. 10, 16–17, 233; Bloom: *The Visionary Company* (1971), pp. xiii–xvi; Lucas: *The Decline and Fall of the Romantic Ideal* (1991), p. 42; Wilson: *Axel's Castle* (1961), pp. 9–10; Stephen: *Hours in a Library* (1991), III, pp. 334–5.

3 Holmes: *Coleridge* (1998), II, p. 320.

4 Shelley: 'A Discourse on the Manners of the Ancient Greeks Relative to the Subject of Love', in *Prose*, pp. 217–18, 223; Shelley: *A Defence of Poetry*, in R & P, p. 508; Ullman: *Mad Shelley* (1930), pp. 11, 25–30; Hazlitt: *The Spirit of the Age* (1894), p. 58; Hazlitt: *On Thompson and Cowper*, in Waller and Glover (eds): *The Collected Works of William Hazlitt* (1992), V, p. 98; Brett-Smith (ed.): *Peacock's Four Ages of Poetry* (1921), p. 14.

5 Elton: *A Survey of English Literature 1780–1830* (1912), I, p. 6; Brett-Smith (ed.), p. 17; Arnold: *Essays in Criticism* (1895), II, p. 110; Williams: *Culture and Society* (1963), pp. 48–9; Gill: *William Wordsworth* (1989), p. 197; Curran: *Poetic Form and British Romanticism* (1989), p. 15; Barton: *Byron and the Mythology of Fact* (1968), p. 4; Thomas: *Man and the Natural World* (1983), p. 149; Byron: *Beppo*, ll. 415–16, *CPW*, IV, p. 145.

6 Gibbon: *Memoirs of My Life* (Bonnard ed. 1966), p. 162.

7 Schama: *Citizens* (1989), pp. 390–3; J. Thompson (ed.): *English Witnesses of the French Revolution* (1939), p. 53; Goodwin: *Friends of Reform* (1979), pp. 20, 120; Coleridge: *Lectures on Politics and Religion* (1974), pp. 30–1.

8 Keane: *Tom Paine* (1995), pp. 307–8; E. P. Thompson: *The Making of the English Working Class* (1980), pp. 117–18; Wordsworth: *The Prelude* X, ll.

340

123–4; Marshall: *William Godwin* (1989), p. 155; Gray: *The Socialist Tradition* (1946), p. 114; Gill, pp. 71–3; Elwin: *The First Romantics* (1947), pp. 55–9; Moorman: *William Wordsworth* (1968), I, pp. 226–8.

9   Wollstonecraft: *Political Writings* (Todd ed. 1999), pp. 8–9, 225; Elwin: *The Noels and the Milbankes* (1967), pp. 297, 320, 350; Cannon: *Aristocratic Century* (1989), pp. 161–2, 169–79.

10 Peacock: *Memoirs of Percy Bysshe Shelley* (*Fraser's Magazine* 1858–62), p. 647; Cannon: *Parliamentary Reform 1640–1832* (1972), p. 108; Sack: 'The House of Lords and Parliamentary Patronage in Great Britain, 1802–1832' *Historical Journal*, 23, 2 (1980), pp. 918–19; Gilmour: *Riot, Risings and Revolution* (1992), pp. 209, 434; Dobree (ed.): *The Letters of George III* (1935), p. 128; *ST* XXII, p. 384.

11 Coleridge, pp. 30–1; Hole: *Pulpits, Politics and Public Order in England 1760–1832* (1989), p. 128; Schenk: *The Aftermath of the Napoleonic Wars* (1997), pp. 4–5.

12 Foreman: *Georgiana, Duchess of Devonshire* (1998), pp. 291–2; Godwin: *Political Justice* (1992), p. 850; Marshall, p. 220; Paulson, p. 115; Soboul: *The Parisian sans-Culottes and the French Revolution 1793–4* (1964), p. 246; Clutton-Brock: *Shelley, The Man and the Poet* (1910), p. xiv; Mee: *Dangerous Enthusiasm* (1994), p. 144; Lindsay: *William Blake* (1978), p. 80; *AR* 1798, p. 229; *Journal* II, p. 751.

13 Gelpi: *Shelley's Goddess* (1992), p. 58; Philp: *Godwin's Political Justice* (1986), pp. 223–4; *AR* 1798, p. 229; *Conversations*, p. 69; Bage: *Hermsprong or Man As He Is Not* (1796), Ch. 24; *Records*, p. 32; Elmsley: 'An Aspect of Pitt's Terror', *SH* 6, no. 2 (1981), pp. 155–74; Bryant: *The Years of Endurance* (1942), p. 140; Coleridge, p. 288; Gilmour, pp. 412–14; Spater: *William Cobbett* (1982), I, p. 368.

14 Butterfield: 'Charles James Fox and the Whig Opposition in 1792', *Cambridge Historical Journal*, 9, nos 1, 2, 3, p. 325; Dozier: *For King, Constitution & Country* (1983), pp. 100–1, 174–5; Godwin: *Caleb Williams* (World's Classics, 1982), p. 79; Paine: *Rights of Man* (Penguin Classics, 1985), pp. 236–70; Coleridge, p. 10; E. P. Thompson, pp. 174–6.

15 Marshall, pp. 229, 232; Leask: 'The Godwins and the Shelleys', *K–SR* (1990), p. 78; Byron: Dedication to *Don Juan*, ll. 3–4, 134–6; *CPW*, V, pp. 3, 8.

16 Smith, I, p. iv.

17 Langford: *Englishness Identified* (2000), pp. 268, 274–5; Boswell: *Life of Johnson* (1953), p. 404; Byron: *Beppo*, l. 374, *CPW*, IV, p. 144; Halévy: *England in 1815* (1949), pp. 588–91; Holmes: *Shelley: The Pursuit* (1974), p. 540; *Letters*, I, pp. 489; White: *The Age of George III* (1968), p. 203 (Albert Sorel).

18 Simmons: *Southey* (1995), p. 152; *Letters*, I, pp. 219, 223, 513; Hutchinson, pp. xxi, 33.

19 *BLJ*, VII, pp. 44, 62, 80; McCalman: *Radical Underworld* (1993), pp. 137–9: Thompson, pp. 769–75; *Letters*, II, pp. 176, 345; I, p. 513; Holmes: *Shelley*, p.

359; Motion: *Keats* (1997), p. 139; Reiman: *Romantic Texts and Contexts* (1987), pp. 260–74; Webb: *Shelley, A Voice Not Understood* (1977), pp. 92–3; Stocking: 'New Shelley Letters', *K–SMB*, 31, pp. 4, 8; Dawson: *The Unacknowledged Legislator* (1980), pp. 172–3; Gisborne, p. 47; Woodward: *The Age of Reform* (1962), pp. 65–6; *HC*, I, p. 275.

20 *HVSV*, p. 147; *Laon and Cythna*, l. 3685, and Preface, E & M, II, pp. 215; Rutherford: *Byron the Best-Seller* (1964), p. 13; *BLJ*, III, p. 242; VIII, pp. 26, 74; P. A. Brown: *The French Revolution in English History* (1965), pp. 211–13.

21 'Ode to Liberty', ll. 211–12, R & P, p. 234; E & M, II, p. 35; *PH*, XXX, 394–5; *Don Juan*, VIII, ll. 1076–7; *CPW*, V, p. 406; Boyd Hilton: 'Manchester's Moment', *LRB*, 20 August 1998; Bayly: *Imperial Meridian* (1989), pp. 2–4, 160–2, 248–50; *PD*, XI, 888.

22 Hogg: *The Life of P. B. Shelley* (1858), I, pp. 212–13, *BLJ*, X, p. 69; Merle: 'A Newspaper Editor's Reminiscences' (*Fraser's Magazine*, June 1841), p. 706; Brightfield: *John Wilson Croker* (1940), p. 276; Smiles: *A Publisher and His Friends* (1911), pp. 158–9; Hazlitt, pp. 132–3; Franklin: *Byron, A Literary Life* (2000), p. 8; Hazlitt: *Table-Talk* (World's Classics, 1901), pp. 199–201; Everett (ed.): *Shelley Revalued* (1983), pp. 78–9.

23 *PD*, XXXV, p. 591; Lefebvre: *The Coming of the French Revolution* (1947), p. 3; Lovell: *Byron, The Record of a Quest* (1949), pp. 161–4; Jeaffreson (1885), I, pp. 139–40, 151–2; James: Preface to *Letters from America* (1916), by Rupert Brooke, p. xiii.

24 *LBAR*, p. 471; Buxton: *Shelley and Byron* (1968), pp. ix–x.

I The Byrons and Gordons
Pages 12 to 20

 1 *BLJ*, VIII, p. 108; IX, p. 87; Moore, I, pp. 19, 34–6, II, p. 36; *L & J*, I, p. 4; cf. Watson: *The Literature of Scotland* (1964), pp. 242–3; Hugh McDiarmid's Foreword to N. K. Wells: *George Gordon, Lord Byron, A Scottish Genius* (1961), pp. 7–8.

 2 T. S. Eliot: *On Poetry and Poets* (1957), pp. 224–5, 238; Moore, I, p. 36; C.R.L.F: *Mr Gladstone at Oxford 1890* (1908), p. 39; Leigh Hunt: *Lord Byron and Some of His Contemporaries* (1828), I, p. 179; *HVSV*, pp. 610, 621; *Conversations*, pp. 34–5; Moore, *Letters*, II, p. 714; Minchin: *Old Harrow Days* (1898), p. 192; Byron: *Don Juan*, c. X, ll. 135, 151–2; *CPW*, V, p. 442.

 3 Leigh Hunt, I, p. 158.

 4 Lockhart: *Memoirs of the Life of Sir Walter Scott* (1878), p. 3; 'The Duel', ll. 15–17; *CPW*, IV, p. 207; *BLJ*, X, pp. 208–9, II, p. 27; *Don Juan*, c. X, ll. 226–9; *CPW*, V, p. 445.

 5 Moore, I, pp. 1–3; Walker: *The House of Byron* (1988), pp. 1–7, 16–18, 29; Rowse: *The Byrons and Trevanions* (1978), pp. 3–4, 8–9; *Don Juan*, c. X, ll.

278, 282–4, *CPW*, V, pp. 447–8; Byron: 'On Leaving Newstead Abbey', ll. 6, 11, 13; *CPW*, I, pp. 35, 364.

6 Knowles: *The Monastic Order in England* (1949), pp. 174–5; Knowles: *The Religious Orders in England* (1959), III, p. 465; Shelley: 'Essay on the Revival of Literature', in *Prose*, p. 179; Walker, pp. 26–7; Rowse, pp. 10–11; 'Elegy on Newstead Abbey', ll. 37, 40; *CPW*, I, p. 108.

7 Jeaffreson, pp. 8–10; Walker, pp. 24, 30–1, 34, 45, 50; Rowse, pp. 12–14.

8 Wedgewood: *The King's War* (1958), pp. 203, 229–30, 290, 338–43, 357; Gibb: *The Lord General* (1938), pp. 60–3, 75–9; *The Complete Peerage* (1912), II, p. 454; Rowse, pp. 54–6, 58, 65–6, 72, 78–80, 104–5.

9 Clarendon: *History of the Rebellion and Civil Wars in England*, I, p. 534; Latham and Matthews (eds): *The Diary of Samuel Pepys* (1970–83), V, p. 336; VIII, pp. 181–2; Davies: *The Restoration of Charles II 1658–1660* (1955), pp. 128–39; Rowse, pp. 105–14; Walker, pp. 91–4, 97, 105–11; Jeaffreson, p. 18; Johnson: *Berkeley Square to Bond Street* (1952), pp. 1, 43, 48–50.

10 Holmes: *British Politics in the Age of Anne* (1987), p. 255; Johnson, p. 154; Walker, pp. 117–19, 122, 172–5; Rowse, pp. 115–16.

11 *The Complete Peerage* (1913), III, pp. 35–6; Halsband (ed.): *The Complete Letters of Lady Mary Wortley Montagu* (1966), II, p. 312; III, p. 184; Walker, pp. 118, 152–3, 168–9; Rowse, pp. 127–8.

12 Hunting Smith: *Originals Abroad* (1952), pp. 97–112; Jesse: *George Selwyn and His Contemporaries* (1882), III, p. 392; IV, pp. 11, 47–9, 218–22, 249–52; Lewis (ed.): *Lady Louisa Stuart's Notes on Jesse's George Selwyn* (1928), pp. 46–9; Walker, pp. 169–71.

13 Walker, pp. 118–19, 122–6; Rowse, pp. 122–3; Burford: *Wits, Wenchers and Wantons* (1990), pp. 176–8; Boswell: *Life of Johnson* (1953), pp. 1252–3; *Boswell in Holland 1763–4* (1952), p. 172.

14 *ST*, XX, pp. 1178, 1185–6, 1196, 1213, 1216, 1218, 1220, 1234–6; *AR* 1765, pp. 208–12; Walker, pp. 126–9; Kiernan: *The Duel in European History* (1988), p. 137; Rowse, pp. 123–5; Gilmour, pp. 266–7.

15 Moore, I, pp. 29–33, 39–40, 247–9; Prothero: 'The Childhood and Schooldays of Byron', *The Nineteenth Century*, January 1898, p. 70; Jeaffreson, pp. 14–15; Walker, pp. 133–9, 144; Coope: 'Newstead Abbey in the Eighteenth Century', *Transactions of the Thoroton Society*, 83 (1979), pp. 57–9; Beckett: *Byron The Aristocrat and the Abbey* (2001), pp. 57–60, 67–83; Rowse, pp. 128–9; Smiles: *A Publisher and His Friends* (1911), p. 101.

16 *Narrative of the Hon. John Byron* (1812); *DNB*; Williamson: *Cook and the Opening of the Pacific* (1946), pp. 54–6; Rowse, pp. 130–4, 136–9; Walker, pp. 149–58; *Thraliana* (1942), p. 407.

17 Gittings: *John Keats* (1970), p. 416.

18 *Thraliana*, pp. 444, 470, 787, 739; *The Town and Country Magazine*, 5 (December 1773), pp. 625–7; Rowse, pp. 132–3, 138–45, 148.

19 Boswell: *On the Grand Tour, Italy, Corsica and France* (1955), p. 58.

20 Walker, pp. 135, 153–6, 161–2, 166–7,; Rowse, pp. 138, 148; Prothero, pp. 69–70; *Thraliana*, p. 787.

21 Walker, pp. 124, 159; Rowse, pp. 134–6, 142, 146, 150; I am indebted to Major M. A. T. Hibbert-Hingston, Regimental Adjutant of the Coldstream Guards: MacKinnon: *Origin and Services of the Coldstream Guards* (1833), I, pp. 433–4; *BLJ*, X, p. 208; *Thraliana*, p. 739n; Bakewell: *Augusta Leigh* (2000), pp. 7–8; BL Add. Ms. 19038, f. 54.

22 L & J, I, pp. 3–4; *The Town and Country Magazine*, 11 (January 1779), pp. 9–11; Bakewell, pp. 9–16; *The Complete Peerage* (1929), VII, pp. 515–16; Clinton: *Memoirs of the Life and Writings of Lord Byron* (1826), pp. 34–5; Rosebery: *Pitt* (1891), p. 46; Jeaffreson, p. 20.

23 *BLJ*, VII, p. 204; Bulloch: *The House of Gordon* (1903), I, pp. 5–9, 13–17, 38–48, 51–6; Ford: *Political Murder* (1985), pp. 167–73.

24 Bulloch, I, pp. 73, 87–8, 100, 103, 118; Boyes: *My Amiable Mamma* (1991), p. 3; Massie: *Byron's Travels* (1988), pp. 17–19; *BLJ*, VIII, p. 73; cf. 'The Duel', ll. 15–20, *CPW*, IV, p. 207.

25 Bulloch, I, pp. 115–22; L & J, I, p. 3; *BLJ*, VIII, p. 217; Boyes, pp. 1–11; Pryse Gordon: *Personal Memoirs* (1830), II, p. 330; Moore, I, pp. 7–8; III, pp. 159–60.

26 Dryden: *King Arthur*, iii; *EBSR*, l. 113, *CPW*, I, p. 232; *Don Juan*, c. I, l. 1633; *CPW*, V, p. 74; Prothero, p. 66; Walker, p. 178; Bage: *Hermsprong*, ch. 46.

II Childhood in Aberdeen
Pages 21 to 38

1 *Scottish Notes and Queries*, 1, no. 6 (December 1899), pp. 81–2; Moore, I, pp. 7–9; Newton Hanson's Narrative in the Murray Archive, Box 13A; Galt: *The Life of Lord Byron* (1830), p. 9; Boyes, pp. 11–15; Walker, p. 178.

2 Moore, I, pp. 9–10; Bulloch, I, pp. 124–32; *DNB*; Symon: *Byron in Perspective* (1924), pp. 7–10; Boyes, pp. 16–18.

3 BL Add. Ms. 19038, f. 54; Moore, I, p. 9; Jeaffreson, p. 21; Bulloch, I, pp. 129–31; Symon, pp. 8–10; Walker, p. 165.

4 Bulloch, I, p. 128; Symon, p. 19; *LBAR*, pp. 13, 21; Gunn, *My Dearest Augusta* (1968), pp. 29–30; Boyes, pp. 23–4; Pratt: *Byron at Southwell* (1948), p. 5.

5 Gunn, p. 30; Symon, pp. 12, 18; *LBAR*, p. 21.

6 Marchand, I, p. 23; Bulloch, I, p. 132; Gunn, pp. 12, 30; Boyes, p. 24; Pratt, p. 5; *LBAR*, pp. 50–1.

7 Symon, pp. 12–13; L & J, I, pp. 5, 8; Prothero, p. 68; Boyes, p. 27.

8 *Recollections*, pp. 223–5; Bornand (ed.): *The Diary of W. M. Rossetti 1870–1873* (1977), p. 171; Elze: *Lord Byron* (1872), p. 335; *LLB*, pp. 435–6.

9 *Records*, p. 233; *LLB*, pp. 92–3, 430; Nicolson: *Byron: The Last Journey* (1940), pp. 269–70; in *Trelawny The Incurable Romancer* (1977), William St

Clair, pp. 176, 218–19, is inclined to accept Trelawny's story, pointing out that the date both of his arrival at Missolonghi, on which Doris Langley Moore relied for his demolition of his claim, and of the sealing of the coffin are doubtful. Nevertheless, in the many letters that he wrote at the time Trelawny never mentioned having seen the body. And his two later accounts differ so markedly that the likelihood is that both are false. In his biography *Lord Byron's Jackal* (1998), pp. 135–6, 363–4, David Crane leaves the matter open.

10 *L & J*, I, pp. 11–12; Kemble: 'Byron: His Lameness and Last Illness', *QR*, 257 (1931), pp. 231–3; Knebworth: *Boxing* (1931), p. 26; *Conversations*, p. 9; *Blessington*, p. 6; Barber: *Byron and Where He Is Buried* (1939), p. 137.

11 *L & J*, I, pp. 11–12; *HVSV*, pp. 15–16, 611; Symon, pp. 39–40; *Don Juan*, c. VIII, sts 83–4; *CPW*, V, p. 390; Marchand, I, pp. 54–5; *Journal*, III, p. 1121; Browne: 'The Problem of Byron's Lameness', *Proceedings of the Royal Society of Medicine*, 53, no. 6 (June 1960), pp. 1–3; Mills: 'Byron's Last Illness', *BJ*, 2000, pp. 56–7; Kemble, pp. 233–5 (who thought the boots pointed to a club foot).

12 Moore, I, p. 347; *Conversations*, p. 9; *S and C*, I, p. 186; Tomalin: *The Life and Death of Mary Wollstonecraft* (1992), pp. 274–5; Boyes, p. 27.

13 Symon, p. 38; Moore, I, p. 104; Boyes, pp. 28, 31–2.

14 Moore, I, pp. 9–10; Bulloch, I, pp. 131–2; Symon, pp. 16–25; Boyes, pp. 29–30.

15 Moore, I, pp. 11–12; Symon, pp. 26–7; Marchand, I, pp. 27–8; *LBAR*, p. 12.

16 Moore, I, pp. 11–16; Jeaffreson, pp. 27–8; Symon, pp. 30–2; Marchand, I, pp. 29–30.

17 *Conversations*, pp. 55–7; *BLJ*, X, pp. 208–9; Massie, p. 17; Byron: 'Childish Recollections', ll. 219–20, *CPW*, I, p. 165; Prothero, p. 71.

18 Moore, I, pp. 15–16; Bulloch, I, pp. 133–4; Symon, pp. 33–5.

19 *LBAR*, pp. 25–6, 42–3, 46.

20 *Conversations*, p. 55.

21 *LBAR*, pp. 24–30.

22 Ibid., pp. 26, 34–5; Symon, pp. 35–6.

23 *LBAR*, pp. 28, 31, 35, 37–42; L'Estrange: *The Literary Life of the Rev. William Harness* (1871), pp. 32–3.

24 Murray Ms. 23.8.1791; Boyes, pp. 38–9; Moore, I, p. 16; 'The Destruction of Sennacherib', l. 21, *CPW*, III, p. 310.

25 Simpson: *Education in Aberdeenshire before 1872* (1947), p. 1; Pryse Gordon, I, pp. 2–3; II, p. 320; *LBAR*, pp. 12, 53–4; Symon, p. 31; Boyes, p. 40; Wells, pp. 14–15.

26 *Recollections of the Table Talk of Samuel Rogers* (1856), p. 245.

27 *CPW*, VI, p. 519.

28 Moore, I, pp. 14–15; Symon, p. 43.

29 Kaplan: *Thomas Chatterton* (1987), pp. 5–6, 261.

30 BL Ms. 2612, f. 98; Symon, p. 63.

31 Goodwin: *The Friends of Liberty* (1979), pp. 283–306; Ehrman: *The Younger*

Pitt (1983), II, pp. 237–9; P. A. Brown: *The French Revolution in British History*, pp. 95–9; Hall: *British Radicalism 1791–7* (1976), pp. 224–9; *ST*, XXIII, pp. 117–239; *ST*, XXIII, p. 766; Mackay: *Burns* (1993), pp. 534, 539–41; Gilmour, pp. 399–402.

32 Thomis: *Politics and Society in Nottingham, 1785–1835* (1969), pp. 144–5, 156–8, 164–5; *LBAR*, p. 67; E. P. Thompson: *The Making of the English Working Class* (1980), pp. 140–1; Marchand, I, p. 74.

33 Moore, I, pp. 13–14, 28–9; *BLJ*, VIII, p. 238; IX, p. 18; Marchand, I, p. 18; Boccaccio: *The Decameron*, trans. G. H. McWilliam (1972), p. 831; *Childe Harold's Pilgrimage*, c. IV, st. 58; *CPW*, II, pp. 143, 241–4; *K–SMB*, 14, pp. 30–3; Lewis: *The Monk* (The World's Classics, 1995), pp. viii-ix, 259–60; Perrin: *Dr Bowdler's Legacy* (1992), pp. 118–21; *ST*, XXV, p. 166; Erdman (ed.): *The Complete Prose and Poetry of William Blake* (1988), p. 611; Hill: *The English Bible and the 17th Century Revolution* (1993), passim.

34 Perrin, p. 119; Lewis, p. ix.

35 Shelley: 'A Refutation of Deism', in *Prose Works*, I, pp. 101–2; Newman: *Apologia Pro Vita Sua* (1946), p. 3. Newman was writing particularly of the doctrine of 'final perseverance'; *CHP*, c. III, ll. 303–4; *CPW*, II, p. 135; *LBAR*, p. 445; Marchand, I, p. 39; *Poetry*, II, p. 74n; Stocking (ed.): *The Journals of Claire Clairmont 1812–1827* (1968), p. 226; M. Foot: *The Politics of Paradise* (1988), pp. 93–4.

36 *BLJ*, VIII, pp. 107–8; Moore, I, p. 17; Simpson, pp. 111–12; Smout: *History of the Scottish People 1560–1830* (1969), p. 458; Symon, pp. 50–1.

37 Moore, I, pp. 28–9, 33; *L & J*, I, pp. 5–6; Oman: *Nelson* (1947), pp. 147–51; Symon, p. 67; *LBAR*, p. 50.

38 *BLJ*, X, p. 108; Moore, I, pp. 19–21; Bulloch, I, p. 141; Graham-Campbell: 'Shelley's Eton Days', *K–SR*, 8 (1993–4), p. 155.

39 Moore, II, p. 7; *L & J*, I, pp. 2–3; Symon, pp. 60–2; Byron: 'Preface to Cain', *CPW*, VI, p. 228; Marchand, I, pp. 38–9.

40 Elwin: *The First Romantics*, p. 71.

41 Symon, p. 69; Moore, I, pp. 12–13, 101–2; Prothero, p. 72; Kings I, chs XI, XXI; Kings II, ch. II.

42 Moore, I, pp. 25–8; Pryse Gordon, II, pp. 321–2; Ruskin: *Praeterita* (1949), p. 91; *BLJ*, III, pp. 221–2; Byron: 'Song', ll. 9–10, *CPW*, I, pp. 47, 366–7.

43 *BLJ*, III, p. 222; Hobhouse's notes titled 'Lord Byron' with his manuscript diary of the summer of 1824, Marchand, I, pp. 57–8; Hobhouse's marginal comments on Moore in Nicolson: p. 299; *BLJ*, IX, p. 40.

44 *BLJ*, VII, p. 216; *CPW*, I, p. 81; *BLJ*, III, p. 246; Kipling: 'The Ladies', st. 8.

45 Moore, I, pp. 29–30; Marchand, I, pp. 43–4; Magnus: *Gladstone* (1954), p. 21.

46 'Lachin Y Gair', ll. 33–4, 37–8; *CPW*, I, pp. 103–4; 'The Island', c. II, ll. 280–1, 290–1; *CPW*, VII, pp. 44, 145; Pryse Gordon, II, p. 321; Moore, I, p. 35; *HVSV*, pp. 145–6; Smout, pp. 473, 478–9; *BLJ*, III, p. 64.

47 L'Estrange, p. 30; Moore, I, pp. 38–9, 347; *Blessington*, pp. 80–1.

48 Moore, I, p. 12; Symon, p. 70; Page (ed.): *Byron* (1985), p. 4; Galt, pp. 19–20.

III The Shelleys and Field Place
Pages 39 to 51

1 Byron: 'The Vision of Judgement', ll. 4–5; *CPW*, VI, p. 312; Marshall, p. 76; Galt: *Annals of the Parish*, quoted in Brinton: *Political Ideas of the English Romanticists* (1926), p. 221; Shelley: Preface to *Laon and Cyntha*, E & M, II, p. 35; Norman: *Flight of the Skylark* (1954), pp. 103–4, 232n; W. H. White: 'Notes on Shelley's Birthplace', *Macmillan's Magazine*, 1879, p. 453; J. M. Thompson: *The French Revolution* (1943), p. 283; cf. Salt: *Shelley's Principles* (1892), p. 3.

2 Medwin, pp. 7, 10; Lady Shelley (ed.): *Shelley Memorials* (1875), p. 1; Jeaffreson, I, pp. 13–19.

3 N. I. White: *Shelley* (1947), I, pp. 7–9; Jeaffreson, I, pp. 19–21; Ingpen: *Shelley in England* (1917), p. 4; *Medwin*, p. 8.

4 *Medwin*, p. 8; Jeaffreson, I, p. 22.

5 Stone: *Road to Divorce* (1990), pp. 107–28.

6 Ingpen, pp. 7n, 13, 451; *Medwin*, pp. 8–10; Jeaffreson, I, pp. 22–3; Dowden: *The Life of Percy Bysshe Shelley* (1886), II, p. 540; White, I, pp. 9–10; *S & C*, III, pp. 444–5.

7 Ingpen, pp. 10–11; White I, pp. 8–9; Boswell: *Johnson*, p. 681; *HC*, V, p. 141; Austen: *Pride and Prejudice*, ch. 3.

8 Habakkuk: *Marriage, Debt and the Estates System: English Landownership, 1650–1950* (1994), pp. 277–80; Colvin: *A Biographical Dictionary of English Architects* (1954), p. 485; *Medwin*, pp. 10–12; Jeaffreson, I, p. 24; Ingpen; pp. 18, 21; Robinson: *Shelley: His Links with Horsham and Warnham* (1983), p. 4; Sir T. Browne in *Shorter Oxford Dictionary* under 'avarice'; Merle: 'A Newspaper Editor's Reminiscences', *Fraser's Magazine*, June 1841, p. 702.

9 *Letters*, I, p. 239; Hogg: *Life of P. B. Shelley*, I, p. 139; Dowden, I, p. 4; Medwin, pp. 12–13; Symonds: *Shelley* (1878), p. 5; Pope: *The Dunciad*, IV, ll. 301–24; Hibbert: *The Grand Tour* (1987), pp. 235–6; Buzard: *The Beaten Track* (1993), p. 99; Hudson (ed.): *The Grand Tour 1592–1796* (1993), pp. 17–18.

10 Robinson: *The Dukes of Norfolk* (1982), pp. 171–4; Albery: *A Parliamentary History of the Ancient Borough of Horsham, 1295–1880* (1927), pp. 114–15, 123, 128, 142–56, 177, 183–4, 191; *HC*, II, p. 394; V, pp. 140–1.

11 *Medwin*, p. 104; Hogg, I, p. 2; Gelpi: *Shelley's Goddess*, p. 88; Bieri: 'Shelley's Older Brother', *K–SJ*, 39 (1990), pp. 29–33; Brown: *Sexuality and Feminism in Shelley* (1979), p. 252.

12 Holmes: *Shelley*, p. 11; Longford: *Wellington* (1969), I, pp. 13–16; Hogg, I, p. 2; Cameron (ed.): *Romantic Rebels* (1973), pp. 267–79.

13 Rolleston: *Talks with Lady Shelley* (1977), pp. 95–6; Hogg, II, p. 459; Ingpen, p. 347; *Letters*, I, p. 5.

14 GM XXII (1844), pp. 205–6; Lovell: *Captain Medwin* (1962), p. 17; *Medwin*, p. 105.

15 GM XXII, p. 206; XXI, pp. 419–24.

16 Hogg, I, p. 307; W. H. White, p. 461; Rossetti: *Memoir of Shelley* (1886), p. 5; Austen: *Mansfield Park*, ch. 4; HC, V, pp. 140–1; Reiman: *Romantic Texts and Contexts*, pp. 266–7; *Hints from Horace*, l. 247; CPW, I, p. 298.

17 *Letters*, I, p. 72; Hogg, I, p. 350; Dowden, I, p. 5; *Medwin*, p. 13.

18 *Medwin*, pp. 104, 113; Shelley: 'Notes on Queen Mab', M & E, I, pp. 370–1; Brown: *Sexuality and Feminism in Shelley*, p. 98; Cameron: *The Young Shelley* (1950), pp. 3–5; Sharp: *Shelley* (1887), p. 56; Campbell: *Shelley and the Unromantics* (1924), p. 70.

19 Hogg, I, pp. 5–22; *Medwin*, p. 14; *Letters*, I, p. 2.

20 Cameron (ed.): *Romantic Rebels*, pp. 3–4.

21 Feiling: *The Second Tory Party, 1714–1832* (1938), pp. 166, 168; see Chapter II above; ST XXIII, 231; Rubinstein: 'The End of "Old Corruption" in Britain 1780–1860', *Past and Present*, 101 (1985), pp. 55–85; Porter: *English Society in the Eighteenth Century* (1982), pp. 70–81; Phelps Brown: *Egalitarianism and the Generation of Inequality* (1988), pp. 310–20; Gilmour, pp. 435–6.

22 Christie: *Stress and Stability in Late Eighteenth Century Britain* (1984), pp. 91–2; PR XLIV, 31; Norman, p. 163; Wells: *Wretched Faces* (1988), pp. 1, 65; Elwin, pp. 280–1; Gilmour, pp. 249, 436–7.

23 Wollstonecraft: *A Vindication of the Rights of Man* in Todd (ed.): *Mary Wollstonecraft: Political Writings* (1994), p. 57.

24 Schenk: *The Aftermath of the Napoleonic Wars*, pp. 4–6; Burke: *Reflections on the Revolution in France*, ed. O'Brien (1986), p. 372; Hole: *Pulpits, Politics and Public Order in England 1760–1832* (1989), pp. 90, 128–30; Gibson: *Church, State and Society, 1760–1850* (1994), pp. 10, 36, 46–7; Hogg, I, pp. 308–9; Schilling: *Conservative England and the Case against Voltaire* (1976), pp. 82–3.

25 Hole, pp. 84–92, 186; Gibson, pp. 5–13, 47; Norman, pp. 103–4; *Medwin*, p. 13; Dowden, I, p. 5n; Chadwick: *The Secularization of the European Mind in the Nineteenth Century* (1975), pp. 10, 104.

26 Dinwiddy: 'Charles James Fox and the People', *History*, 55 (1970), pp. 342–59; Goodwin: *The Friends of Liberty*, pp. 20, 120; Mitchell: *Charles James Fox* (1992), pp. 150–3; PH, XXIX, pp. 409–11.

27 Roe: *Wordsworth and Coleridge, The Radical Years* (1990), p. 187; see Chapter II above; Feiling, p. 281; Prothero, pp. 64–5.

28 HC, II, pp. 148–9; IV, p. 587; Elwin: *The Noels*, pp. 341–4, 374, 424, 426; Elwin: *Lord Byron's Wife* (1974), pp. 78–9.

29 Elwin: *The Noels*, p. 342.

30 Moorman: *William Wordsworth*, I, pp. 503–4; Burke: *A Letter to a Noble Lord* (1796), p. 196; Hazlitt: *The Spirit of the Age*, p. 186; Leigh Hunt, II, pp. 23–7.

31 Houston: *A Woman's Memories of World-Known Men* (1883), I, pp. 99–107;

Letters, I, p. 230; Hogg, I, pp. 298–9; Grabo: *The Magic Plant* (1936), pp. 2, 10; Engelberg: *The Making of the Shelley Myth* (1988), p. 261.

IV Isleworth and Dulwich
Pages 52 to 70

1 *Medwin*, pp. 14–16; Gittings, pp. 14, 17, 23–4; Peacock, p. 646.
2 Jeaffreson, I, pp. 44–5; *HC*, II, p. 398; *Medwin*, p. 33.
3 *Medwin*, pp. 14–15; Santayana: *Winds of Doctrine* (1912), p. 158: Dowden, I, p. 16.
4 Pevsner: *The Buildings of Middlesex* (1951), p. 117; A. Cameron: *Hounslow* (1995), p. 112; Hogg, I, p. 22; Gittings, p. 24; *Medwin*, pp. 19–22.
5 *Medwin*, p. 17; Rennie: *Autobiography* (1875), p. 2; *Medwin*: 'Memoirs of Shelley', *Athenaeum*, 1832, p. 472.
6 *Medwin*, pp. 15–17; King-Hele: *Shelley, His Thought and Work* (1971), p. 3.
7 Rennie, pp. 1–2.
8 Hogg, I, pp. 8–9; *Medwin*, pp. 28–9; Gelpi, pp. 100–1, 133; Rennie, pp. 1–2; White, I, pp. 22–4.
9 *Medwin*, pp. 22–4, 447; Lovell: *Captain Medwin* (1962), p. 18; *Letters*, I, p. 1.
10 *Medwin*, p. 28; Peacock, pp 656–8.
11 *Medwin*, pp. 16, 24–5; Hogg, I, p. 15; Praz: Introductory Essay to *Three Gothic Novels* (1968), pp. 8–9, 32; Austen: *Northanger Abbey*, chs 6, 9, 25; Drabble: *The Oxford Companion to English Literature* (1985), p. 757.
12 *Medwin*, pp. 26–8.
13 E & M, II, ll. 19–42, pp. 50–1.
14 Auden and MacNeice: *Letters from Iceland* (1985), p. 48.
15 M & E, I, ll. 49–63, pp. 530–1.
16 *Letters*, II, p. 310; I, p. 517; Rennie, p. 2; Mary Shelley's 'Note on Poems of 1816', in Hutchinson, pp. 535–6; Webb: *Shelley: A Voice not Understood* (1977), pp. 34–5; Cranston: *The Romantic Movement* (1994), p. 116; M & E, I, pp. 530–1; Longford, I, pp. 16–17.
17 *Medwin*, p. 20; Rennie, pp. 1–2; Dowden, I, p. 16n.
18 *Medwin*, p. 31; Hogg, I, p. 22; Peacock, pp. 646; S & C, I, p. 477; Ingpen, pp. 49–50.
19 Beckett: *Byron The Aristocrat and the Abbey*, p. 82; Marchand, I, pp. 37, 43–7; Prothero, p. 73; Pratt, p. 2; *LBAR*, p. 53; Boyes, pp. 52–3.
20 Byron: 'Elegy on Newstead Abbey', l. 38, *CPW*, I, p. 108; Knowles: *Religious Orders*, II, pp. 8, 400.
21 Moore, I, pp. 29, 37–40; Beer (ed.): *The Diary of John Evelyn*, III (1995), p. 126; Symon, pp. 73–5; Drinkwater: *The Pilgrim of Eternity, Byron – A Conflict* (1925), pp. 83–4.
22 Marchand, I, p. 48; *LBAR*, pp. 97–9; Pratt, p. 2.
23 Moore, I, pp. 32–3; Newton Hanson's Narrative, p. 18, in Murray Archive;

Coope: *Lord Byron's Newstead* (n.d.), p. 134; Cannadine: *Aspects of Aristocracy* (1994), p. 13; Prothero, p. 74; Beckett, pp. 82–3, 107–12.
24 Prothero, pp. 74–5; Moore, I, p. 39; Bakewell, p. 51; *LBAR*, p. 52.
25 Newton Hanson's Narrative; Moore, I, pp. 43–4; Prothero, p. 74; *LBAR*, pp. 52–3.
26 See Chapter III above; *LBAR*, p. 53; *BLJ*, I, p. 201.
27 Newton Hanson's Narrative; Galt: *The Life of Lord Byron* (1830), pp. 23–4; *LBAR*, pp. 53–7, 97–8; Symon, pp. 23–4; Coope, p. 133.
28 Beckett: 'Byron's Nottingham', *NBSR*, July 2000, p. 51; Boyes, pp. 60–1; Moore, I, p. 4; Prothero, p. 73; *L & J*, I, pp. 78n.
29 *BLJ*, I, pp. 39–40; Moore, I, p. 41; *L & J*, I, p. 78n.
30 Moore, I, pp. 41–2; Boyes, pp. 62–3.
31 Marchand, I, p. 54.
32 Newton Hanson's Narrative; *L & J*, I, pp. 9–10; Prothero, pp. 75–6; Moore, I, p. 40.
33 Newton Hanson's Narrative; *L & J*, I, pp. 11–12; Moore, I, pp. 44–5.
34 Blanche: *Ye Parish of Camberwell* (1875), pp. 375, 386–8; Prothero, p. 76.
35 Newton Hanson's Narrative; *L & J*, I, p. 10.
36 See Chapter II above; *BLJ*, I, p. 40; Boyes, p. 69.
37 Hobhouse's marginal note in his copy of Moore; *LBAR*, p. 57; Prothero, p. 75; *Journal*, III, pp. 1044–5; Moore, I, p. 70.
38 Moore, I, pp. 45–6.
39 *HVSV*, pp. 14–18, 611; Moore, I, pp. 44–5; *Journal*, III, pp. 1044–5.
40 Moore, I, pp. 46, 54; Symon, pp. 80–1.
41 Newton Hanson's Narrative; Prothero, p. 77; Marchand, I, p. 60; Boyes, p. 70.
42 Moore, I, pp. 49–50; Symon, p. 82.
43 Moore, I, pp. 47–9: *Journal*, III, p. 1045.
44 Moore, I, pp. 48–9; *LBAR*, pp. 57–8.
45 *BLJ*, IX, p. 40; Moore, I, pp. 42–3; *CPW*, I, pp. 1, 355.
46 *BLJ*, IX, p. 40; Moore, I, pp. 52–3; *CPW*, I, pp. 125, 377; VII, pp. 99, 158.
47 Moore, I, pp. 53–4, 57–8; *BLJ*, I, p. 41; Marchand, I, p. 63.
48 *Medwin*, p. 16; Medwin in the *Athenaeum*, p. 472; Lindsay, p. 4; Gelpi, p. 101.

V Harrow and Eton
Pages 71 to 93

1 Salt: *Memories of Bygone Eton* (1928), p. 129; Rose: *Superior Person* (1969), p. 30; Meredith: 'Shelley at Eton', an unpublished lecture in Eton College Library (hereafter cited as Meredith); *Harrow*, pp. 152, 157.
2 *ER*, 32 (1810), p. 327; Ryscamp: *William Cowper of the Inner Temple Esquire* (1959), pp. 28–9; Cowper: 'Tirocinium', ll. 292–5; Chandos: *Boys Together* (1984), pp. 22–3; Black: *Pitt the Elder* (1992), pp. 2–3.

3 Bullett: *Sydney Smith* (1951), pp. 22–3.

4 *ER*, pp. 331, 332.

5 Rowcroft: *Confessions of an Etonian* (1852), pp. 112–27; Chandos, p. 103; Fischer Williams: *Harrow* (1901), p. 84; Tyerman: 'Byron's Harrow', *BJ*, 17 (1989), p. 29.

6 Gathorne-Hardy: *The Public School Phenomenon, 1597–1977* (1977), pp. 20–1, 60–3; Chandos, p. 138; Minchin, pp. 255–6.

7 *ER*, p. 331; Chandos, p. 86; Hollis: *Eton* (1960), pp. 196–8, 222–4; Tyerman, pp. 23–7; Moore, I, p. 19; Marples: *Romantics at School* (1967), p. 180.

8 St Clair: *The Godwins and the Shelleys* (1989), pp. 7–8; Thornton: *Harrow School and its Surroundings* (1885), pp. 207–8; Maxwell Lyte: *A History of Eton College* (1911), pp. 353–4, 364–5; Tyerman, pp. 21–3.

9 Pope: *The Dunciad*, III, 333–4; Steele: 'On Flogging Schoolboys', quoted in Craig (ed.): *The Oxford Book of Schooldays* (1994), p. 145; Hollis, pp. 206–7: Simmons, *Southey*, pp. 26–7; *Don Leon*, ll. 920–1; Ziegler: *Melbourne* (1976), pp. 106–7, 110; Chandos, p. 237; Gathorne-Hardy, pp. 38–9.

10 Jenkins: *Gladstone* (1995), pp. 13, 103–7, 115.

11 Cheetham and Parfitt (eds): *Eton Microcosm* (1964), pp. 92–4; Hollis, p. 233; Grosskurth: *John Addington Symonds* (1964), p. 32–4; Chandos, pp. 307–8, 287–8; *Harrow*, p. 159.

12 Gathorne-Hardy, p. 45; *Harrow*, p. 159; Hollis, p. 178.

13 Rowcroft, p. 39; Fischer Williams, pp. 84–5; Cranston: *John Locke* (1985), p. 243; Craig (ed.), p. 10; Cowper: 'Tirocinium', ll. 618–19.

14 *BLJ*, I, p. 41; IX, p. 37.

15 *Harrow*, pp. 160, 162; ibid. pp. 144–7, 161; Fischer Williams, pp. 73–4; Thornton, pp. 195–6; Tyerman, pp. 21, 23, 26; Bourne: *Palmerston: The Early Years, 1784–1841* (1982), pp. 8–11.

16 Tyerman, p. 23; *Harrow*, p. 148; Moore, I, pp. 57–8.

17 Ch. 1, 3rd (1831) edition of *Frankenstein*.

18 *L & J*, I, p. 13n; *Harrow*, p. 151; Tyerman, pp. 18, 22; Thornton, pp. 207–8, 202; *BLJ*, I, p. 53; Howson (ed.), *Harrow School* (1898), p. 64.

19 *Harrow*, pp. 142–4, 149, 152–3; Labourde: *Harrow School* (1948), pp. 44–5; Thornton, pp. 194–5; Tyerman, p. 21; Marchand, I, p. 67.

20 Moore, I, pp. 64, 69–70; Tyerman, p. 29; *Harrow*, p. 145.

21 Marples, p. 121; *BLJ*, IV, p. 49; Leigh Hunt, I, p. 152; *Harrow*, p. 157.

22 Albemarle: *Fifty Years of My Life* (1876), p. 217.

23 L'Estrange, pp. 4–5; Moore, I, pp. 70–1; Gash: *Mr Secretary Peel* (1961), p. 44; Tyerman, p. 35.

24 Trollope: *Autobiography* (The World's Classics, 1968), pp. 3–4; Gash, p. 46.

25 Gash: *Sir Robert Peel* (1972), pp. 175–81.

26 *BLJ*, IX, p. 43; Moore, I, p. 62; Tyerman, pp. 27, 32–4; Fischer Williams, pp. 84–5, 108–9; Thornton, pp. 244–5; Hunter: 'Byron the Classicist', *ad famillaris*, Spring 1995, p. xiv; *CHP*, c. IV, ll. 671–3; *CPW*, II, p. 149.

27 Chandos, pp. 155–8; Kelly: *Richard Brinsley Sheridan* (1997), pp. 20–1;

Tyerman, pp. 32, 28; *Harrow*, pp. 158, 160; Howson (ed.), p. 186; Moore, I, p. 62; Minchin, p. 310; Marples, p. 21; Trollope, p. 16; Stürzl: 'How Good was Lord Byron's Greek?' in Raizis, I, pp. 79–80; Blackstone: *Byron* (1970), I, p. 19.

28 Hobhouse's Diary, BL Add. Ms. 56538, f. 6. I am indebted to Dr Cochran for this reference.

29 *CMP*, pp. 1–7, 255–69; Moore, I, pp. 140–4.

30 Marginal Notes in Hobhouse's copy of Moore: Marchand, I, p. 85; *BLJ*, IX, p. 42; Ruskin: *Praeterita* (1949), p. 131.

31 *BLJ*, I, pp. 49, 53; see Chapter II above and cf. Galt: *Lord Byron*, p. 15; 'To the Duke of D[orset]', ll. 23–4, *CPW*, I, p. 67.

32 'To the Duke of D[orset]', ll. 13–16, *CPW*, I, pp. 67, 369; Cowper: 'Tirocinium', ll. 379–418; Letter of 19 January 1803, Murray Archive, Box 13A.

33 *L & J*, I, pp. 12–13; Minchin, pp. 227–8.

34 Marples, p. 123; *BLJ*, I, pp. 41–3; *CMP*, p. 196; Murray Archives; *L & J*, I, p. 13n.

35 *BLJ*, I, p. 43; *L & J*, I, p. 12n.

36 Marchand, I, p. 70; *CPW*, VII, p. 145; Pratt, pp. 5–6; Pryse Gordon, II, pp. 332–3.

37 Moore, I, p. 79: Murray Archive; BL Egerton Mss. 2610, f. 75; *LBAR*, p. 63; Marchand, I, pp. 74–5; Boyes: *Love without Wings* (1988), pp. 1–2, 4, 20–1; *L & J*, I, p. 25.

38 Marchand, I, pp. 75, 77; Moore, I, p. 98; Boyes, *Love without Wings*, pp. 4–5.

39 Boyes: *Queen of a Fantastic Realm* (1986), pp. 14, 21–2, 26; Marchand, I, pp. 49–50; *BLJ*, IX, p. 34; Elze, p. 49.

40 Boyes, pp. 16, 20–3, 76; Nimrod: *Hunting Reminiscences* (1926), pp. 171–2.

41 Moore, I, pp. 80–3; Marchand, I, pp. 75–6; Boyes, *Queen of a Fantastic Realm*, pp. 26–8; BL Egerton Ms. 2612, f. 36.

42 *BLJ*, I, pp. 43–4; Murray Archive, 30.10.1805; *L & J*, I, p. 16; Moore, I, p. 83; Boyes, *Queen of a Fantastic Realm*, pp. 28–9.

43 'To My Dear Mary Anne', l. 23, *CPW*, I, pp. 2, 355; 'The Dream', ll. 156–65; *CPW*, IV, pp. 27–8, 455–6; Moore, I, pp. 83–5; III, pp. 140–1; Wordsworth: 'Nutting', ll. 48–9; Nicolson, p. 300; *BLJ*, IX, p. 24; Grebanier: *The Uninhibited Byron* (1971), pp. 38–9.

44 BL Egerton Ms. 2612, f. 136; *LBAR*, pp. 77–8; Crompton: *Byron and Greek Love* (1985), pp. 82–5; Hobhouse in Nicolson, p. 300.

45 Tyerman, p. 27; Note on 'To the Duke of Dorset', *CPW*, I, p. 369: *ER*, 32, 1810, p. 327.

46 Minchin, pp. 192–3; Thornton, pp. 273, 358–60; Moore, I, pp. 62–3; *Conversations*, pp. 63–4.

47 'On a Distant View of the Village and School of Harrow on the Hill', l. 14, *CPW*, I, p. 138; Minchin, p. 239; Moore, I, pp. 77–8; *L & J*, I, pp. 18–19; Bakewell, pp. 55–6; *BLJ*, I, 44–8.

48 Moore, I, pp. 63, 65; *Harrow*, p. 145; *BLJ*, IX, p. 44; I, pp. 54–5; *The Complete Peerage* (1913), III, p. 256; (1916) IV, p. 163.

49 *BLJ*, I, p. 53; *CPW*, I, pp. 126, 168, 383; Elledge: *Lord Byron at Harrow School* (2000), pp. 72–4; Moore, I, pp. 71–6; *The Autobiography of Leigh Hunt* (1850), pp. 143–4; Wordsworth: *The Prelude*, Bk II, l. 334.

50 *BLJ*, II, p. 6; Moore, I, pp. 65–6; Marchand, I, p. 90.

51 *BLJ*, VIII, p. 124; *CPW*, I, pp. 51–2, 367; L'Estrange, pp. 32–3; Noakes: *Jonathan Swift: A Hypocrite Reversed* (1985); Grebanier, p. 33; *LLB*, p. 243; Hobhouse: *Recollections of a Long Life* (1909), I, p. 325; Crompton, pp. 63–106.

52 *BLJ*, IX, p. 44; I, p. 48; VII, p. 177; Marchand, I, p. 76; *The Poetical Works of the Late Thomas Little Esq.* (1802), p. 40; *BLJ*, IX, p. 40; Vail: *The Literary Relationship of Lord Byron and Thomas Moore* (2001), pp. 18–28; see Chapter II above.

53 *BLJ*, I, pp. 49, 53; Moore, I, p. 59; Marples, p. 137; *L & J*, I, p. 52n–53n.

54 BL Egerton Ms. 2612, f. 163; *BLJ*, I, pp. 45–6, 54–5; *LBAR*, pp. 78–9.

55 *BLJ*, I, 53–4, 68; Murray Archive, 12.5.1804.

56 *BLJ*, I, p. 47; Pratt, pp. 12–16; *CPW*, I, pp. 131, 154–5, 366, 378; Boyes: *Love without Wings*, pp. 6–12, 46–7, 52–4, 61; *Lord Byron's 'Fugitive Pieces' Rare Quarto Edition, Described by Herbert C. Roe* (1919), pp. 24–5.

57 Tyerman, pp. 35–7; *Harrow*, pp. 164–5; Chandos, pp. 178–89; Gathorne-Hardy, pp. 56–8; Jarrett: *England in the Age of Hogarth* (1986), p. 71. For the traditional view see *Journal*, III, p. 1039; Fischer Williams, pp. 74–5; Howson (ed.), pp. 66–7.

58 *BLJ*, IX, pp. 24–5; Graham: *The Harrow Life of Montague Butler* (1920), p. xv; Murray Archive, letter to Hanson, 13.8.1804; Tyerman, p. 36; *L & J*, I, pp. 27–9, 68; Elledge, pp. 1, 16–17, 64; Gunn, p. 54; *BLJ*, I, pp. 69–70, 72–3; Byron: 'On a Distant View ... of Harrow', ll. 23–4, *CPW*, I, p. 139.

59 Lines 7–13, *CPW*, I, pp. 132, 161–2, 172–3, 382; *Harrow*, pp. 164–5; Tyerman, p. 37; *BLJ*, I, p. 155.

60 *Harrow*, pp. 159–60; Ashley-Cooper: *Eton v. Harrow at the Wicket* (1927), p. 24; Bernard Darwin in Home Gordon (ed.): *Eton v. Harrow at Lord's* (1926), p. 1; Thornton, pp. 238–9, 319–20; *L & J*, I, pp. 69–71; *BLJ*, I, pp. 70–2.

VI Eton and Harrow
Pages 94 to 118

1 Mary Shelley's note on Queen Mab, Hutchinson, p. 835; Meredith; Blunden (ed.): *Shelley and Keats, As They Struck Their Contemporaries* (1925), pp. 1–3; White, I, p. 44.

2 Browning: 'Memorabilia', l. 1; Symonds, *Shelley*, p. 25; Thornton Hunt in Blunden (ed.), pp. 49–51; Peacock, pp. 649; Rossetti, pp. 15–16; White,

I, pp. 17–18, II, p. 560; Hughes: *The Nascent Mind of Shelley* (1947), p. 17; Meredith; Cory in *The Shelley Society's Notebook*, 1886, p. 14.

3   Hogg, I, p. 27; Nitchie: 'Shelley at Eton: Mary Shelley vs Jefferson Hogg', *K-SMB*, II (1960), pp. 53–4; *Medwin*, p. 32; Lady Shelley (ed.), pp. 6–7; Graham-Campbell: 'Shelley's Eton Days', *K–SR*, 8 (1994), p. 153; Gash: *Mr Secretary Peel* (1961), p. 44; Blunden (ed.), p. 8.

4   Peacock, p. 647; *Shelley Society's Notebook*, pp. 127–8; pp. 70–1, 85; Nitchie, p. 52.

5   *Shelley Society's Notebook*, p. 14; Merle's Letter to the *Athenaeum*, March 1849, commenting on Medwin's biography in Blunden (ed.), pp. 3–4; Hutchinson, pp. 835–6.

6   Jeaffreson, I, pp. 83–5; Meredith; Finlayson: *The Seventh Earl of Shaftesbury* (1981), p. 20; White, I, pp. 58, 571.

7   Moorman, I, p. 28; Dowden, I, pp. 22–35; Meredith; Blunden (ed.), pp. 6–9.
8   Peacock, pp. 645, 698–9; Hogg, I, p. 13; II, pp. 668–75.
9   Hogg, I, pp. 43–5, 48; 'Written in Very Early Youth', ll. 9–14, M & E, I p. 5.
10 Nitchie, pp. 52–3; 'Hymn to Intellectual Beauty', ll. 49–51, M & E, I. p. 530; *Letters*, I, p. 303; *Medwin*, p. 58; Hogg, I, pp. 33–4, 141.
10a Wordsworth: *The Prelude*, BkI, ll. 329–32.
11 White, I, pp. 40, 572; Meredith; *Medwin*, p. 34.
12 Blunden (ed.), pp. 4–7; Dowden, I, pp. 29–30.
13 Hogg, I, pp. 40–2; Dowden, I, pp. 21–2, 30–1; *Shelley Society's Notebook*, pp. 14–15; Blunden: *Shelley* (1946), p. 35; Graham-Campbell, pp. 154–5; Meredith.

14 *Letters*, I, p. 227; Grabo: *A Newton among Poets* (1930), pp. 5–6; Hough, p. 138; Marples, p. 157; Ullman, pp. 86–8; Hogg, I, pp. 110–11; Peck, I, p. 23; Cameron: *The Young Shelley*, p. 5.

15 Blunden (ed.) p. 7; Hogg, I, p. 44; Meredith; Thompson (Woof (ed.)): *Wordsworth's Hawkshead* (1970), pp. 342–3.

16 White, I, p. 36; Rowcroft, p. 39; Maxwell Lyte, pp. 382–3; Books in Eton College Library.

17 Nitchie, p. 54; *Medwin*, pp. 34–5; Dedication to *Laon and Cyntha*, ll. 39–40, E & M, II, p. 51; p. 38; *Who Was Who* (1972), VI, p. 1040; Hollis, p. 209.

18 White, I, p. 32; *DNB*; Hogg, I, pp. 31–2; Blunden (ed.), p. 44; King-Hele: 'Shelley and Dr Lind', *K–SMB*, 18 (1967), pp. 1–6; St John-Stevas (ed.): *The Collected Works of Walter Bagehot* (1986), I, p. 442.

19 Hogg, I, p. 28; *Medwin*, pp. 69; Hughes, pp. 26–9; Shelley: 'Henry and Louisa', ll. 144–6; *Esdaile*, pp. 136–7, 267; M & E, I, ll. 13, 19,; Dowden, I, pp. 28–9; King-Hele: 'Erasmus Darwin's Influence on Shelley's Early Poems', *K–SMB*, 16 (1965), p. 26; King-Hele: 'Shelley and Dr Lind', *K–SMB*, 18 (1967), p. 5; Marshall, pp. 156–63, 198–201, 232; P. A. Brown: *The French Revolution in English History*, pp. 183–4.

20 Motion: *Keats* (1997), p. 29.
21 *Laon and Cyntha*, c. III, ll. 1348–9; E & M, II, p.120; 'Prince Athanase', ll.

126, 172, Hutchinson, pp. 162–3; Hogg, I, p. 32.

22 Popper: *The Open Society and its Enemies* (1943), II, pp. 217, 355–6; White, I, pp. 48, 574; Hogg, I, p. 332; Peacock, p. 648.

23 Hogg, I, pp. 136–8; Smith, I, p. vi; Dowden, I, p. 29; Jeaffreson, I, pp. 90–2; 'Henry and Louisa', ll. 186–7, *Esdaile*, pp. 8, 131–7, 260–70; M & E, I, pp. 13–26; King-Hele: *Shelley, His Thought and Work*, pp. 9–10; Jaeger: *Before Victoria* (1956), p. 109; Quinlan: *Victorian Prelude* (1941), p. 181; *Don Juan*, c. I, ll. 123–4; *CPW*, V, p. 13.

24 Chandos, pp. 268–75; Hollis, pp. 197–9; Thornton, pp. 242–3; Hughes, pp. 23–4.

25 *Letters*, I, p. 230; White, I, p. 35; Meredith; *ER* 16 (1810), p. 327; *CPW*, I, p. 369.

26 *Medwin*, p. 38; Hogg, I, pp. 31, 124; Peacock, p. 656; 'The Boat on the Serchio', ll. 78–83; Hutchinson, p. 656; Graham-Campbell, pp. 155–6.

27 Information kindly given by Sir John Smith, CH, who owns and showed me two of the books.

28 'An Essay on Friendship', in *Prose*, p. 338; Hogg, I, pp. 22–4; Meredith.

29 *Prose*, p. 338.

30 Ibid.

31 Ibid., pp. 338, 347–8, 350; Symonds, p. 10; Carpenter and Barnefield: *The Psychology of the Poet Shelley* (1925), p. 76; Brown: *Sexuality and Feminism in Shelley*, pp. 20–1, 226.

32 Carpenter and Barnefield, pp. 17–21; Hutchinson, p. 427; 'The Witch of Atlas', st. 36; R & F, p. 357; Praz: *The Romantic Agony* (1970), pp. 332–3, 414.

33 Jaeger, p. 81; Godwin: *Memoirs of Wollstonecraft* (1993), pp. 54–5; Wollstonecraft: *A Vindication of the Rights of Women* (1992), pp. 173–7; Cheetham and Parfitt (eds), p. 93; Carpenter and Barnefield, p. 37; Crompton, pp. 294–9.

34 Hickson: *The Poisoned Bowl* (1995), p. 191 (Roxburgh of Stowe); *GM*, February 1798, p. 95; Crook and Guiton: *Shelley's Venomed Melody* (1986), pp. 32–3; Cowper: 'Tirocinium', l. 217; Gathorne-Hardy, p. 45; Hollis, p. 178; Brown: *Sexuality and Feminism in Shelley*, pp. 210–11, 284; Holmes (ed.): *Shelley on Love* (1996), p. 185 – Holmes thinks the incident occurred at Oxford or just afterwards.

35 Thornton Hunt in Blunden (ed.), pp. 30–1; Cameron: *The Young Shelley*, pp. 125–6; Crook and Guiton, *passim*; their book is a brilliant survey of the evidence.

36 Tatchell: 'Thornton Hunt', *K–SMB*, 20 (1969), p. 15; Blunden (ed.), p. 44; *Epipsychidion*, ll. 56–66, R & F, p. 380; Cameron, pp. 125–6; *Prose*, pp. 359–61; *Medwin*, pp. 233–4.

37 Leigh Hunt: *Lord Byron and some of his Contemporaries*, II, p. 83; Blunden (ed.), p. 44; *Epipsychidion*, II, 256–70, R & P, p. 380; Hutchinson, p. 808; *Prose*, p. 223; Magarshack: *Dostoevsky* (1962), pp. 271–3; Brown: *Sexuality*

and Feminism in Shelley, p. 202; the best treatment of the whole question is in Crook and Guiton.

38 Gittings, pp. 49, 157, 446–50; Motion, pp. 196–8, see Chapters VII, VIII and IX, below: Andrews: 'Keats and Mercury', *K–SMB*, 20 (1949), pp. 37–42; *BLJ*, II, p. 46; Ashton: *Samuel Taylor Coleridge* (1969), pp. 37, 207, 228; Hogg, I, p. 175; II, p. 332; Crook and Guiton, pp. 30, 41, 44–7.

39 The Critical Review in Barcus (ed.): *Shelley: The Critical Heritage* (1975), p. 49; Maxwell Lyte, p. 58; Meredith; R & F, I, p. 180; *Medwin*, pp. 30–1; *Letters*, I, pp. 4–5; Hughes: 'Shelley's Zastrozzi and St Irvyne', *Modern Language Review*, 7 (1912), pp. 53–9.

40 *Letters*, II, p. 58; 'Venice: An Ode', ll. 12–13, *CPW*, IV, pp. 201, 494.

41 Barcus (ed.), pp. 46–9; *Letters*, I, 5–6; Wahrman: 'Percy's Prologue', *Past and Present*, 159 (1998), p. 123; Gelpi, pp. 46–60; Dacre: *Zofloya* (1997), pp. 87, 96, 129, 144, 153; Crook and Guiton, pp. 33–5; Brown: *Sexuality and Feminism in Shelley*, p. 52; Chesser: *Shelley and Zastrozzi* (1965), pp. 82–3, 89, 92–4, 101, 106, 108, 114–16, 130–3, 139, 141, 143–4, 151, 154; McGann: 'My Brain is Feminine', in Rutherford (ed.), *Byron: Augustan and Romantic* (1990), pp. 27–30.

42 Barcus (ed.), p. 49; Hogg, I, p. 18; II, p. 55; S & C, II, pp. 476–7, 497, 505; *Medwin*, p. 47; 'Julian and Maddalo', l. 59; E & M, II, p. 693.

43 S & C, II, pp. 511, 526; *Esdaile*, p. 306; *Letters*, I, p. 2.

44 S & C, II, p. 517; Hawkins: *Shelley's First Love* (1992), pp. 14–15, 18, 124–5; 'Melody to a Scene of Former Times', l. 28, M & E, I, p. 128.

45 *Medwin*, pp. 58–9; Raizis, I, (ed.), p. 138; White, I, p. 61; Hawkins, pp. 19, 24–5, 125–6; King-Hele in *K–SMB*, 28, p. 6; Cochran: 'Byron, the Vampire, and the Vampire Women', *NBSR*, July 2000, p. 60.

46 'Song', ll. 21–4; M & E, I, pp. 29–30; R & F, I, p. 189; *Medwin*, p. 49: S & C, II, pp. 571–4.

47 S & C, II, pp. 573–6; Hawkins, p. 126.

48 Hogg, II, pp. 550–1; 'How swiftly through Heaven's wide expanse', ll. 21–32, M & E, I, pp. 87–9.

49 S & C, II, pp. 576–8.

50 *Prose*, p. 223; Crook and Guiton, p. 210.

51 *Letters*, I, pp. 266, 412–14; Hogg, I, p. 33; Crook and Guiton, pp. 31–2; *Records*, p. viii.

52 Maxwell Lyte, pp. 373–7; Hollis, pp. 190–2; Meredith.

53 *Medwin*, p. 68; Hogg, I, p. 12; Lady Shelley (ed.), *Shelley Memorials*, p. 6; Sharp, p. 36; White, I, p. 379; Meredith; Ms Diary of Miss Margarette Brown (Keats's sister-in-law) in the Eton College Library.

54 *Letters*, I, p. 228; Peacock, p. 647; Buchanan: *A Poet's Sketchbook* (1883), p. 108; Bennett (ed.): *The Letters of Mary Wollstonecraft Shelley* (1980), I, p. 475.

55 Marchand, I, p. 93.

56 Jeaffreson, I, pp. 77–9, 108–9.

57   Gittings, pp. 110–14; Motion, pp. 138–9; Grayling: *The Quarrel of the Age* (2000), pp. 266–7; Holmes, *Shelley*, p. 359.

58   'Lines Written among the Euganean Hills', l. 356; E & M, II, p. 442; *CMP*, p. 25; 'To the Rev. J. T. Beecher', *CPW*, I, p. 178.

59   'Thoughts Suggested by a College Examination', ll. 17–18, *CPW*, I, p. 92; *Letters*, I, pp. 279, 340–1; *Prose*, p. 219.

60   Langford, p. 295; Dowden, I, p. 26n; White, I, pp. 54–5; Shelley: *Henry and Louisa*, Pt. II, l. 186, pt I, ll. 145–56; *Esdaile*, pp. 131–44, 260–70; M & E, I, pp. 13–26; *Conversations*, p. 235.

61   *BLJ*, III, pp. 210, 217; Shelley: 'Henry and Louisa', Pt I, l. 72, *Esdaile*, p. 134; *CPW*, I, pp. 45–6, 132, 140–1.

62   Byron: 'On a Distant View of the Village and School . . .', ll. 1–2, *CPW*, I, pp. 138–9; Shelley: 'The Boat on the Serchio', ll. 78–83; Hutchinson, p. 656; Bate: *John Keats* (1992), p. 5; Motion, p. 22; Cowper: 'Tirocinium', l. 292; Ackroyd: *Blake* (1995), p. 23; Lindsay, pp. 4–5.

VII Oxford and Cambridge
Pages 119 to 145

1   Johnston: *The Hidden Wordsworth* (1998), p. 13; *The Prelude*, Bk. III, ll. 327–8; VI, ll. 25–7; Elwin: *The First Romantics*, pp. 83–4; Ashton, p. 41; Simmons, p. 41; Sackville West: *A Flame in Sunlight* (1974), pp. 59–60; Elwin: *Landor* (1958), pp. 49–50.

2   Edgecumbe (ed.): *The Diary of Frances Lady Shelley 1787–1817* (1912), p. 21; Gash: *Mr Secretary Peel*, pp. 55–60; Lamb: *The Essays of Elia*, 'Oxford in the Vacation', in Kent (ed.): *The Works of Charles Lamb* (1882), p. 333.

3   Winstanley: *Unreformed Cambridge* (1935), pp. 256–8; Mack: *Jeremy Bentham, 1748–1792* (1962), pp. 43–4; Mitchell and Leys: *A History of the English People* (1950), p. 548; Davis: *The History of Balliol College* (1963), p. 154; J. Jones: *Balliol College* (1988), p. 164; *Letters of Chesterfield*, ed. P. M. Jones (1929), pp. 220, 260.

4   Williamson (ed.): *The Poetical Works of Christopher Smart* (1980), I, p. 15.

5   Hough, p. 10; Ketton-Cremer: *Thomas Gray* (1955), pp. 229–33.

6   Morritz: 'Travels, Chiefly on Foot, through Several Parts of England in 1782', in Pinkerton (ed.): *A General Collection of the Best and Most Interesting Voyages and Travels in All Parts of the World* (1808), pp. 541–3.

7   Winstanley, pp. 317–18; Trevelyan: *Trinity College* (1943), p. 78; Masterman: *To Teach the Senators Wisdom* (1952), p. 178; Gash, pp. 50–1; Perkin: *The Origins of Modern English Society 1780–1880* (1969), p. 298.

8   Cameron: *The Young Shelley*, p. 18; White, I, pp. 76, 586; Slatter's letter in Montgomery: *Oxford with Biographical Notes and Other Poems* (6th edn, 1843), p. 172.

9   Cameron, *The Young Shelley*, pp. 33–4; Dowden, I, pp. 50–2; *Stockdale's Budget* (1826–7), pp. 1, 2, 26; Grant Robertson (ed.): *Selected Cases, Statutes*

and Documents (1947), pp. 524–33; MacCarthy, *Shelley's Early Life* (1872), pp. 13–14.

10   Victor and Cazire: *Original Poetry* (1898, facsimile of the original edition), pp. 10–13; *S & C*, II, pp. 590, 628; Hawkins, pp. 46–9.

11   Barcus (ed.), pp. 41–5.

12   Victor and Cazire, pp. 37–44; *Stockdale's Budget*, p. 2; Jones: *Letters*, I, p. 13; R & F, I, pp. 154–5, 178; Cameron: *The Young Shelley*, pp. 305–6; Hogg, I, p. 15; White: *The Unextinguished Hearth* (1938), p. 32; White, I, p. 59.

13   *Medwin*, pp. 13, 67; Bieri: 'Shelley's Older Brother', *K–SJ*, 39 (1990), pp. 29–33; Hughes: *The Nascent Mind of Shelley*, pp. 49–50; Carr: *University College* (1902), pp. 185–93; Peck: *Shelley His Life and work* (1927), I, p. 63.

14   Bornand (ed.): *The Diary of W. M. Rossetti 1870–1873* (1977), p. 50; Mary Shelley: *Westminster Review* II (Oct. 1829), reproduced in Mary Shelley's *Lodore*, ed. Vargo, p. 464; Humbert Wolfe's Introduction to *The Life of Percy Bysshe Shelley* (1933), pp. vii–xxxi.

15   Winifred Scott: *Jefferson Hogg* (1951), pp. 13–21; Hogg, I, pp. 51–66.

16   Hogg, I, pp. 54, 66, 205; Mary Shelley's Preface to *Shelley's Poems*, Hutchinson, p. XXIII.

17   Rossetti, p. 16; Lucas: *Literature and Psychology* (1951), p. 201; Ingpen, p. 107; Peacock, p. 649; *Recollections*, pp. 140–1; Bornand (ed.), pp. 167–8; Mary Shelley: *The Last Man* (1993), pp. 17, 30; Gray and Walker: 'Haydon on Byron and Others' *K–SMB*, 7 (1956), p. 20; Mayne: *Byron* (1912), I, p. 140; Medwin: *The Angler in Wales* (1834), II, p. 212.

18   Information kindly given to me by Robin Darwall-Smith, the Archivist of University College; Hogg, I, pp. 72–3, 124, 322–3; Blunden (ed.): *On Shelley* (1938), p. 33; White, I, p. 82.

19   Hogg, I, pp. 48–51, 57, 91–7, 124, 126, 258–9, 277–8; *Letters*, I, p. 53; Sackville West, p. 93.

20   Congreve: *Love for Love*, V, ii; Davis, p. 155; J. Jones, pp. 174–5; Dowden, I, pp. 55–6.

21   *Letters*, I, pp. 21, 21n, 277–8; White, I, p. 98; Hughes: *The Nascent Mind of Shelley*, p. 38. For Godwin's *Political Justice*, see Chapter XIV below; Gray: *The Socialist Tradition* (1946), pp. 114–17, 120; Mills: *Peacock, his Circle and his Age* (1969), p. 59.

22   *University College Buttery Book 1810–11*, UC BU4/F/80; Hogg, I, pp. 72, 85–6, 192; White, I, p. 116; Holmes: *Shelley*, p. 38; W. Scott, p. 31; Grant: *Memoirs of a Highland Lady* (1992), p. 167.

23   Hogg, I, pp. 130–1, 217–21 290, 322,; UC BU4/F80; Ingpen, pp. 176–9.

24   *Letters*, I, p. 13; *S & C*, II, p. 588; Hawkins, pp. 46–9, 129; M & E, I, pp. 122–4, 127–8.

25   *S & C*, III, pp. 444–5; R & F, I, p. 240.

26   Hogg, I, pp. 261–6; MacCarthy, pp. 34–40; Ingpen, p. 122.

27   M & E, I, pp, 113–28; *Esdaile*, pp. 251–4, 267, 269; Hogg, I, p. 265; II, p. 69; AR 1786, pp. 233–5.

28 'Epithalamium', ll. 82–90, 96, M & E, I, pp. 117–22; Hogg, I, p. 267; *Letters*, I, p. 23; Cameron: *The Golden Years* (1974), p. 223; Hamilton: *The Infamous Essay on Woman* (1978), pp. 241–3; Brown, pp. 52–3, 248; Crook and Guiton, pp. 42–3, 236; R & F, I, p. 254.

29 *Letters*, I, pp. 22–3; Hogg, I, p. 268; Montgomery, p. 172; Dowden, I, p. 92; Bury: *The Diary of a Lady in Waiting* (1908), I, pp. 35–6; Ingpen, p. 192; Allardyce (ed.): *Letters to and from Charles Kirkpatrick Sharpe* (1888), I, pp. 38–9, 442–3.

30 Hogg, II, pp. 335–6; Crook and Guiton, pp. 86–9.

31 Crook and Guiton, pp. 44–52; *Letters*, I, p. 22; Hogg, I, pp. 68–74; *Medwin*, pp. 68–9.

32 Porter: *The Greatest Benefit to Mankind* (1997), pp. 280–1; *Prose*, p. 223.

33 Hogg, I, pp. 75, 115, 306; Wordsworth: *The Prelude* (1850), Bk VII, l. 65; Johnston: *The Hidden Wordsworth*, pp. 136–47; Coleridge: 'Progress of Vice', and 'Sonnet on Quitting School for College', *Poetical Works*, ed. E. H. Coleridge (1969), pp. 12–13, 29; Lefebure: *Samuel Taylor Coleridge: A Bondage of Opium* (1977), pp. 83–4; Crook and Guiton, pp. 41–4, 47–8.

34 *Letters*, I, pp. 24–5; Hughes, p. 30; Forman (ed.): *The Prose Works of P. B. Shelley* (1880), I, pp. 174, 208, 217, 218, 265, 294–5; White: *The Unextinguished Hearth*, pp. 35–8; Bury, pp. 35–6.

35 *Letters*, I, pp. 17–21; *Stockdale's Budget*, pp. 2, 9; Jeaffreson, I, pp. 155–67; White, I, pp. 89–92.

36 *Letters*, I, pp. 20, 23–4; R & F, I, pp. 41–87; 189–91, 196–9; M & E, I, pp. 38–83; CHP, c. II, l. 854, CPW, II, p. 40; Thompson: *The Making of the English Working Class*, pp. 502, 511; Feiling, p. 263–4; Dinwiddy: *Radicalism and Reform in Britain, 1780–1850* (1992), pp. 110–12; PD, XVI, pp. 547–8, XVII, pp. 592; BLJ, I, p. 186.

37 MacCarthy, pp. 75–106; Hughes, pp. 51–3; White, I, pp. 107–8; *Letters*, I, pp. 54–5.

38 *Letters*, I, pp. 26–7; *Stockdale's Budget*, pp. 9, 26; Dowden, I, pp. 95–6.

39 Hawkins, pp. 55–60, 129; S & C, II, 488–9; Dowden, I, pp. 50, 100–2; 'Melody to a Scene of Former Times', ll. 1–2; M & E, I, pp. 122–4, 127–8.

40 Peacock, p. 647; Nicolson, p. 300; M. Crompton: *Shelley's Dream Women* (1967), p. 21; see Chapter VI. above.

41 Friedenthal: *Goethe* (1993), p. 138.

42 Holmes, p. 40; W. Scott, p. 26; Hill: *Milton and the English Revolution* (1977), pp. 30–2; *Letters*, I, pp. 29–30, 96; *St Irvyne*, pp. 265, 294–5.

43 Gill: *William Wordsworth*, pp. 18, 43, 202–3; Reiman, pp. 183–205; Shelley: 'Peter Bell the Third', ll. 314, 351; R & P, pp. 335, 341; Brown, pp. 47–8, 241, 246; Shelley: Preface to *Laon and Cythna*, E & M, II, p. 47; Lucas, pp. 110, 120–2; Holmes: *Coleridge*, I, pp. 69–70; Ashton, p. 277; Griggs (ed.), *Collected Letters of Samuel Taylor Coleridge* (1959), III, 375–77.

44 Holmes, pp. 40, 44, 96; W. Scott, pp. 26, 148–64, 272; *Letters*, I, pp. 96, 227; Lady Shelley (ed.), *Shelley Memorials*, p. 62; Cameron: *The Young Shelley*, pp. 16, 106–7, 298.

45 Jones, I, pp. 26–48; *S & C*, II, pp. 668–717.

46 *S & C*, II, pp. 681–2; *St Irvyne*, p. 294; *Letters*, I, pp. 28, 42, 76.

47 *S & C*, II, pp. 681–2; Shelley: *St Irvyne*, p. 94; *Letters*, I, pp. 28, 42, 76.

48 *Letters*, I, p. 48.

49 Ibid., I, p. 239; Griggs (ed.), I, p. 281.

50 Hole, p. 137; Harris: *Romanticism and the Social Order 1780–1850* (1969), pp. 129–30; Shelley: 'A Sabbath Walk', ll. 34–42; *Esdaile*, pp. 39, 176–9; M & E, I, pp. 198–200; Merle, pp. 703, 704.

51 Hogg, II, p. 304; Peacock, p. 658.

52 UC BU4/F/480: Hogg, I, pp. 322–3; Berkeley: *Principles of Human Knowledge*, Introduction, S. 5; Ingpen, p. 192; Grant, p. 129.

53 Hogg, I, p. 79; *Letters*, I, p. 36.

54 Blunden (ed.), p. 54; Hogg, I, pp. 270–3; Rossetti, pp. 21–2.

55 Hogg, I, pp. 270–4; MacCarthy, pp. 107–8; *Letters*, I, p. 47; Jones: 'Hogg and the Necessity of Atheism', *PMLA*, 52 (1937), pp. 423–6.

56 *Letters*, I, p. 228; 'Notes on Queen Mab', VII, 13, Hutchinson, p. 813.

57 Hume: *Dialogues Concerning Natural Religion*, part XII, in Wollheim (ed.): *Hume on Religion* (1963), pp. 192–4; *Letters*, I, pp. 44–5; *Prose Works*, I, pp. 1–5, 319–27.

58 Hole, p. 60; Erdman (ed.), p. 648; Godwin: *Political Justice*, p. 12; Coburn (ed.): *The Philosophical Lectures of Samuel Taylor Coleridge* (1949), p. 383; *Prose Works*, I, pp. 1–5, 324.

59 Montgomery, p. 173; Ingpen, pp. 193–5.

60 Allardyce (ed.), I, p. 443; Bury, I, pp. 35–6; *DNB*; *Letters*, I, p. 228; *ER*, 31, pp. 158–87; C. C. Southey (ed.): *The Life and Correspondence of Robert Southey* (1850), III, p. 325.

61 Hogg, I, pp. 281–6; Rossetti, p. 24; Symonds, p. 55; Blunden (ed.), pp. 24, 26; Priestley (ed.): *Tom Moore's Diary* (1925), p. 14.

62 Rossetti, p. 23; Blunden (ed.), p. 30; *Letters*, I, pp. 27, 53, 55.

63 *Letters*, I, pp. 228; Merle: 'A Newspaper Editor's Reminiscences', *Fraser's Magazine* (1841), p. 704; Carr, p. 197.

64 Holmes: *Coleridge*, I, p. 59; *Medwin*, p. 84.

65 Nicolson: *Swinburne* (1926), pp. 56–7; Faber: *Jowett* (1957), pp. 366, 371–2.

66 *Letters*, I, pp. 50–1; Ashton, pp. 338–9.

67 *Conversations*, p. 247; *Medwin*, p. 84.

68 Blunden (ed.), p. 2; Dowden, I, pp. 123–5; W. S. Scott (ed.): *New Shelley Letters* (1948), p. 27.

VIII Cambridge and Oxford
Pages 146 to 163

1 *BLJ*, VII, p. 230; Marples, p. 140.

2 *BLJ*, VII, p. 230; I, pp. 78–80; *LBAR*, pp. 82–3.

3 *BLJ*, VIII, pp. 23–4; VII, p. 230; I, pp. 108–9, 111; Byron: 'To E[dward] N[oel] L[ong]', l. 3; *CPW*, I, p. 116.

4 Wordsworth: *The Prelude*, Bk IX, ll. 224–8; Bk III, ll. 543–4; *BLJ*, I, pp. 78, 81; IV, p. 168; VI, p. 12; A Trinity Man (Wright): *Alma Mater* (1827), p. 12; Byron: 'Thoughts suggested by a College Examination', ll. 55–60; *CPW*, I, pp. 93–4; Lane-Poole: *The Life of Stratford Canning* (1888), p. 293; Joyce: *My Friend H.* (1948), p. 5; Barton: 'Lord Byron and Trinity, a Bicentenary Portrait', *Trinity Review*, 1988, p. 4; Taylor: *Bacchus in Romantic England* (1999), p. 194.

5 Trevelyan, pp. 83, 90; Winstanley, pp. 199, 257; Barton, p. 4; 'Granta, a Medley', ll. 36, 45–9; *CPW*, I, pp. 99–100; Bourne, pp. 34–6, 43; *BLJ*, I, pp. 80–1, 108.

6 Berkeley: *Principles of Human Knowledge*, Introduction S. 22; *Conversations of Goethe with Eckermann and Soret*, trans. John Oxenford (1850), I, p. 272.

7 *Don Juan*, c. XI, ll. 29–32; *CPW*, V, p. 466.

8 *BLJ*, I, pp. 114–15, 124.

9 Byron: 'Damaetas', l. 9; 'Granta, a Medley', ll. 52–6; *CPW*, I, pp. 52, 100; *BLJ*, VII, p. 232; I, pp. 81, 80.

10 *BLJ*, IX, p. 37; Byron: 'To the Sighing Strephon', ll. 25–30; *CPW*, I, p. 149; Cochran: *Byron at Cambridge*, a booklet designed to accompany the Byron Society tour of Cambridge in 1996.

11 Cochran, p. 10; *LBAR*, p. 84; *BLJ*, I, p. 85; *L & J*, I, p. 95.

12 *BLJ*, VIII, p. 24; I, p. 122; VII, p. 230; Elwin: *Lord Byron's Wife*, pp. 107–9, 117; Crompton: *Byron and Greek Love*, pp. 100, 347, 357–8; Eisler: *Byron* (1999), p. 95; 'To Thyrza', ll. 29–32; *CPW*, I, p. 347; Wasserman: 'William John Bankes', *NBSR*, July 2000, pp. 71–2.

13 *BLJ*, I, pp. 86–89n; II, pp. 154–5; Gunn, pp. 56–9; Walker, p. 4.

14 *BLJ*, I, pp. 88–9; C. Hobhouse: *Oxford* (1944–5), p. 51; *L & J*, I, p. 95; Pratt, pp. 23–4.

15 See Chapter XI below; *BLJ*, I, pp. 87–8; IX, p. 38; Porter: *Mind Forg'd Manacles* (1987), pp. 88–9; Wain: *Samuel Johnson* (1974), pp. 286–7; Ober: *Bottoms Up* (1988), p. 196.

16 *BLJ*, I, p. 92; Marchand, I, pp. 110, 112; Winstanley, p. 205.

17 *BLJ*, VIII, pp. 23–4; I, p. 123; Pratt, pp. 13n, 24; Paston and Quennell (eds): *To Byron* (1939), p. 5; *L & J*, I, pp. 117–18.

18 *BLJ*, I, pp. 93–5, 97, 99–100, 107; Nicholson: 'That Suit in Chancery', *BJ*, 1998, pp. 50–3. I am indebted to Professor J. V. Beckett; Beckett, p. 258.

19 Moore, I, pp. 97–8, 123–4; *BLJ*, VII, p. 117; Vail, pp. 23–8; Byatt: *Wordsworth and Coleridge in their Time* (1970), pp. 220–1; McGann in

Rutherford (ed.), pp. 27–30; Boyes: *Love without Wings*, pp. 44–6; *BLJ*, I, pp. 105, 97; Pratt, pp. 36–41, 49–50; Nicolson: *Byron, The Last Journey*, p. 300; *BLJ*, XIII, p. 2; *L & J*, I, pp. 182n–183n; 'To a Knot of Ungracious Critics', ll. 48, 77; 'To Mary', ll. 13–15, 18–19, 37–40; *CPW*, I, pp. 21, 132–3, 179.

20 Cochran: *Byron Tastes the Freedom of Southwell* (2002), pp. 3–5; *BLJ*, I, pp. 103–6; Pratt, pp. 41–7; 'To Caroline'; 'To Miss E[lizabeth] P[igot]', l. 16; *CPW*, I, pp. 137, 145.

21 *BLJ*, I, pp. 102–4, 115; Marchand, I, pp. 123–6; Moore, I, p. 138; Austen: *Mansfield Park*, ch. 9; Longford: *Wellington*, I, p. 100.

22 *BLJ*, I, pp 106–7, 113, 117, 119; *Recollections*, pp. 225–7; Murray Archive Medical Report, 19.11.1806.

23 Boyes: *My Amiable Mamma*, pp. 126–7; Eisler, pp. 120–2; 'The Adieu', ll. 86–9, 120; *CPW*, I, pp. 182–6, 385.

24 *BLJ*, I, p. 106; Ober: *Boswell's Clap* (1988), p. 29; Masters: *Casanova* (1969), p. 282.

25 Mayne, I, p. 140.

26 *BLJ*, I, pp. 103, 110–13, 118; Blackstone: *Byron: Lyric and Romance* (1970), p. 11; Cochran, pp. 5–6; Vail, pp. 31–4; Pratt, pp. 65–7; *CPW*, I, pp 31–181, 364–84; McGann in Rutherford (ed.), pp. 27–30; *EBSR*, ll. 755–7, *CPW*, I, p. 253.

27 *BLJ*, I, p. 109; *Hours of Idleness* (1807 edn), pp. v–x; *CPW*, I, pp. 14, 26, 31–4, 358–9.

28 *BLJ*, I, pp. 110, 111, 119–23; *L & J*, I, pp. 128–9; Peters: *Byron* (2000), p. 21.

29 'To Thyrza', ll. 33–6; *CPW*, I, p. 347; *BLJ*, I, pp. 122–5; Crompton, pp. 104–6.

30 *BLJ*, I, pp. 124–6; *LBAR*, p. 88; *Don Juan*, c. VI, ll. 35–40; *CPW*, V, p. 300.

31 Byron: 'To E———', l. 8; [Pignus Amoris] ll. 21–4; *CPW*, I, pp. 124, 182, 376–7.

32 Ashton, p. 367; Kinsey: *Sexual Behaviour in the Human Male* (1948), pp. 629–30; Crompton, p. 104; *CPW*, I, p. 117; *BLJ*, I, pp. 123–5; Paston and Quennell (eds), p. 9.

33 *BLJ*, I, pp. 126, 132; VII, pp. 230–1; Joyce, p. 6; Burnett: *The Rise and Fall of a Regency Dandy* (1981), pp. 29–30.

34 *BLJ*, I, pp. 136–7; Kenyon Jones: 'Kindred Brutes', *NBSR*, January 2001, pp. 88–9; A Trinity Man, *Alma Mater*, pp. 166–7; *CPW*, I, p. 262; Marchand, I, pp. 136–7.

35 C. Hobhouse, p. 84.

36 Graham (ed.): *Byron's Bulldog*, p. 250; Burnett, p. 38; Cochran: 'O Did I Ever No I Never', *NSBR* 1998, p. 49.

37 *BLJ*, II, p. 93; I, pp. 135–9; VII, pp. 230–1; Marchand, I, pp. 137–41; Joyce, p. 6; Burnett, p. 31; Ward: Byron's *Hours of Idleness*, *MLN*, December 1944, pp. 547–50.

38 Sackville West, p. 94; Dowden: *Southey* (1902), p. 29.

39 *S & C*, II, pp. 820–3.

IX Post-University Blues I
Pages 164 to 184

1 'Lara', ll. 13–24; *CPW*, III, pp. 214–15; *Conversations*, p. 72.
2 Moore, I, pp. 176–7; Dallas: *Recollections of the Life of Lord Byron* (1824), pp. 3–9; *BLJ*, I, pp. 148–9, 151; *LLB*, p. 117; *LBAR*, p. 107.
3 *BLJ*, I, pp. 114–15, 146–7,; L'Estrange, pp. 33–4; Grierson: *Essays and Addresses* (1940), p. 7; *CPW*, I, pp. 28–30.
4 Dallas, pp. 10–15; *BLJ*, I, p. 148.
5 *L & J*, I, p. 168n; *BLJ*, I, pp. 158–9, 165; IX, p. 39; Graham (ed.), p. 29; *The Reminiscences and Recollections of Captain Gronow* (1984), I, pp. 55–7, 131; II, 81–2, 93–4; Bryant: *The Age of Elegance*: (1950), p. 327.
6 *LBAR*, p. 89; Crompton, p. 110.
7 Jeger: *Before Victoria* (1956), p. 121; L'Estrange, pp. 83–5.
8 *Byron, The Critical Heritage*, ed. Rutherford (1970), pp. 27–32; New: *Life of Henry Brougham to 1830* (1961), pp. 35, 45; Virgin: *Sydney Smith* (1994), pp. 2, 50–1; Perrin: *Dr Bowdler's Legacy*, pp. 5, 59–65.
9 *CPW, I, p. 364.*
10 *Letters*, I, p. 514; Elton: *A Survey of English Literature 1780–1830* (1948), I, pp. 393, 454; Galt, p. 50; *L & J*, I, p. 183n; Byron: *Hours of Idleness* (1807 edn), p. 3; *CPW*, I, pp. 35–6; Jeaffreson, p. 98; *LLB*, pp. 110, 125–7.
11 *BLJ*, I, pp. 158–62; III, p. 213; VIII, pp. 102–3; *CPW*, I, p. 398; Joseph: *Byron the Poet* (1964), p. 131.
12 *BLJ*, I, pp. 145–6, 153–5; *CPW*, I, p. 382; *Poetry*, VII, pp. 249–50; Vail, pp. 34–7; Marchand, I, p. 155.
13 *BLJ*, I, pp. 160–1; Moore, I, pp. 211–12; Joyce, pp. 10–11; *Conversations*, p. 67; Marchand, I, p. 151; *CPW*, I, pp. 215–18, 390; Burnett, p. 47.
14 *CPW*, I, pp. 210–11; *Poetry*, I, p. 260n; Marchand, I, pp. 165–6; *BLJ*, I, pp, 187, 189, 191; *NBSR*, 2000, p. 64; *Don Juan*, c. XVI, l. 533, *CPW*, V, p. 638.
15 Ober: *Boswell's Clap*, pp. 4, 89; Johnson: *The Hidden Wordsworth* (1998), pp. 295–302, 311–12, 316–7, 327; Nichol: *Byron* (1894), p. 46; *BLJ*, I, p. 165; L'Estrange, p. 31; Galt, pp. 51, 54–5.
16 *BLJ*, VII, p. 224.
17 Ibid., I, pp. 158–64; Burnett, pp. 36–7; Eisler, p. 145; Boyes: *My Amiable Mamma*, pp. 126–7; *L & J*, I, p. 221, 221n.
18 *BLJ*, I, pp. 163, 195, 196, 198; *L & J*, I, pp. 205–6; Marchand, I, pp. 169–70, 177.
19 *BLJ*, I, p. 161; *L & J*, I, p. 221; Montgomery: *Oxford* (6th edn), p. 139; Marchand, I, 177; Vulliamy: *Byron* (1948), p. 43; Hogg, I, pp. 302–3; Langford: *Englishness Identified*, p. 79; K. Jones: *The Passionate Sisterhood* (1997), p. 121; Ashton, p. 207; Rollins (ed.): *The Letters of John Keats* (1958), I, p. 404; Moore, I, p. 233; Dallas, pp. 49–50; *LBAR*, p. 106.
20 *BLJ*, I, pp. 147, 161, 197; *Conversations*, p. 67; Hobhouse's Diary, BL Add. Ms 56530, f. 25.

21 'To an Oak', II, ll. 6, 10; *CPW*, I, pp. 204–5; *BLJ*, I, pp. 81, 151, 171–2, 179–80; Beckett: 'Byron's Nottinghamshire', *NBSR*, July 2000, pp. 52–3.

22 *BLJ*, I, 173–4; Boyes: *My Amiable Mamma*, pp. 137–40; Mayne, I, pp. 138–9; Holmes: *Coleridge*, II, p. 426; Boyes: *Queen of a Fantastic Realm*, pp. 42–3.

23 *BLJ*, I, p. 179; *CPW*, I, pp. 221–3, 225–6, 391, 392; Byron: *Beppo*, l. 474, *CPW*, IV, p. 148; Boyes: *Queen of a Fantastic Realm*, pp. 44–5, 70; Wilson Knight: *Lord Byron's Marriage* (1957), pp. 27–8; *Conversations*, p. 64; Moore, I, p. 79.

24 Moore, I, pp. 221–2; *BLJ*, I, pp. 176–8, 180–2; *CPW*, I, pp. 224–5, 391–2; BL Egerton Ms. 2611, ff. 55, 77.

25 *CPW*, I, pp. 396–8; Moore, I, p. 226; J. T. Hodgson: *Memoir of the Rev. Francis Hodgson* (1878), I, p. 67.

26 *CPW*, I, pp. 393–9; *BLJ*, I, pp. 136, 141; X, p. 70; Dallas, pp. 17–48.

27 *BLJ*, XIII, p. 4; I, pp. 177–8, 201–2; *CPW*, I, p. 261.

28 *BLJ*, I, pp. 49, 52, 56, 133, 173, 186, 196; Bakewell, pp. 81–2; *HVSV*, p. 612; *CPW*, I, pp. 252, 258, 416; *L & J*, I, p. 217n; Mayne, I, pp. 141–2; Beckett, pp. 85, 308.

29 Foord: *Her Majesty's Opposition 1714–1830* (1964), pp. 443–4; *HC*, I, pp. 345–6.

30 Dallas, pp. 50–1; *BLJ*, I, pp. 186–7; Roberts: *The Whig Party, 1807–1812* (1965), pp. 1–6; *LBAR*, p. 469; *EBSR*, ll. 1011–16; *CPW*, I, p. 261.

31 Dallas, pp. 52–4; Davis: *The Age of Grey and Peel* (1929), pp. 141, 147; *BLJ*, IX, p. 28; *Journals of the House of Lords*, XLVII (1809–10).

32 *BLJ*, III, p. 213; *CMP*, pp. 3, 6–9; *CPW*, I, pp. 236–7, 404; *L & J*, I, p. 183n.

33 Greig: *Francis Jeffrey of The Edinburgh Review* (1948), pp. 289–90; Jack: *English Literature 1815–1832* (1963), p. 326.

34 *EBSR*, II, 94, 689–90, 693–4; *CPW*, I, pp. 228, 232, 251, 255; Beaty: *Byron The Satirist* (1985), pp. 41–2; Christie in *BJ* 1997, pp. 25–6; Highet: *A Clerk of Oxenford* (1954), p. 121; Fleming: *Bright Darkness* (1983), p. 17.

35 *CPW*, I, p. 228, 398; Manning: 'Byron's *EBSR*', *K–SMB*, XXI (1968), pp. 7–10; Highet: *Juvenal the Satirist* (1954), pp. 220–1; Beaty, pp. 34–8; Nichol, p. 52; *EBSR*, ll. 1027–33; *CPW*, I, p. 261.

36 *BLJ*, I, p. 189; Burnett, pp. 74–96; *LBAR*, pp. 459–71; Graham (ed.), pp. 158–60, 170–2; Dallas, pp. 223–5, 249; Boyes: *My Amiable Mamma*, p. 162.

37 Marchand: 'Byron's Ordeal with Lady Falkland', *BJ*, 1988, pp. 21–2; Marchand, I, 169–70; Marchand in *K–SMB*, VII, p. 41; *LLB*, pp. 213–14; *LBAR*, pp. 106, 202; *BLJ*, I, p. 213; II, pp. 45, 162; Burnett, pp. 53, 74–83, 89–96.

38 Jeaffreson, pp. 122–3; *BLJ*, I, p. 199; VII, p. 231; *L & J*, I, pp. 153–5; Moore, I, p. 127; Guiccioli: *My Recollections of Lord Byron* (1869), pp. 227–8; Nicolson, p. 301; Treloar: *Wilkes and the City* (1917), pp. 239–44; Kemp: *Sir Francis Dashwood* (1967), pp. 130–6.

39 *BLJ*, I, pp. 202–5; *LLB*, pp. 291, 240–6; Gatrell: *The Hanging Tree* (1994),

pp. 100–1; Gilmour, pp. 11–13, 156; *Don Leon*, ll. 165–76.

40 *BLJ*, I, p. 206; *ESBR*, ll. 699–700; *CPW*, I, p. 251.

41 *BLJ*, I, pp. 204–5, 210; Lees-Milne: *William Beckford* (1990), pp. 28–46; *Medwin*, p. 258; Hodgson, I, pp. 159–60.

42 Crompton, pp. 126–9; *BLJ*, I, pp. 206–10.

43 *CHP*, c. I, ll. 82–5; *CPW*, II, pp. 11–12; BL Egerton Ms. 2611; Burnett, p. 82; *BLJ*, I, p. 206.

44 [Lines to Mr Hodgson], II, 65–80, *CPW*, I, pp. 268–70; *BLJ*, I, pp. 210–43; Joyce, p. 18; Gamba: *Lord Byron's Last Visit to Greece* (1825), pp. 148–9; *CMP*, pp. 4–5.

45 *BLJ*, I, pp. 89, 135, 151, 173.

46 Ibid., I, pp. 192, 199, 200–2, 232; Egerton Ms. 2611, f. 105.

47 *BLJ*, I, pp. 200–1: *CHP*, c. I, sts 4, 6, *CPW*, II, pp. 9–10.

48 'Stanzas to [Mrs Musters] on Leaving England', ll. 5–6; *CPW*, I, pp. 266–8, 419; Longford: *Byron* (1976), pp. 17–18; Massie, p. 27.

X Post-University Blues II
Pages 185 to 209

1 See note 1, Chapter IX above.

2 Ackroyd: *Blake*, p. 99; Rieger: *The Mutiny Within* (1967), pp. 155–7.

3 Hogg, I, pp. 296–8; Djabri and Knight: *Horsham's Forgotten Son, Thomas Medwin* (1995), p. 11; *Medwin*, pp. 87–8.

4 *S & C*, II, pp. 730–2; Hogg, I, p. 309; *Letters*, I, pp. 53, 55–6.

5 W. Scott: *Jefferson Hogg*, pp. 33–4; *S & C*, II, pp. 736–9.

6 Hogg, I, pp. 299–300.

7 See Chapter III above; Gilmour, pp. 156–7; Peck, I, p. 116.

8 Hogg, I, pp. 304–9, 314–15; Ingpen, pp. 241–3.

9 Ingpen, pp. 225–7; *S & C*, II, pp. 739–40; *Letters*, I, p. 57.

10 *Letters*, I, pp. 56–7; Moore, I, p. 58.

11 *S & C*, II, p. 745; Ingpen, pp. 228–31.

12 Erdman (ed.), p. 471; Lucas, p. 117.

13 Ingpen, pp. 229–30; Peacock, p. 656; Austen: *Northanger Abbey*, ch. 30; Rolleston: *Talking with Lady Shelley* (1977), p. 95; *Stockdale's Budget*, p. 9.

14 *Letters*, I, p. 60; Ingpen, pp. 235–7.

15 W. Scott, pp. 33–4; *S & C*, II, pp. 736–9; Ingpen, pp. 237–8.

16 *Letters*, I, pp. 64, 72; Ingpen, pp. 241–3; *BLJ*, II, p. 34.

17 Habakkuk, 1–19, and *passim*; Wollstonecraft in Todd (ed.), p. 21; Jane Austen: *Sense and Sensibility*, ch. 1; *Pride and Prejudice*, chs, 7, 13, 23 and 50.

18 Godwin: *Political Justice*, p. 486; Lady Shelley (ed.), *Shelley Memorials*, p. 63; *S & C*, II, pp. 751–2, 755; *Letters*, I, pp. 62–5.

19 Ingpen, pp. 253–4; Porter: *Mind-Forg'd Manacles*, p. 16; Habakkuk, p. 62.

20 *Letters*, I, pp. 64, 78, 77.

21 Ibid., I, pp. 77, 40; Langford: *Englishness Identified*, p. 253; Hogg, I, p. 25; Ingpen, pp. 268–9, 515–16.

22 Hogg, II, p. 552; *Letters*, I, p. 274; Peacock, p. 652.

23 Mark Twain: 'In Defence of Harriet Shelley', in *How To Tell A Story and Other Essays* (1898), pp. 16–22, 61; Lady Shelley (ed.): *Shelley Memorials*, pp. 20–2, 65–6; Leigh Hunt: *Lord Byron and Some of His Contemporaries*, II, pp. 34–7; H. Wolfe: Introduction to *The Life of Shelley*, pp. xv–vi; Norman, pp. 195, 210–72, 224–6; St Clair: *The Godwins and the Shelleys*, pp. 493–4; Hamilton: *Keepers of the Flame* (1992), pp. 131–8; Boas: *Harriet Shelley* (1962), pp. v–viii, 28; Crook in *K–SR*, 3 (1988), p. 84.

24 Hogg, I, pp. 25–6; II, p. 5; P. Foot: *Red Shelley* (1984), pp. 124–5; Shelley: 'To November', l. 8; 'To Harriet on her birthday', l. 1; *Esdaile*, pp. 50, 88; M & E, I, pp. 186, 229; Peacock, p. 96; Austen: *Pride and Prejudice*, ch. 6.

25 *Letters*, I, p. 64; Peacock, p. 652; M & E, I, pp. 165–6; Dowden, I, p. 140.

26 *Letters*, I, pp. 66, 76.

27 Ibid., p. 66, 77, 79.

28 Ibid., I, pp. 66–70, 383; Ingpen, p. 243; Hughes, p. 80; Merle, p. 705.

29 *Letters*, I, pp. 71, 77, 80; Ingpen, pp. 290–1; Hughes, pp. 82–3; Shelley: *St Irvyne*, pp. 265, 294–5; *S & C*, II, pp. 866–7.

30 *Letters*, I, p. 67; Ingpen, pp. 240, 255.

31 Hogg, II, p. 553; I, pp. 205–6; *Medwin*, p. 101; Byron: 'The Devil's Walk', l. 143, *CPW*, IV, p. 100; *HC*, II, p. 395; Byron: *Hints from Horace*, II, pp. 579–83; *CPW*, I, p. 310.

32 Dawson, pp. 13–14; Holland: *Further Memoirs of the Whig Party 1807–1821* (1905), p. 15; *PD*, XI, 1106–8; XIV, 712; XVII, 592; Hogg, I, pp. 206–7; II, p. 553; *Letters*, I, pp. 54–5.

33 *Letters*, I, pp. 121, 144; Motion: *Keats*, pp. 45–6; *K–SR*, 13 (1999), p. 60; Storey: *Robert Southey* (1997), pp. 41–3; Crook and Guiton, pp. 19–20, 69.

34 *Medwin*, p. 136; Milton: *Paradise Lost*, XI, ll. 479–82; Crook and Guiton, p. 69; Blunden (ed.), pp. 30–1.

35 The date of the poem is probable, not certain; 'Zeinab and Kathema', ll. 33, 101–2, 107–8; M & E, I, pp. 171–7; *Esdaile*, pp. 148–59, 275–8; Crook and Guiton, pp. 60–3.

36 *Letters*, I, pp. 63, 67, 74–5; Holmes: *Shelley*, pp. 64n, 637–8; Holmes: *Shelley on Love*, p. 185; *Letters*, I, p. 216; Crook and Guiton, p. 20.

37 *Letters*, I, pp. 74, 82–3, 84, 90; Hawkins: *Pilfold* (1998), pp. 24–30, 36, 42–5.

38 *Letters*, I, pp. 83–5, 90; W. B. Pope in *K–SMB*, 15 (1964), pp. 45–8; *S & C*, II, p. 827.

39 *S & C*, II, pp. 780–1; *Letters*, I, pp. 80–2; Houston, I, pp. 99–101; Rolleston, pp. 124–5; *K–SMB*, 19 (1968), p. 16; Langford, p. 113; Wollstonecraft: *A Vindication of the Rights of Women*, ch. 11.

40 *Letters*, I, pp. 79–82, 116; Veeder: *Mary Shelley & Frankenstein* (1988), p. 16; *S & C*, II, pp. 780–1.

40 *Letters*, I, pp. 79–82, 116; Veeder: *Mary Shelley & Frankenstein* (1988), p. 16; *S & C*, II, pp. 780–1.

41 *Letters*, I, pp. 85–7, 123; *S & C*, II, pp. 824–7; M & E, I, pp. 166–70.

42 *Letters*, I, p. 87; R & F, I, pp. 318–19; Ingpen, pp. 343–7; Gelpi, pp. 116–18.

43 *S & C*, II, pp. 789–827; *Letters*, I, pp. 90–2, 106–8, 113–15, 123–4, 128–9; Ingpen, p. 415; Gelpi, pp. 113–15.

44 *Letters*, I, pp. 104–5, 107–8, 113.

45 Grabo, p. 4; Hogg, I, p. 16; Merle, p. 707; Hughes, p. 22; Gelpi, pp. 97–8.

46 *Letters*, I, p. 104; Ingpen, pp. 276–7.

47 *Letters*, I, pp. 97–102, 116–17; Hawkins: *Pilfold*, p. 54.

48 *Letters*, I, pp. 105, 117; R & F, I, p. 323; Ingpen, pp. 292–3; *S & C*, II, pp. 818–20.

49 *Letters*, I, pp. 105–6, 110, 116–17, 119; *S & C*, II, pp. 851–2; Hughes, p. 96; Smith: *George IV* (1999), pp. 133–4; Hogg, II, pp. 556–7; R & F, I, pp. 448–51.

50 *K–SMB*, 19 (1968), p. 16; *Letters*, I, p. 118.

51 *Letters*, I, pp. 122–3, 129; Tomalin, pp. 249–51, 293–4; St Clair: *The Godwins and the Shelleys*, p. 322; *K–SR*, 1 (1986), pp. 68–9; Boas, pp. 36–9.

52 Allen: *The Wages of Sin* (2000), pp. 7–8, 16.

53 *Letters*, I, p. 119; Crook and Guiton, pp. 71–5; *K–SR*, 12 (1998), p. 32; 13 (1999), p. 61; 'The Retrospect: Cwm Elan, 1812', ll. 39–42, M & E, I, pp. 222–3; *Esdaile*, p. 156.

54 *Medwin*, p. 109; *Letters*, I, pp. 90, 92, 96, 111, 118, 122–3, 177, 180–1; *S & C*, III, pp. 46–54.

55 *Letters*, I, pp. 177, 180–1.

56 *Letters*, I, pp. 131; Boas, p. 27.

57 *Letters*, I, p. 131; Boas, pp. 43–4; *K–SMB*, 21 (1970), p. 23.

58 *S & C*, III, p. 48; *Letters*, I, pp. 119, 124–7, 132, 135–6.

59 Ingpen, p. 301; Djabri and Knight, pp. 15–16; *Letters*, I, pp. 133–4, 158–9.

60 Dowden, I, pp. 172–3; Hogg, II, pp. 554–5; *Letters*, I, pp. 137–8; Ingpen, pp. 301–2, 306–8.

61 *S & C*, II, pp. 868–70; Ingpen, p. 302; Holmes, p. 78; Boas, p. 48; Hogg, II, pp. 554–5.

62 *Letters*, I, pp. 134–5, 323; Hogg, I, pp. 466–7.

63 Ibid., I, pp. 162–3; Boas, pp. 45–8; Hogg, I, p. 422; Cameron: *The Young Shelley*, pp. 98–9; Dowden, I, p. 173.

64 *Conversations*, p. 247; Webb, p. 65; Cameron: *The Young Shelley*, p. 37; Hamilton: *Percy Bysshe Shelley* (2000), p. 3; Shelley: *A Defence of Poetry*, in *Prose*, p. 297; Eliot: *The Use of Poetry* (1933), pp. 25–6.

65 Schroeder: 'Byron's Sense of Time and Age before 1810', *BJ*, 1983, pp. 4–19; *CMP*, p. 206; 'To a Youthful Friend', ll. 22, 25; ['There Was a Time I Need

Not Name'], ll. 10–11; 'Inscription on the Monument of a Newfoundland Dog', ll. 15–20; Dallas, p. 61.

XI Poetic Madness
Pages 210 to 221

1 Housman: *The Name and Nature of Poetry* (1933), pp. 38–9; Jamison: *Touched with Fire* (1994), pp. 51, 62–3, 92–5; Erdman (ed.), pp. 724, 728–31; Storey, p. 210; Holmes: *Coleridge*, II, p. 474; Ackroyd: *Blake*, p. 325; Cecil: *The Stricken Deer* (1943), pp. 223–5; Porter: *Mind-Forg'd Manacles*, pp. 265–7; Rosen: *Romantic Poets, Critics and Other Madmen* (1998), pp. 105–12, 126.

2 Johnson: *Lives of the English Poets* (1906), II, pp. 398–402; Lucas: *The Decline and Fall of the Romantic Ideal* (1936), p. 98; *BLJ*, III, p. 179, IV, p. 332; Ober: *Boswell's Clap*, p. 138: Williamson (ed.): *The Poetical Works of Christopher Smart*, I, pp. xviii–xix; Rosen, pp. 120–3; Porter: *Mind-Forg'd Manacles*, pp. 99, 146, 234, 265–7; Bett: *The Infirmities of Genius* (1952), pp. 33–8; Boswell: *Johnson*, p. 281.

3 Porter: *Mind-Forg'd Manacles*, pp. x, 1, 17–18, 21–4; Rosen, pp. 113–19; Jamison, p. 51; Lucas: *Literature and Psychology*, pp. 1, 67; *Letters*, II, p. 29; Boswell, p. 1088; White: *The Unextinguished Hearth*, p. 289.

4 *BLJ*, III, pp. 157, 179, V, p. 52; *A Midsummer Night's Dream*, V, i, ll. 7–8; *Blessington*, Intro., pp. 6–7, 61–2, 108–11; pp. 115; St Clair: 'Bamming and Humming', *BJ*, 1979, pp. 38–47.

5 *Letters*, I, p. 491; II, pp. 57–8; E & M, II, p. 445; *BLJ*, VII, p. 174; Wordsworth: 'Resolution and Independence', ll. 48–9; Spence: 'The Maniac's Soliloquy', *K–SR* (1989), IV, p. 84; Rosen, p. 113.

6 Jamison, pp. 61–72, and *passim*; Walters: 'Keats and Cyclothymia', *K–SR* 3 (1988), pp. 70–5; Nicolson: 'The Health of Authors', *The Lancet*, 1947, p. 710.

7 Jamison, pp. 7–8, 13–16, 58–9; Goodwin and Jamison: *Manic-Depressive Illness* (1990), pp. 337, 339.

8 Jamison, pp. 2–3, 54, 125.

9 Black: *Pitt the Elder*, p. 271; Porter: *Mind-Forg'd Manacles*, pp. 233–4; *Journal*, II, p. 556.

10 Jamison, pp. 105, 152–3, 240; Rosen, pp. 120–1; Mary Shelley's Preface to Second Collected Edition of *Poetical Works*, Hutchinson, p. xxiii.

11 Andrews: 'Keats and Mercury', *K–SMB*, 20 (1969), p. 42; Jamison, p. 51; Miller: 'Manic Depressive Cycles of the Poet Shelley', *Psycho-Analytic Forum*, I (1966), pp. 197–8.

12 *BLJ*, I, pp. 58, 62–3, 88, 114.

13 Dallas, pp. 190; Moore, I, pp. 38–9, 264–5; 'Childish Recollections', ll. 221–2; *CPW*, I, p. 165; *BLJ*, II, p. 110; I, p. 181; Marchand in *K–SMB*, 7 (1956), pp. 41–2; Pope: *An Essay on Man*, Epistle, III, ll. 147–68.

14 Eliot: *The Use of Poetry*, p. 154.

15 *BLJ*, II, p. 110; I, pp. 47, 181; *Beppo*, ll. 593–608; *CPW*, IV, 152–3; Moore, I, p. 264; *BLJ*, III, p. 64; *CHP*, c. I, ll. 826–7, *CPW*, II, p. 39; Dallas, pp. 61, 198; *BLJ*, V, p. 268; Lovell: *Byron, The Quest* (1949), pp. 125–6; Byron: 'Prometheus', *CPW*, IV, pp. 31–3; *CPW*, II, pp. 99, 306; V, p. 112.

16 Dallas, p. 196; Galt: *Lord Byron*, p. 51; *BLJ*, VIII, p. 216; VII, p. 189; see Chapters I and II above; *Conversations*, p. 55.

17 Moore, I, p. 336; Rutherford: *Byron, a Critical Study* (1961), p. 10; Galt: *Lord Byron*, pp. 130–1; Grierson (ed.): *The Letters of Sir Walter Scott 1815–1817* (1933), IV, p. 297; Page (ed.): *Byron*, pp. 145, 147; *HVSV*, pp. 469–70; Blessington, pp. 33, 47, 47n, 71–2, 75n, 195–7, 205–6, 219.

18 *BLJ*, III, pp. 62, 215; Ward: *Letters to Ivy*, ed. Romilly (1905), p. 163; *CHP*, I, ll. 64–70; *Don Juan*, c. II, ll. 1705–12; *CPW*, II, pp. 10–11; V, p. 156.

19 *Beppo*, l. 508; *CPW*, IV, p. 149; *Don Juan*, c. XVI, ll. 819–21; *CPW*, V, pp. 649, 769; Kenyon Jones: 'James Holmes and the Byron Circle', *BJ*, 1997, pp. 84–5.

20 *Medwin*, p. 31; R & F, I, pp. 135–6, 296–301; Crook: 'Shelley's Earliest Poem?', *Notes & Queries*, December 1987, pp. 486–90; *S & C*, IV, pp. 813–19; M & E, I, pp. 3–4.

21 King-Hele: *Erasmus Darwin 1731–1802* (1963), pp. 55–6; Smith, I, pp. 84–112; Porter: *Mind-Forg'd Manacles*, pp. 32–3.

22 Hogg, II, p. 117; Ingpen, pp. 273, 329, 368–71; Boswell, p. 1235; Thompson, pp. 511–13; *The Examiner*, 14 November 1813, quoted by Carnall in Bold (ed.): *Byron: Wrath and Rhyme* (1983), p. 133; White, II, p. 170.

23 *Medwin*, p. 237; Hogg, I, p. 441; II, pp. 46–8, 304; 'Death-Spurning Rocks!', ll. 11, 29; 'The Retrospect: Cwm Elan, 1812', ll. 37–8; M & E, I, pp, 181–2, 222.

24 Edel: 'The Madness of Art', *American Journal of Psychiatry*, October 1975, pp. 1006–7; Mary Shelley's Preface to the 1824 edition, Hutchinson, pp. xxv–vii; Hogg, p. 111; 'The Retrospect: Cwm Elan 1812', ll. 28, 129–31; M & E, I, pp. 1–2, 220–7; *Esdaile*, pp. 73, 155–60, 211–15, 281–4; *Letters*, I, p. 119; *Medwin*, p. 269.

25 *Medwin*, p. 313; *Letters*, II, p. 288; Rossetti, p. 68; White, II, pp. 255, 370, 606; I, p. 644; Miller, pp. 197–203.

26 Rennie, p. 2; White, II, p. 419; *K–SMB*, 19 (1968), p. 16; *Letters*, I, p. 165, 383; Merle, p. 704; Buchanan: *A Poet's Sketch-Book* (1883), pp. 108–9.

27 White, I, p. 316; Lea: *Shelley and the Romantic Revolution* (1945), p. 19; Peacock, pp. 643–4; Jeaffreson, I, pp. 172–3; Symonds, p. 33; Medwin in the *Athenaeum*, p. 554.

28 *Leigh Hunt's Letter on Hogg's Life of Shelley With Other Papers* (1927), pp. 28–9; Shelley: *A Defence of Poetry*, in *Prose*, p. 277; Engelburg: *The Making of the Shelley Myth* (1988), pp. 44–6.

XII Byron's Grand Tour
Pages 222 to 261

1   *BLJ*, I, pp. 208, 216, 218; *CHP*, c. I, l. 217, *CPW*, II, p. 16; Broughton: *Recollections of a Long Life* (1909), pp. 6–9.

2   Roberts: *The Whig Party 1807–1812* (1965), pp. 3–4, 118, 122–3, 133–5, 139–43, 163–71; Taylor: *The Troublemakers* (1957), p. 34; PD, XI, 888; Butler: *Sheridan* (1935), p. 273; Kelly: *Sheridan* (1997), pp. 276–7; Turberville: *The House of Lords in the Age of Reform, 1784–1837* (1958), pp. 148–53; Holland, pp. 105–6; Feiling, p. 258.

3   [D. Roberts:] *The Military Adventures of Johnny Newcome by An Officer* (1904), pp. 25–6, 54; Gronow, II, 195–6; Marchand, I, p. 187.

4   *BLJ*, I, pp. 208, 218; Hinde: *Castlereagh* (1981), pp. 148–53; Granville (ed.): *Lord Granville Leveson-Gower Correspondence* (1916), II, p. 330; Longford: *Wellington*, I, pp. 155–8; Bryant: *The Great Duke* (1971), pp. 114, 122–3, 129–30, 135–8.

5   *CHP*, c. I, st. 26 and lines deleted from *CHP*; *CPW*, II, p. 20; Longford: *Wellington*, I, p. 146; Elwin: *Landor*, p. 115; Kent Thomas: *Lord Byron's Iberian Pilgrimage* (1983), p. 9; White (ed.): *Political Tracts of Wordsworth, Coleridge and Shelley* (1953), pp. 142, 149, 190.

6   *CHP*, c. I, sts 19–21, 29; c. II, st. 44; *CPW*, II, pp. 17–18, 21–2, 58, 188; Gibbon: *Decline and Fall of the Roman Empire*, ch. 37; Broughton, I, pp. 7–8.

7   Hodgson, I, p. 163; Beckford: *Vathek* (The World's Classics, 1983), p. 102; *CHP*, c. I, sts 22–3, *CPW*, II, pp. 18–19, 276; R. Macaulay in *Blue Guide to Portugal* (1996), p. 146; Crompton, pp. 120–1.

8   Hobhouse Diary, BL Add. Ms. 56527, f. 6; White (ed.), *Political Tracts*, p. 125; Longford: *Wellington*, I, p. 146; Kent Thomas, p. 12.

9   Hobhouse Diary, ff. 6, 8; Broughton; I, p. 9; *CHP*, c. I, sts 16, 18; *CPW*, II, pp. 17, 187–8; *BLJ*, I, p. 218; Baker: 'Byron and Childe Harold in Portugal', *BJ*, 1994, pp. 43–4, 47.

10 *BLJ*, I, p. 215; Hobhouse: *A Journey through Albania and Other Provinces of Turkey* (1813), II, p. 808.

11 Gore (ed.): *Creevey* (1948), p. 267; Ward: *Letters to 'Ivy'*, p. 317; *Journal*, 12 September 1827, III, p. 1055.

12 *BLJ*, I, pp, 214–19; *Letters to 'Ivy'*, p. 163; Borst: *Lord Byron's First Pilgrimage* (1969), p. 20; Broughton, I, p. 10; *CHP*, c. I, st. 43; *CPW*, II, p. 26; Bryant: *Great Duke*, pp. 261–4.

13 *BLJ*, I, pp. 219, 217; Steffan and Pratt: *Byron's Don Juan* (1957), II, pp. 3–6.

14 *CHP*, c. I, st. 40; *CPW*, II, p. 25; *BLJ*, I, p. 219; Bryant: *Great Duke*, pp. 166–7, 172–3; Longford: *Wellington*, pp. 193–7; Davis: *The Age of Grey and Peel* (1929), p. 121; PD, XV, 357–8.

15 *BLJ*, I, p. 219; Hobhouse Diary, ff. 13–15; *CHP*, c. I, st. 57, *CPW*, II, p. 30; *CMP*, pp. 221, 549–50; *CHP*, c. II, 6 p. 305, *CPW*, II, p. 55; Moore, I, pp. 281–4.

16 *BLJ*, IX, p. 85.

17 Powell: *A Jane Austen Compendium* (1993), p. 7; *Blessington*, Intro., pp. 25–6; *K–SMB*, 31 (1980), pp. 61–7; Seymour: *Mary Shelley* (2000), p. 315.

18 Hobhouse Diary, f. 13; Kent Thomas, p. 44; *Poetry*, II, pp. 79–80; *CPW*, II, p. 41; *BLJ*, V, p. 269; Bryant: *The Years of Victory* (1944), pp. 267–8, 273; Holland, pp. 19–20; Day: *The Life of Sir John Moore* (2001), pp. 141–2, 146–53, 159–61, 165.

19 *BLJ*, I, pp. 219–20; Ford: *Gatherings from Spain* (2000), pp. 141, 150, 342; Broughton, I, p. 13; *CPW*, II, p. 291; Hobhouse: *A Journey through Albania* (1813).

20 *BLJ*, I, pp. 216, 220–1; *CHP*, c. I, sts 65–6; *Don Juan*, II, st. 5; *CPW*, II, p. 33, V, p. 90; Broughton, I, pp. 11–12.

21 Pollock: *Wilberforce* (1977), pp. 59–66; Quinlan: *Victorian Prelude* (1991), pp. 202–6, 212–13; Jaeger, pp. 14–17; Smith: 'The Suppression of Vice', in Bullett (ed.), pp. 165–6.

22 Hobhouse Diary, f. 16; *EBSR*, ll. 632–7; *CPW*, I, p. 249; Broughton, I, p. 11; Blackstone, p. 19; *CHP*, c. I, sts 68, 77, 80; *CPW*, II, pp. 34–8; Usher: *Spanish Mercy* (1959), p. 25; *Poetry*, II, pp. 521–2.

23 Shubert: *Death and Money in the Afternoon* (1999), p. 156; Carr: *Spain 1808–1939* (1966), p. 70.

24 Hobhouse Diary, ff. 17, 18, 19, 21; Information from Peter Cochran; *CHP*, c. I, st. 33; *Don Juan*, c. II, st. 81; *CPW*, II, p. 33, V, p. 114; Cochran: 'O Did I Ever No I Never', *NBSR*, 1998, pp. 53–4.

25 *BLJ*, I, pp. 216, 221–2; Hayter: *Coleridge's Journey to Malta* (1993), pp. 106–7, 112–17; Hobhouse Diary, ff. 19, 21.

26 *BLJ*, I, pp. 218, 221; Hobhouse: Diary, f. 22; Broughton, I, p. 12.

27 Bessborough (ed.): *Lady Bessborough and Her Family Circle* (1940), p. 209; Borst, p. 20; *CHP*, c. II, st. 40, *CPW*, II, p.57; Barton: *Byron and the Mythology of Fact*, pp. 8–9; *BLJ*, XIII, p. 4; I, pp. 49, 117–18, 215; II, p. 57; Schmidt: *Lives of the Poets* (1998), p. 192.

28 'To the Rev. J. T. Becher', ll. 13–14; *CPW*, I, p. 178; 'Adieu to the Muse', ll. 25–8; *CPW*, I, 127; Elwin: *Landor*, pp. 116–19; Hogg, I, pp. 201–2.

29 Gronow, I, p. 1; Lovell: *Captain Medwin*, p. 24; *BLJ*, I, p. 221; Kent Thomas, pp. 61–2; Hobhouse, 'Notes of Expenses of Tour in Turkey 1809', BL Add. Ms. 56528.

30 Hobhouse Diary, f. 23; Graham (ed.), pp. 36, 47; Gordon: *John Galt* (1972), pp. 4, 11–12, 22, 51–2, 88–97, 106–7; Elton, I, p. 363; *LLB*, pp. 356–9.

31 Galt: *Lord Byron*, pp. 59–61; *BLJ*, I, p. 220.

32 Galt, pp. 59–61; *BLJ*, III, p. 210; IV, p. 57; Saglia: 'Spain and Byron's Construction of Place', *BJ*, 1994, pp. 36–7; *CHP*, c. I, sts 38, 44, 52, 53, 57, 85, 86, 90; *CPW*, II, pp. 24, 26, 29, 41–3; see Chapter VII, above; M & E, I, p. 115.

33 Galt, pp. 60–1; *Blessington*, p. 146, 146n; *LLB*, p. 480; Hobhouse Diary, f. 58; *BLJ*, III, pp. 216–17; Kent Thomas, p. 63; Wilson Knight: *Byron and*

Shakespeare (1966), pp. 146–7; Nicolson: *Byron, The Last Journey*, p. 298; *CPW*, I, pp. 270–2, 420; *BLJ*, I, p. 220.

34 Galt, p. 62; Hobhouse Diary, ff. 25–6; *Conversations*, p. 11; *K–SMB*, 28 (1977), p. 46; Holmes: *Coleridge*, II, p. 18; *BLJ*, I, p. 230; Oman: *Nelson*, pp. 279–80.

35 Broughton, I, pp. 13–14; *BLJ*, I, pp. 223–5, 239, 240, II, pp. 198–9; Burnett, pp. 218–20; Galt, p. 68; *CPW*, II, pp. 54–5; I, pp. 273–8; Hobhouse Diary, ff. 31–2; Paston and Quennell, pp. 1–5; *CMP*, pp. 221, 549.

36 'To Florence', l. 8; *CPW*, I, p. 273; *BLJ*, I, p. 223; Hobhouse Diary, f. 27; Byron: 'Notes to CHP', *CPW*, II, p. 192; Hobhouse: *Journey through Albania*, I, p. 1.

37 Cochran: 'Nature's Gentler Errors: Byron, the Ionian Islands and Ali Pacha', *BJ*, 1995, pp. 23–4; 'Cochran in Newstead Abbey', *Byron Society Newsletter*, January 1999; Adair: *The Negotiations for the Peace of the Dardanelles, in 1808–9* (1845), I, p. 20; II, pp. 128–33; *DNB*: Leake; Hourani: *A History of the Arab People* (1991), p. 273; Mansel: *Constantinople* (1995), p. 231.

38 Cochran: 'Nature's Gentler Errors', pp. 25–7; Sultana: *Samuel Taylor Coleridge in Malta and Italy* (1969), pp. 104, 159, 210–11; Hobhouse Diary, ff. 28, 31–4; Adair, II, p. 132; Sultana (ed.): *New Approaches to Coleridge* (1981), pp. 214–17; Metaxas: 'Byron's Intelligence Mission to Greece', *BJ*, 1982, pp. 72–4.

39 Hobhouse Diary, ff. 34, 36, 41; Journey, I, pp. 25–7, 114; Travels, I, p. 3; *CHP*, c. II, ll. 385, 677–80; *CPW*, II, pp. 58, 68, 290; Minta: *On a Voiceless Shore* (1998), p. 10; Angelomatis-Tsougarakis: *The Eve of the Greek Revival* (1990), p. 63.

40 *CHP*, c. II, st. 47; *CPW*, II, p. 59; W. H. Malloch: *Memoirs of Life and Literature* (1920), pp. 23–4.

41 Hobhouse Diary, ff. 44, 48; Travels, I, p. 43; *CPW*, II, p. 195; Borst, pp. 57, 62–3; *BLJ*, I, p. 231; Sultana: *Coleridge*, pp. 210, 226–7, 231, 291; Lefebvre: 'Samuel Taylor Coleridge: A Bondage of Opium', pp. 425–6; Angelomatis-Tsougarakis, pp. 5–6, 20, 86; Minta, pp. 30–3.

42 Hobhouse Diary, f. 52; Travels, I, pp. 66–7, 70–2; *BLJ*, I, pp. 226–7; 'Stanzas', ll. 5, 31–2; *CPW*, I, pp. 275–6; *CHP*, c. II, sts 48–52; *CPW*, II, pp. 59–60.

43 *BLJ*, I, pp. 226–7; Hobhouse Diary, f. 58; *BJ*, 1992, p. 92–4; Adair, II, p. 129; Angelomatis-Tsougarakis, p. 191; Hobhouse: Travels, I, pp. 114, 114n.

44 *CHP*, c. II, st. 62; *CPW*, II, p. 63; Hobhouse Diary, f. 59; *BLJ*, I, pp. 227–8; Travels, I, pp. 97–8; Borst, p. 84n.

45 Metaxas, p. 74; Hobhouse, Travels, I, pp. 98–9; Diary, f. 60; Journey, I, p. 43; *BLJ*, I, p. 228; Angelomatis-Tsougarakis, pp. 49, 64–5, 75, 82; Massie, p. 45.

46 *BLJ*, I, p. 228; Hobhouse, Diary, f. 60; Travels, I, pp. 99–100; but see Cochran, 'Nature's Gentler Errors', pp. 29–31.

47 *CHP*, c. III, sts 60–4 and deleted lines; *CPW*, II, pp. 62–4.

48 Lang: 'Narcissus Jilted', in McGann (ed.): *Historical Studies and Literary*

Criticism (1985), pp. 145–79; Cochran, 'Natures Gentler Errors', p. 22; Fleming: *The Myth of the Bad Lord Byron*, pp. 12–13.

49   *CPW*, II, pp. 5, 269, 272; Cochran in *NBSR*, Winter 1998, p. 97; Lang, p. 150.

50   *EBSR*, ll. 1055–6; *CPW*, I, p. 261; *BLJ*, I, p. 49; Broughton, I, p. 19; Hobhouse Diary, f. 65; *CPW*, II, pp. 4–5, 266; Smith and de Selincourt (eds): *Spenser: Poetical Works* (1970), p. lxii; E & M, ll, pp. 30–1, 42; Marchand, I, p. 212, Notes 22; Grierson, pp. 7–8; Joseph: *Byron, the Poet*, p. 20; *BLJ*, II, p. 210.

51   *CHP*, Preface, c. I, st. 2; *CPW*, II, pp. 4, 5; *BLJ*, II, pp. 75–6; Keats: 'To Byron'; Gittings: 'Byron and Keats's Eremite', *K–SMB*, 7 (1956), p. 9; Elton, II, pp. 141–3; Rutherford: *Byron the Best Seller* (1964), pp. 8, 10; Smith and de Selincourt (eds), pp. lxi–ii; Cronin: 'Mapping Childe Harold, I, and II', *BJ*, 1994, pp. 16–17; Schmidt, pp. 133, 138–9; Edgecumbe: *Byron: the Last Phase* (1909), pp. 102–3; *LLB*, pp. 12–56; Hamilton: *Keepers of the Flame*, pp. 115–18.

52   *CHP*, c. II. st. 36; *CPW*, II, p. 55; *Don Juan*, c. IX, st. 42, *CPW*, V, p. 421.

53   *BLJ*, I, pp. 229, 233; Minta, pp. 88–9; Borst, pp. 80–1; *Recollections*, I, p. 21; Angelomatis-Tsougarakis, p. 15; *CPW*, I, p. 278.

54   *BLJ*, I, pp. 331, 333.

55   Hobhouse Diary, f. 77; Journey, I, p. 193, II, pp. 46–7; Finlay: *History of the Greek Revolution*, II, p. 35, in *HVSV*, p. 502; *CHP*, c. I, sts 52–64, 75; *CPW*, I, pp. 330–2; II, pp. 29–55, 69, 201, 280.

56   *CPW*, II, pp. 200, 266; Borst, p. 91.

57   Angelomatis-Tsougarakis, p. 57; Borst, p. 93; *CHP*, c. II, sts 84; *CPW*, II, pp. 72, 200.

58   *CHP*, c. ll, sts 3–8; *CPW*, II, pp. 45–7, 283; *BLJ*, II, p. 216n; de Quenen (ed.): *Lucy Hutchinson's Translation of Lucretius: De Rerum Natura* (1996), Bk III, ll. 739–67, pp. 107–8.

59   Hobhouse, Journey, I, p. 244; *CPW*, II, p. 190; Borst, p. 96; St Clair: *Lord Elgin and the Marbles* (1998), pp. 6–9, 89–95.

60   *EBSR*, l. 1030; *CPW*, I, pp. 261, 418; St Clair: *Lord Elgin*, pp. 40–1, 160, 169–72, 181; Dunn: 'Lord Byron and Lord Elgin', in Calder (ed.): *Byron and Scotland* (1989), p. 99; Broughton, I, p. 25; Borst, pp. 94–8; *CHP*, c. II, sts 11–12; *CPW*, II, pp. 47–8, 190, 200.

61   Hobhouse Diary, 28 January 1810, f. 19; Travels, I, pp. 299–301; Borst, pp. 98–9, 145; St Clair: *Lord Elgin*, pp. 88–97, 123–5 158–9, 199, 207–9, 212; Deleted lines from *CHP*, c. II; *CPW*, II, p. 48; I, pp. 323–4.

62   *BLJ*, I, p. 237; *CPW*, II, p. 198; Lucas: *The Decline and Fall of the Romantic Ideal*, p. 234; Hobhouse, Journey, I, p. 439; Diary, ff. 30–1; Broughton, I, p. 27; Galt, ff. 111, 122; Borst, p. 106.

63   *CHP*, c. II, l. 280; 'Stanzas Written in passing the Ambracian Gulf', l. 20; 'Written at Athens', l. 1; *CPW*, II, p. 54; I, pp. 278–81; V, pp. 311, 721; Borst,

pp. 103–5; Galt, p. 119; *CHP*, c. I, st. 59, *CPW*, II, p. 31; *BLJ*, I, p. 240; II, p. 13.

64 *CPW*, I, p. 199; Hobhouse, Travels, II, pp. 22, 29, 31, 55, 69, 75; *Don Juan*, c. IX, st. 27; *CPW*, V, p. 417; *BLJ*, I, pp. 235, 240; Borst, p. 110; Galt, pp. 130–1; Hobhouse, Diary, f. 39.

65 Hobhouse, Travels, II, p. 93, 86–200; Adair, I, pp. vii–viii; Bruun: *Europe and the French Imperium 1799–1814* (1938), pp, 183–4; Mansel, pp. 231–2; St Clair: *Lord Elgin*, pp. 151–6.

66 *BLJ*, IV, pp. 325–6; I, pp. 236–8, VIII, pp. 21–2; Lloyd-Jones: 'Byron's Battlefields', *BJ*, 2000, p. 85; *CMP*, pp. 204–5; Hobhouse Diary, ff. 41, 43; Sotheby's Catalogue of Sale on 24 February 2000; Hobhouse, Journey, II, p. 808.

67 *BLJ*, II, p. 18, I, pp. 236–54; *CPW*, I, pp. 281–2; Lane-Poole: *The Life of Stratford Canning* (1888), I, pp. 18, 84; Borst, p. 117; Hobhouse Diary, 17 and 19 May, ff. 44–5; Travels, II, p. 262; Masters, pp. 48, 224–7.

68 *BLJ*, I, pp. 251–2; see Chapter VIII; *EBSR*, ll. 699–700, *CPW*, I, p. 251.

69 Hobhouse Diary, ff. 50, 63–6; Lane-Poole, I, pp. 85–6; Galt, p. 111; *BLJ*, I, pp. 108, 256–7; Marchand, I, pp. 244–7; Hobhouse, Travels, II, pp. 358–68; Journal, I, p. 176; *The Taming of the Shrew*, III, iii, ll. 101–4.

70 'Mazeppa', ll. 156–66; *CPW*, IV, pp. 178–9.

71 Moore, I, pp. 130–1, 336; Mayne, I, p. 91; Wells: *George Gordon, Lord Byron*, p. 47; Habakkuk, p. 59; St Clair: *Lord Elgin*, p. 9.

72 Moore, I, p. 336; Galt, pp. 130–2; *BLJ*, I, pp. 246, 256–7, II, p. 92; Marchand, I, pp. 245–6; BL Egerton Ms. 2611; Donovan: 'Don Juan in Constantinople', *BJ*, 1993, pp. 14–17; Boyes: *Love without Wings*, p. 66; Borst, p. 125.

73 Graham (ed.), I, pp. 37–8; II, pp. 4, 9; Burnett, p. 219; *BLJ*, I, p. 180; Hobhouse Diary, f. 68.

74 *BLJ*, II, p. 3; I, p. 159.

75 *BLJ*, II, pp. 3–4, 9–10.

76 Graham (ed.), p. 61; Nicolson, p. 301; *LBAR*, p. 138n.

77 Ibid., II, pp. 3–11; T. H. White: *The Age of Scandal* (1962), p. 20.

78 *BLJ*, II, pp. 11–14; Marchand, I, pp. 253–4.

79 *BLJ*, II, pp. 21, 23, 49–50; Borst, p. 130; Hobhouse Diary, f. 70; Lane-Poole, I, p. 292.

80 *CPW*, II, p. 193; *BLJ*, II, pp. 14–16, 18–19, 23.

81 *BLJ*, II, pp. 17–18, 25, 30–1; Borst, pp. 132–4; *CPW*, II, pp. 284–5; III, pp. 421–2.

82 *DNB*, *xvi*, p. 56.

83 *BLJ*, I, p. 236; II, pp. 26–7, 40–1, 51–2; III, p. 250.

84 *CPW*, II, p. 266; *BLJ*, I, pp. 238, 248; II, p. 35.

85 'Adieu to the Muse', l. 1; *CPW*, I, p. 206; *BLJ*, II, pp. 42–6; 'Hints from

Horace', ll. 339–48; CPW, I, pp. 288, 301–2, 427, 435, 436; Highet: *Poets in a Landscape* (1957), pp. 114, 159–60; CHP, c. IV, l. 685; CPW, II, p. 150.

86 Beaty, pp. 51–2; *Don Juan*, c. X, st. 19; CPW, V, p. 442.

87 Grant: *The Founders of the Western World* (1991), p. 187; *Hints from Horace*, ll. 139–40, 231–4; CPW, I, pp. 298, 426; *The Curse of Minerva*, ll. 138, 151; CPW, I, pp. 325, 445–7; Calder (ed.), p. 2; St Clair: *Lord Elgin*, pp. 193–9; BLJ, II, pp. 73–4, 80; VII, p. 179.

88 BLJ, II, p. 55; Drinkwater: *The Pilgrim of Eternity* (1925), pp. 125–6.

89 CPW, II, p. 202.

90 McGann: *Fiery Dust*, Frontispiece, pp. 27–8; CPW, II, pp. 200–4.

91 CHP, c. II, st. 92; CPW, II, p. 74; BLJ, II, pp. 23, 26, 27, 29, 31, 33; Borst, pp. 134–6.

92 BLJ, II, pp. 38–9, 41, 46; Borst, pp. 146–8; St Clair: *Lord Elgin*, p. 160.

93 BLJ, II, pp. 44, 47–9, 198–9; Cheetham: *Byron in Europe* (1988), p. 56; Marchand, I, pp. 264–5, 270–2; Paston and Quennell, pp. 12–14.

94 BLJ, II, pp. 47–8; CHP, c. II, l. 137; CPW, II, p. 49; 'Farewell to Malta', ll. 26–30; CPW, I, p. 339.

95 BLJ, II, pp. 51–60; St Clair: *Lord Elgin*, pp. 160, 201; Graham (ed.), p. 66.

96 *Records*, p. 32.

97 LLB, pp. 438–9; Crompton: *Byron and Greek Love*, pp. ix–x, 8–9.

98 BLJ, II, pp. 34, 40–1; XIII, p. 4.

XIII Return and Luddism
Pages 262 to 276

1 BLJ, II, pp. 45, 59.

2 Ibid., pp. 20, 56–60; Dallas, pp. 103–4, 113–18; EBSR, ll. 877–80; CPW, I, pp. 256, 415; II, pp. 207, 270; Gibbon: *Memoirs of my Life*, ed. Bonnard, pp. 133–5; Hazlitt: *The Spirit of the Age*, p. 126; Morley (ed.): *Henry Crabb Robinson on Books and Their Writers* (1938), I, p. 2.

3 See Chapter XII above; BLJ, II, p. 84.

4 CPW, II, p. 266; McGann: *Fiery Dust*, pp. 94–100; BLJ, II, pp. 43, 58, 59–60; VII, pp.178–9; Dallas, pp. 103, 113–18; Joyce, p. 28; Marchand, I, pp. 281n, 293; Beaty, p. 51.

5 BLJ, II, p. 63; I, p. 248; Franklin: 'An English Bard Goes East', in Procházka (ed.): *Byron: East and West* (2000), pp. 21–5; Dallas, pp. 119–22; *Journal*, I, p. 94; Smiles: *A Publisher and His Friends*, pp. 84–8.

6 BLJ, II, pp. 54, 59–61; Burnett, p. 83; see Chapter IX above; Joyce, pp. 26–8; Graham (ed.), pp. 66–7; Hodgson, I, pp. 179–81.

7 Chapter XII above; BLJ, II, p. 57; Joyce, p. 26.

8 CPW, I, p. 428

9 EBSR, ll. 174–6, CPW, I, pp. 234, 430; Johnson: *Sir Walter Scott* (1970), I, pp. 386, 392; L & J, II, pp. 131–5; LBAR, pp. 121, 144, 180; BLJ, II.

Franklin: *Byron: A Literary Life* (2000), pp. 29, 47–8; *S & C*, III, pp. 270–3; IV, pp. 828–31.

10   *LBAR*, pp. 113, 117–18; *BLJ*, II, pp. 61, 62, 66–7; Boyes, pp. 167–71; Beckett in *NBSR*, July 2000, pp. 53–4.

11   Graves: *The Greek Myths* (1988), pp. 37, 122.

12   *BLJ*, II, p. 67; Boyes: *My Amiable Mamma*, 171–4; Moore, II, p. 31; *LBAR*, p. 112; *BLJ*, I, pp. 93–4; Melchiori: *Byron and Italy* (1958), p. 19; *CPW*, I, pp. 11, 357; *CMP*, p. 1.

13   Moore, II, p. 34; Boyes, pp. 117, 174; *CHP*, c. I, ll. 82–3; *CPW*, II, p. 11; Galt, pp. 161–2.

14   Moore, II, pp. 38–42; 'Childish Recollections', l. 243; *CPW*, I, p. 166.

15   *BLJ*, II, pp. 62, 68, 75, 84, 88, 94, 96, 105, 107, 110, 115, 119–20; Beckett, pp. 156–7; ll. 48–50, *CPW*, I, pp. 344–6, 456.

16   *BLJ*, II, pp. 90–1, 99, 110, 114, 116, 117; Dallas, pp. 114–26; Smiles, pp. 86–7; *CHP*, c. I, ll. 338–41; c. II, sts 8–9; *CPW*, II, pp. 22, 46–7.

17   Dallas, pp. 118, 122, 153–4, 173–9; *Prose Works*, I, p. 30; *Letters*, I, p. 208; *L & J*, II, pp. 24–5; *CHP*, c. I, sts 24–7, *CPW*, II, pp. 19–21, 188; *BLJ*, II, pp. 75–6, 90–2, 103–4, 106, 109, 121; *Letters*, I, p. 214.

18   *CHP*, c. I, ll. 904–5, *CPW*, II, p. 75; *BLJ*, II, p. 114; Peters: *Byron* (2000), p. 43.

19   McGann: *Fiery Dust*, pp. viii, 75, 104–5; Marchand: *Byron's Poetry* (1966), pp. 12, 14; Joseph, pp. 15–16, 21–2; *BLJ*, II, p. 75; Curran: *Poetic Form and British Romanticism*, pp. 151–7.

20   *CHP*, c. IV, ll. 974–5, c. I, l. 64, *CPW*, II, pp. 160, 10; Joseph, pp. 15–16, 21; Jump (ed.): *Byron, A Symposium* (1975), pp. 90–1.

21   Moore, *Letters*, I, pp. 102–6, 134–5; *EBSR*, ll. 460–7, and note, *CPW*, I, pp. 243–4, 407; Flynn: *Francis Jeffrey* (1978), pp. 82–3; Greig: *Francis Jeffrey of The Edinburgh Review*, pp. 150–1; Marchand, I, p. 245.

22   *Recollections of the Table-Talk of Samuel Rogers*, pp. 232–3; Graham (ed.), pp. 77–97; Joyce, p. 33; Palinurus (Connolly): *The Unquiet Grave* (1945), p. 44; Highet: *A Clerk of Oxenford*, pp. 123–4; Hogg, II, p. 426; *Journal*, III, p. 1074; *LBAR*, p. 152.

23   Moore, *Letters*, I, pp. 161–2, 165–8, 170, 185; *Journal*, I, pp. 93–4; *BLJ*, II, pp. 51, 118–22, 128–9.

24   *HVSV*, p. 72; Hodgson, I, pp. 147–8

25   *EBSR*, ll. 881–90, *CPW*, I, pp. 256–7, 415; *BLJ*, II, pp. 88–9, 97–8, 112, 129–30, 149; IX, pp. 25–6; Lloyd-Jones: 'Byron's Friend Bland', *BJ*, 1997, pp. 89–100; Hodgson, I, pp. 198–200; *L & J*, I, pp. 271–2.

26   *The Curse of Minerva*, ll. 271–2. These lines were probably written in November. The poem was not published until 1815, and then only in a pirated text; *CPW*, I, pp. 329, 445–7.

27   *BLJ*, II, pp. 141, 148, 150–1.

28   L'Estrange, pp. 11–12, 46–7, 83–5; Hodgson, I, pp. 219–21; *L & J*, I, pp. 177–9; Chew: *Byron in England* (1924), pp. 87–8, 290; Chadwick: *The*

Secularisation of the European Mind in the Nineteenth Century (1975), pp. 166, 182; Lane Fox: *The Unauthorised Version* (1992), p. 21.

29 L'Estrange, pp. 12–13; Hodgson, I, pp. 220–1; *L & J*, I, pp. 177–9; Paston and Quennell: 'To Lord Byron', p. 33; *BLJ*, II, pp. 151, 159.

30 Paston and Quennell, pp. 34–9; Moore, II, pp. 116–17; *BLJ*, II, pp. 163–4; *CPW*, III, pp. 1–3, 389.

31 *LBAR*, pp. 179–80; *BLJ*, II, pp. 151–3; Darvall: *Popular Disturbances and Public Order in Regency England* (1969), pp. 80, 244, 338; Erdman: 'Lord Byron as Rinaldo', *PMLA*, 57 (1992), p. 210; Thomis: *The Luddites* (1972), p. 75; Bailey: *The Luddite Rebellion* (1998), pp. 39, 112–13, 154–9.

32 Reid: *Land of Lost Content* (1986), pp. 56–9, 72; Hammond: *The Skilled Labourer*, p. 213; Darvall, pp. 64–75; *PD*, XXI, 811.

33 Hobsbawm: *Labouring Men* (1986), pp. 6–13; Thomis, pp. 138, 166–7; Gilmour, pp. 256–9; Ricardo: *Principles of Political Economy*, Ch. 31, 'On Machinery'.

34 Felkin: *A History of the Machine-Wrought Industry and Lace Manufacturers* (1867), pp. 34–41, 117–18; Peel: *The Risings of the Luddites* (1968), pp. 22–3, 28–32; Thompson: *The Making of the English Working Class*, pp. 581–2; Darvall, pp. 4–6, 37–42; *PD*, XXVI, 814.

35 Thompson, pp. 578, 592–8; Hammond, pp. 64–5, 212–13; Thomis, p. 65; Darvall, pp. 47–8, 65–9, 168; Perkin: *The Origins of Modern English Society 1780–1880* (1972), pp. 186–7.

36 Emsley: *British Society and the French Wars 1793–1815* (1979), pp. 130–1, 153–4; *The Curse of Minerva*, ll. 267–8, *CPW*, I, p. 328; Halévy: *England in 1815*, pp. 314–18; New, pp. 39–43, 58–60.

37 Thomis, pp. 21–4, 43–8, 75; Darvall, pp. 44–8, 95–7, 198–204; Felkin (an eyewitness), pp. 230–1, 239; Stevenson: *Popular Disturbances in England 1700–1870* (1979), pp. 103–4.

38 Halévy, p. 149; Palmer: *The Age of Democratic Revolution* (1964), II, p. 491.

39 Darvall, p. 1; Thomis, p. 107; Boyes: *Queen of the Fantastic Realm*, pp. 47–9.

40 Reid, pp. 151–2; Anglesey: *A History of the British Cavalry*, I, *1816–1850* (1973), pp. 56–7.

41 *Letters*, I, p. 213.

XIV Marriage and Exile
Pages 277 to 304

1 Ingpen, pp. 308–10; *Letters*, I, pp. 137, 139; Hogg, I, p. 425; White, I, pp. 155, 611; Peck, I, pp. 172–4; Peacock, p. 652; Boas, p. 50.

2 *Report of the Royal Commission on the Laws of Marriage* (4059, 1867–68), pp. xvi–xix; Stone: *Road to Divorce*, pp. 131–4, 276–7; *Pride and Prejudice*, ch. 46; Harvey: *Sex in Georgian England* (1994), p. 59; *BLJ*, III, p. 247; IX, p. 44; *Blessington*, pp. 129–31.

3 *Letters*, I, p. 139; Hogg, I, pp. 425, 434–6; *S & C*, III, pp. 7–8; W. Scott, p. 43.

4 Hogg, I, pp. 437–8; Veeder, p. 13; Cameron: *The Young Shelley*, pp. 106–7; W. Scott, pp. 43–5; *Prose*, pp. 222–3; Wilde: *The Importance of Being Earnest*, I; Brown, pp. 117–18.

5 Hogg, I, pp. 437, 439–40, 457–8; *Letters*, I, p. 182; W. Scott, pp. 52–61; Holmes: *Shelley*, p. 90; Boas, pp. 55, 61; P. Foot: *Mad Shelley*, pp. 124–5.

6 Hogg, I, pp. 1, 455–6, 464; II, p. 5; W. Scott, p. 49; *Letters*, I, p. 151; Hogg, I, pp. 268–9, 279; G. Scott-Moncrieff: *Edinburgh* (1947), pp. 81–8; *Boswell's London Journal 1762–1763* (1951), p. 117; Peck, I, pp. 174–5.

7 Stephen Jay Gould in *New York Review of Books*, 22 October 1998, pp. 83–90; King-Hele: *Erasmus Darwin*, pp. 65–7.

8 Hogg, I, pp. 445–52.

9 Ibid., pp. 458–60; Boas, p. 54.

10 Hogg, I, pp. 465–71; *Letters*, I, p. 151; White, I, pp. 161–2.

11 Chapter X above; Ingpen, pp. 307–8; *Letters*, I, pp. 137–8; *S & C*, III, p. 11.

12 Hogg, I, p. 466; Ingpen, p. 316.

13 *Medwin*, p. 13.

14 Cameron: *The Young Shelley*, pp. 102, 343; *Letters*, I, pp. 137–8, 158.

15 *Letters*, I, pp. 137–43; Freeman: 'Shelley's Letters to his Father', *K–SMB*, 34 (1983), pp. 2–6; *S & C*, III, pp. 14–15; *EBSR*, l. 690, *CPW*, I, p. 251.

16 *Letters*, I, pp. 144–6, 149–52, 331–2; Boas, pp. 103, 222.

17 *Letters*, I, p. 147.

18 Ibid., pp. 143, 146–9; Freeman, pp. 6–8; Ingpen, pp. 334–5.

19 Ingpen, pp. 319–20; Gelpi, p. 120.

20 Hogg, I, p. 467.

21 Freeman: 'Shelley's Early Letters', in Everest (ed.): *Shelley Revalued* (1983), p. 114; *Letters*, I, p. 2; *Henry IV*, *Pt I*, I, iii; *Hints from Horace*, l. 134, *CPW*, I, p. 294; Hogg, II, p. 68; Clutton-Brock, pp. 40–2.

22 Ingpen, pp. 333–5; *Letters*, I, pp. 148–9, 175; Holmes: *Shelley*, p. 90; Holmes (ed.): *Shelley on Love*, p. 24; *S & C*, III, p. 44; Boas, pp. 59–60; W. Scott, pp. 52, 56–7; Rossetti (ed.): *The Diary of Dr John William Polidori* (1911), p. 128.

23 M & E, I, pp. 185–7.

24 Horsham Museum, Ms. 512, 10.9.1811; *Letters*, I, pp. 151, 152–3; Hawkins: *Pilfold*, p. 45; *S & C*, III, p. 21; Ingpen, pp. 347–8; White, I, pp. 166–7.

25 *Letters*, I, p. 158; Gelpi, pp. 121–3; Holmes: *Shelley*, p. 88; Freeman in *K–SMB* 34, pp. 9–10; Ingpen, pp. 344–7.

26 Ingpen, p. 338; *Letters*, I, pp. 154–6; Hogg, I, p. 477; Djabri and Knight, p. 16.

27 *Letters*, I, pp. 154–6, 158–9; *S & C*, III, pp. 20–3; Hogg, I, p. 447; Ingpen, pp. 347–8.

28 Hogg, I, p. 473; II, pp. 1–2.

29 Wolfe's Introduction to *The Life of Percy Bysshe Shelley As Comprised In The*

Life of Shelley by Thomas Jefferson Hogg etc. (1933), I, pp. xv–xvii.

30 *Letters*, I, pp. 183, 186; Hogg, I, pp. 474–6, II, pp. 1–8; Boas, pp. 62–4.

31 *Letters*, I, pp. 166–7; Hogg, II, pp. 8–13; W. Scott, p. 56.

32 M & E, I, pp. 187–8; Hogg, II, p. 13; *Letters*, I, pp. 166–71, 182.

33 *Letters*, I, pp. 171–2; Webb: *Shelley: A Voice Not Understood*, p. 8.

34 *Letters*, I, pp. 173, 174–5, 176–7, 184; Boas, pp. 61–2; Tomalin, p. 23; P. Foot: *Mad Shelley*, pp. 146–7.

35 M & E, I, pp. 189–91; *Letters*, I, pp. 180, 183–4, 192, 207–8; W. Scott, pp. 62–5.

36 *Letters*, I, pp. 188, 196.

37 Chapter X above; M & E, I, p. 222; *Letters*, I, p. 149; Hughes, pp. 60–1; Carpenter and Barnefield, pp. 92–3; Brown, pp. 26–43, 108–9; Stovall: 'Shelley's Doctrine of Love', *PMLA*, 45 (1950), pp. 300–1; Lea, pp. 172–4; Hough, p. 134; Hogg, II, p. 365; Austen: *Northanger Abbey*, ch. 7.

38 Brown, p. 226; Grabo, p. 271; *Julian and Maddalo*, ll, pp. 463–9, E & M, II, p. 687; Barber: *Byron and Where He Is Buried*, pp. ix–x, 129–36; Longford: *Byron*, pp. 215–19; Wordsworth: *The Prelude*, Bk III, ll. 305–7; Joseph Shorthouse in *Oxford Book of Quotations*.

39 Lucas: *Literature and Psychology*, p. 122; *Letters*, I, pp. 194, 195; Holmes: *Shelley on Love*, pp. 97, 117–22.

40 MacCarthy, pp. 119–24; Robinson: *The Dukes of Norfolk* (1982), p. 177; *Letters*, I, pp. 198–9, 212, 247–8; Hogg, II, pp. 23–4; White, I, pp. 177, 181–2.

41 Ingpen, pp. 347–8; *Stockdale's Budget*, p. 9.

42 *Letters*, I, pp. 205–6.

43 Ibid., I, pp. 209, 213–14, 238; Peck, I, pp. 198–9; White, I, pp. 177–8.

44 *Letters*, I, pp. 194, 196, 201–2, 212–14, 248–9, 259; Holmes: *Shelley*, pp. 95–7.

45 *Letters*, I, p. 194; White, I, p. 183; C. C. Southey (ed.): *The Life and Correspondence of Robert Southey* (1850), III, pp. 325–6; Storey: *Robert Southey* (1997), p. 212; Peck, I, p. 204.

46 Hogg, II, p. 29; Grierson (ed.): *The Letters of Sir Walter Scott 1808–1811*, II, p. 346; Byron: *EBSR*, ll. 202, 230, 127; *CPW*, I, pp. 233–6; *Medwin*, pp. 44, 316; *Letters*, I, p. 208; *BLJ*, II, p. 137; C. C. Southey (ed.), VI, p. 200; Southey: *Essays, Moral and Political* (1832), I, p. 224; Brinton: *Political Ideas of the English Romanticists*, p. 102; Gilmour: *Britain Can Work* (1983), pp. 19–22.

47 Southey (ed.), III, pp. 325–6; *Letters*, I, pp. 210–12, 241; Simmons, pp. 135–7; Holmes: *Shelley*, pp. 100–1; Hogg, II, pp. 29–33.

48 *Letters*, I, pp. 215, 249, 220, 28; Simmons, pp. 15–17; Cameron: *Shelley v Southey, New Light On An Old Quarrel*, pp. 489–90; Mills: *Peacock*, p. 71; White, I, pp. 186–7.

49 Marshall, pp. 9–11, 28–30, 43–4, 46–51, 55; St Clair: *The Godwins and the*

Shelleys, pp. 1–2, 7–17, 36–7; Brailsford: *Shelley, Godwin and their Circle* (1951), pp. 79–80.

50 Godwin: *Political Justice*, pp. 846–7.

51 St Clair: *The Godwins and the Shelleys*, pp. 51–4; Marshall: *William Godwin*, pp. 82–4, 117; Godwin: *Political Justice*, pp. 380, 458, 603–4, 771, 790–5, 844, 848–52; Gray, pp. 114, 134; Joll: *The Anarchists* (1979), pp. 16, 23; Fletcher: *Montesquieu and British Politics* (1980), p. 255.

52 Ibid., pp. 202–4, 206–16, 452–3, 593, 886–8; Roe: *Wordsworth and Coleridge: The Radical Years* (1990), pp. 167–8; Brailsford, pp. 109–10; Gray, pp. 121, 132–30.

53 *The Novels of Thomas Love Peacock*, ed. Garnett, 1998, p. 85.

54 Godwin, *Political Justice*, pp. 807–12, 821–3, 845, 850–2, 862–71, 879–80, 891–5; Marshall, pp. 76, 417; Hume: *An Enquiry Concerning Human Understanding*, Section VIII; Gray, p. 115; Evans: 'Shelley, Godwin, Hume and the Doctrine of Necessity', *Studies in Philology*, 37, no. 14 (October 1940), pp. 635, 638–40.

55 Hume: 'Idea of a Perfect Commonwealth', in *Essays* (1963), p. 500; Hogg, I, p. 99; Wordsworth: *The Prelude*, Bk X, ll. 848–50; Hazlitt: *Spirit of the Age*, p. 23; Marshall, pp. 155, 156–63, 198–201, 211–31; Philp: *Godwin's Political Justice* (1986), pp. 99–100, 223–4; Brailsford, pp. 50–1; St Clair: *The Godwins and the Shelleys*, pp. 70, 192–7, 208, 219–20; Hole, p. 102; Glynn Grylls: *William Godwin and his World* (1953), p. 49.

56 Godwin, *Political Justice*, pp. 316, 849–52; St Clair: *The Godwins and the Shelleys*, pp. 163–79, 497–503; see Introduction above; Tomalin, pp. 259–70; Godwin: *Memoirs of Wollstonecraft* (1798), pp. 74–93, 154–65; Marshall, pp. 185–90, 396–7.

57 Marshall, pp. 229, 232, 238–9; Pearson: *The Smith of Smiths* (1945), p. 240; Lovell: Byron: pp. 154–5; P. A. Brown: *The French Revolution in English History*, pp. 183–4; Godwin: *Political Justice*, pp. 848–9; Kilgour: *The Rise of the Gothic Novel* (1995), pp. 96–7; Cannon: *Aristocratic Century*, p. 165; Holmes: *Coleridge*, I, p. 258; St Clair: *The Godwins and the Shelleys*, pp. 228–9; *S & C*, I, pp. 431–3.

58 Mills, pp. 77–8; White, I, p. 98; Wordsworth: *The Prelude*, Bk XI, l. 693; Hogg, I, pp. 99–102.

59 *Letters*, I, pp. 201–2, 213–4; Hough, p. 122; Bowra: *The Romantic Imagination* (1961), p. 103.

60 *Letters*, I, pp. 219–21, 227–9; St Clair: *The Godwins and the Shelleys*, pp. 306–14.

61 *Letters*, I, pp. 218, 232, 234–5.

62 Ibid., I, pp. 213, 219, 221–3; Reiman: *Romantic Texts and Contexts*, pp. 260–74; *Queen Mab*, V, ll. 23–64, M & E, I, pp. 311–13.

63 The full title of Godwin's 1794 novel was *'Things as They Are'* or, *The*

Adventures of Caleb Williams; *Letters*, I, pp. 223–6; II, pp. 60, 72–6, M & E, I, pp. 193–8; Gilmour: *Riot, Risings and Revolution*, pp. 228, 439–41.

64 *Letters*, I, p. 213; ll. 13–20, M & E, I, pp. 201–2; Webb: *A Voice Not Understood*, pp. 104–7; *The Mask of Anarchy*, l. 110; 'England in 1819', l. 13; R & P, pp. 304, 311.

65 *Letters*, I, pp. 232–4, 239–40, 271; St Clair: *The Godwins and the Shelleys*, pp. 322–4; White, I, pp. 196–7.

66 *Letters*, I, p. 246; Cameron: *The Young Shelley*, p. 128; Dawson: *The Unacknowledged Legislator*, pp. 24–6; Smith: *George IV*, pp. 140–2, 192; Moore: 'The Sceptic', ll. 57–8.

67 *Letters*, I, pp. 234, 239, 246, 258; Webb: '"A Noble Field": Shelley's Irish Expedition and the Lessons of the French Revolution', in Minerva (ed.): *Robespierre & Co.* (1990), pp. 553–4; Stoval, p. 296; Dawson, pp. 147–9; P. Foot: *Mad Shelley*, p. 207.

68 *Letters*, I, pp. 184, 240–1, 246, 252; Brown: *Sexuality and Feminism in Shelley*, pp. 197–9; Dawson, p. 49; Crook and Guiton, pp. 75–6.

69 Holmes: *Shelley*, pp. 111–14; Dowden, I, p. 227; *Letters*, I, pp. 232, 238, 240; White, I, p. 193.

70 *Letters*, I, p. 248.

XV Maiden Speeches
Pages 305 to 332

1 Ayling: *Edmund Burke* (1988), p. 99; Elliott: *Partners in Revolution* (1982), pp. 3, 7–8; Kee: *The Green Flag* (1972), pp. 35, 41–3; Christie: *Stress and Stability*, pp. 118–20.

2 Pakenham: *The Year of Liberty* (1972), pp. 274, 403; Kee, p. 87; Elliott, pp. 191–3; Gilmour, *Riot, Risings and Revolution*, pp. 414–15, 423–7, 431.

3 *Letters*, I, pp. 248–9, 259; MacCarthy, pp. 139–40; Simmons, p. 95.

4 *Letters*, I, pp. 258, 267, 270–1, 276–7; *Prose Works*, I, pp. 8, 328; Marshall, p. 297; Hughes, p. 138.

5 *Letters*, I, pp. 239, 276; *Prose Works*, I, p. 10; Hughes, p. 131; Grabo, p. 83; Henley Jarvis: *The Gallican Church and the Revolution* (1882), p. 247.

6 *Prose Works*, I, pp. 10–18; Byron: *The Curse of Minerva*, l. 277, CPW, I, p. 329.

7 *Prose Works*, I, pp. 19, 21.

8 Ibid., I, pp. 10, 17, 25–7, 34–6; *Letters*, I, p. 269; Webb: 'A Noble Field', pp. 557–60; Hughes, pp. 128–9; Palmer, II, p. 491.

9 *Letters*, I, pp. 263, 265, 271, 310, 323; Hogg, I, p. 268.

10 MacCarthy, pp. 231, 243; *Prose Works*, I, pp. 291–2; Dawson, pp. 134–5; Hughes, pp. 129, 135.

11 *Letters*, I, p. 275; MacCarthy, pp. 237–48; *Prose Works*, I, pp. 42–3, 291, 542–3; Dawson, pp. 139–40, 151–4.

12 *Letters*, I, pp. 267–8, 276.

13 Ibid., I, pp. 242, 259, 264, 268, 270–1, 287; Kee, p. 169; 'On Robert Emmet's Tomb', ll. 17–20; M & E, I, p. 205; *Esdaile*, pp. 196–8, 215–17; MacCarthy, pp. 149, 154–8; Marshall, pp. 273, 290; Dawson, p. 134; Webb: 'The Bastinadoed Elephant', in Procházka (ed.), p. 49.

14 *Letters*, I, p. 264; Hogg, II, pp. 113–14; *CPW*, II, p. 211; *BLJ*, III, p. 128; IX, p. 20.

15 *Letters*, I, p. 275.

16 Hogg, II, p. 68; *Letters*, I, pp. 251, 258.

17 *Letters*, I, pp. 253–4, 272; 'To the Republicans of North America', ll. 21–30; M & E, I, pp. 206–8; *Esdaile*, pp. 71–2, 201–4; Clutton-Brock, p. 57; *BLJ*, VI, pp. 212, 225–7, 232, 236, 246.

18 St Clair: *The Godwins and the Shelleys*, pp. 305–13; Cameron: *The Young Shelley*, pp. 154–5; Marshall, pp. 257, 266, 276–7, 281–3, 290–1.

19 *Letters*, I, pp. 242–3, 259, 261; Clutton-Brock, p. 56.

20 *Prose Works*, I, pp. 39–55, 338–42; MacCarthy, pp. 263–86; *Letters*, I, pp. 261–2; Hogg, II, pp. 81–90; Dawson, pp. 157, 164–5.

21 *Letters*, I, pp. 2, 66–8.

22 Ibid., I, pp. 267–70; Hogg, II, pp. 95–100; Dawson, p. 140; St Clair, pp. 326–7.

23 *Letters*, I, pp. 276–9; Hogg, II, pp. 104–7; MacCarthy, pp. 319–20; Cameron, pp. 154–7.

24 *Letters*, I, pp. 265, 271, 275, 282.

25 Ibid., I, pp. 270–1.

26 *DNB*; Cameron, pp. 143–5; Holmes: *Shelley*, p. 128; Hughes, p. 137; Boas, p. 78; *Letters*, I, pp. 279, 378; White, I, pp. 222–4.

27 Morton: *Shelley and the Revolution in Taste* (1994), pp. 16, 63–4; Thomas: *Man and the Natural World*, p. 296; *Letters*, I, pp. 274–5, 283; *Prose Works*, I, pp. 77–89, 359–61; *BLJ*, II, pp. 131, 141; see Chapter XIII above; *Blessington*, pp. 35–6, 86; Paterson: 'Was Byron Anorexic?', *World Medicine*, May 1982, pp. 35–8; Baron: 'Illnesses and Creativity', *BMJ*, 20 December 1997, pp. 1697–1703; Kenyon Jones: 'Byron, Food and Culture', in Procházka (ed.), p. 253.

28 MacCarthy, pp. 308–29; *Prose Works*, I, pp. 56–60, 348–53.

29 Lea, pp. 33–4; Grabo, p. 55; Dawson, p. 141; *Letters*, I, pp. 282–4; Redford: *Venice and the Grand Tour* (1996), p. 51; *BLJ*, II, pp. 34, 40–1.

30 *BLJ*, II, pp. 155, 160–1.

31 Darvall, pp. 80–4, 222–6; Reid, pp. 80–1; Thomis, pp. 145–6; Gilmour, pp. 148, 175–6.

32 Halévy, p. 188; Roberts, pp. 349–59, 398–405; Emsley: *British Society and the French Wars 1793–1815*, pp. 129–30; Feiling, pp. 254–5, 265; Smith: 'The Letters of Peter Plymley II', in Bullett: *Sydney Smith*, p. 194; Holland, pp. 132–3; Twiss: *Eldon* (1844), I, pp. 71–7; Harvey: *Sex in Georgian England*, pp. 58–9; Byron: *The Devils Drive*, l. 142; *CPW*, III, p. 100.

33 *BLJ*, I, p. 186; Feiling, pp. 165, 258; New, pp. 32–3, 46, 49, 56, 147; Aspinall:

Lord Brougham and the Whig Party (1927), pp. 7, 13, 29; Foord, p. 454.

34 Roberts, pp. 2–5, 172–83, 205–8, 223–5, 235–7, 261–2, 300–2; *HC*, II, pp. 347, 350; IV, p. 141; Holland, pp. 28–9; *Letters*, I, p. 246; Dinwiddy: *From Luddism to the First Reform Bill* (1986), p. 9; Foord, p. 448; Davis: *The Age of Grey and Peel*, pp. 145–6.

35 Roberts, pp. 3–4, 118, 133–5, 139–43, 163–71; Holland, pp. 118–19.

36 *PD*, XXI, 807, 840, 848, 859–66; Hobsbawm and Rudé: *Captain Swing* (1969), pp. 257–63; Davis, p. 222; Ziegler: *Melbourne*, pp. 106–10; Mitchell, pp. 124, 217–18.

37 Paine: *Rights of Man* (1985), p. 200; Burke: 'Observations on the Conduct of the Ministry', in *Works* (1826), VI, p. 275; Halévy, pp. 196–7; Bickley (ed.): *The Diaries of Sylvester Douglas Lord Glenbervie* (1928), I, p. 384; Holland, p. 115.

38 Roberts, pp. 191–7; Halévy, pp. 198–9; Turberville: *The House of Lords in the Age of Reform, 1784–1837*, p. 130; Bell: *Smith*, pp. 158–9; Romilly: *Memoirs*, II, p. 325; Potter: *Hanging in Judgement* (1993), pp. 36–7, 222; Shelley: *The Mask of Anarchy*, st. iv, R & P, p. 302; *Prose Works* I, p. 64; Davis, pp. 141, 147.

39 Radzinowicz: *A History of English Criminal Law* (1948), I, pp. 503–7, 517, 522–4; Trevelyan: *Lord Grey of the Reform Bill* (1929), pp. 146, 162–4; Davis, p. 124; Turberville: pp. 213–15.

40 *The Curse of Minerva*, ll. 259–76; *CPW*, I, pp. 328–9; *BLJ*, II, pp. 165–6.

41 *PD*, XXI, pp. 965–6; II, pp. 871–2; VIII, pp. 671; Coupland: *Wilberforce* (1945), pp. 253–4, 271–2.

42 Felkin, pp, 50–1.

43 *CMP*, pp. 20–3, 280, 286; *LBAR*, p. 178.

44 *PD*, XXI, pp. 964–972; *CMP*, pp. 22–7.

45 *PD*, XXI, pp. 972–9, 1084; *Lords Journals*, 48, pp. 614, 636; *Commons Journals*, 67, p. 182.

46 *PD*, 3rd series, VIII, pp. 274–5; Turberville, p. 272: Aspinall (in *Lord Brougham and the Whig Party*, p. 191) denounces the story as 'a malicious fabrication'. Yet as Brougham ended his speech with the words 'I pray and exhort you not to reject this measure . . . I implore you – yea, on my bended knees, I supplicate you – reject not this measure,' it is not implausible.

47 Drinkwater, pp. 173–4; M. Foot: *The Politics of Paradise*, pp. 135–7; Kelsall: *Byron's Politics* (1987), p. 46 – an unremittingly hostile account which even manages to claim that Grenville's comparison with Burke was a 'back-handed compliment'; Dallas, pp. 203–4; *BLJ*, II, p. 167; BL Add. Ms. 56530, f. 38.

48 *BLJ*, II, p. 167; Holland; p. 123; Galt, p. 172; Ward: *Letters to 'Ivy'*, p. 199.

49 Grayling, p. 59; Gittings, pp. 167, 319.

50 Dallas, pp. 203–4; Moore, II, p. 148; *Journal*, III, p. 1144; Holland, p. 123; Langford, pp. 210–16; *BLJ*, IX, p. 16; II, p. 167.

51 Finlayson: *The Seventh Earl of Shaftesbury*, pp. 337, 418–19.

52 *PH*, XVIII, 1294–8.

53 *BLJ*, IX, p. 17; VII, p. 205; Reid, p. 82.
54 Reid, pp. 58–9; Darvall, pp. 41, 84, 338; *PD*, XXV, pp. 275; Holland, p. 123; Thomis, pp. 145–6, 160.
55 Darvall, pp. 104, 129–35; Reid, pp. 84, 168–71, 242–3, 254–5, 258, 291; Thomis, pp. 19, 156–60; *Letters*, I, pp. 351, 353; Bohstedt: *Riots and Community Politics* (1983), pp. 161–3; Gattrell: *The Hanging Tree*, pp. 45–51.
56 Lines 9–16, *CPW*, III, pp. 9, 390–1; *Letters*, I, pp. 213, 271, 296–7; P. Foot: *Mad Shelley*, p. 163.
57 St Clair: 'The Impact of Byron's Writings', in Rutherford (ed.): *Byron: Augustan and Romantic*, p. 11; Franklin: *Byron: A Literary Life*, pp. 35–6; Poole: 'What Constitutes the "Real" Child Harold', in Cardwell (ed.): *Lord Byron: The European* (1997), pp. 153–207; Byron: *Childe Harold's Pilgrimage*, tenth edn, 1815, pp. 1–302.
58 Rogers: *Talk Talk*, p. 233; Franklin, p. 50; see Introduction above; *CPW*, II, pp. 9–12.
59 Nicolson: *The Poetry of Byron* (1943), pp. 6–7; Bone: *Byron* (2000), p. 7; Rutherford: *Byron the Best-seller*, pp. 13–14; Dallas, pp. 232, 244; Rutherford (ed.): *The Critical Heritage*, pp. 35–6; Hough, pp. 100–3; Moore: *Letters*, I, p. 187.
60 Moore, II, p. 137; Longford, p. 45; Magarshack: *Dostoevsky*, pp. 144–6.
61 Bowra, pp. 149–50; St Clair: *The Impact of Byron's Writings*, pp. 2–6; Felkin, p. 231; Darvall, p. 33; Rutherford (ed.): *The Critical Heritage*, p. 36.
62 *Laon and Cythna*, Dedication to Mary, ll. 4–10, 118–26, E & M., II, pp. 49, 57.

Epilogue
Pages 333 to 336

1 *Letters*, I, pp. 235–7; Holmes: *Coleridge*, I, pp. 240–2; Peck, I, p. 249.
2 Storey, pp. 133–4; Coleridge: *Poetic Works*, pp. 319–23; Ashton: *Coleridge*, pp. 164–5; Fitzgerald (ed.): *Poems of Southey* (1909), pp. 421, 757–8, R & F, I, p. 281; Chapter VIII.
3 M & E, I, pp. 230–7; R & F, pp. 121–9, Peck, I, pp. 249–51; Holmes: *Shelley the Pursuit*, pp. 106–7.
4 *CPW*, III, pp. 95–104; *BLJ*, VI, p. 12.
5 *BLJ*, III, p. 240; Beaty: *Byron the Satirist*, pp. 77–8.
6 *Letters*, I, p. 235.
7 Stevenson and Quinault (eds): *Popular Protest and Public Order* (1974), pp. 35–6; R & F, I, p. 283.
8 M & E, I, pp. 234, 235–6; *CPW*, III, pp. 101–2.
9 M & E, I, p. 236; *CPW*, III, pp. 98–9.
10 M & E, I, pp. 234–5; *CPW*, III, p. 96.
11 M & E, I, p. 237; *CPW*, III, pp. 100–1.

Index

Bland, Robert, 271
Blessington, Lady, 24*, 211, 234, 316
Boccaccio, Giovanni, 32; *The Decameron*, 32
Boswell, James, 15, 157, 168–9, 279
Bowdler, John, 107
Bowdler family: *Family Shakespeare*, 166, 166*
Braxfield, judge, 31
Brighton, 168
Britain, 2–3, 4, 5, 10, 47, 50, 68, 173, 222, 237, 240, 245, 246, 249, 275, 302, 305 *see also* England; Ireland; Scotland; Wales
Brompton, 168
Brontë, Charlotte: *Shirley*, 276
Brougham, Henry, 319, 326*, 329; attack on Byron's *Hours of Idleness*, 166, 167, 172, 174–5, 176, 269,331
Brown, Charles Brockden, 55
Browne, Felicia (later Hemans), 111
Browne, Sir Thomas, 42
Browning, Elizabeth Barrett, 132
Bruce, Michael, 254
Brummel, Beau, 172
Buffon, Georges, Comte de, 279, 279*
Burdett, Sir Francis, 133, 196, 327
Burgage Manor, 83, 91, 153, 214
Burke, Edmund, 48, 48*, 50, 213, 298, 305, 320–21; *Reflections on the Revolution in France*, 5, 298
Burney, Fanny, 101
Burns, Robert, 3, 12, 31, 119
Buron, Godfrey (or Geoffrey) de (GBB's ancestor), 13,151
Burrard, Sir Harry, 223, 228
Burton: *Anatomy of Melancholy*, 79
Butler, Dr George, 92, 93, 115, 167
Byron, Amelia (Lady Coningsby; first wife of GGB's father), 18
Byron, Lady Anne Isabella (née Milbanke; GGB's wife), 50, 89, 106, 151, 179, 211
Byron, Augusta Mary (GGB's half–sister); birth, 18; childhood, 22, 23, 28; incestuous relationship with Byron, 27*, 136*; Lord Carlisle as guardian of, 61; Byron complains about Southwell to, 83; beginning of correspondence with Byron, 87; Byron complains about mother to, 91, 146; and Byron's temper and

disposition, 92; and Byron's time at Cambridge, 146, 149, 163; and Byron's financial difficulties, 151; estrangement from Byron, 151, 163; and Byron's melancholy, 152, 161, 214; and Byron's view of marriage, 170; not visited by Byron before Grand Tour, 181, and Byron's feelings about Hobhouse, 252
Byron, Catherine (née Gordon; GGB's mother); family and early life, 18–20; relationship and marriage with Jack Byron, 18, 20, 21–3, 25–6, 27, 28; and Augusta, 22, 23, 87, lives alone in London, 23; birth of son, 23–4; and son's lameness, 24*, 25, 30, 37, 82, 214; years in Aberdeen, 26, 29–31, 33, 34, 37; and death of husband, 29; temper, 29–30, 37, 62, 90; political opinions, 30–31; and religion, 31; and son's inheritance 36; hostility to field sports, 49; and move to Newstead, 59–60; receives pension, 61–2; lives at Newstead, 62; and appointment of Rogers as son's tutor, 63; learns about behaviour of May Gray, 65; argues with Glennie, 67–9; and decision to move son to Harrow, 69; and son's failure to return to Harrow, 80, 84–5; relationship with son during schooldays at Harrow, 82, 90–91; at Burgage manor, 83; and son's student years, 146, 150, 151–2, 153–4, 158–9; thinks son should marry, 169–70; not invited to Newstead, 171; and Newstead rents, 178; and son's departure abroad, 181; and son's Grand Tour, 226, 227, 228, 231, 235, 238, 240, 248, 249, 250, 252, 253, 255, 260; son delays visit to, 265–6; death, 266, 269; brief mentions, 92, 167, 172, 199, 220, 258, 298
Byron, Eleanor (wife of 1st Lord Byron of Rochdale), 14
Byron, Frances *see* Leigh, Francis; (Fanny; née Byron; GGB's aunt)
Byron, Frances (née Berkeley; GGB's great–grandmother), 14, 15
Byron, George Anson (GGB's uncle), 17, 23